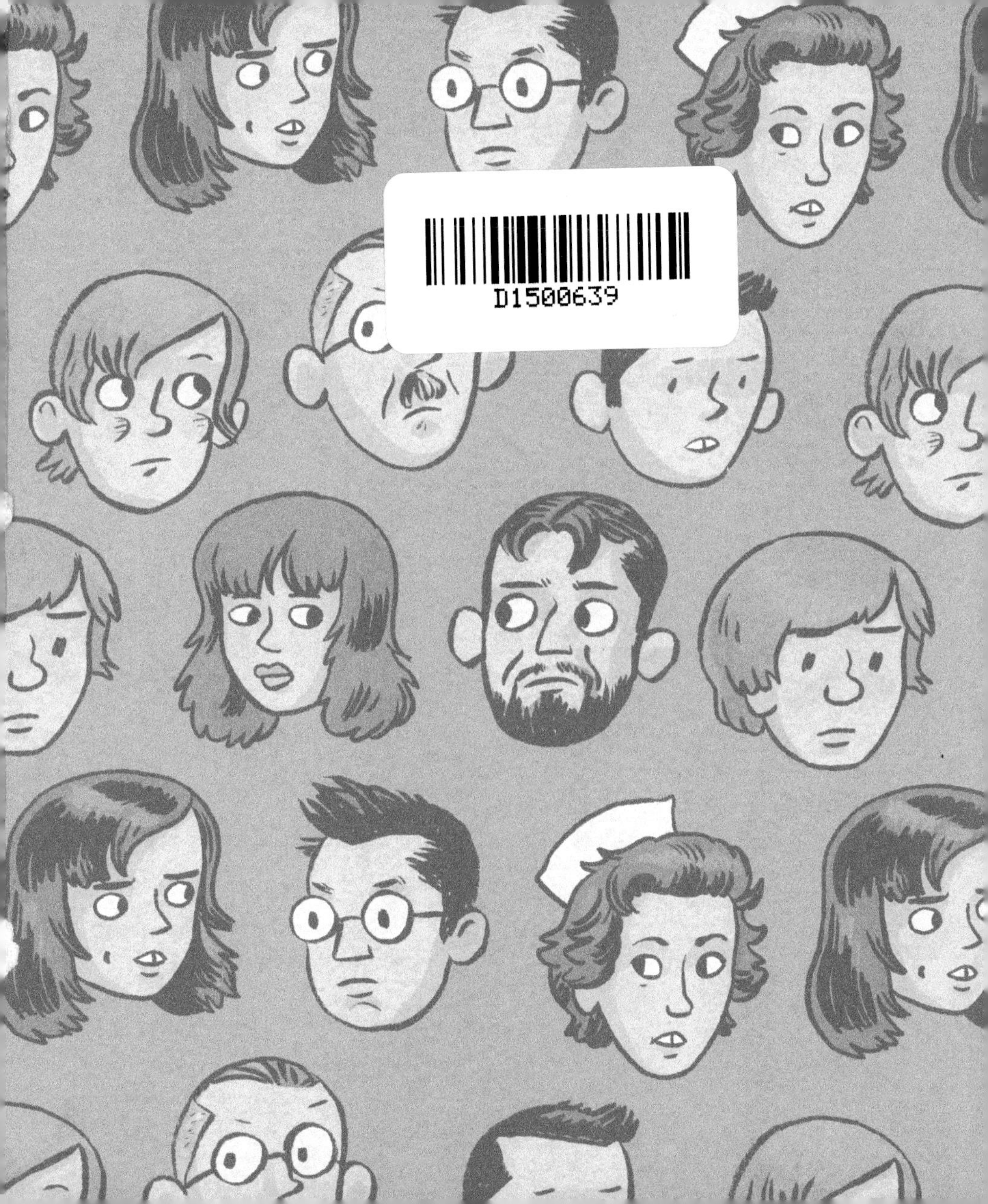

'AT THE SHORE'

Alternative Comics

'AT THE SHORE'

Story and art by Jim Campbell.
Special poetical dialogue editing in chapter one by Michael Herring.
Gabi's drawings and paintings by David V Stevenson.
Production by Ann Xu and Marc Arsenault.

Published by Alternative Comics
21607B Stevens Creek Blvd.
Cupertino, California 95014
IndyWorld.com

———————

Print ISBN: 978-1-68148-518-8
Digital ISBN: 978-1-68148-519-5

comics, music, and more at angryjim.com

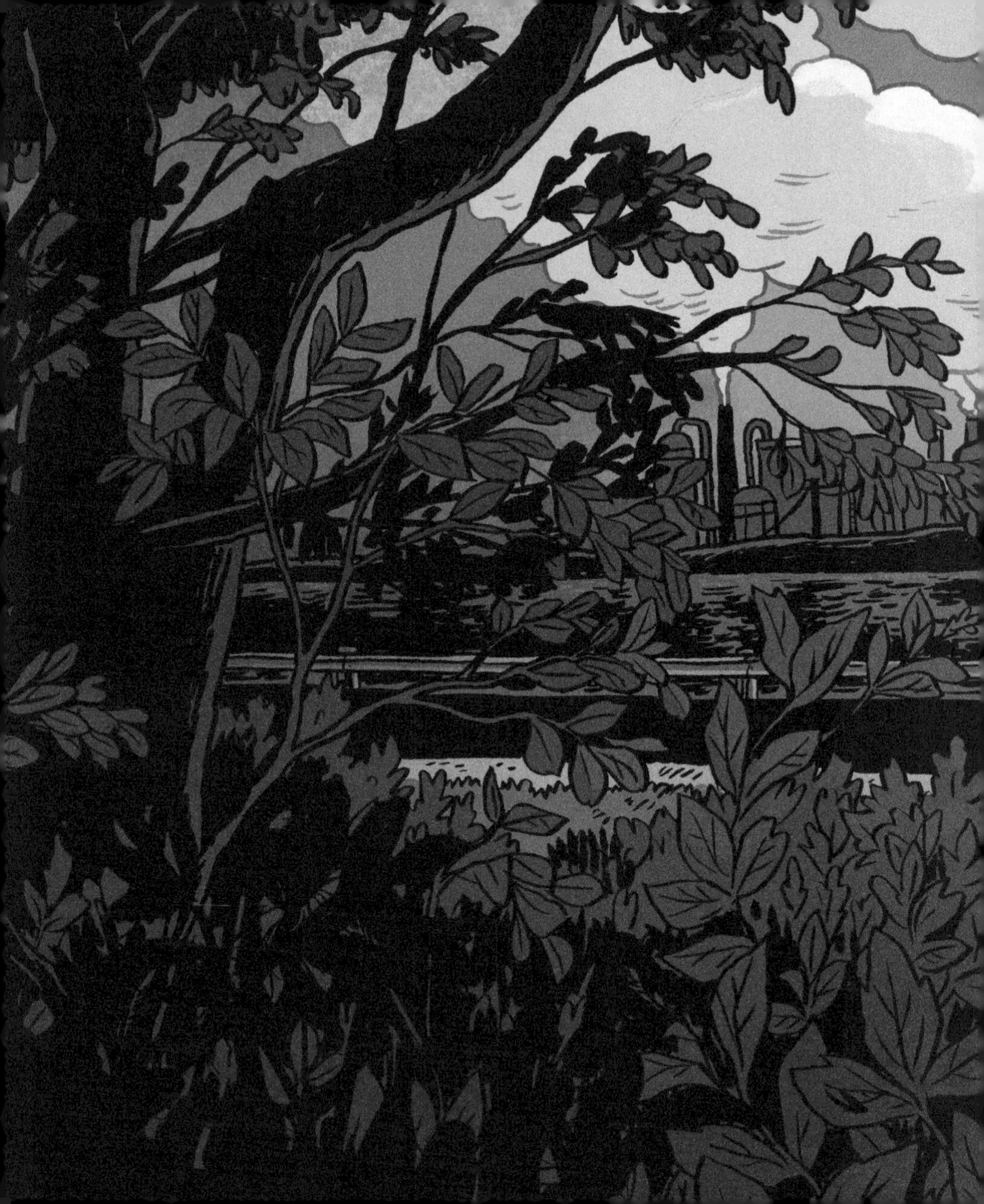

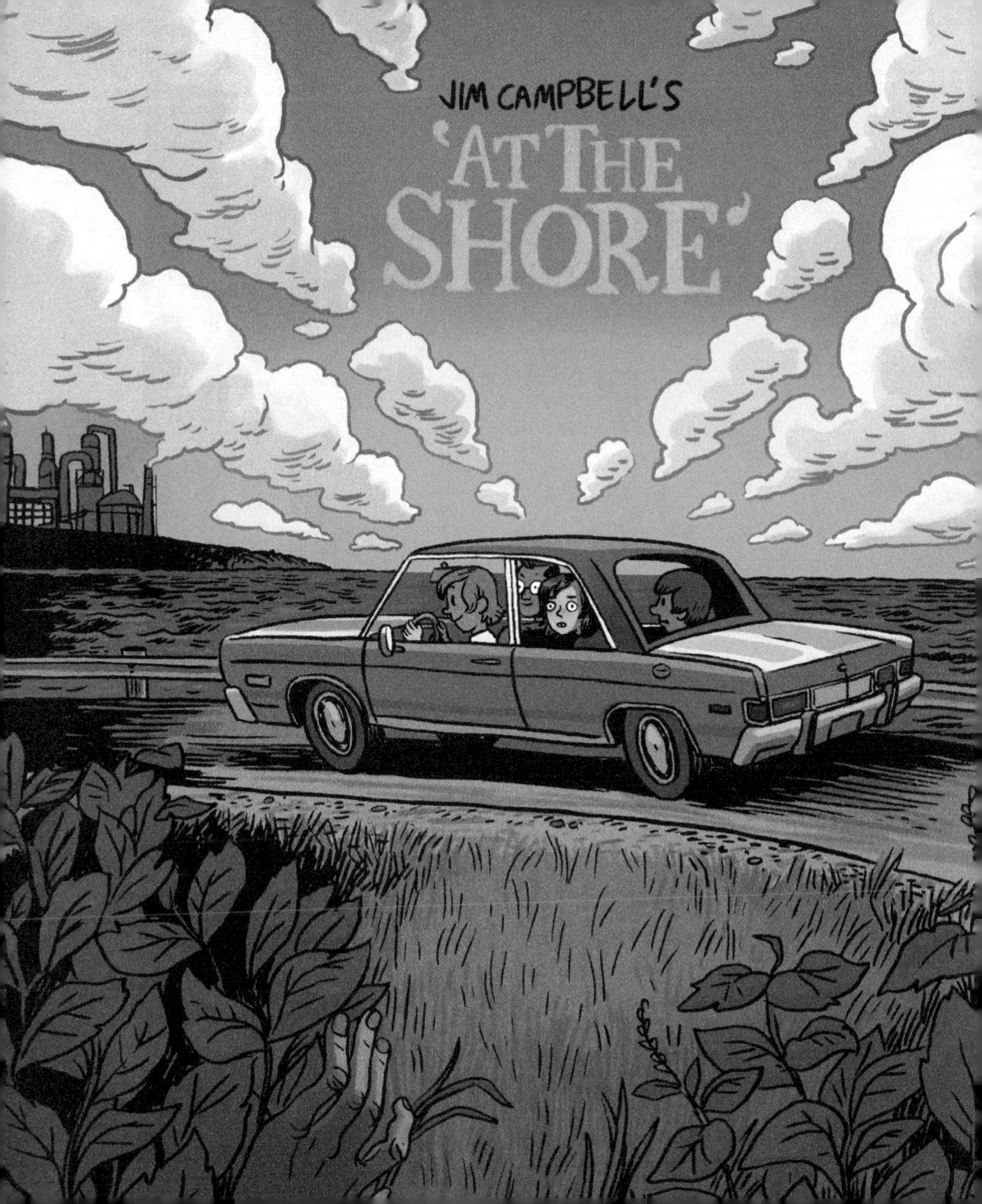
JIM CAMPBELL'S
'AT THE SHORE'

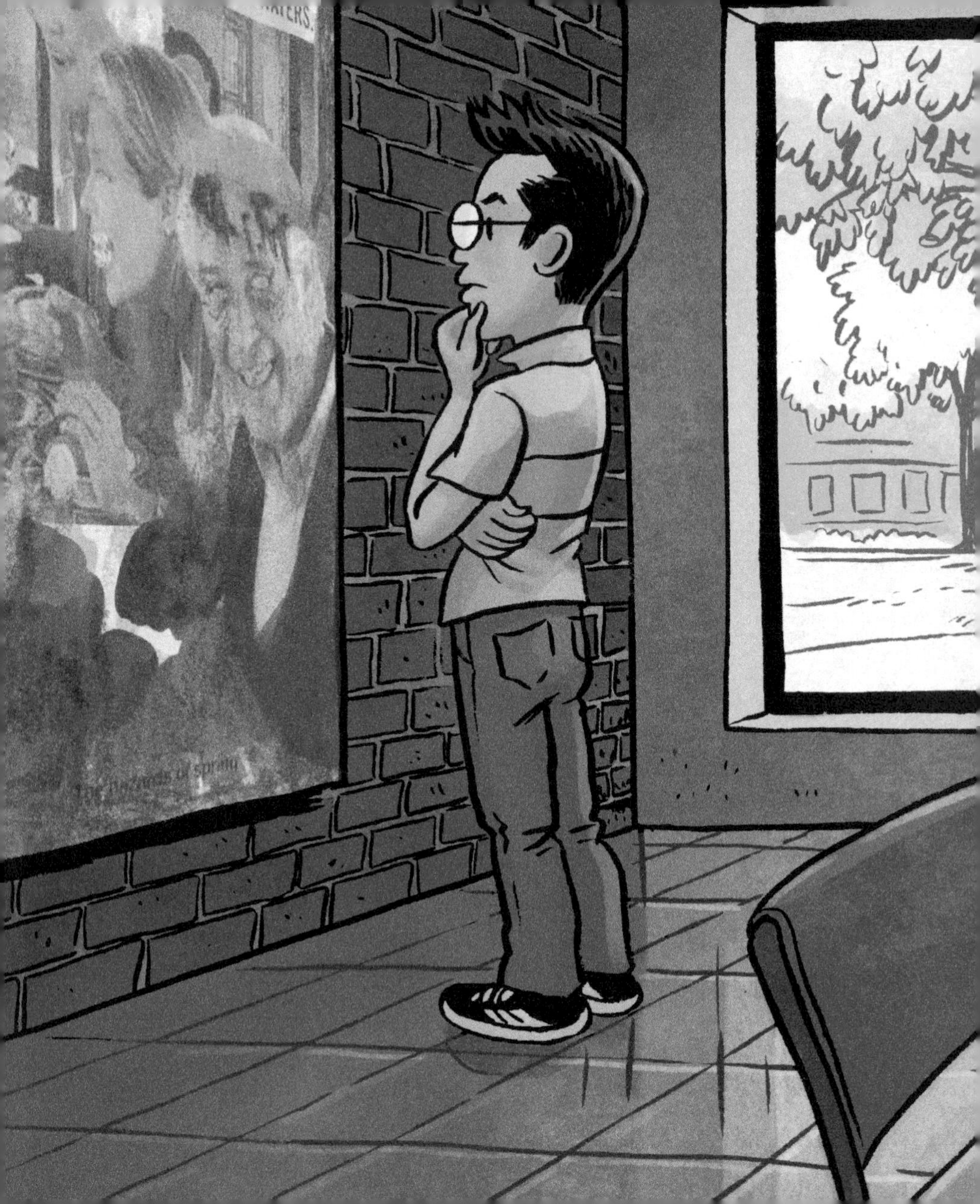

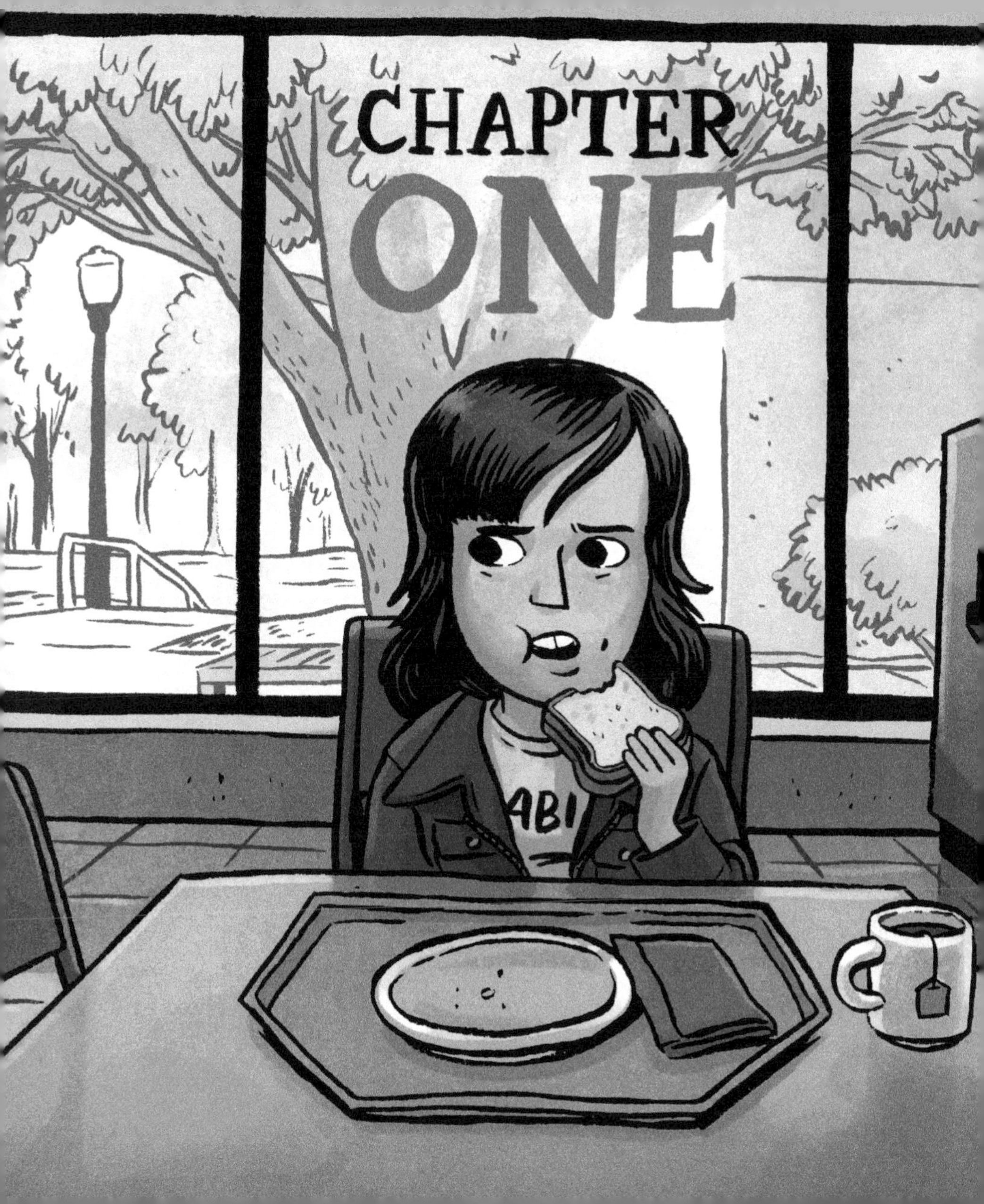
CHAPTER
ONE
ABI

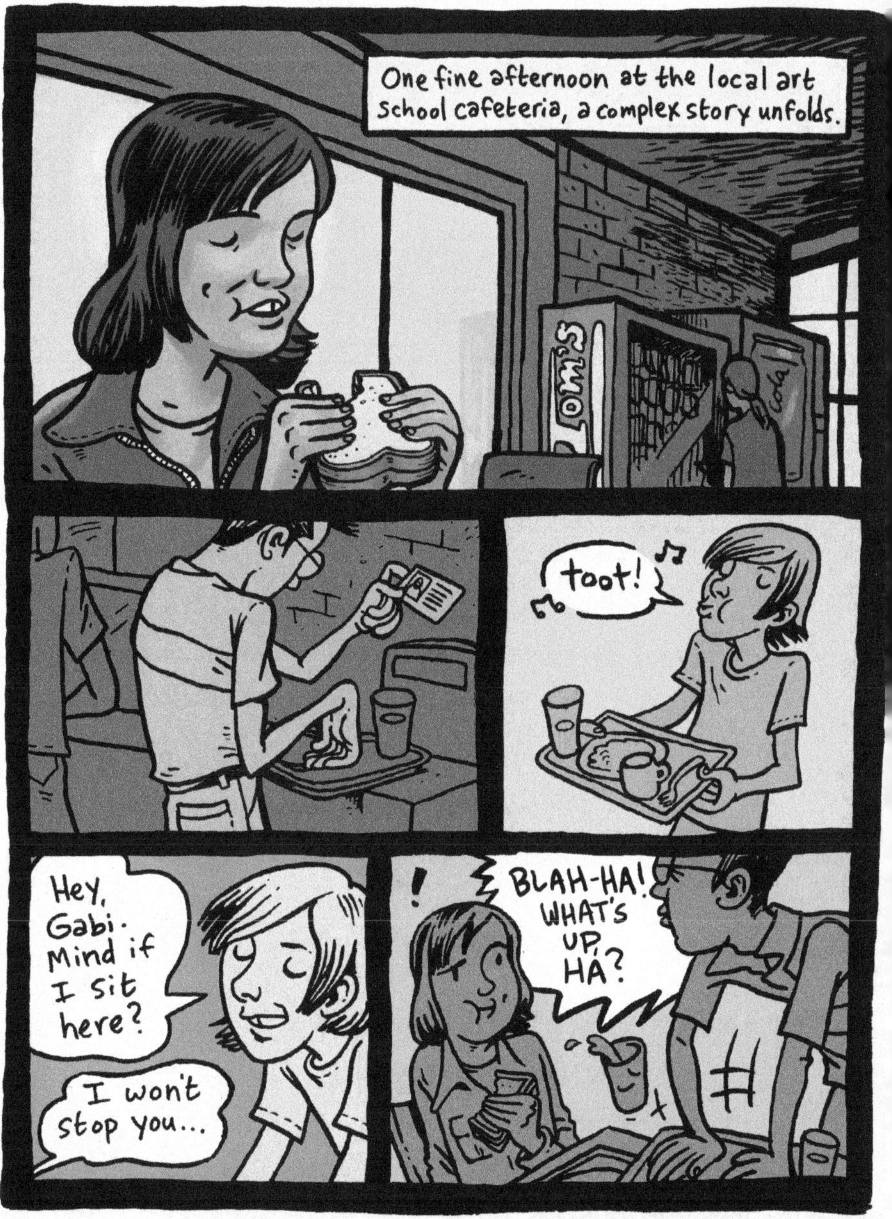
One fine afternoon at the local art school cafeteria, a complex story unfolds.
toot!
Hey, Gabi. Mind if I sit here?
I won't stop you...
!
BLAH-HA! WHAT'S UP, HA?

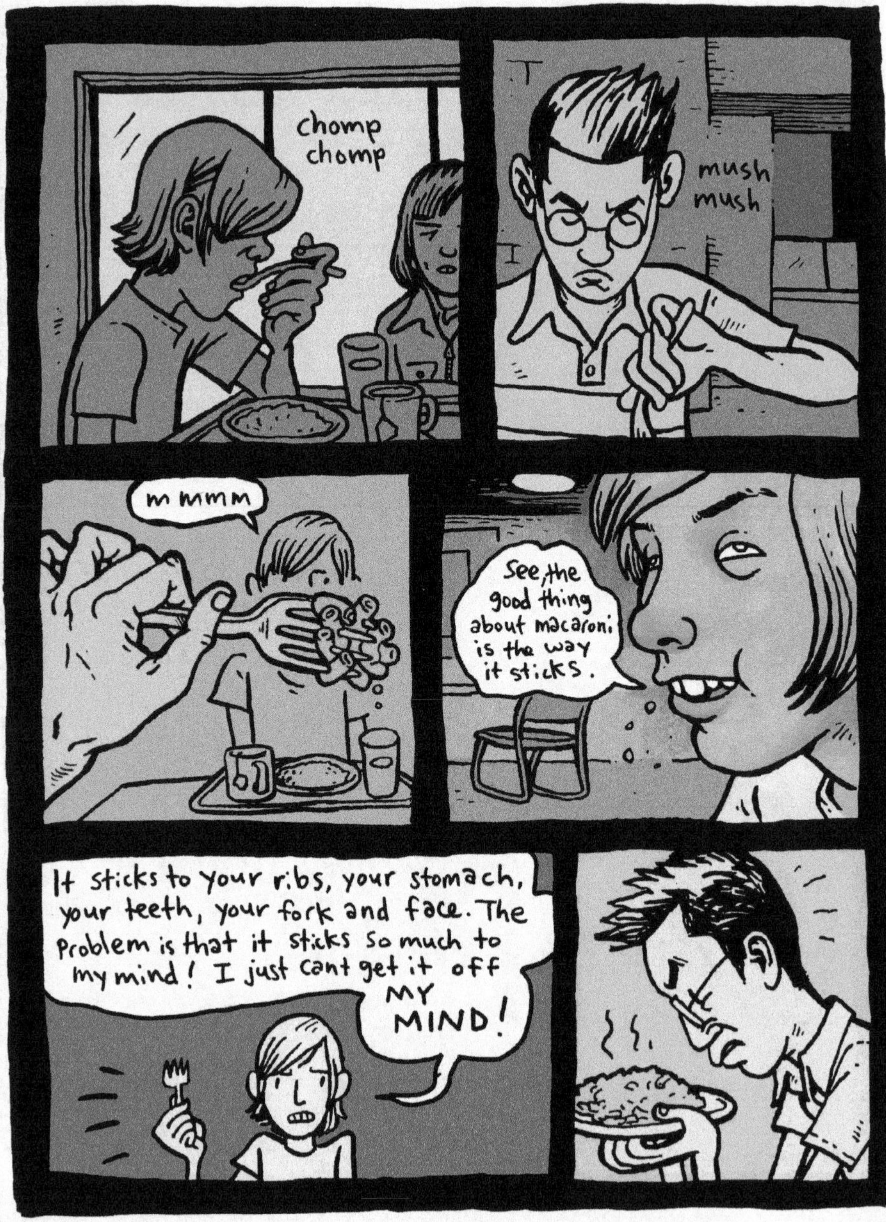
chomp
chomp
mush
mush
mmmm
See, the good thing about macaroni is the way it sticks.
It sticks to your ribs, your stomach, your teeth, your fork and face. The problem is that it sticks so much to my mind! I just cant get it off MY MIND!

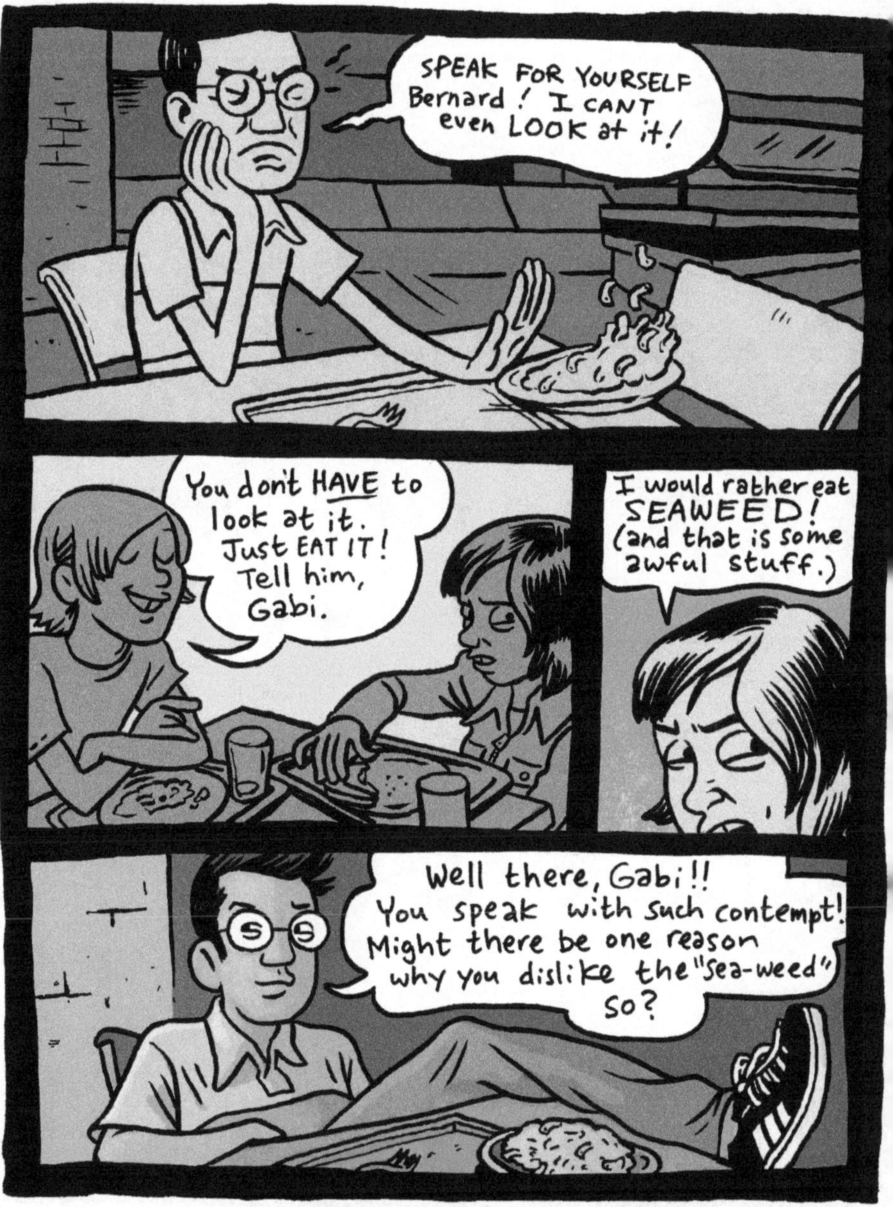
SPEAK FOR YOURSELF Bernard! I CANT even LOOK at it!
You don't HAVE to look at it. Just EAT IT! Tell him, Gabi.
I would rather eat SEAWEED! (and that is some awful stuff.)
Well there, Gabi!! You speak with such contempt! Might there be one reason why you dislike the "sea-weed" so?

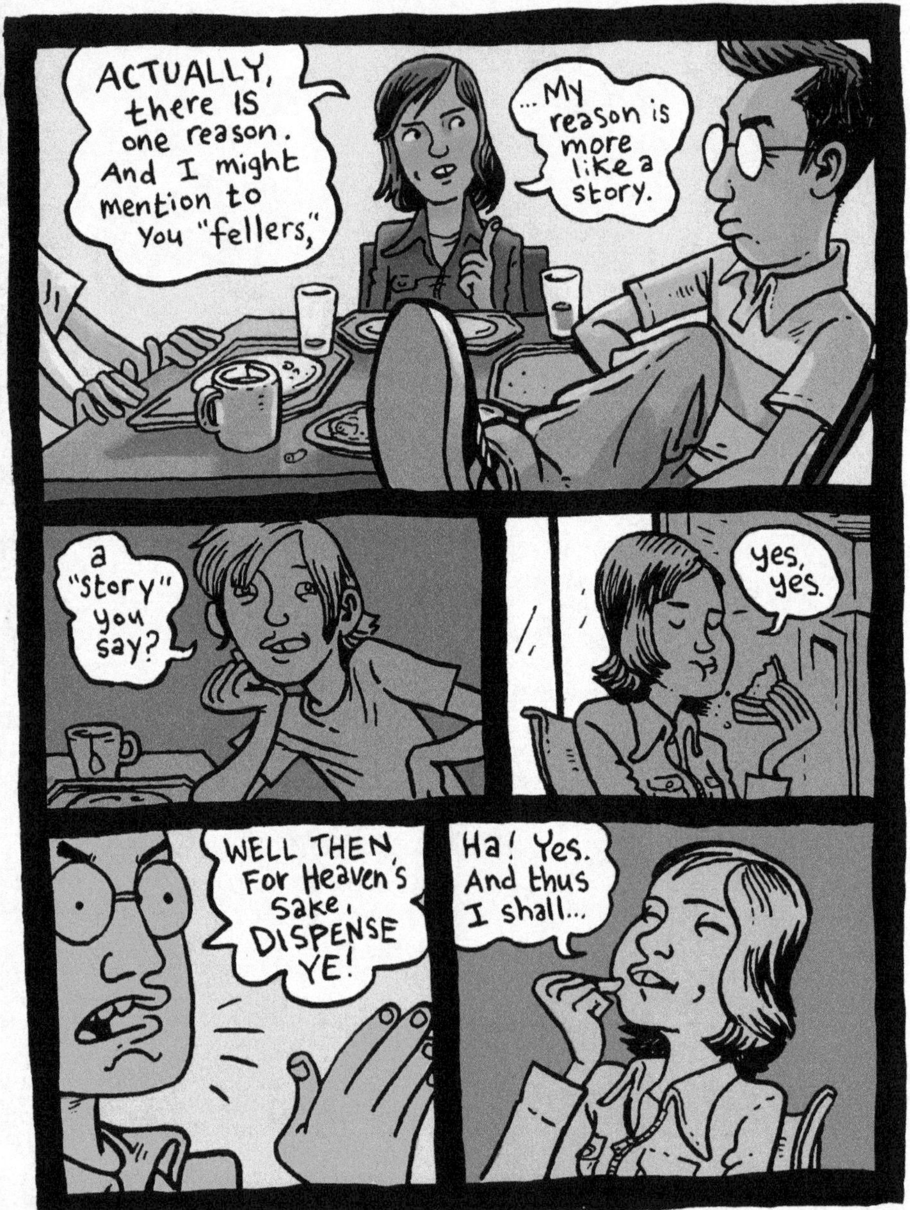
ACTUALLY, there IS one reason. And I might mention to you "fellers,"
...My reason is more like a story.
a "story" you say?
yes, yes.
WELL THEN, For Heaven's sake, DISPENSE YE!
Ha! Yes. And thus I shall...

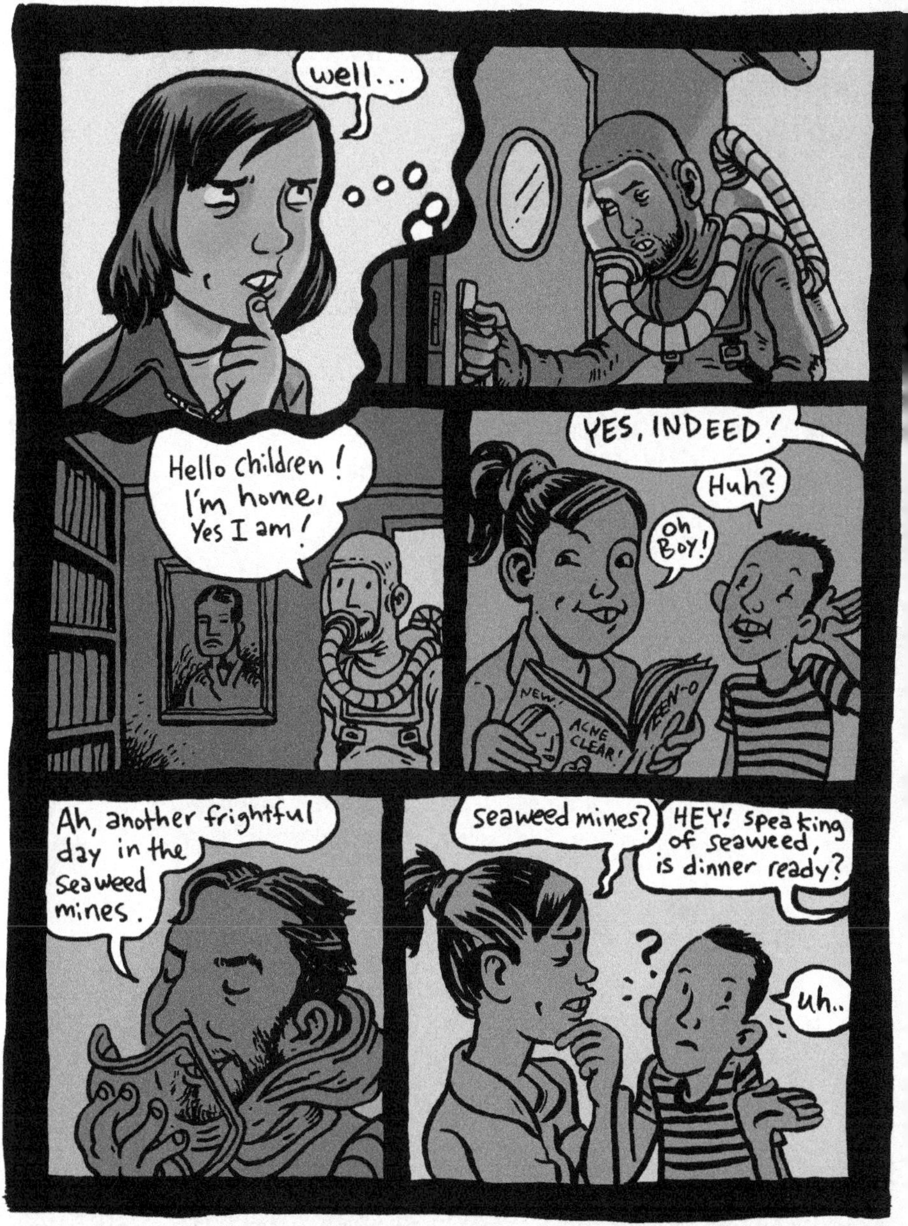

well...
Hello children! I'm home, Yes I am!
YES, INDEED!
Huh?
Oh Boy!
NEW!
ACNE CLEAR!
TEEN-O
Ah, another frightful day in the seaweed mines.
seaweed mines?
HEY! speaking of seaweed, is dinner ready?
?
uh..

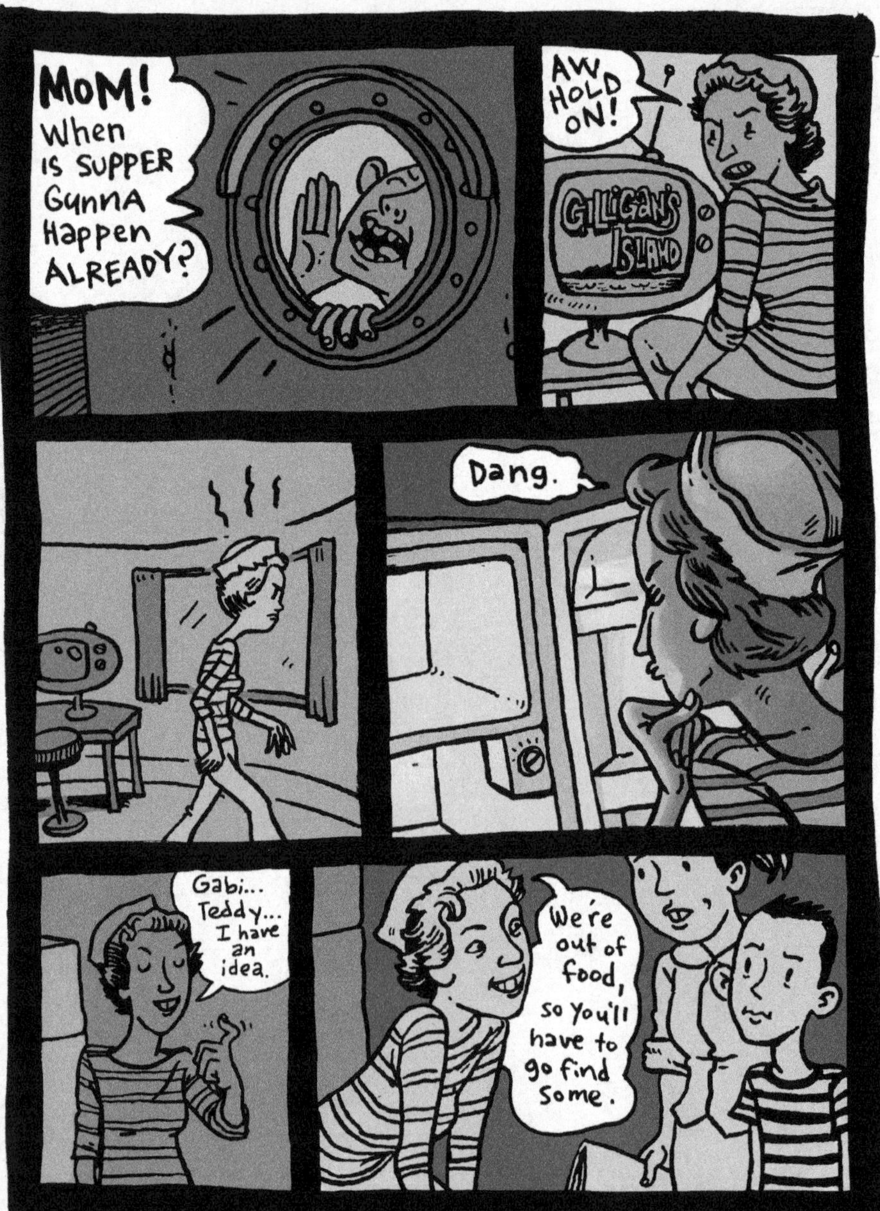
MoM! When IS SUPPER GuNNA Happen ALREADY?
AW HOLD ON!
GILLIGAN'S ISLAND
Dang.
Gabi... Teddy... I have an idea.
We're out of food, so you'll have to go find some.

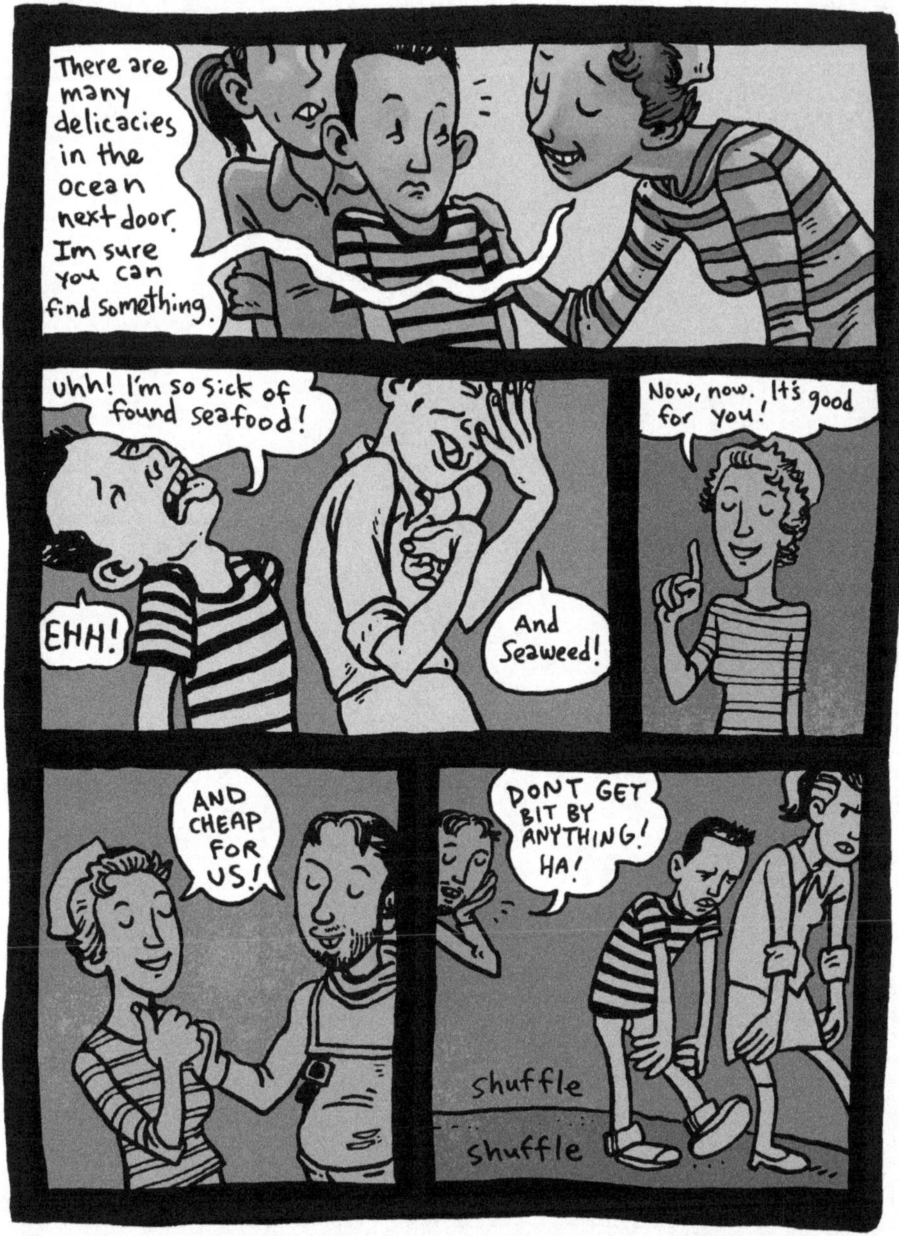
There are many delicacies in the ocean next door. Im sure you can find something.
uhh! I'm so sick of found seafood!
EHH!
And Seaweed!
Now, now. It's good for you!
AND CHEAP FOR US!
DONT GET BIT BY ANYTHING! HA!
shuffle
shuffle

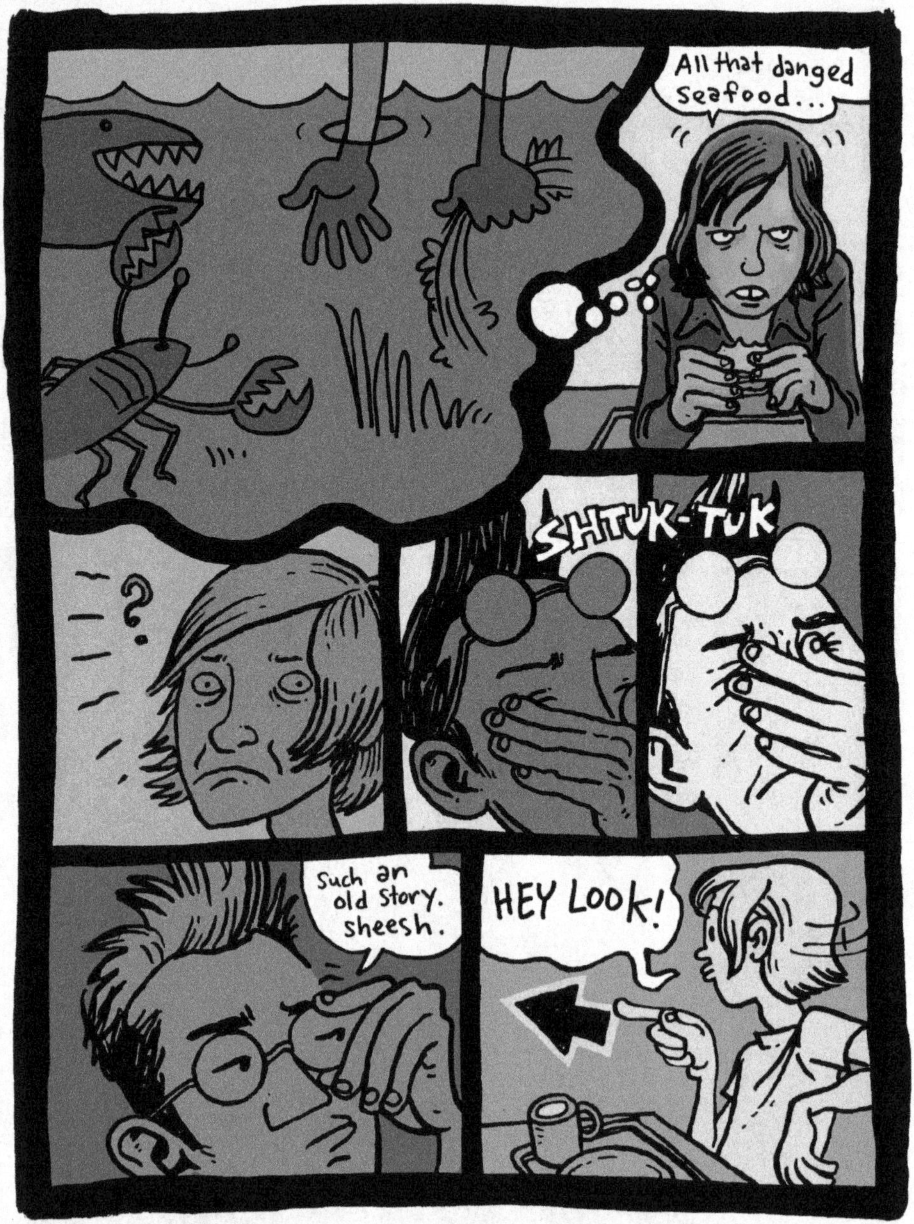
All that danged seafood...
SHTUK-TUK
Such an old story. sheesh.
HEY LOOK!

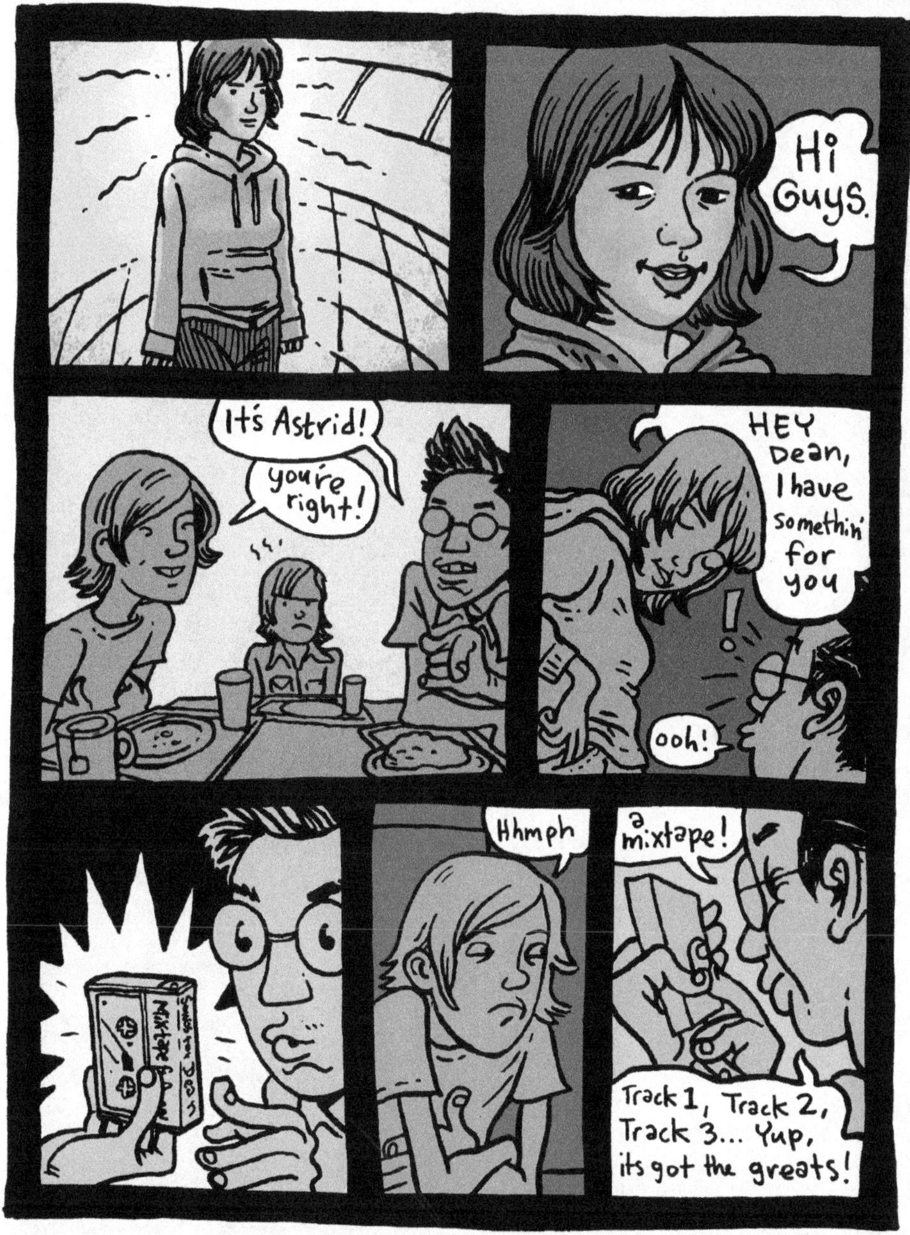
Hi Guys.
It's Astrid!
you're right!
HEY Dean, I have somethin' for you
ooh!
Hhmph
a mixtape!
Track 1, Track 2, Track 3... Yup, its got the greats!

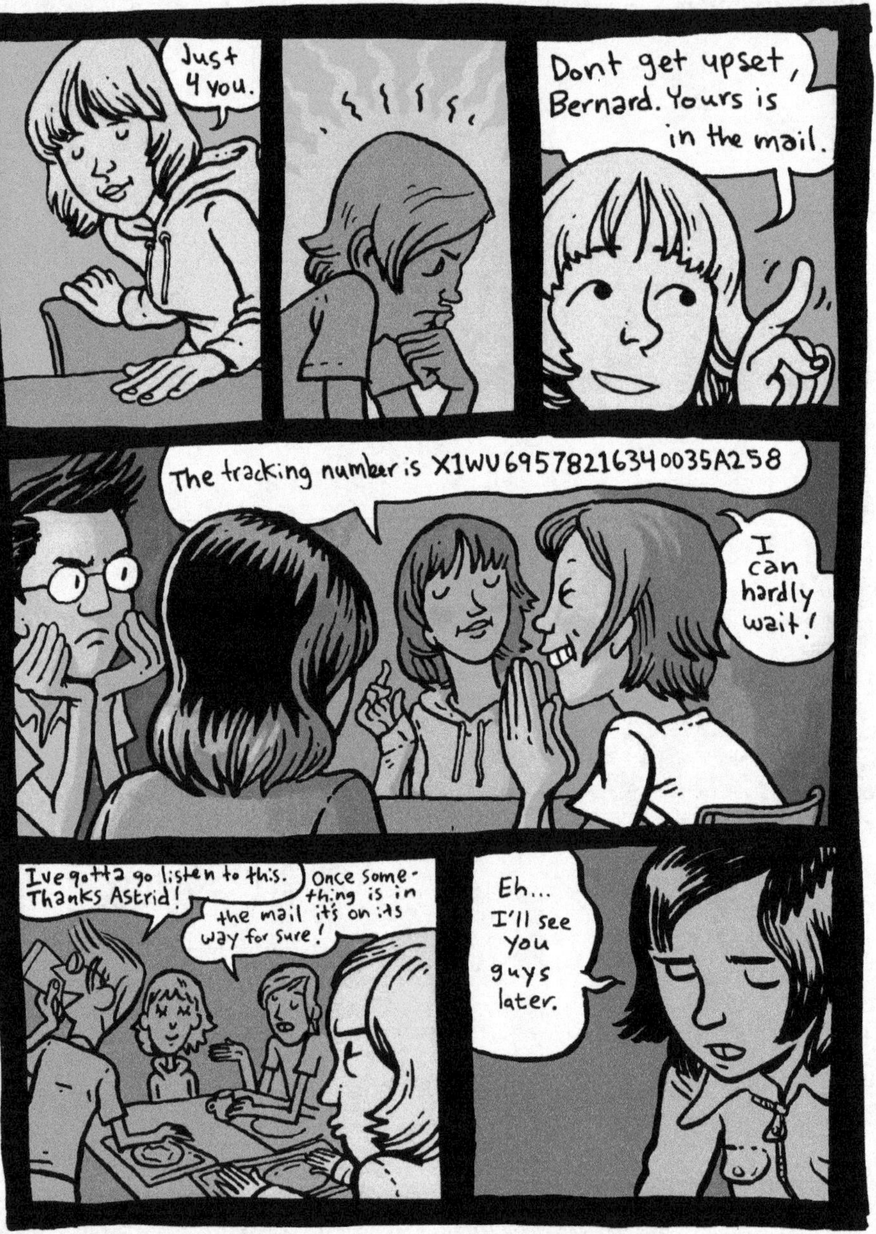

Just 4 you.
Dont get upset, Bernard. Yours is in the mail.
The tracking number is X1WU69578216340035A258
I can hardly wait!
Ive gotta go listen to this. Thanks Astrid!
Once something is in the mail it's on its way for sure!
Eh... I'll see you guys later.

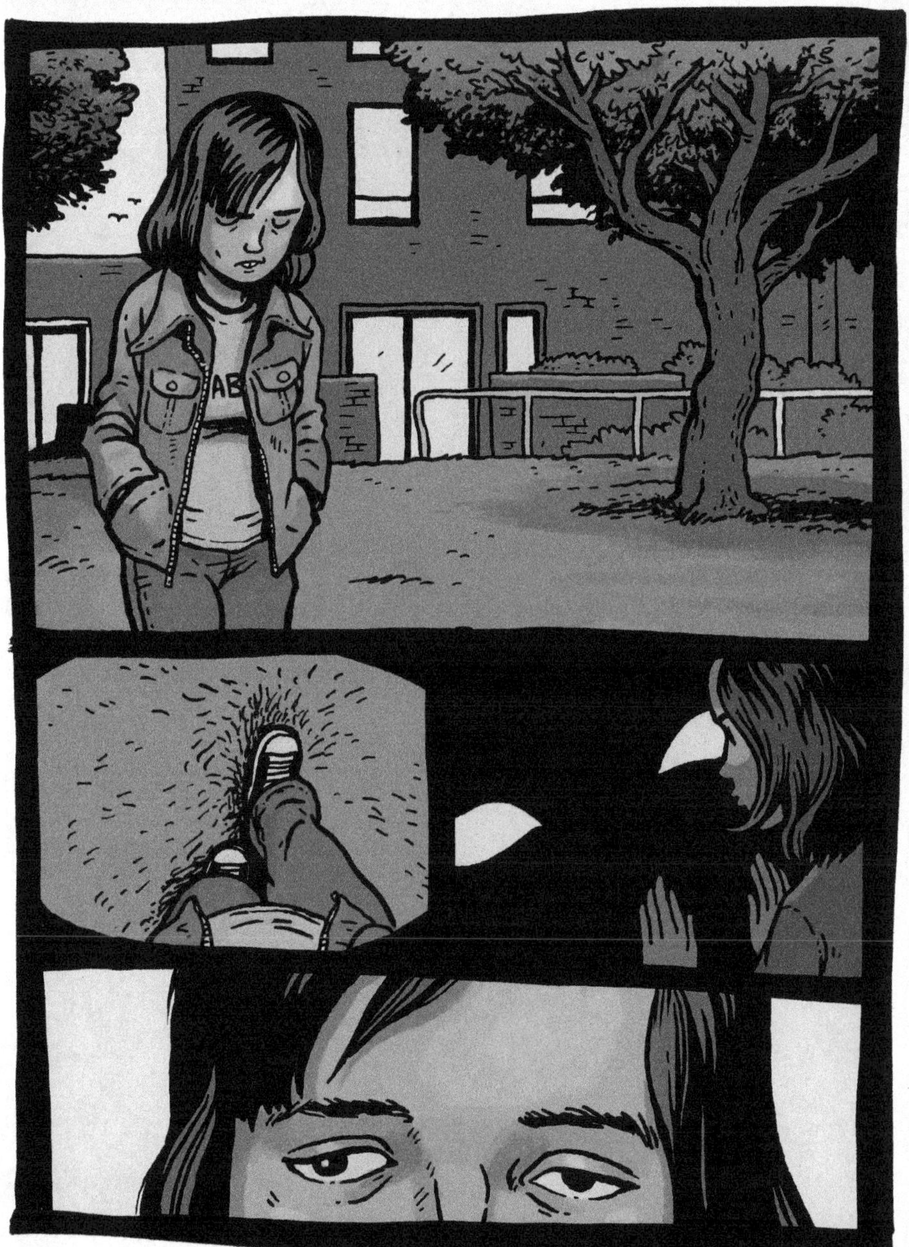

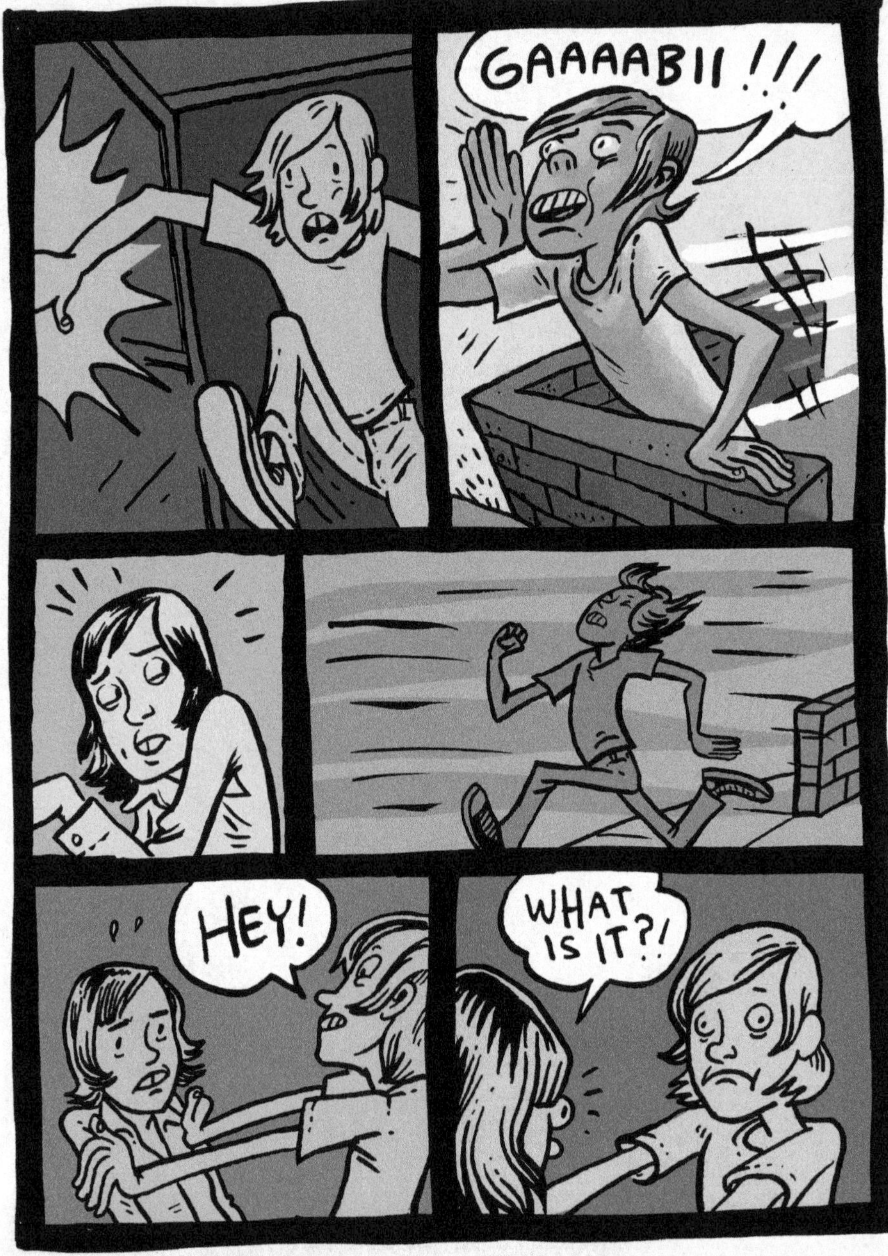
GAAAABII!!!
HEY!
WHAT IS IT?!

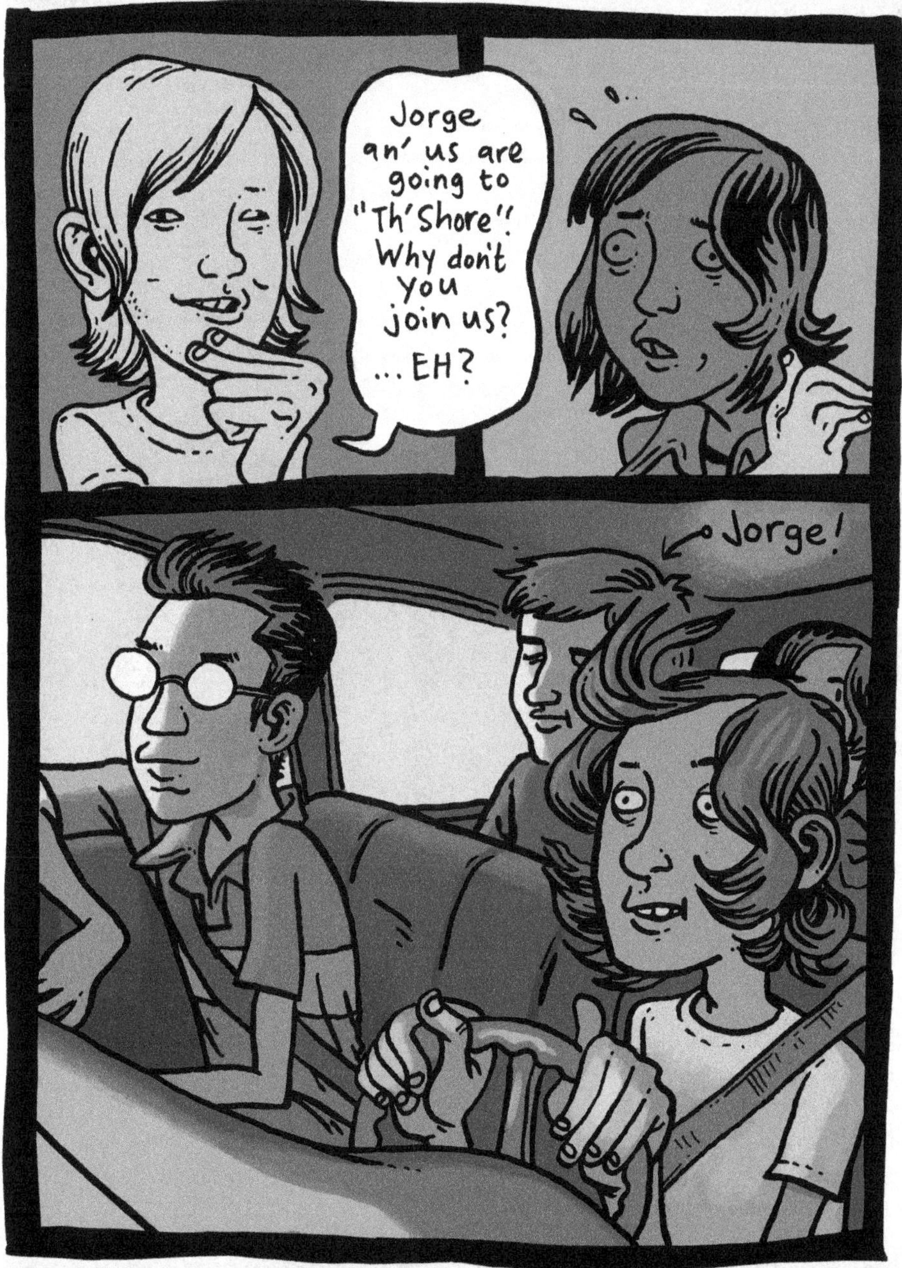
Jorge an' us are going to "Th'Shore"! Why don't you join us? ...EH?
Jorge!

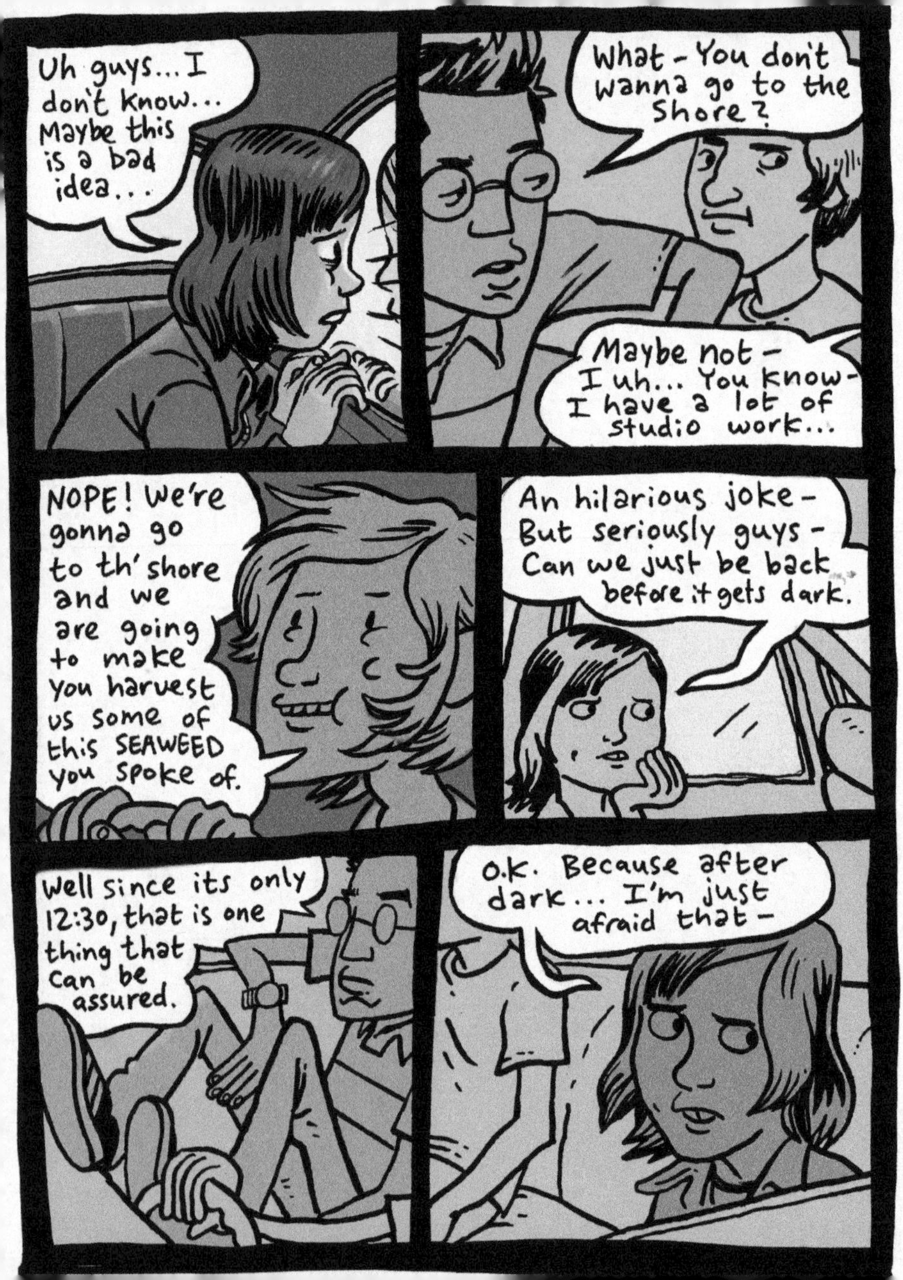
Uh guys... I don't know... Maybe this is a bad idea...
What - You don't wanna go to the Shore?
Maybe not - I uh... You know - I have a lot of studio work...
NOPE! We're gonna go to th' shore and we are going to make you harvest us some of this SEAWEED you spoke of.
An hilarious joke - But seriously guys - Can we just be back before it gets dark.
Well since its only 12:30, that is one thing that can be assured.
O.K. Because after dark... I'm just afraid that -

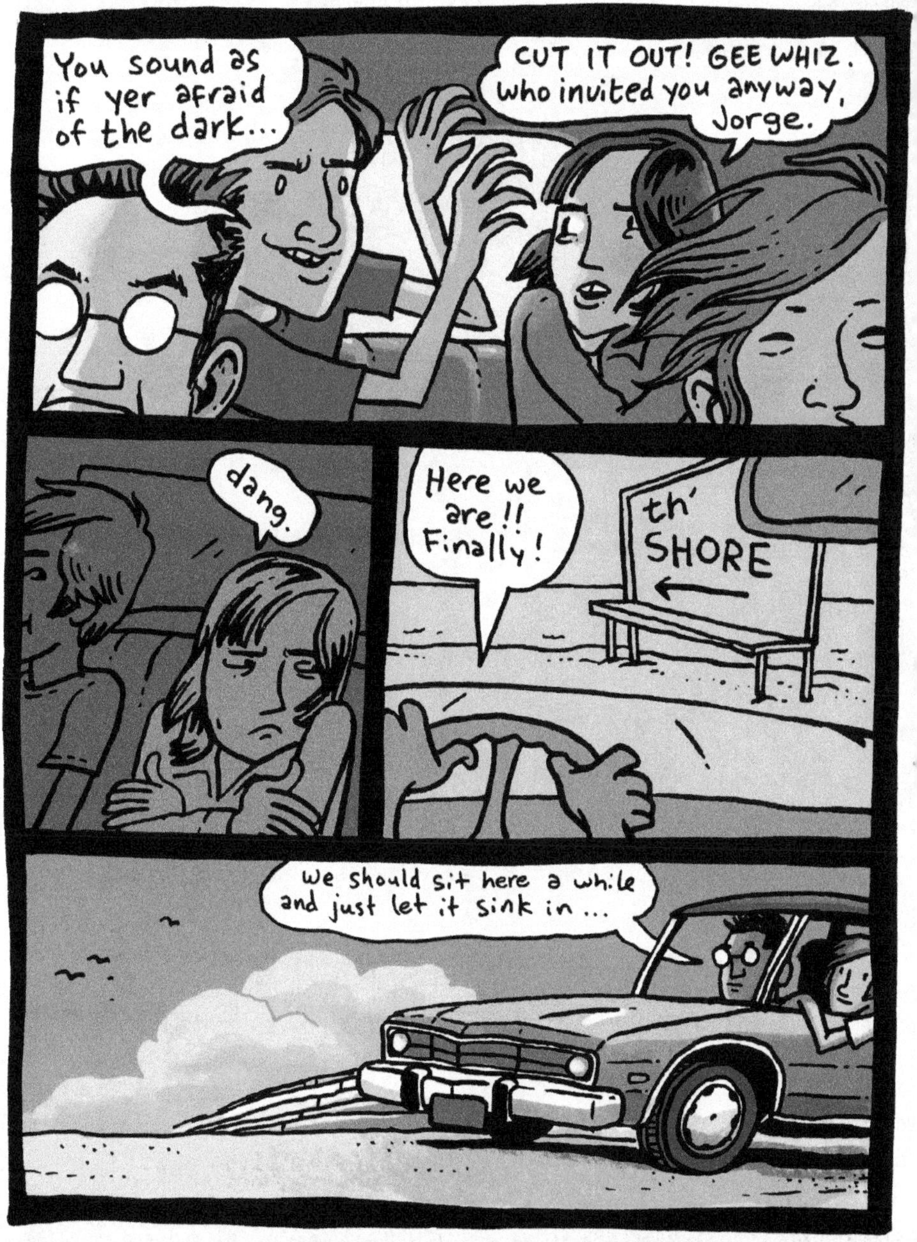
You sound as if yer afraid of the dark...
CUT IT OUT! GEE WHIZ. who invited you anyway, Jorge.
dang.
Here we are!! Finally!
th' SHORE
we should sit here a while and just let it sink in...

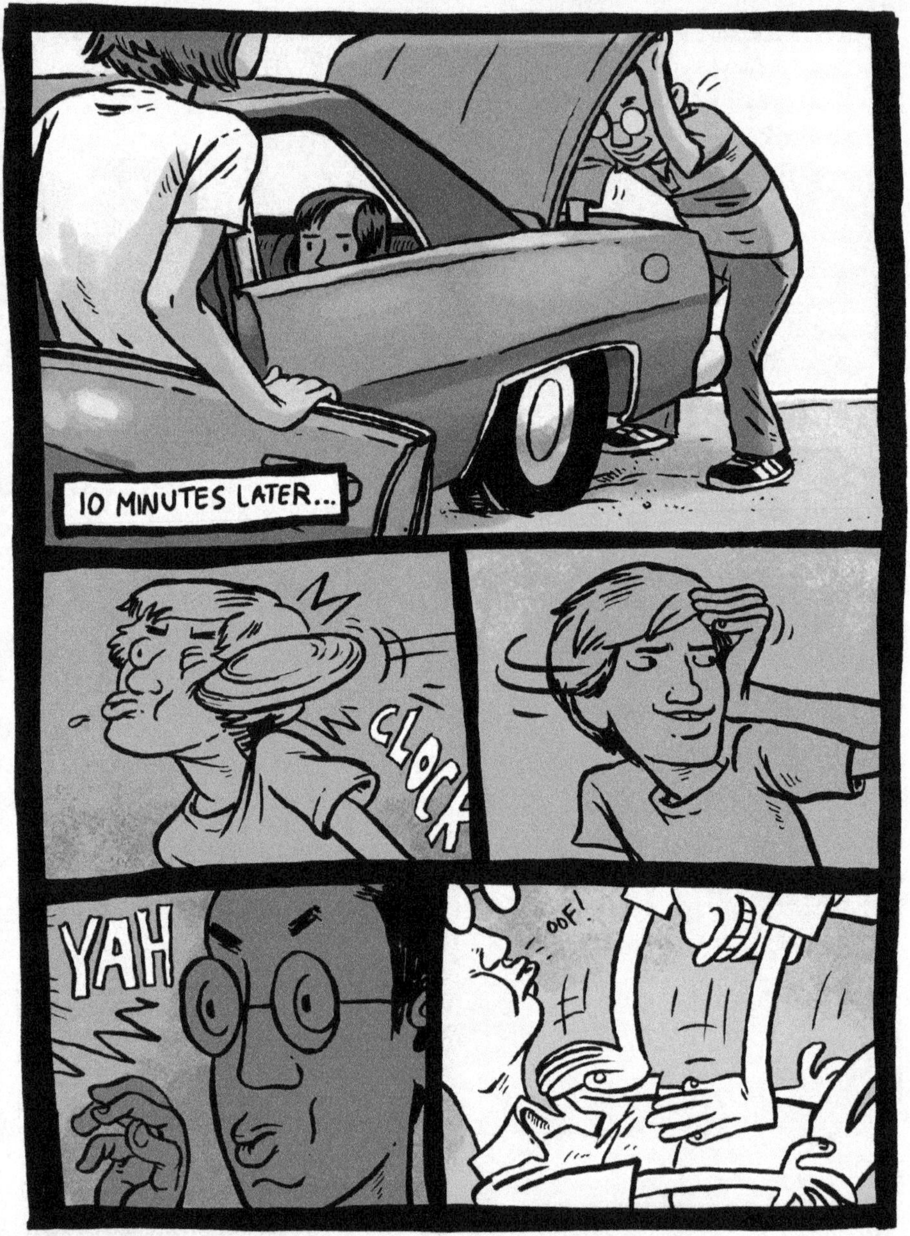
10 MINUTES LATER...
CLOCK
YAH
OOF!

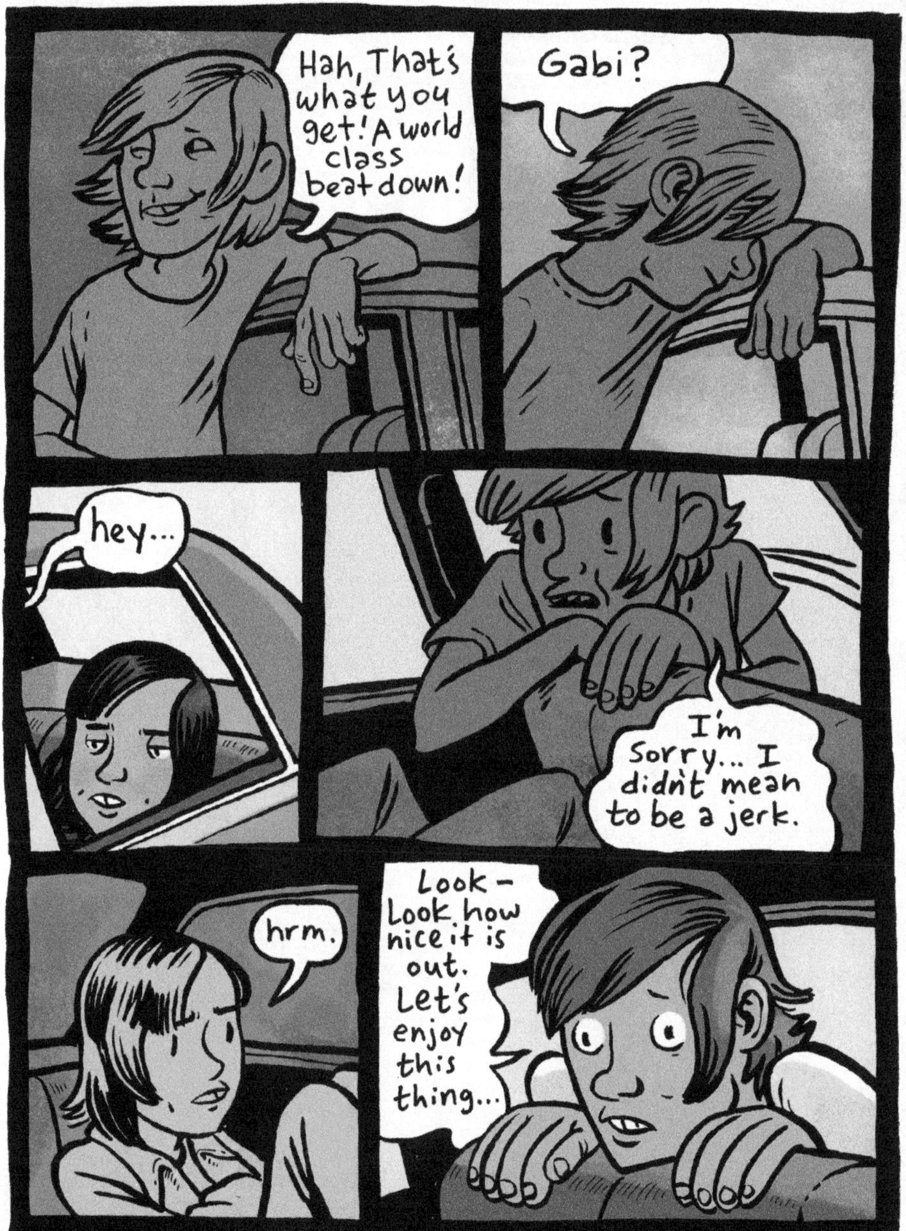
Hah, That's what you get! A world class beat down!
Gabi?
hey...
I'm Sorry... I didn't mean to be a jerk.
hrm.
Look - Look how nice it is out. Let's enjoy this thing...

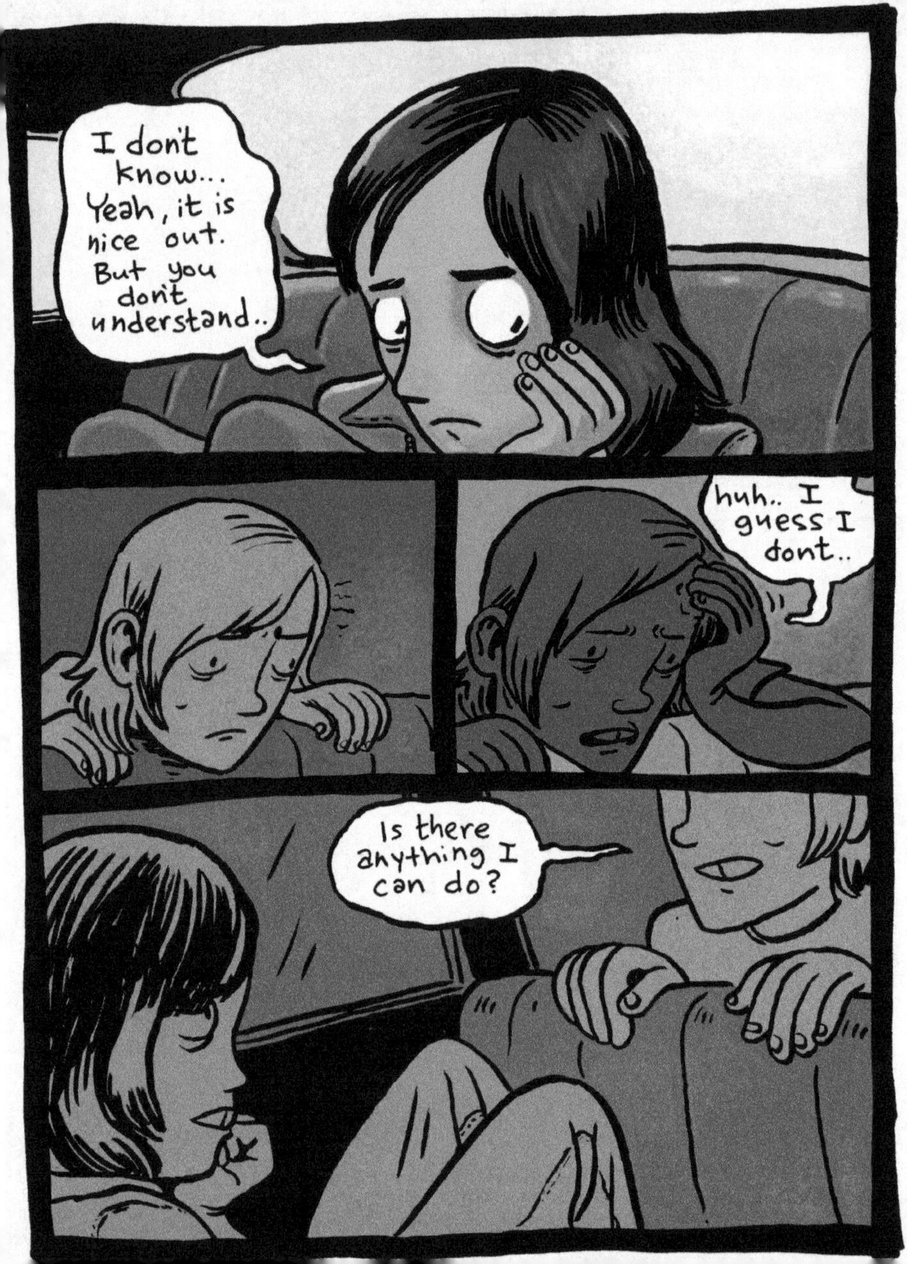
I don't know... Yeah, it is nice out. But you don't understand..
huh.. I guess I dont..
Is there anything I can do?

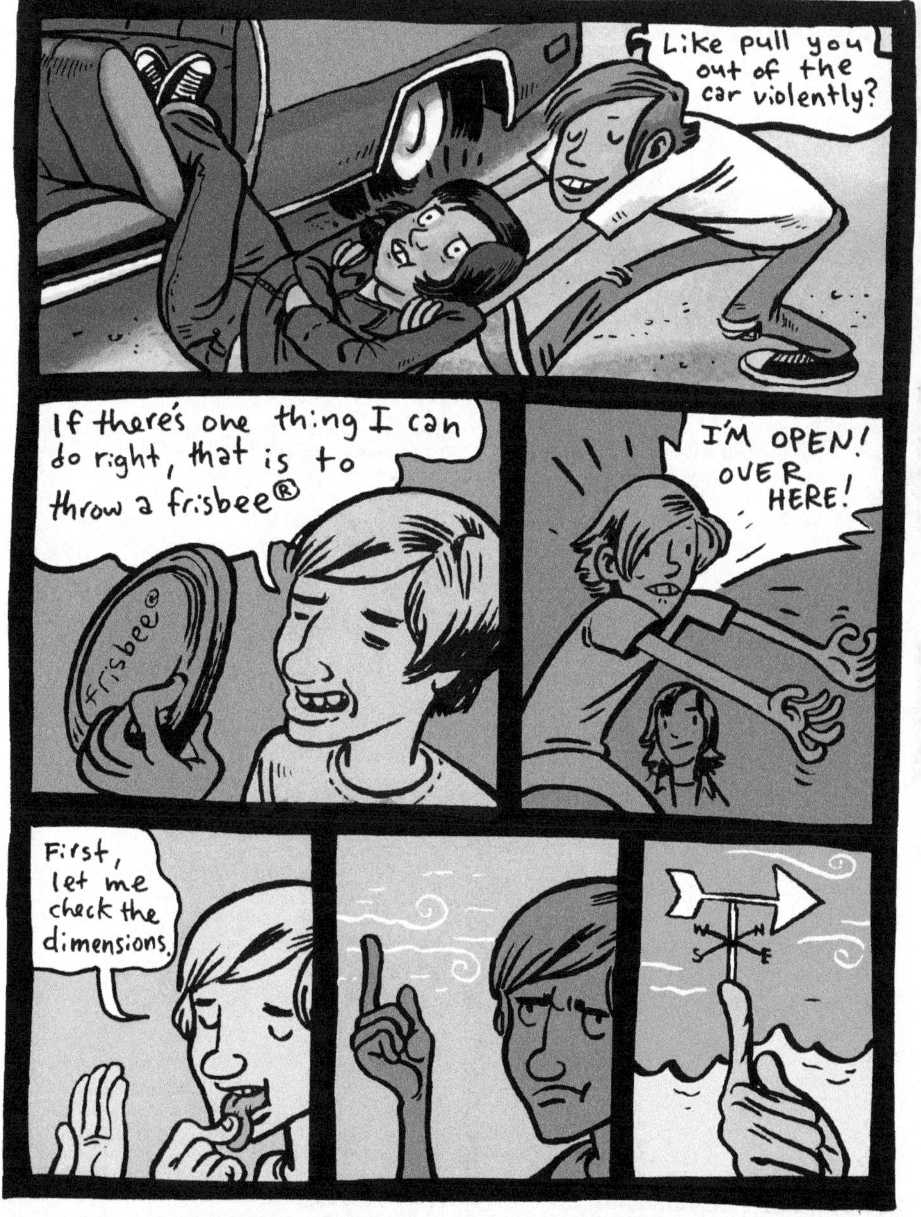
Like pull you out of the car violently?
If there's one thing I can do right, that is to throw a frisbee®
frisbee®
I'M OPEN! OVER HERE!
First, let me check the dimensions.
W
N
S
E

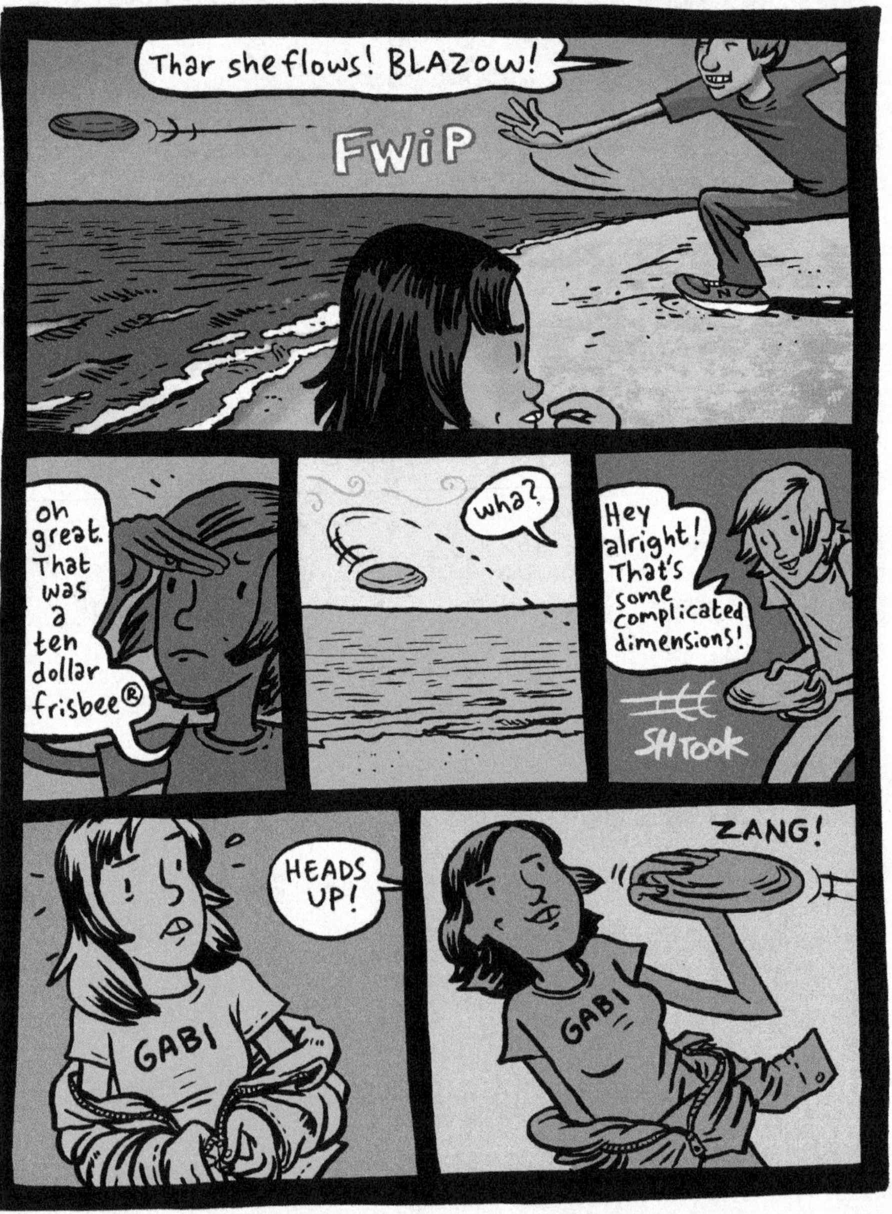
Thar she flows! BLAZOW!
FWIP
oh great. That was a ten dollar frisbee®
wha?
Hey alright! That's some complicated dimensions!
SHTOOK
HEADS UP!
GABI
ZANG!
GABI

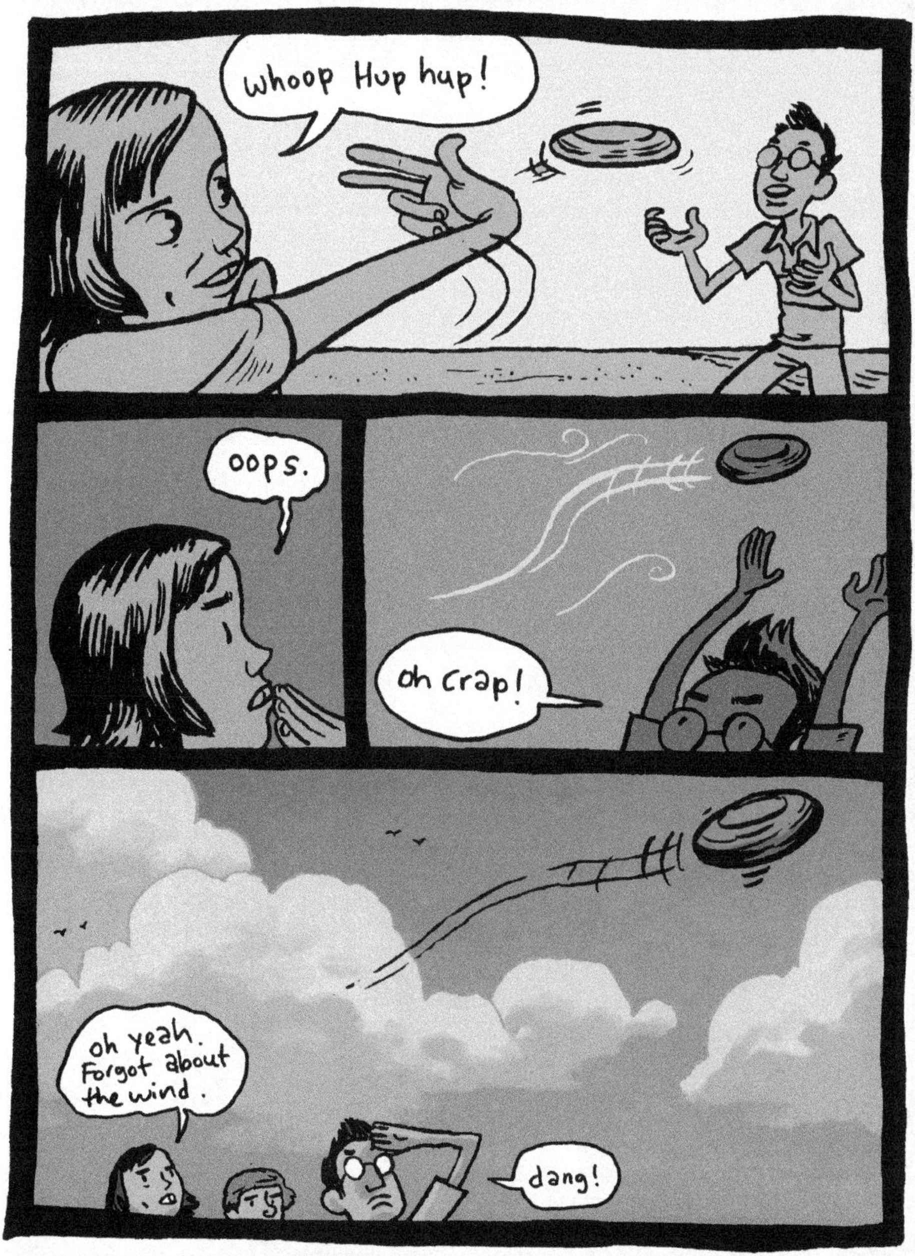
whoop Hup hup!
oops.
oh crap!
oh yeah. Forgot about the wind.
dang!

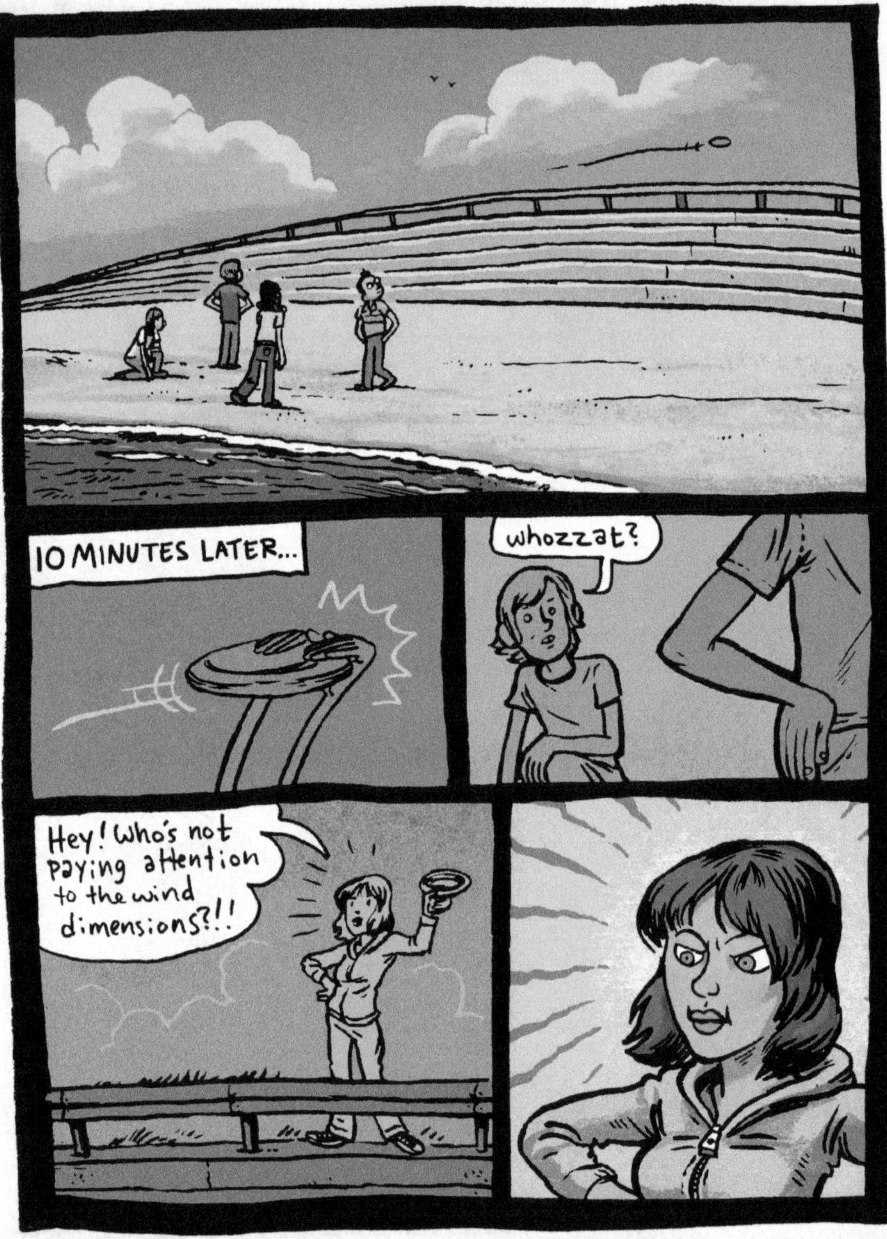
10 MINUTES LATER...
whozzat?
Hey! Who's not paying attention to the wind dimensions?!!

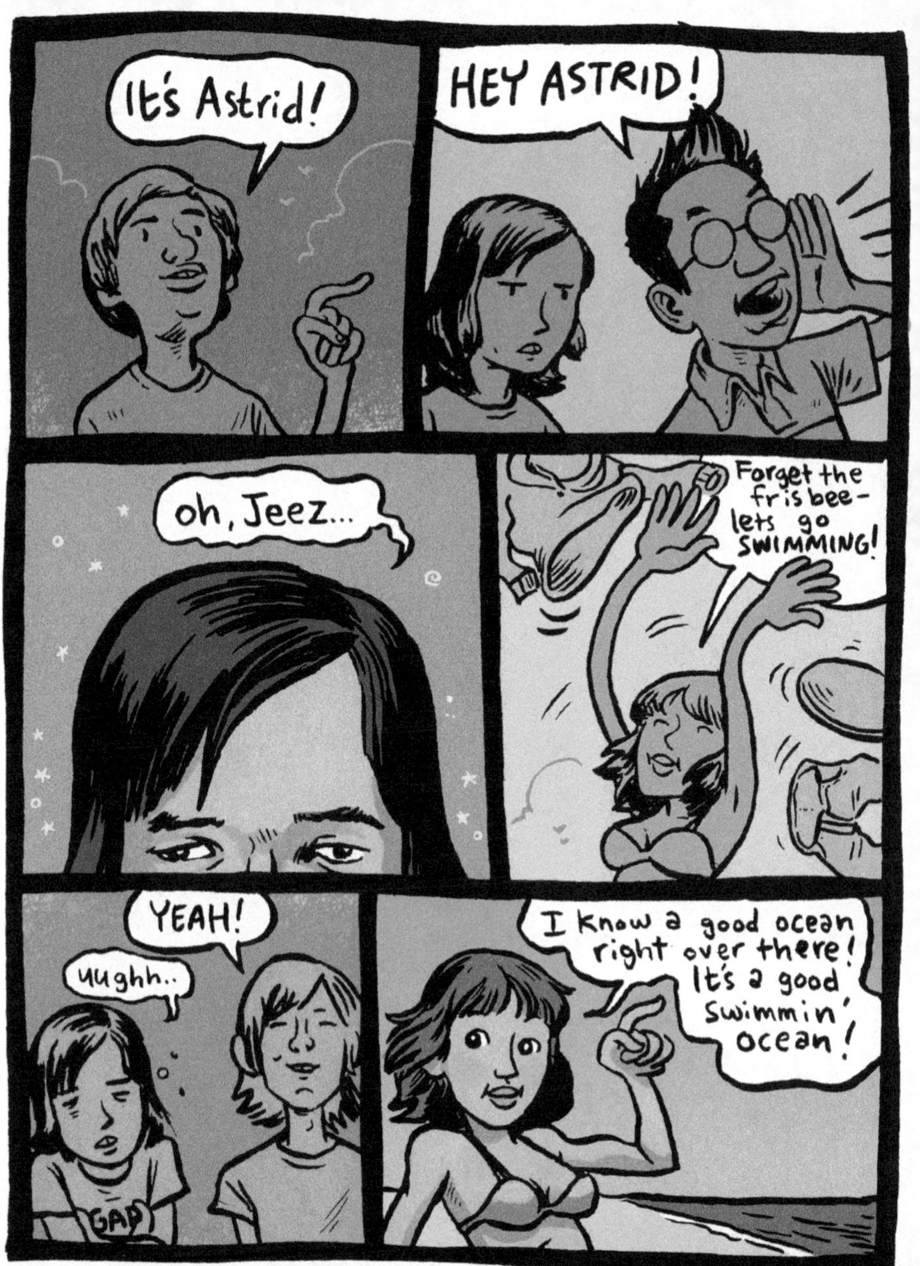
It's Astrid!
HEY ASTRID!
oh, Jeez...
Forget the frisbee- lets go SWIMMING!
YEAH!
uughh..
I know a good ocean right over there! It's a good swimmin' ocean!
GAP

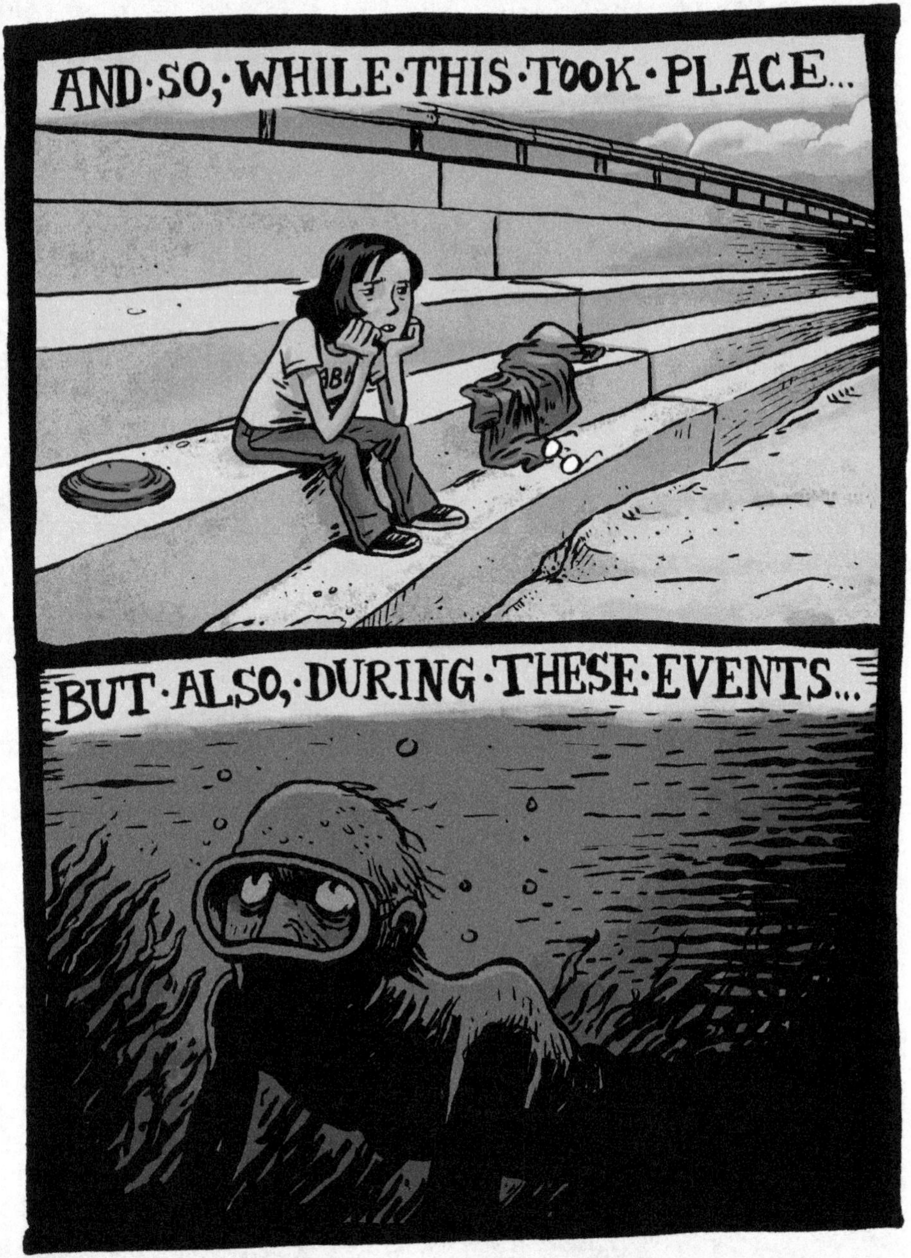
AND·SO,·WHILE·THIS·TOOK·PLACE...
BUT·ALSO,·DURING·THESE·EVENTS...

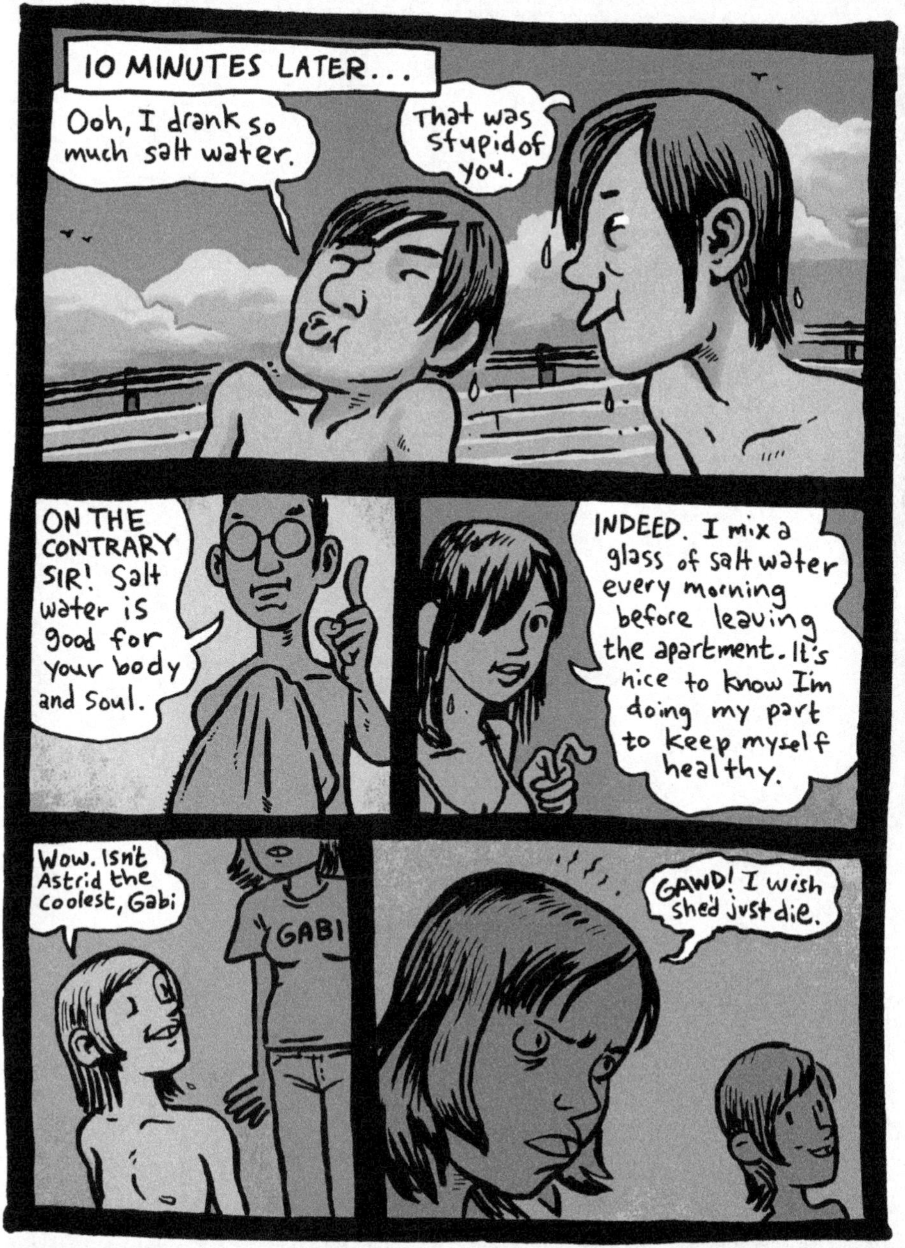

10 MINUTES LATER...
Ooh, I drank so much salt water.
That was stupid of you.
ON THE CONTRARY SIR! Salt water is good for your body and soul.
INDEED. I mix a glass of salt water every morning before leaving the apartment. It's nice to know I'm doing my part to keep myself healthy.
Wow. Isn't Astrid the coolest, Gabi
GABI
GAWD! I wish she'd just die.

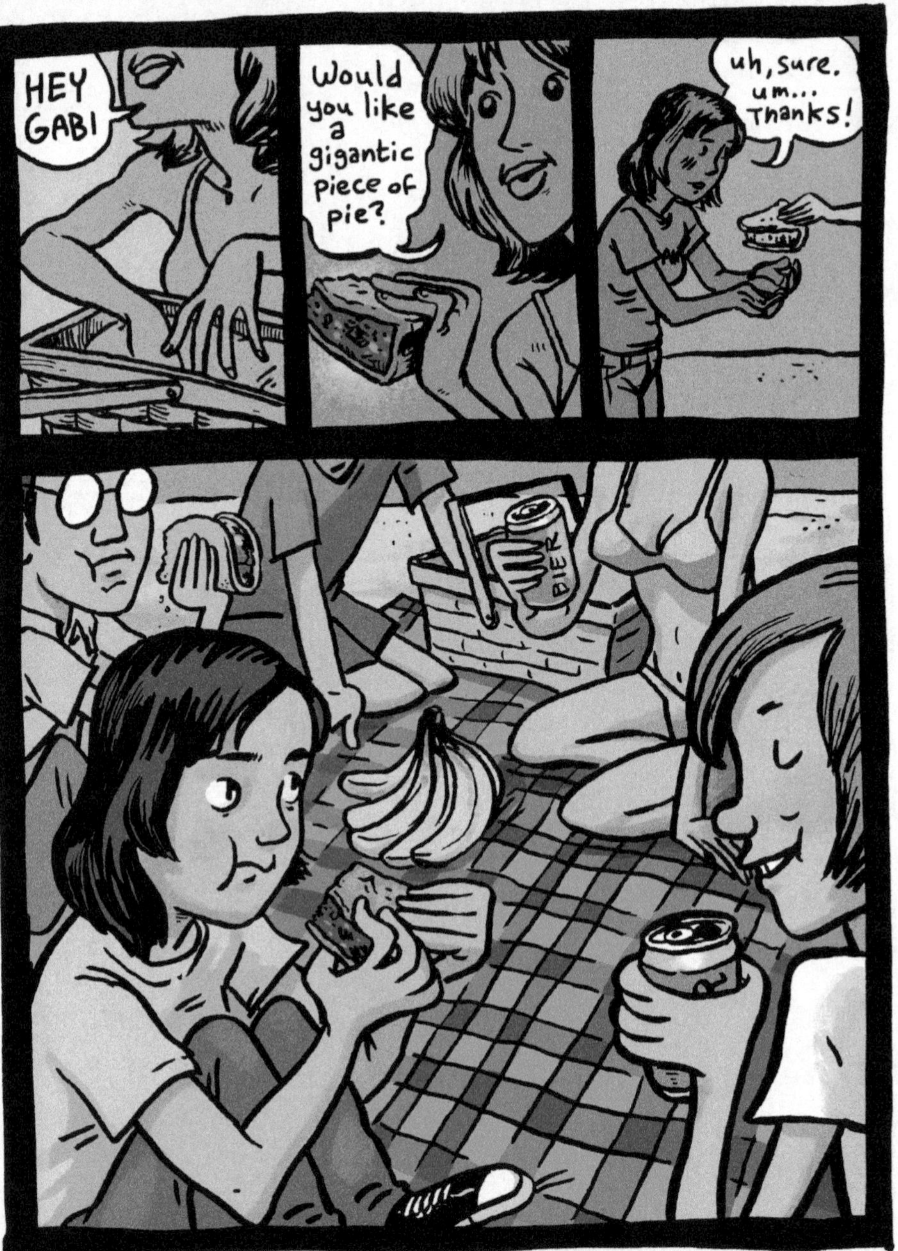
HEY GABI
Would you like a gigantic piece of pie?
uh, sure. um... Thanks!
BIER

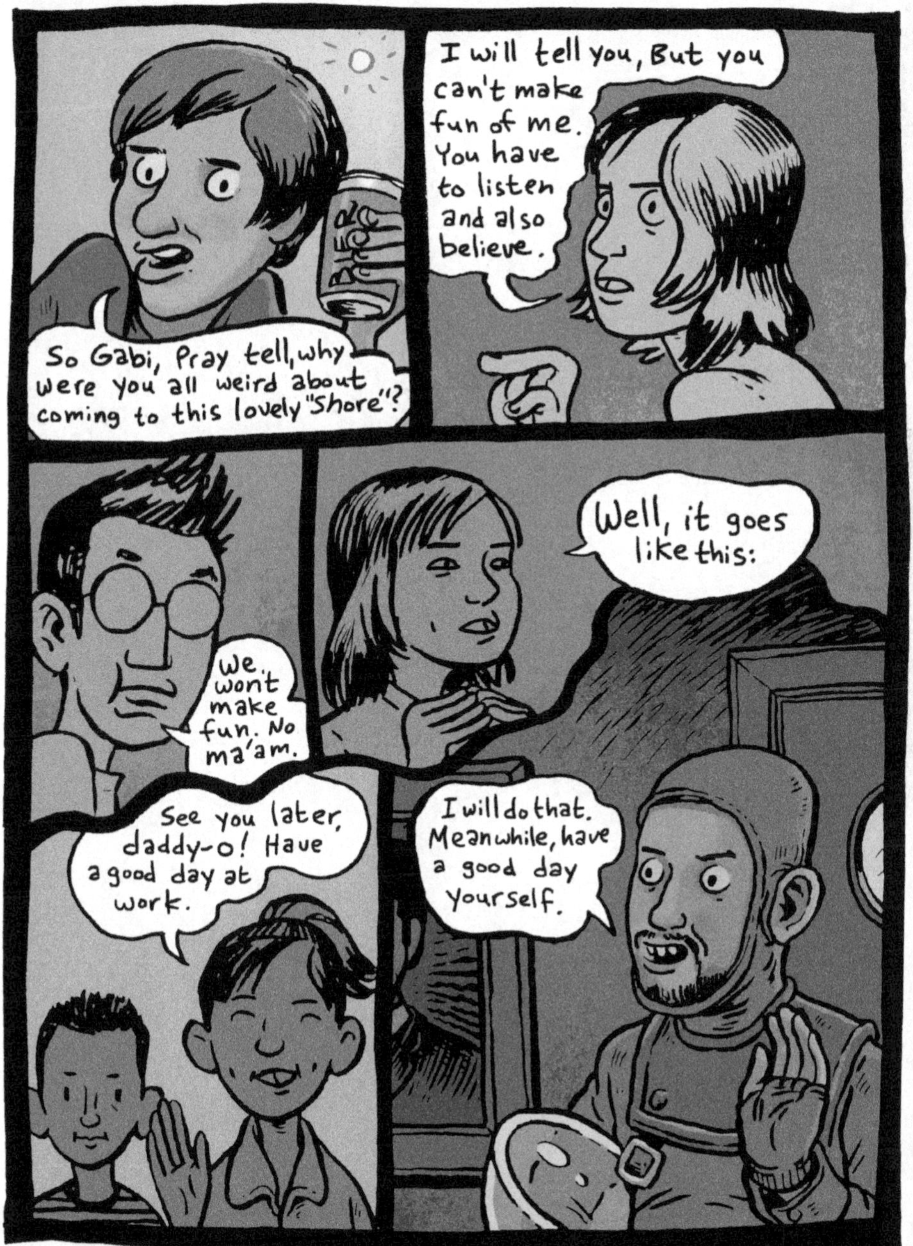
So Gabi, Pray tell, why were you all weird about coming to this lovely "Shore"?
I will tell you, But you can't make fun of me. You have to listen and also believe.
We won't make fun. No ma'am.
Well, it goes like this:
See you later, daddy-o! Have a good day at work.
I will do that. Meanwhile, have a good day yourself.

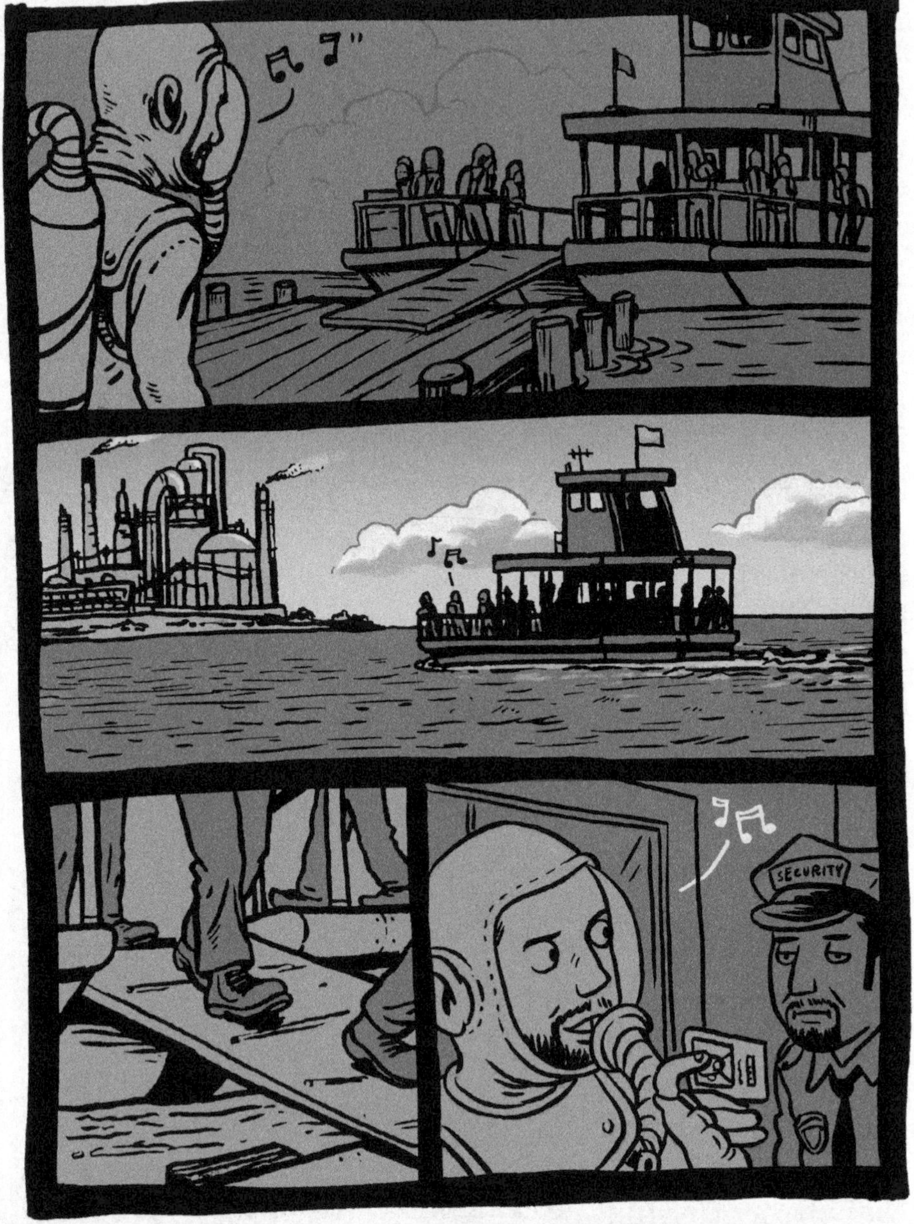
SECURITY

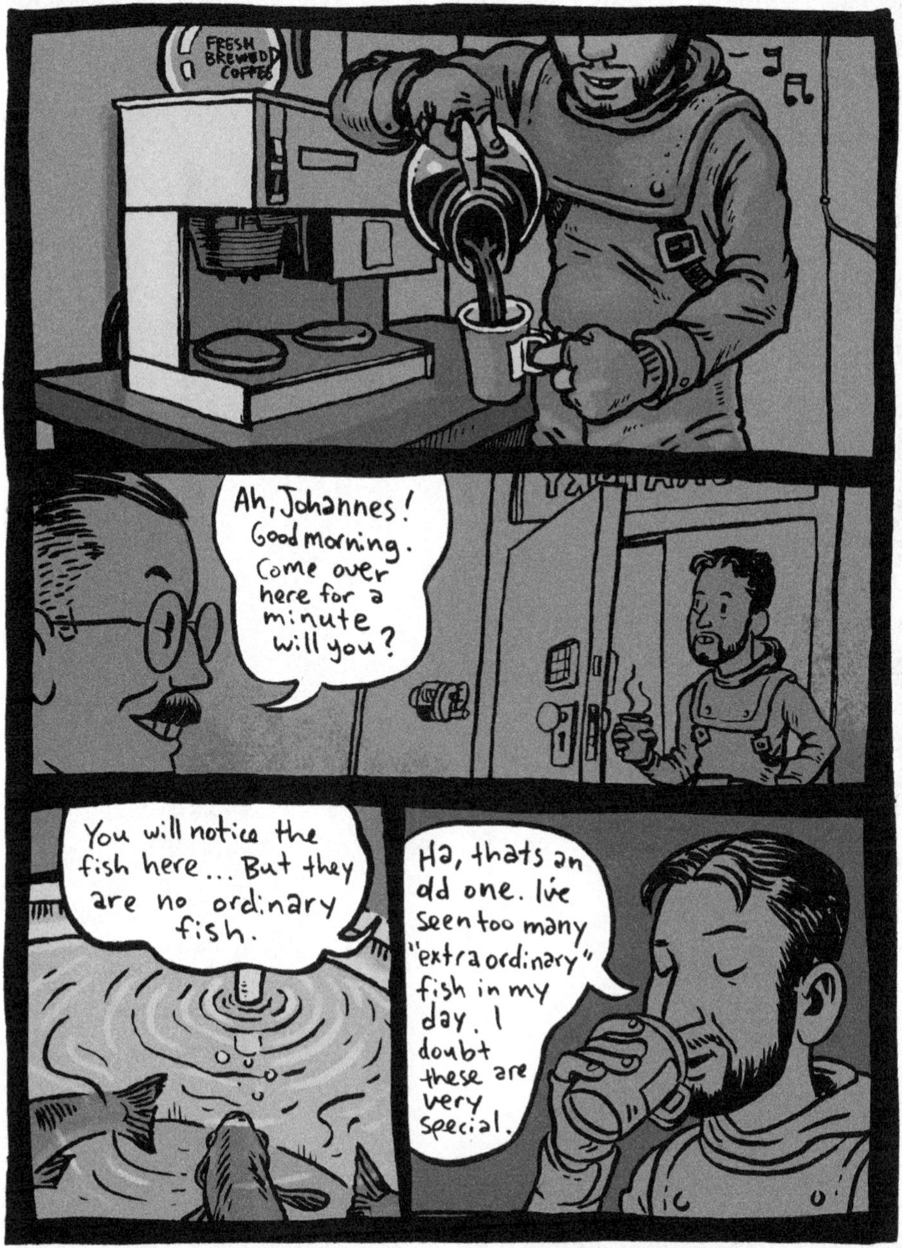
FRESH BREWED COFFEE
Ah, Johannes! Good morning. Come over here for a minute will you?
You will notice the fish here... But they are no ordinary fish.
Ha, thats an odd one. I've seen too many "extraordinary" fish in my day. I doubt these are very special.

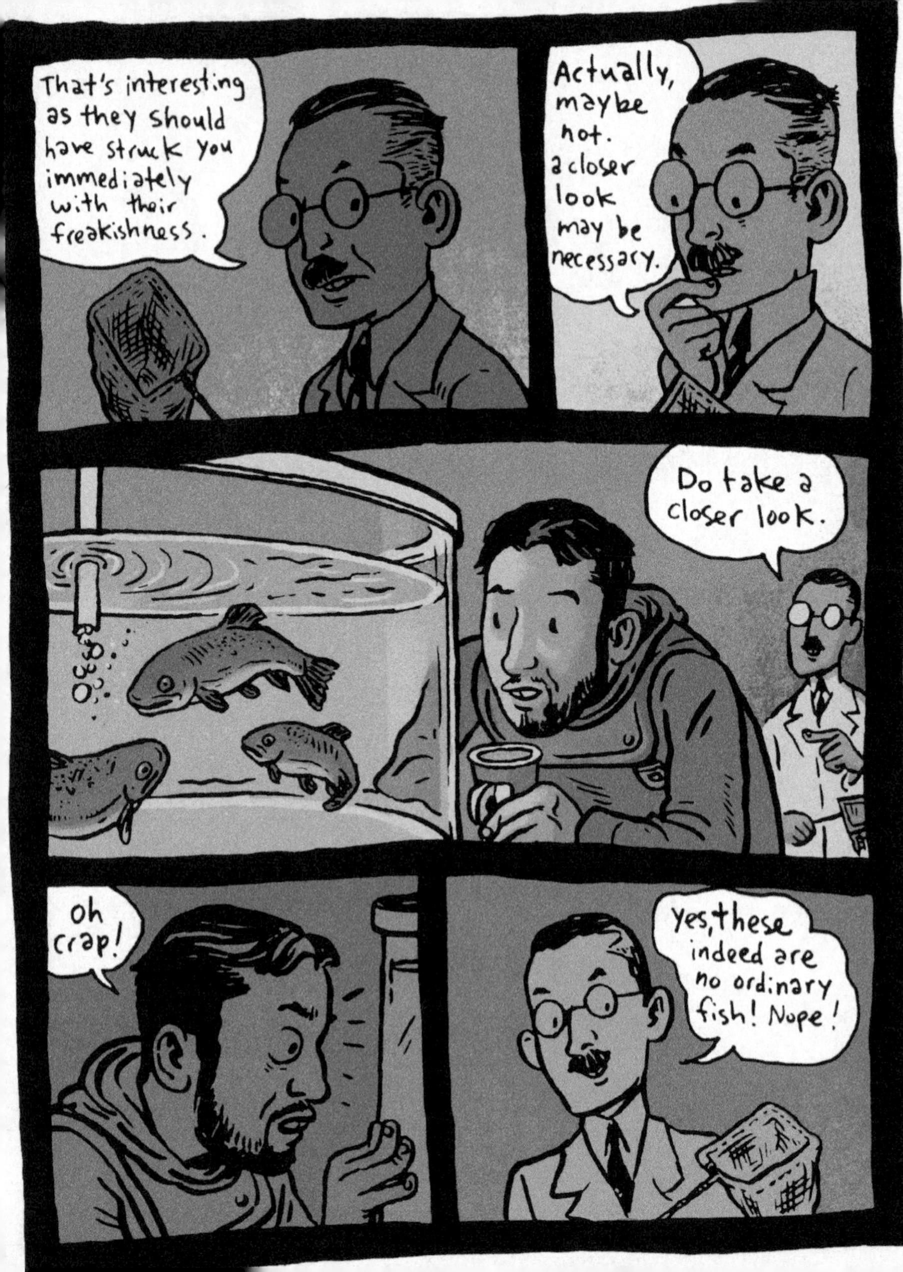
That's interesting as they should have struck you immediately with their freakishness.
Actually, maybe not. a closer look may be necessary.
Do take a closer look.
oh crap!
Yes, these indeed are no ordinary fish! Nope!

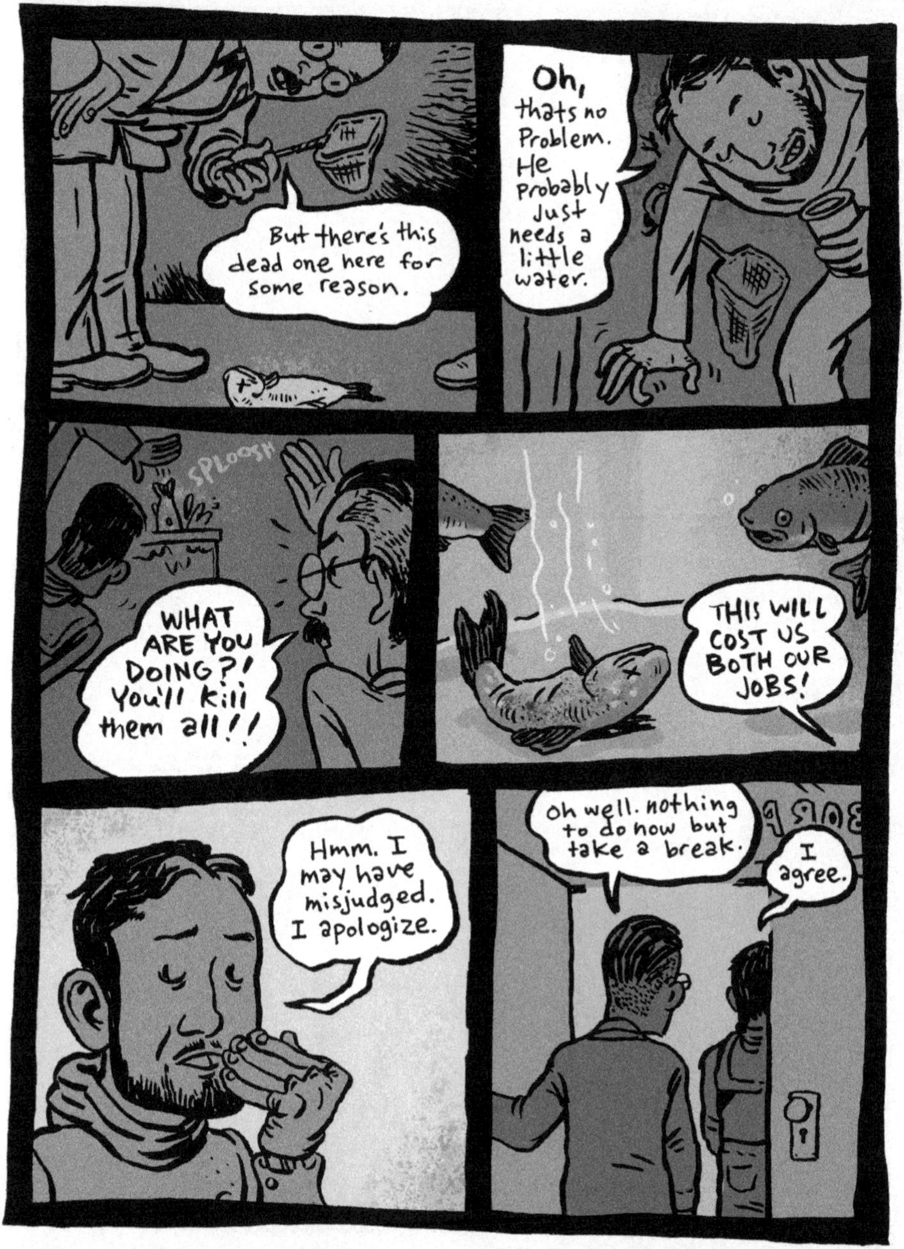
But there's this dead one here for some reason.
Oh, thats no Problem. He Probably just needs a little water.
SPLOOSH
WHAT ARE YOU DOING?! You'll kill them all!!
THIS WILL COST US BOTH OUR JOBS!
Hmm. I may have misjudged. I apologize.
oh well. nothing to do now but take a break.
I agree.

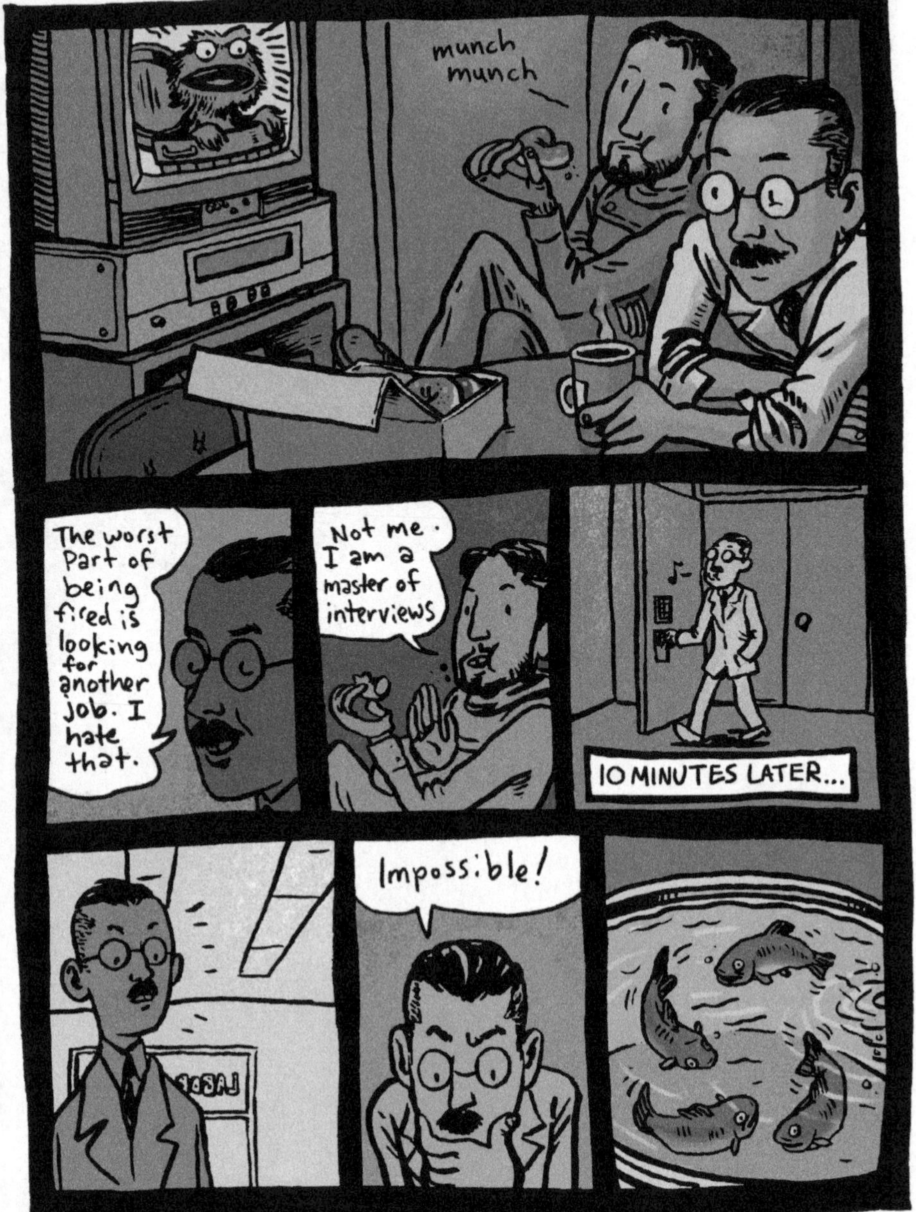
munch munch
The worst part of being fired is looking for another job. I hate that.
Not me. I am a master of interviews
10 MINUTES LATER...
Impossible!

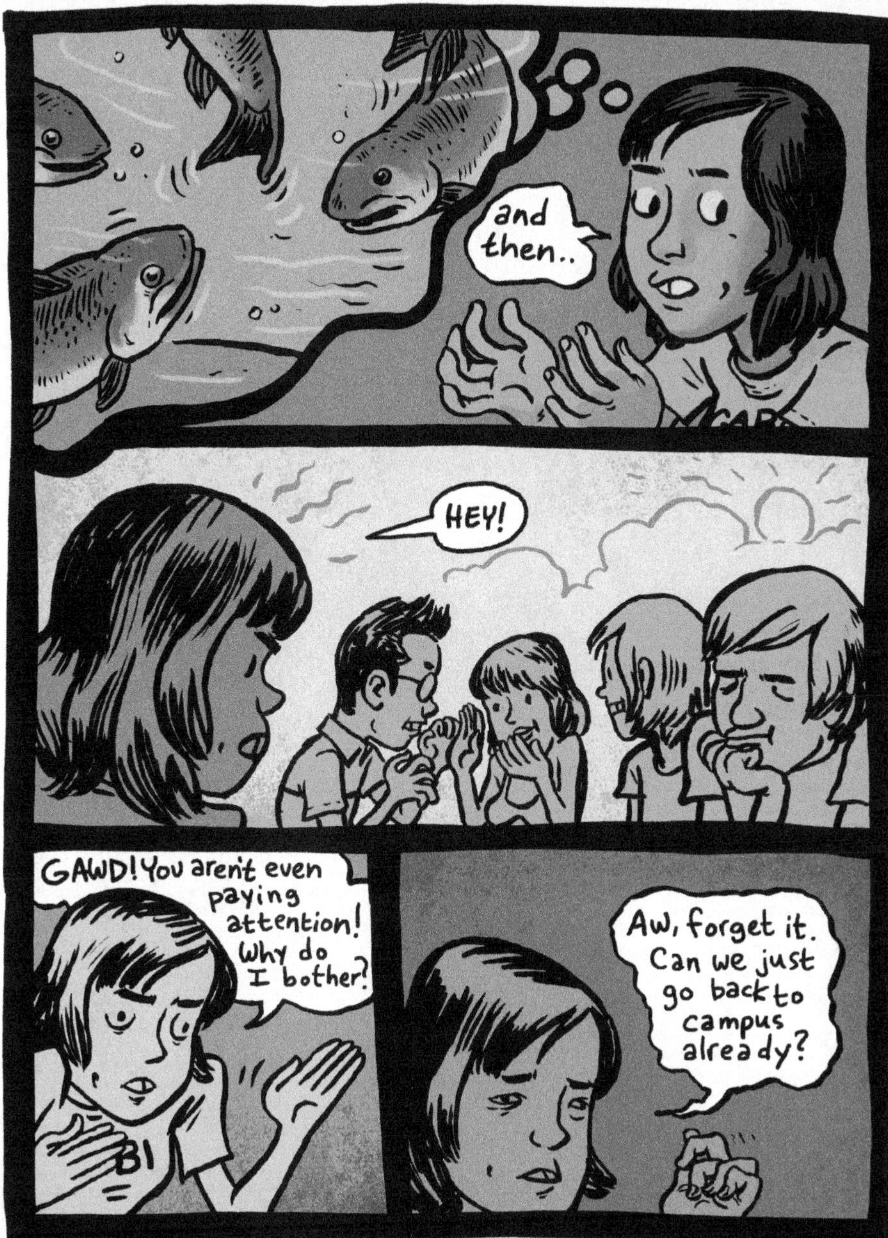
and then..
HEY!
GAWD! You aren't even paying attention! Why do I bother?
Aw, forget it. Can we just go back to campus already?

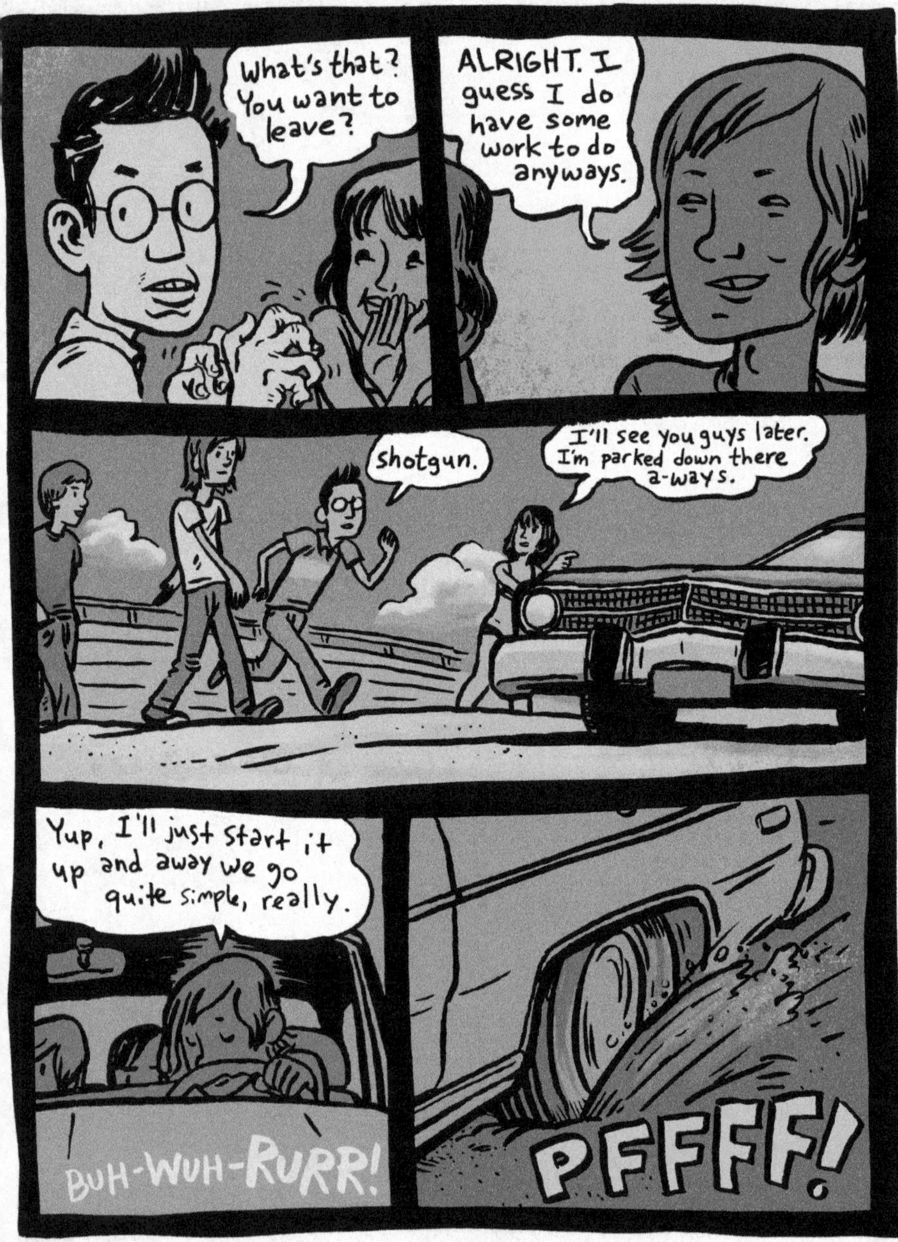
What's that? You want to leave?
ALRIGHT. I guess I do have some work to do anyways.
Shotgun.
I'll see you guys later. I'm parked down there a-ways.
Yup, I'll just start it up and away we go quite simple, really.
BUH-WUH-RURR!
PFFFF!

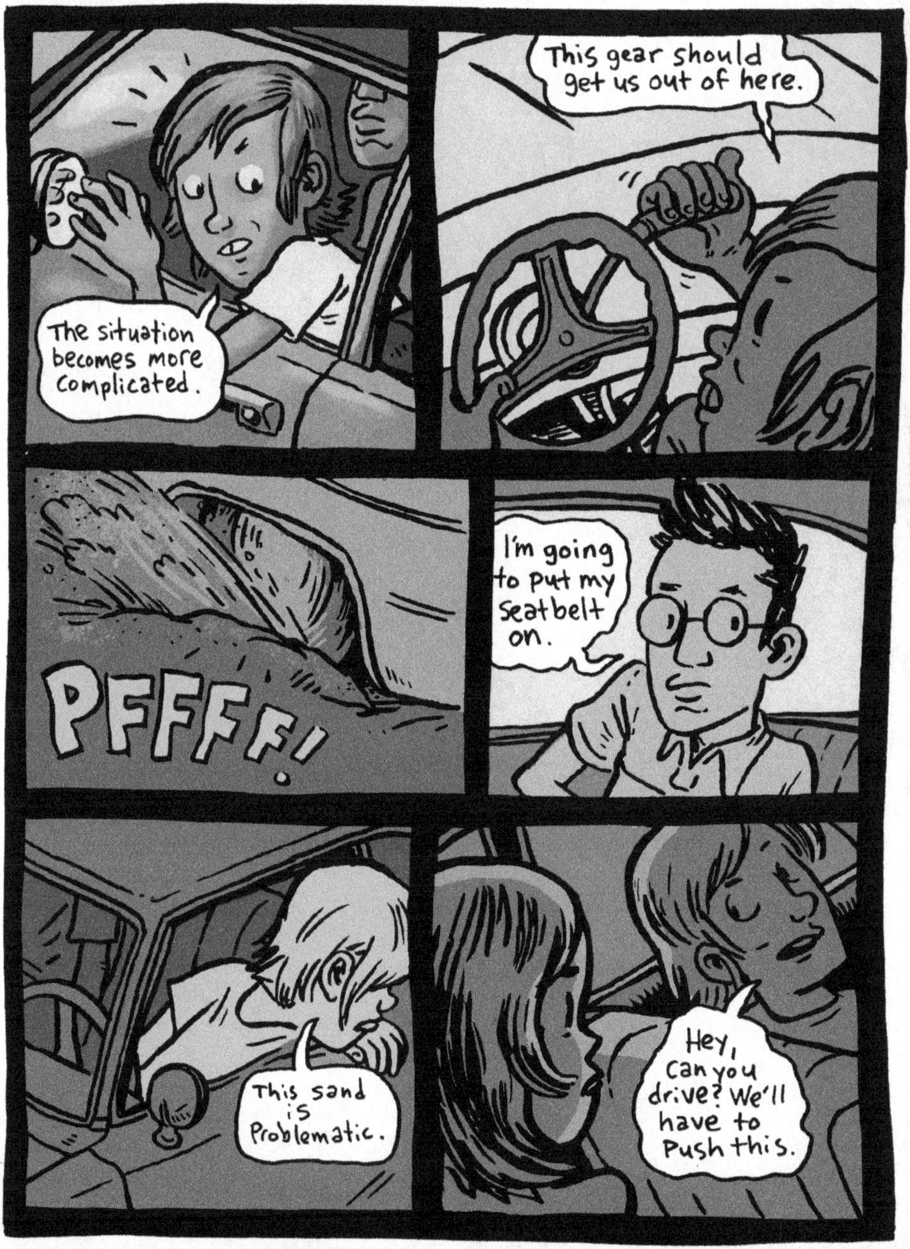
The situation becomes more complicated.
This gear should get us out of here.
PFFFF!
I'm going to put my seatbelt on.
This sand is problematic.
Hey, can you drive? We'll have to push this.

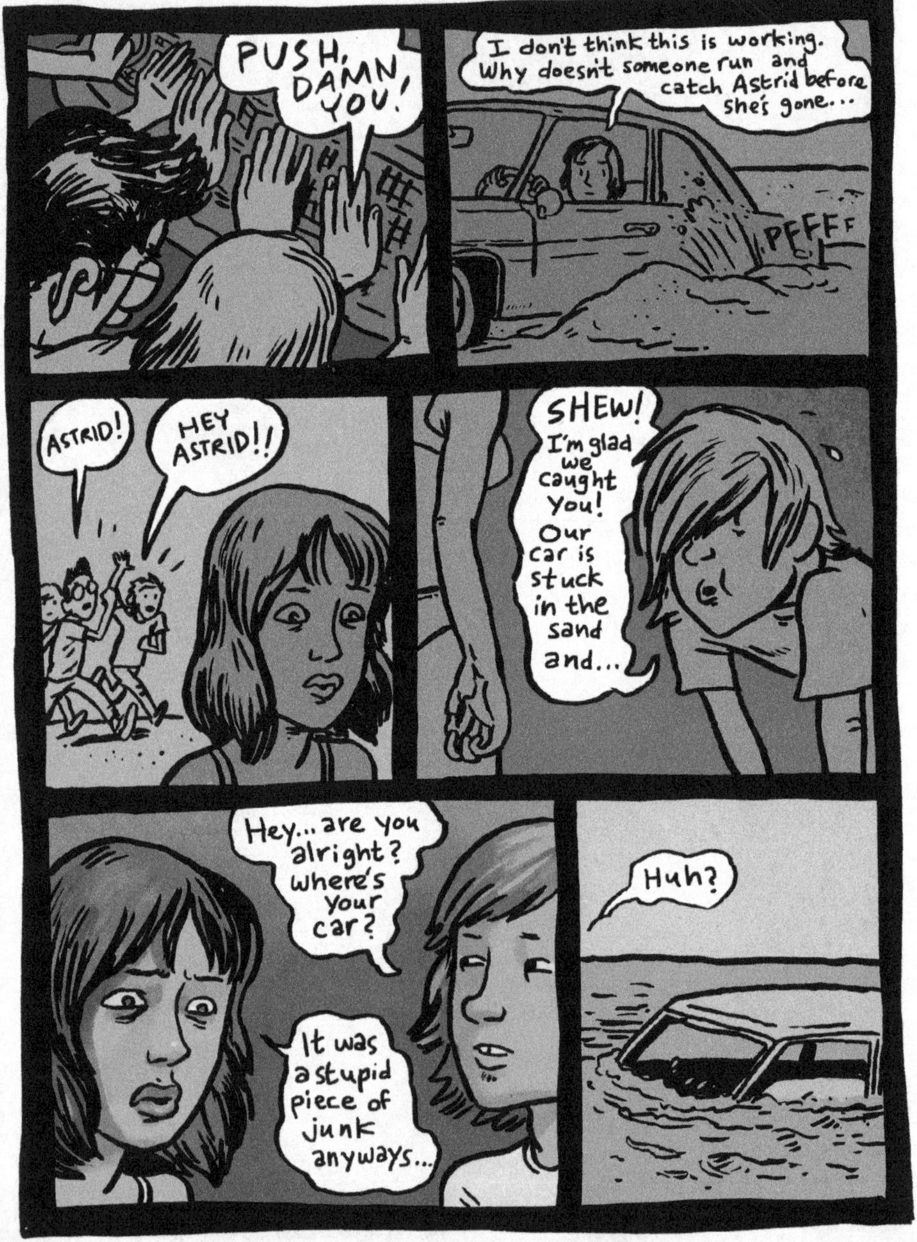
PUSH, DAMN YOU!
I don't think this is working. Why doesn't someone run and catch Astrid before she's gone...
PFFFF
ASTRID!
HEY ASTRID!!
SHEW! I'm glad we caught you! Our car is stuck in the sand and...
Hey... are you alright? where's your car?
It was a stupid piece of junk anyways...
Huh?

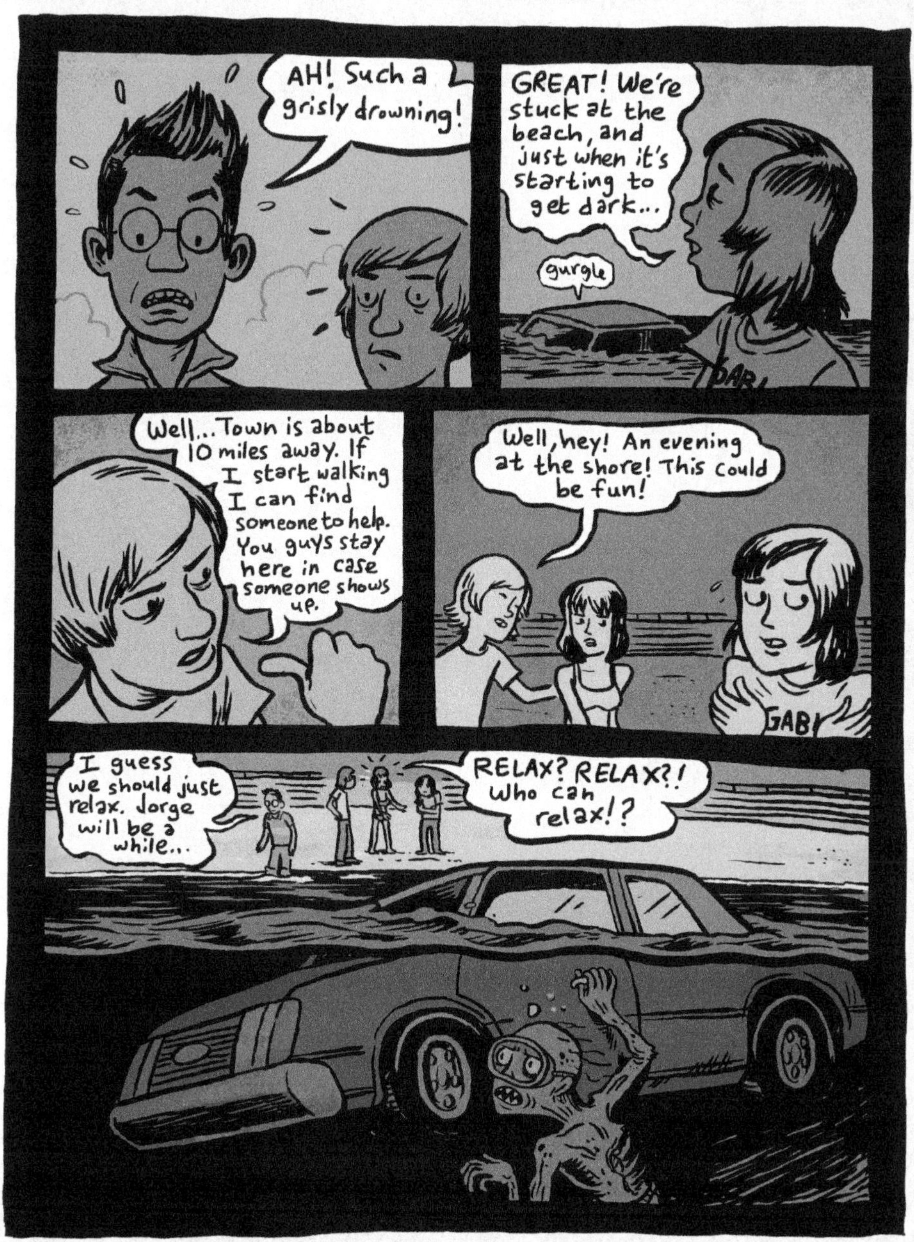
AH! Such a grisly drowning!
GREAT! We're stuck at the beach, and just when it's starting to get dark...
gurgle
DAB
Well... Town is about 10 miles away. If I start walking I can find someone to help. You guys stay here in case someone shows up.
Well, hey! An evening at the shore! This could be fun!
GABI
I guess we should just relax. Jorge will be a while...
RELAX? RELAX?! Who can relax!?

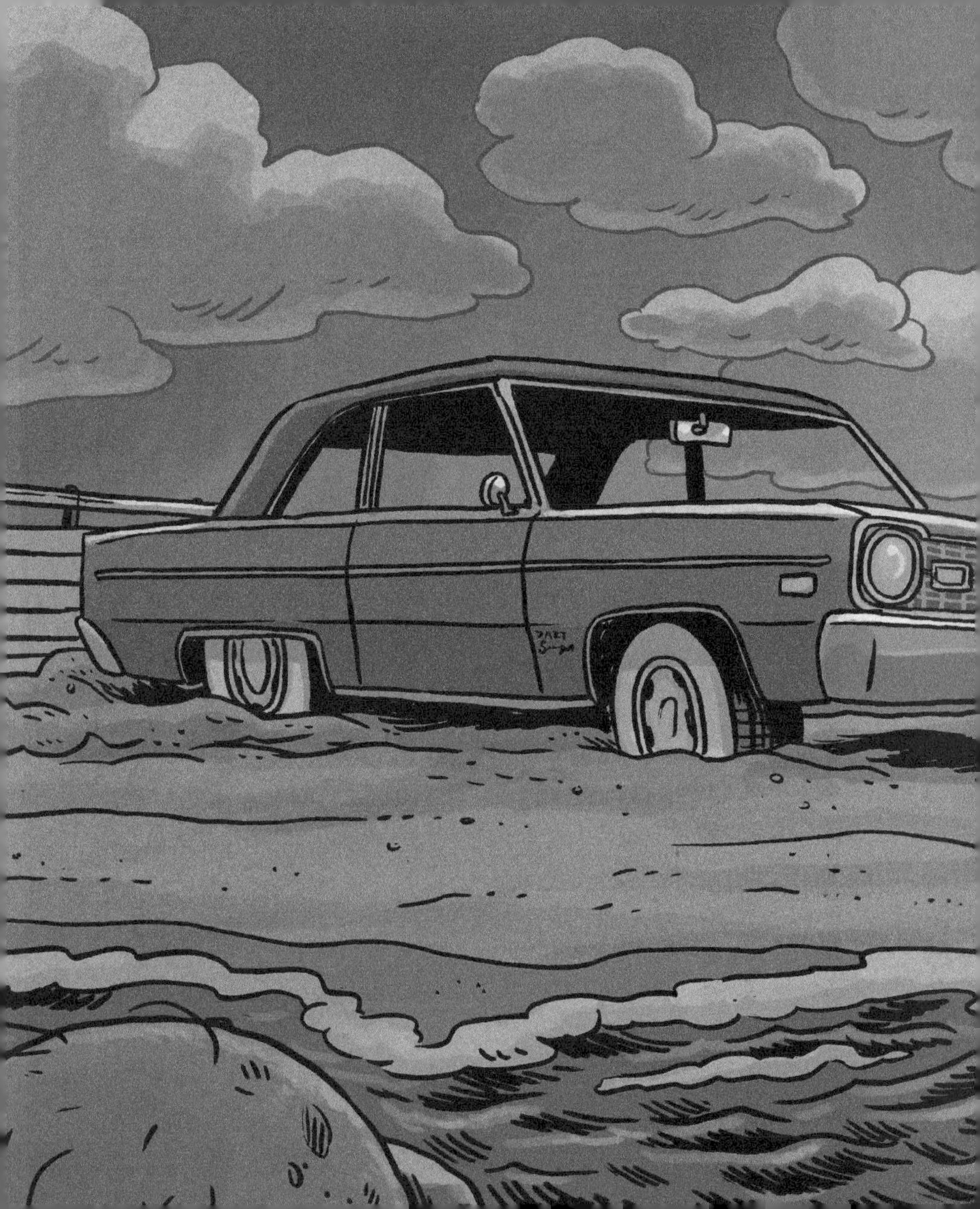

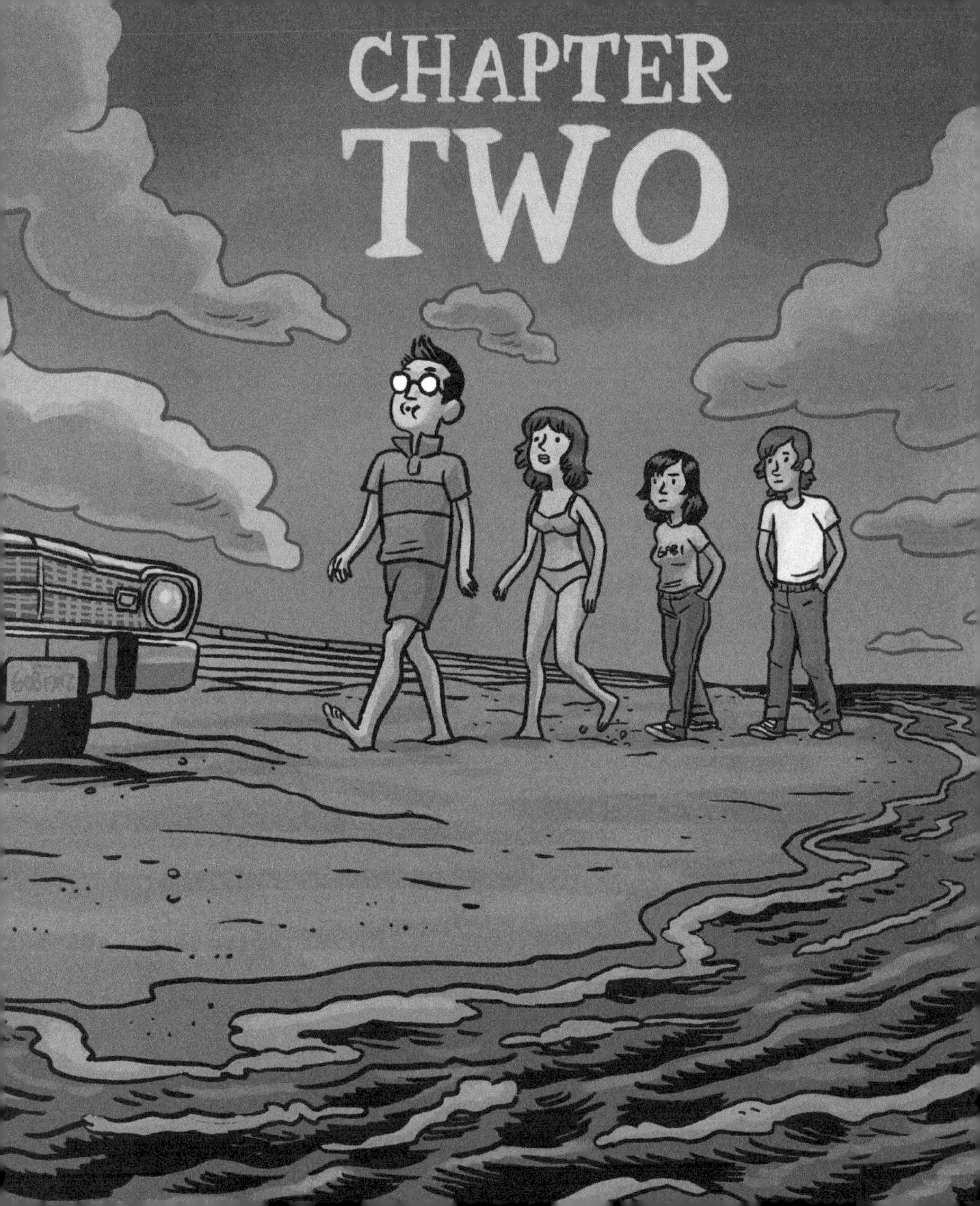
CHAPTER
TWO
GABI

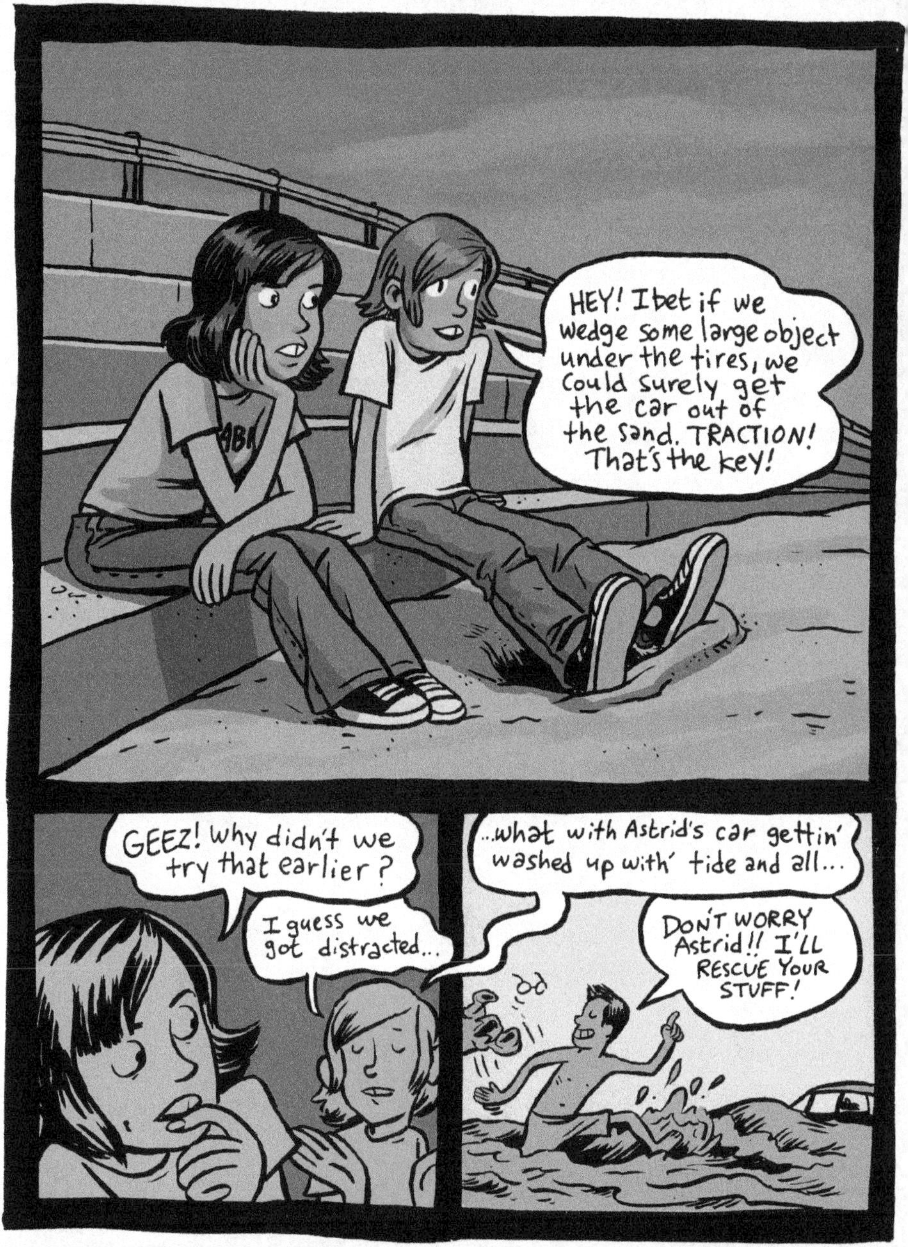
HEY! I bet if we wedge some large object under the tires, we could surely get the car out of the sand. TRACTION! That's the key!
GEEZ! Why didn't we try that earlier?
I guess we got distracted...
...what with Astrid's car gettin' washed up with' tide and all...
DON'T WORRY Astrid!! I'LL RESCUE YOUR STUFF!

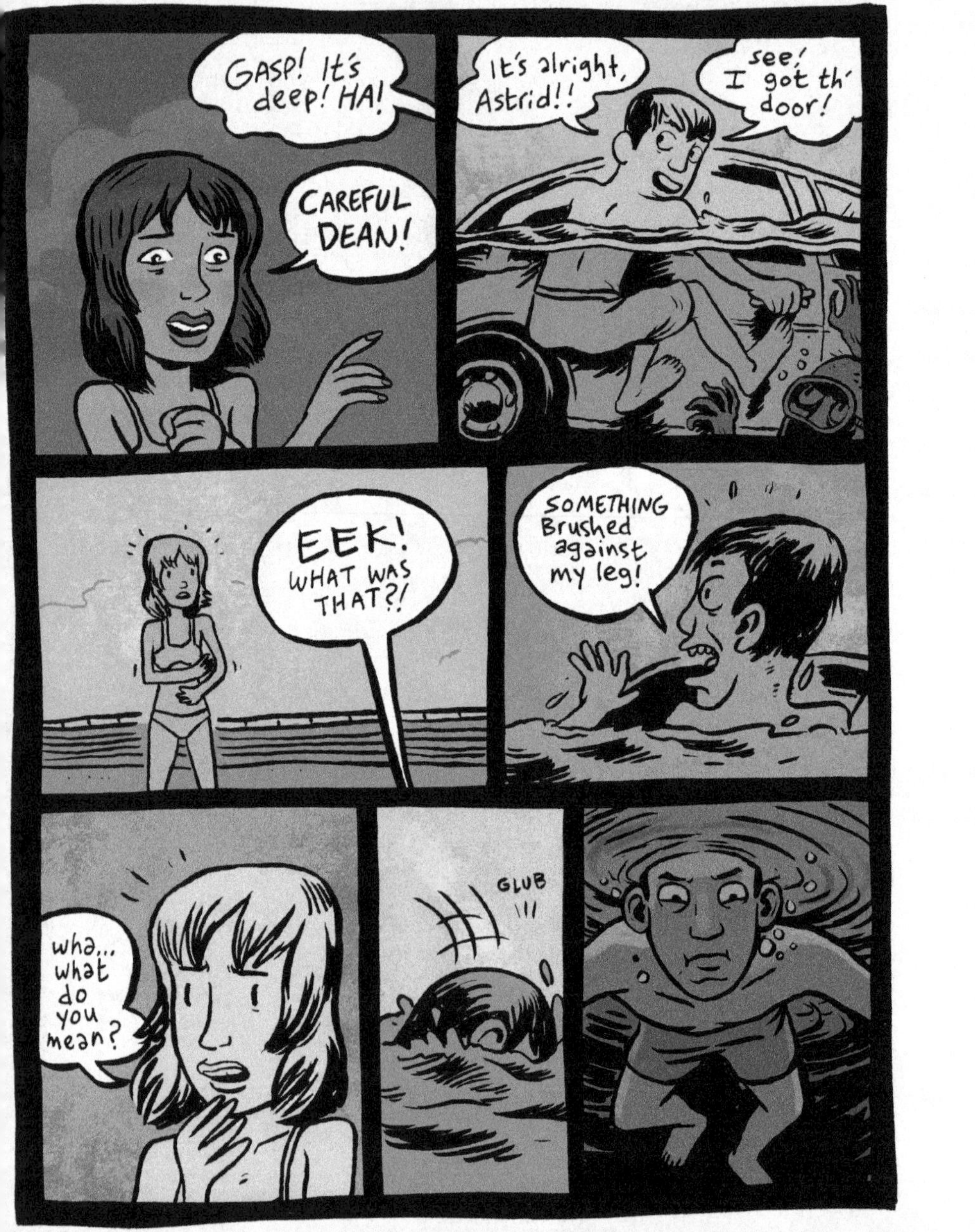
GASP! It's deep! HA!
CAREFUL DEAN!
It's alright, Astrid!!
see! I got th' door!
EEK! WHAT WAS THAT?!
SOMETHING Brushed against my leg!
wha... what do you mean?
GLUB

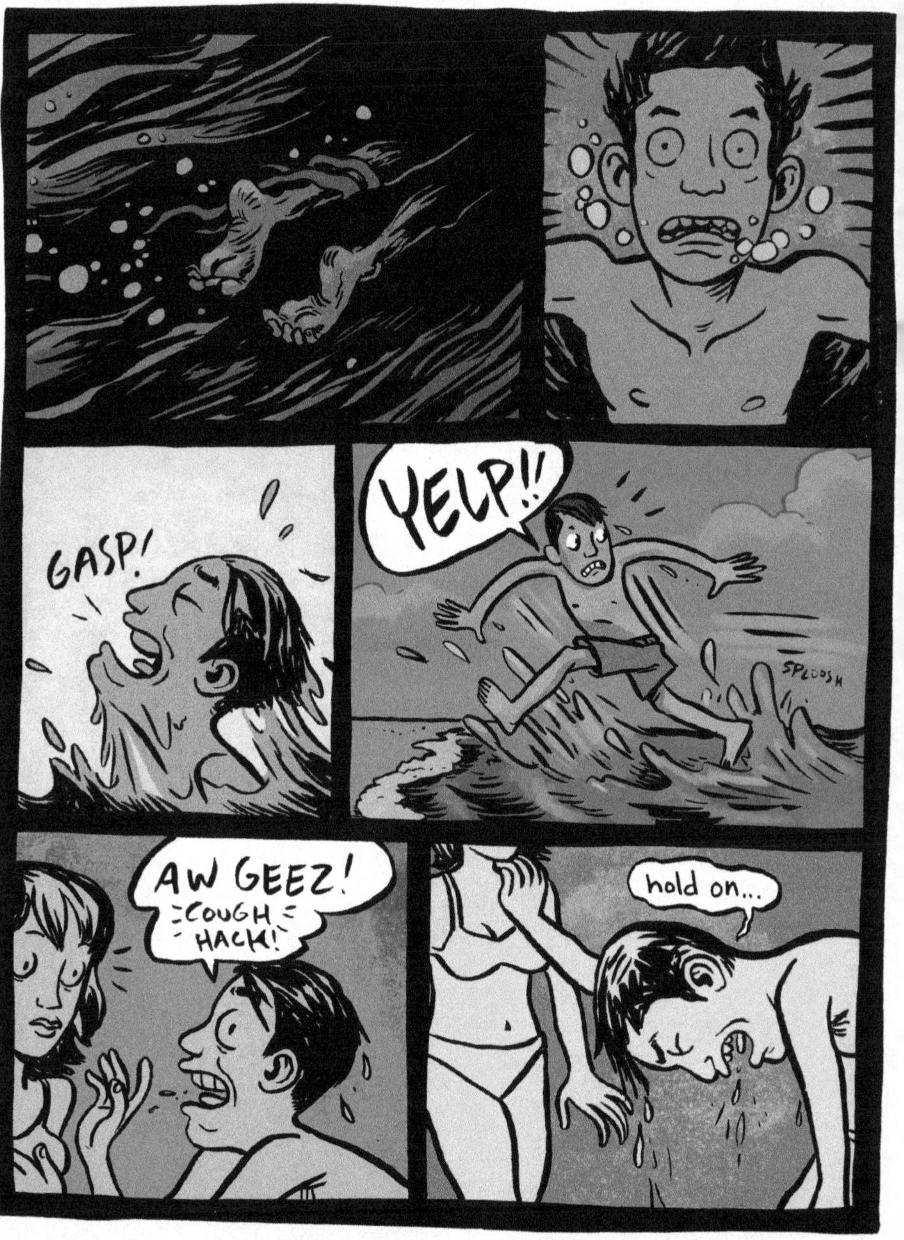
GASP!
YELP!!
SPLOOSH
AW GEEZ!
COUGH
HACK!
hold on...

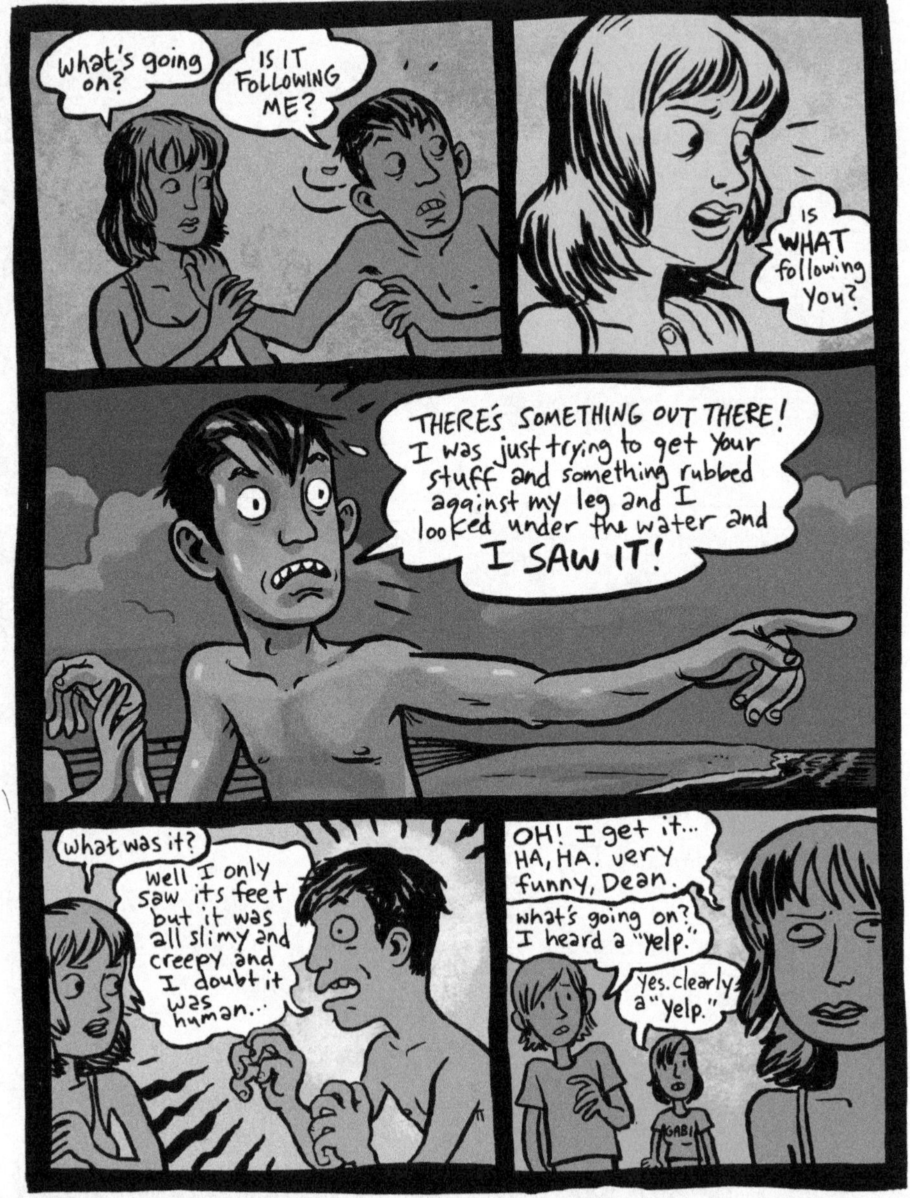
what's going on?
IS IT FOLLOWING ME?
IS WHAT following you?
THERE'S SOMETHING OUT THERE! I was just trying to get your stuff and something rubbed against my leg and I looked under the water and I SAW IT!
what was it?
Well I only saw its feet but it was all slimy and creepy and I doubt it was human...
OH! I get it... HA, HA. very funny, Dean.
what's going on? I heard a "yelp."
yes. clearly a "yelp."
GABI

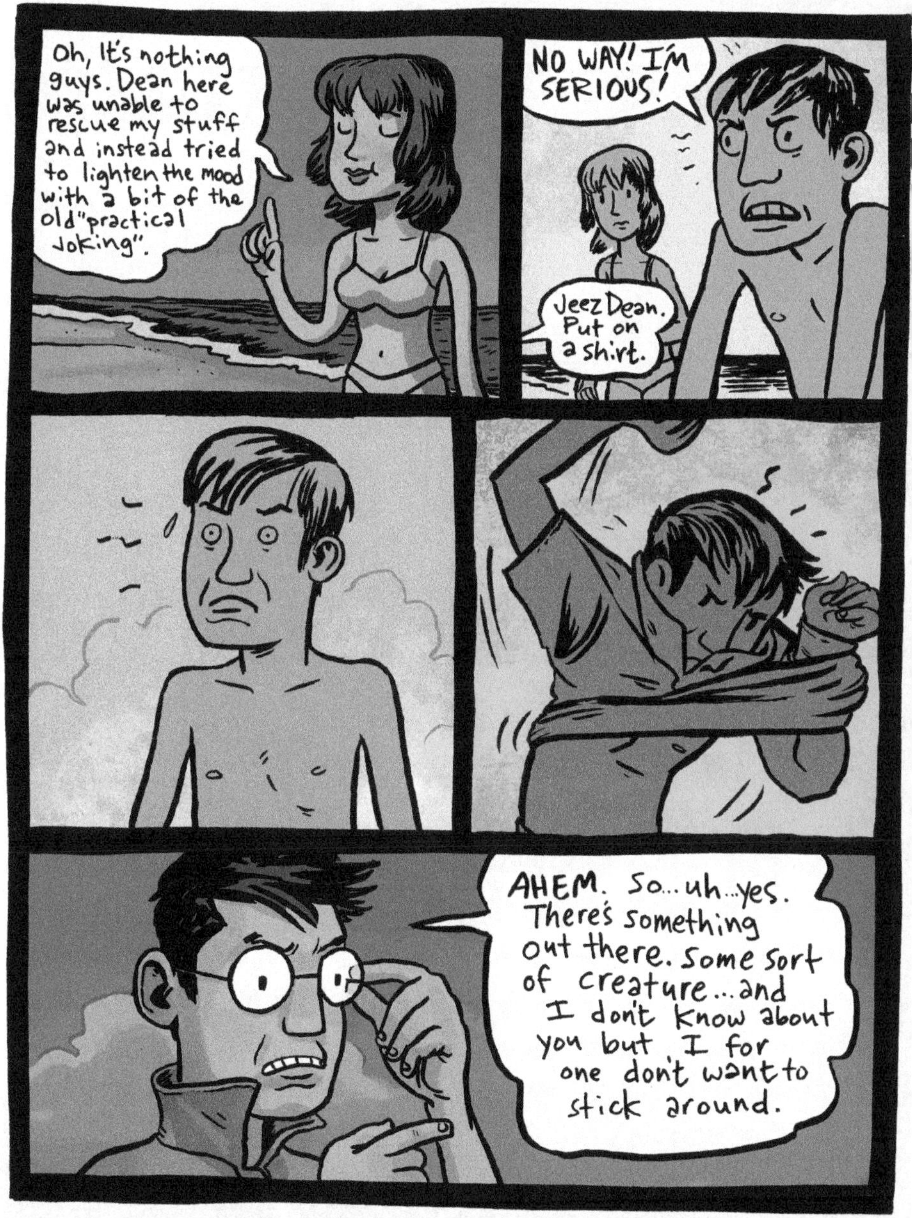
Oh, It's nothing guys. Dean here was unable to rescue my stuff and instead tried to lighten the mood with a bit of the old "practical joking".
NO WAY! I'M SERIOUS!
Jeez Dean. Put on a shirt.
AHEM. So...uh...yes. There's something out there. Some sort of creature...and I don't know about you but I for one don't want to stick around.

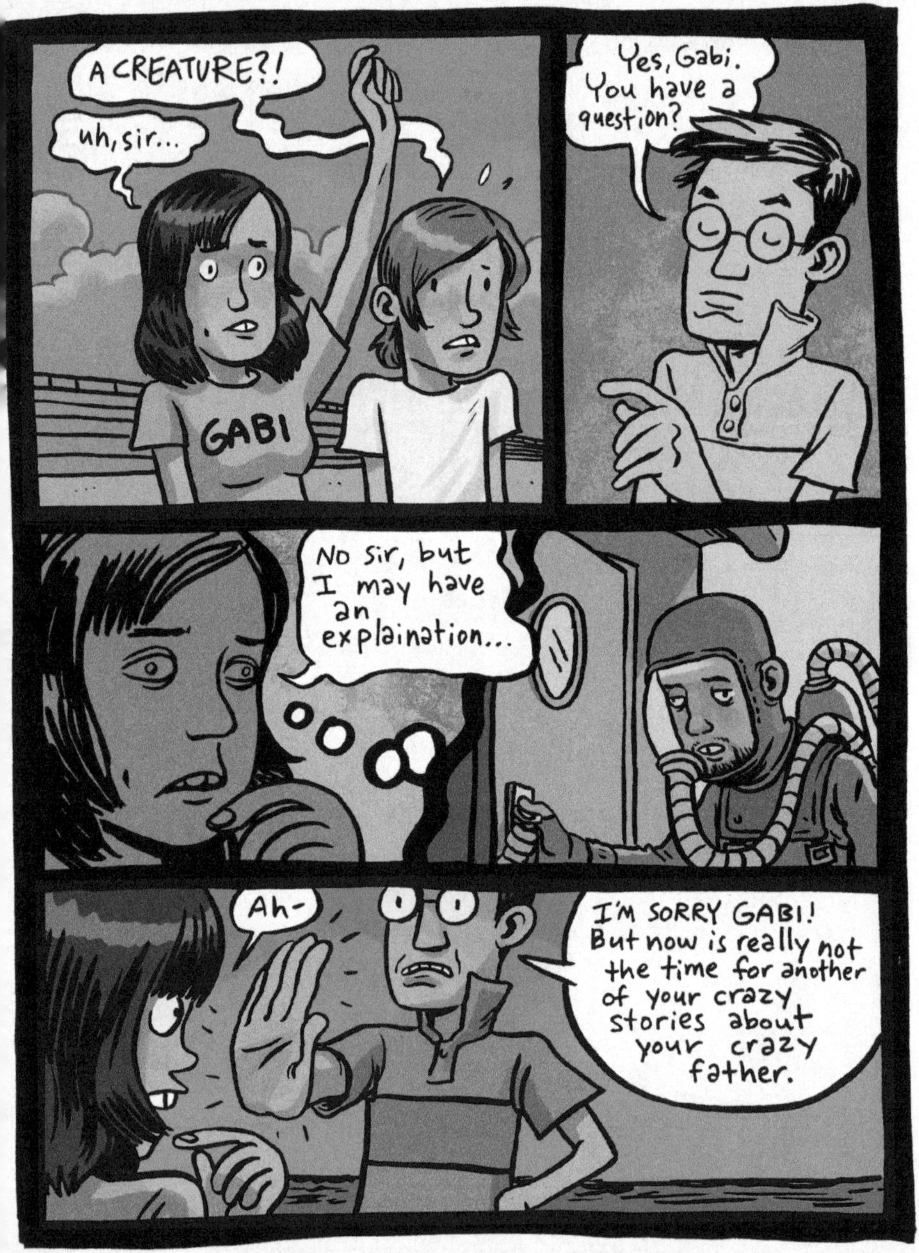
A CREATURE?!
uh, sir...
Yes, Gabi. You have a question?
GABI
No sir, but I may have an explaination...
Ah-
I'M SORRY GABI! But now is really not the time for another of your crazy stories about your crazy father.

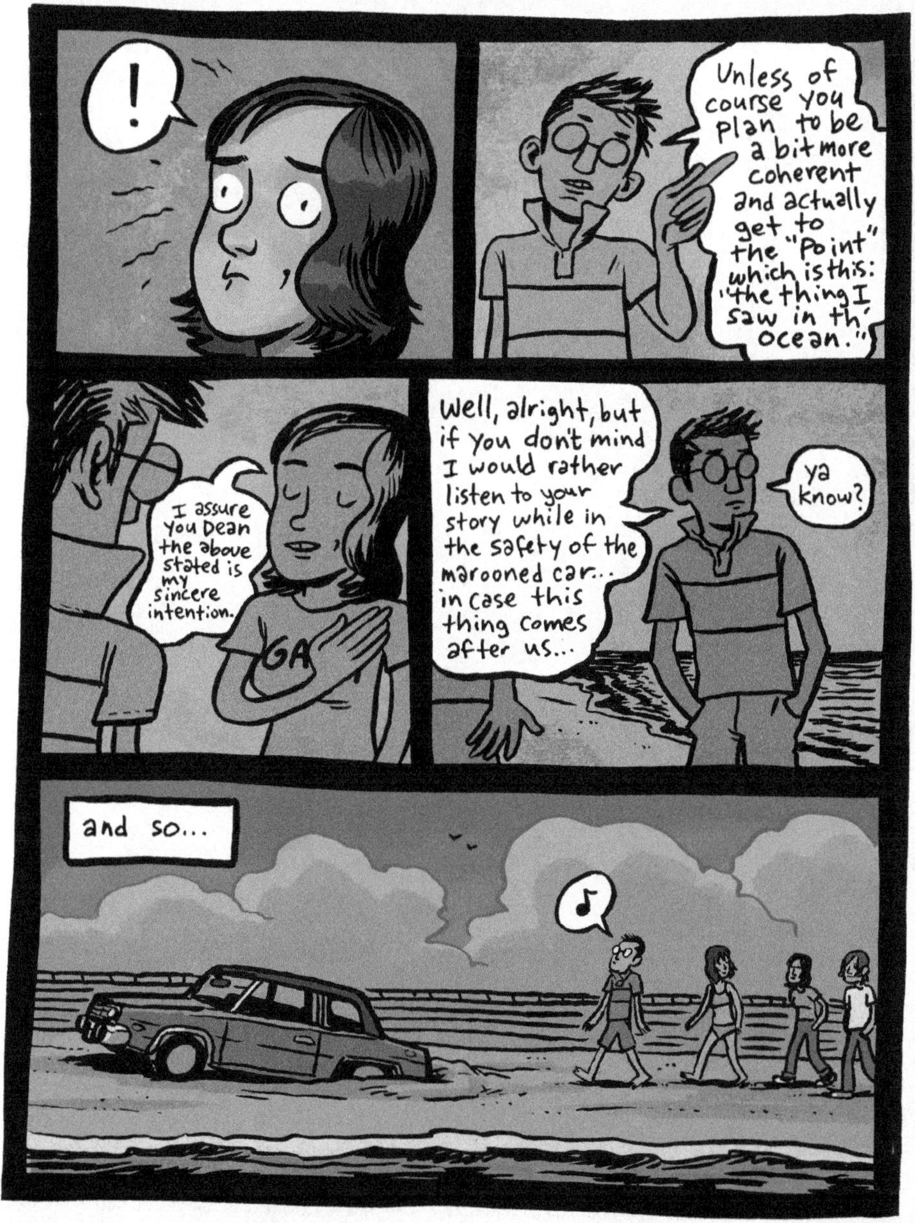
!
Unless of course you plan to be a bit more coherent and actually get to the "Point" which is this: "the thing I saw in th' ocean."
I assure You Dean the above stated is my sincere intention.
Well, alright, but if you don't mind I would rather listen to your story while in the safety of the marooned car... in case this thing comes after us...
ya know?
and so...
♪

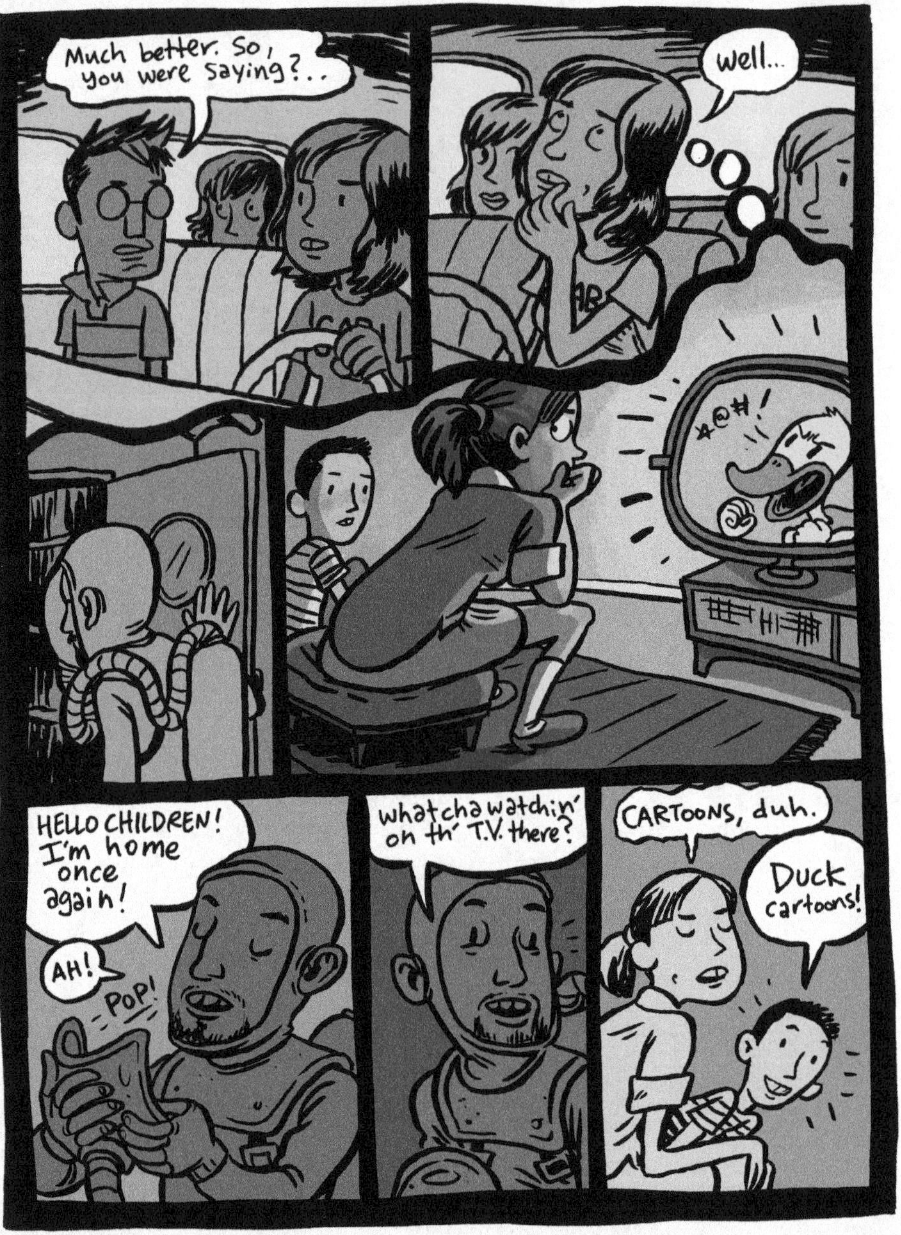
Much better. So, you were saying?...
Well...
*@#!
HELLO CHILDREN! I'm home once again!
AH!
POP!
whatcha watchin' on th' T.V. there?
CARTOONS, duh.
Duck cartoons!

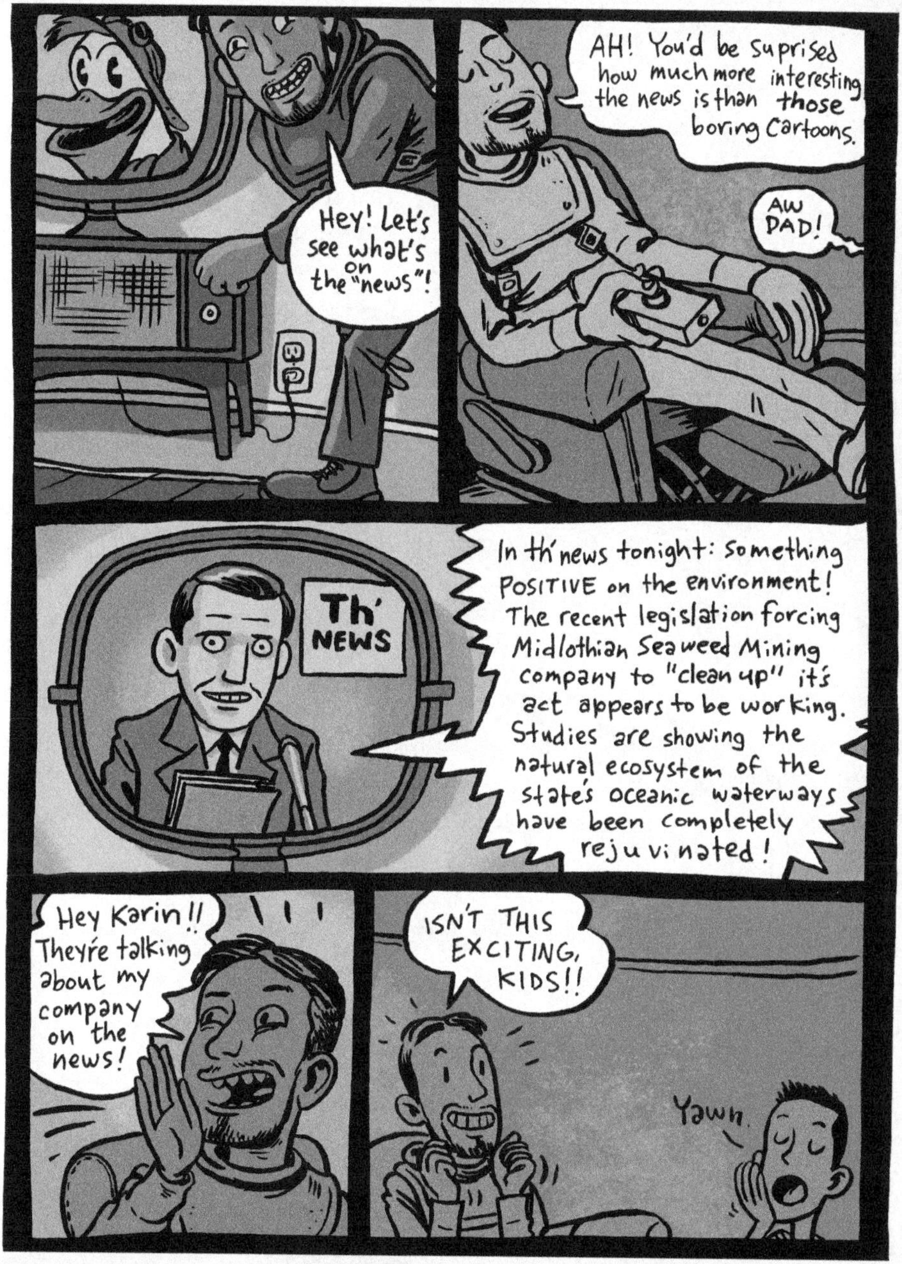
Hey! Let's see what's on the "news"!
AH! You'd be suprised how much more interesting the news is than those boring Cartoons.
AW DAD!
Th' NEWS
In th' news tonight: something POSITIVE on the environment! The recent legislation forcing Midlothian Seaweed Mining company to "clean up" it's act appears to be working. Studies are showing the natural ecosystem of the state's oceanic waterways have been completely rejuvinated!
Hey Karin!! They're talking about my company on the news!
ISN'T THIS EXCITING, KIDS!!
Yawn.

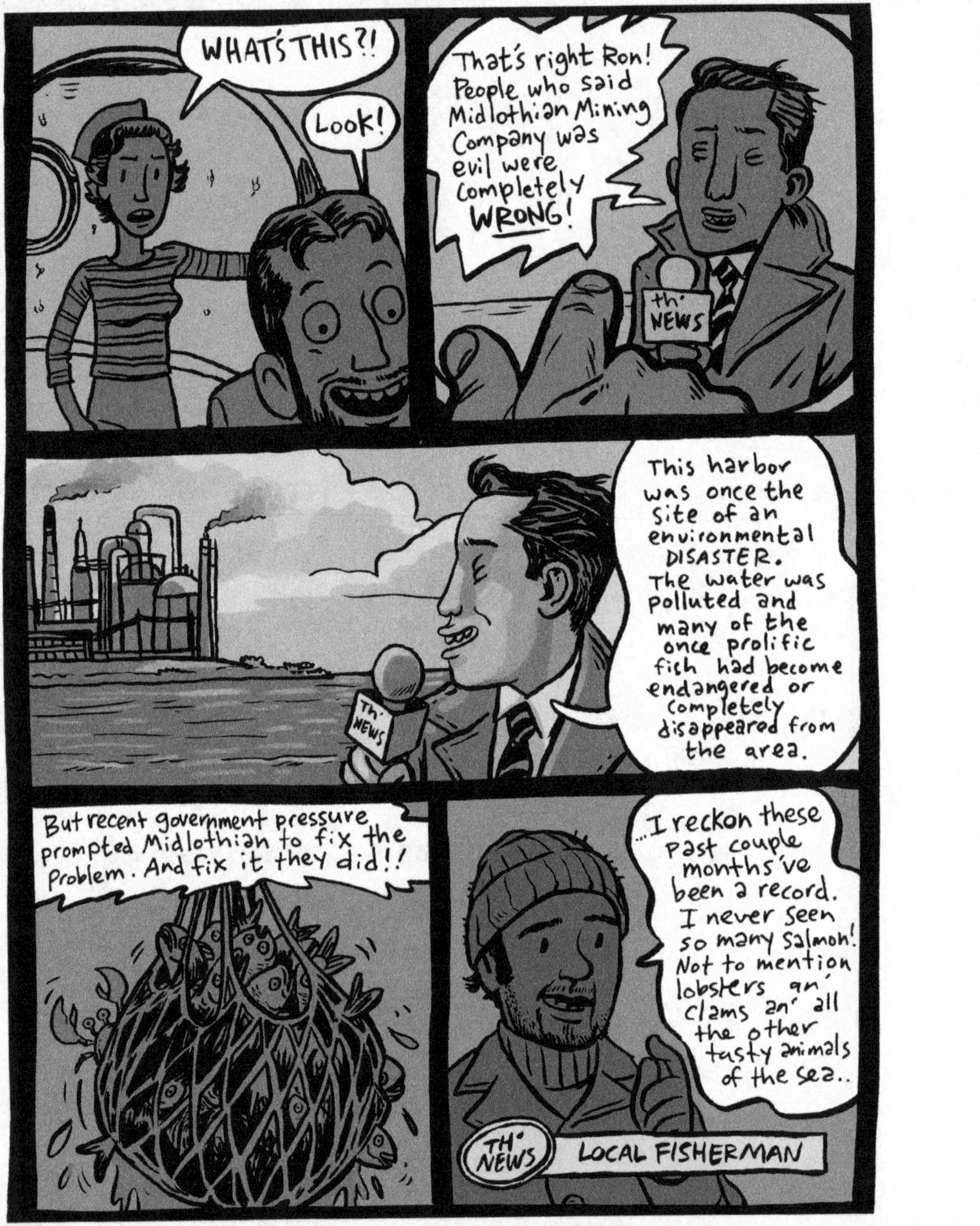
WHAT'S THIS?!
LOOK!
That's right Ron! People who said Midlothian Mining Company was evil were completely WRONG!
TH' NEWS
This harbor was once the site of an environmental DISASTER. The water was polluted and many of the once prolific fish had become endangered or completely disappeared from the area.
TH' NEWS
But recent government pressure prompted Midlothian to fix the problem. And fix it they did!!
...I reckon these past couple months've been a record. I never seen so many salmon! Not to mention lobsters an' clams an' all the other tasty animals of the sea..
TH' NEWS
LOCAL FISHERMAN

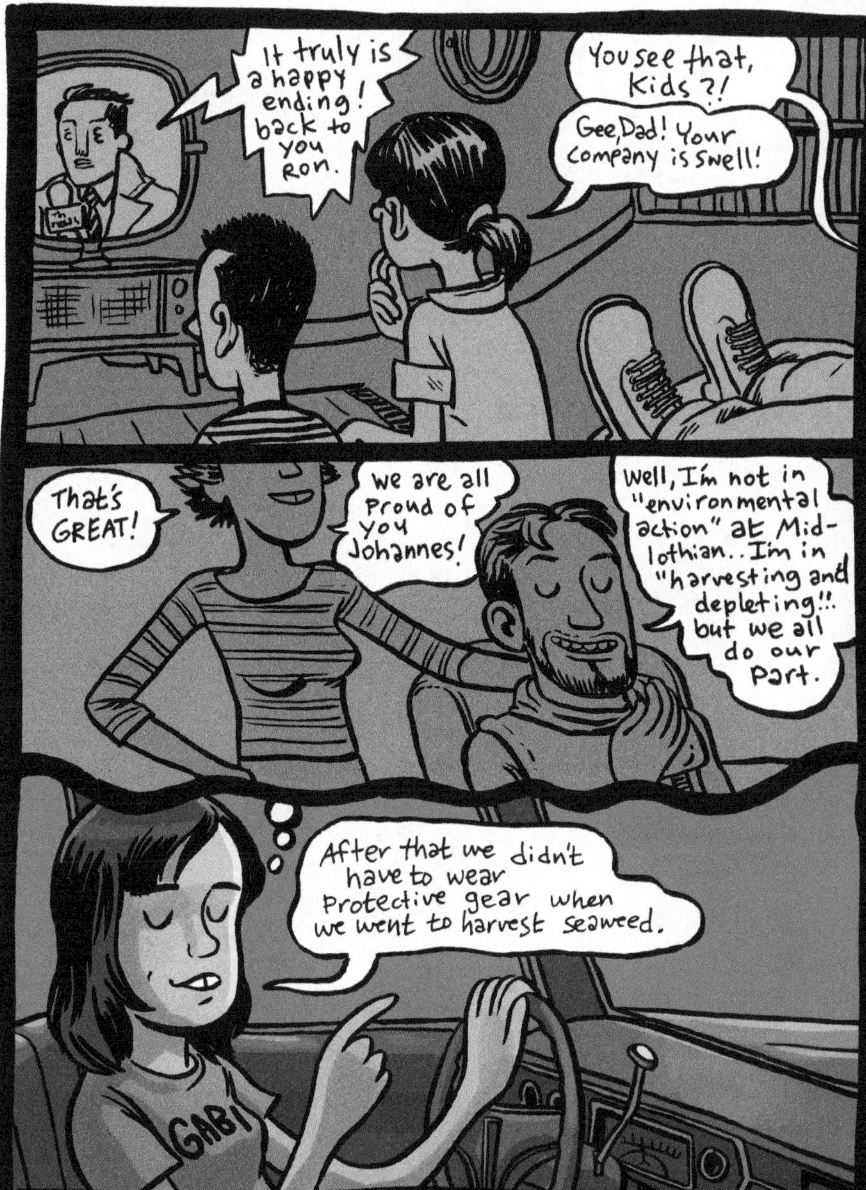
It truly is a happy ending! back to you Ron.
You see that, Kids?!
Gee, Dad! Your company is swell!
That's GREAT!
We are all proud of you Johannes!
Well, I'm not in "environmental action" at Midlothian.. I'm in "harvesting and depleting!" but we all do our part.
After that we didn't have to wear protective gear when we went to harvest seaweed.
GABI

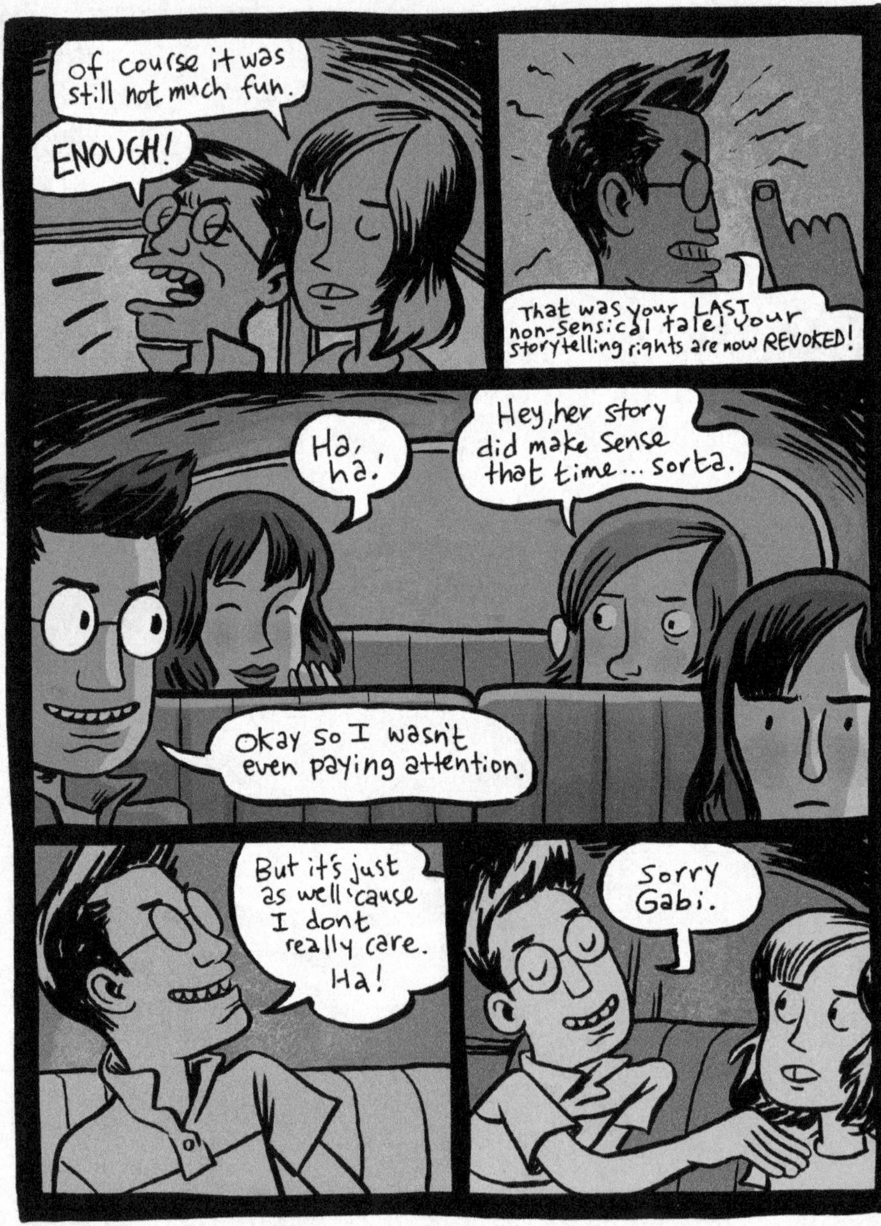
of course it was still not much fun.
ENOUGH!
That was your LAST non-sensical tale! Your storytelling rights are now REVOKED!
Ha, ha.!
Hey, her story did make sense that time... sorta.
Okay so I wasn't even paying attention.
But it's just as well 'cause I dont really care. Ha!
Sorry Gabi.

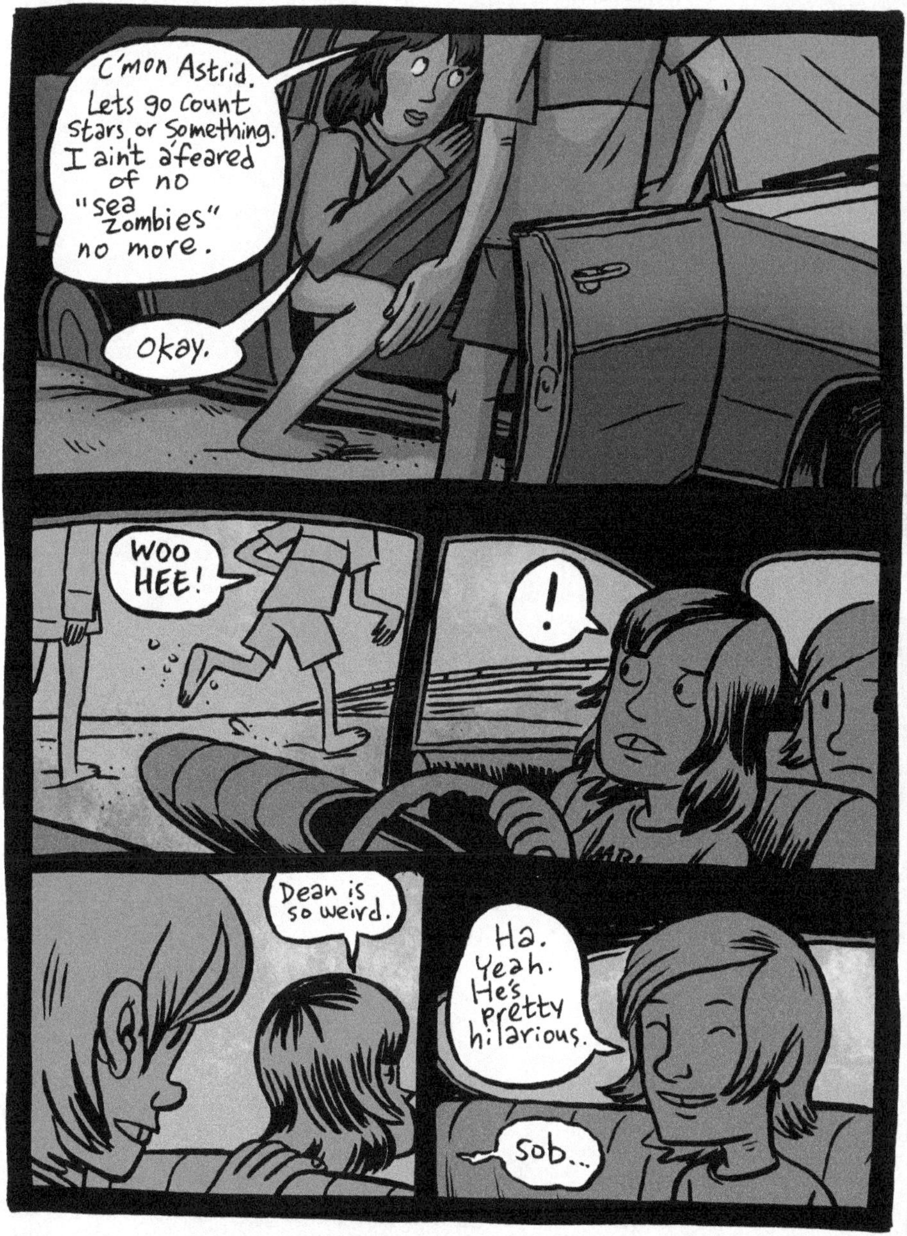
C'mon Astrid. Lets go count stars or something. I ain't a'feared of no "sea zombies" no more.
Okay.
WOO HEE!
!
Dean is so weird.
Ha. Yeah. He's pretty hilarious.
sob...

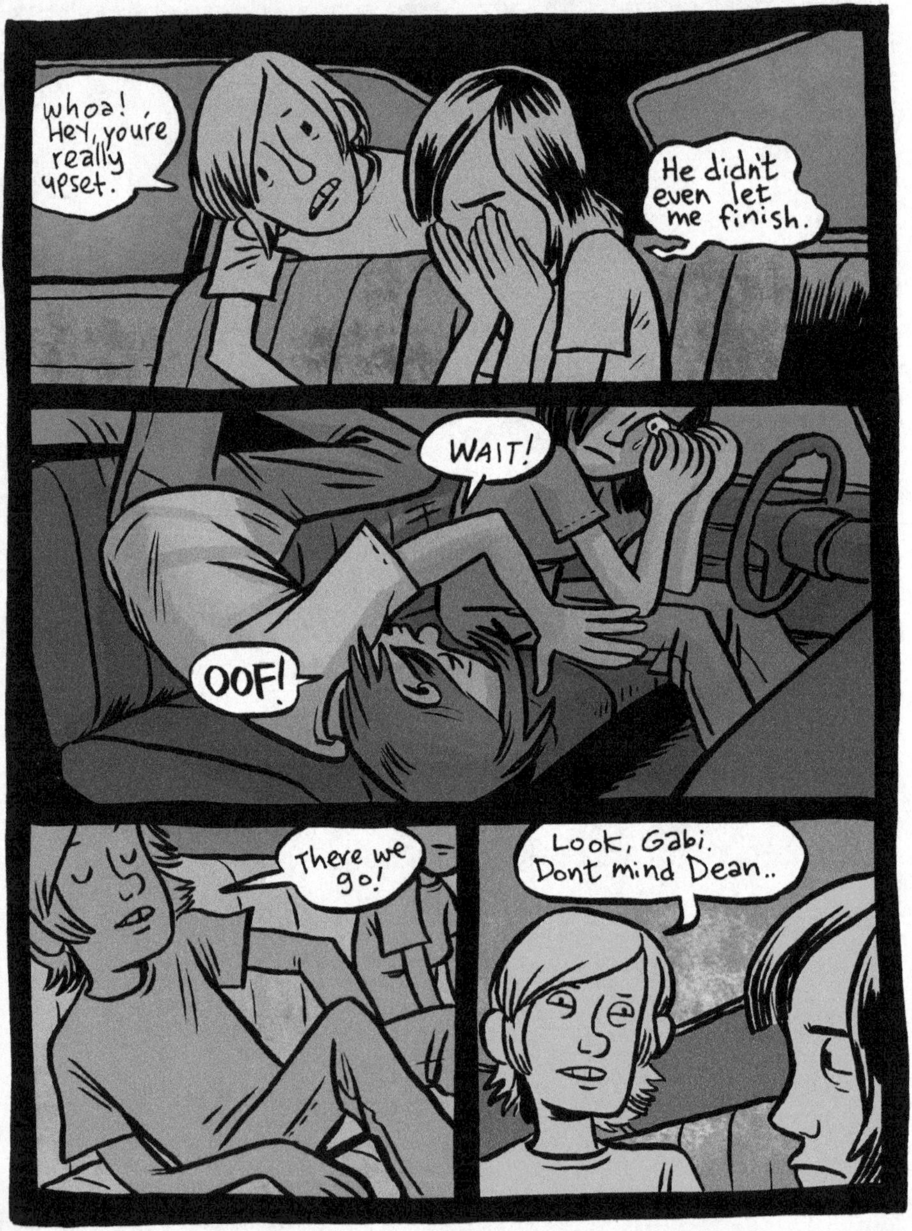
whoa! Hey, you're really upset.
He didn't even let me finish.
WAIT!
OOF!
There we go!
Look, Gabi. Dont mind Dean..

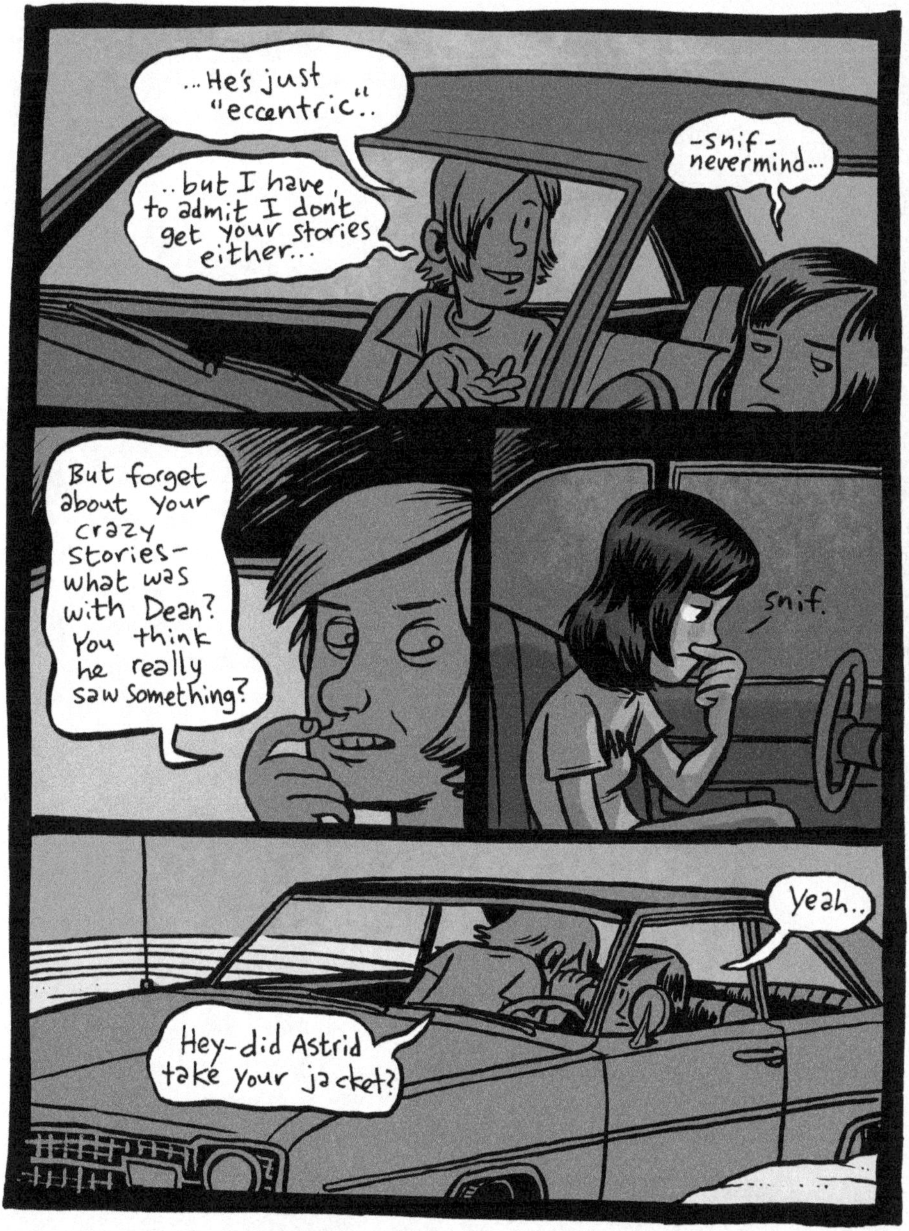
...He's just "eccentric"..
..but I have to admit I don't get your stories either...
-snif- nevermind...
But forget about your crazy stories- what was with Dean? You think he really saw something?
snif.
Hey-did Astrid take your jacket?
Yeah..

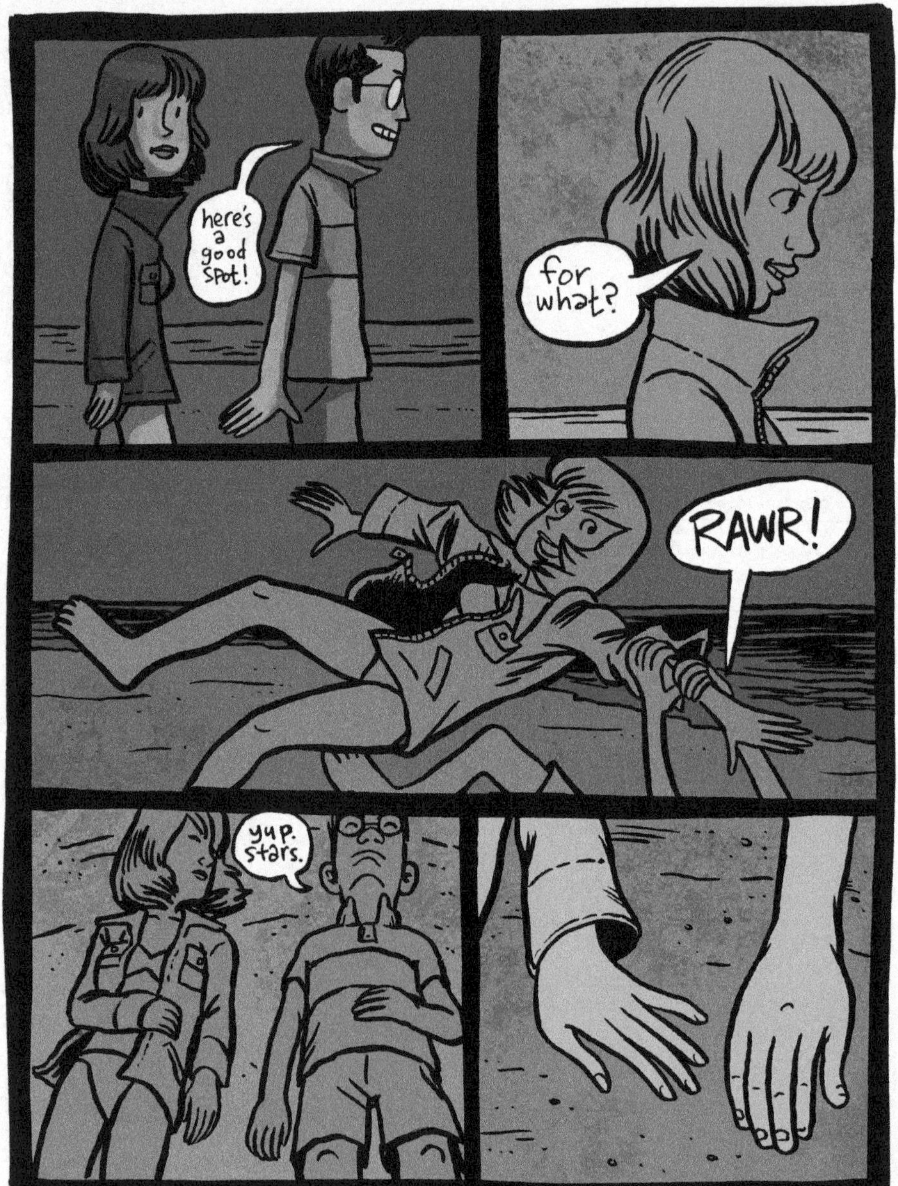
here's a good spot!
for what?
RAWR!
yup. stars.

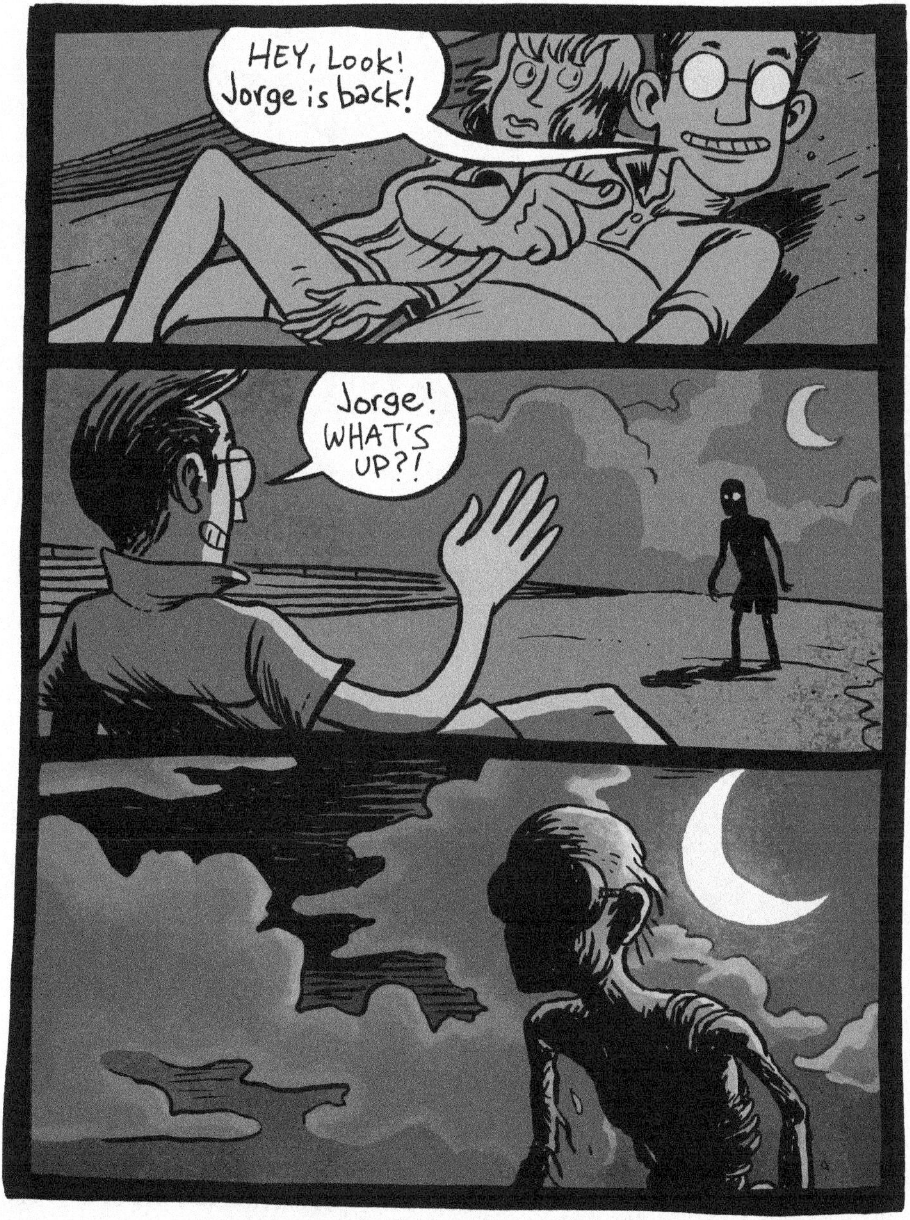
HEY, Look! Jorge is back!
Jorge! WHAT'S UP?!

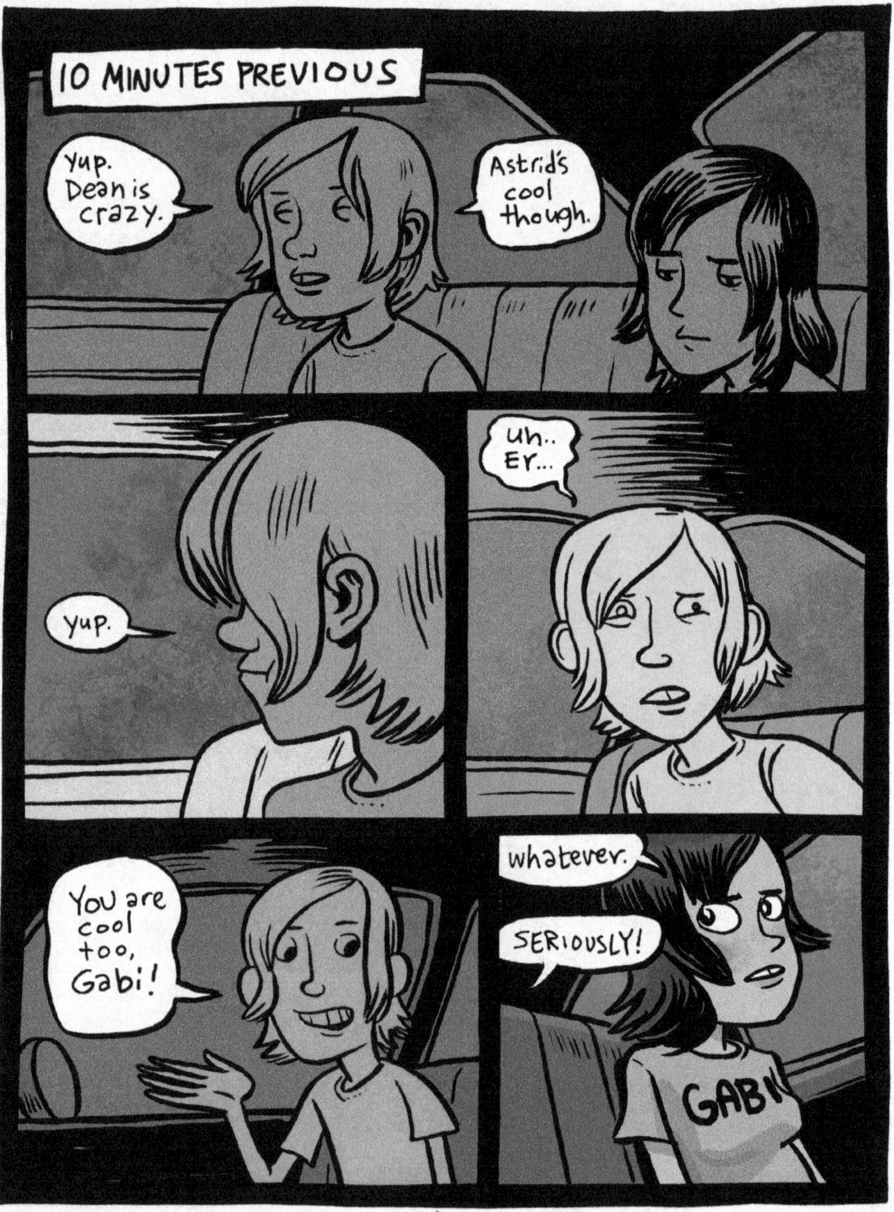
10 MINUTES PREVIOUS
yup. Dean is crazy.
Astrid's cool though.
yup.
uh.. Er...
You are cool too, Gabi!
whatever.
SERIOUSLY!
GABI

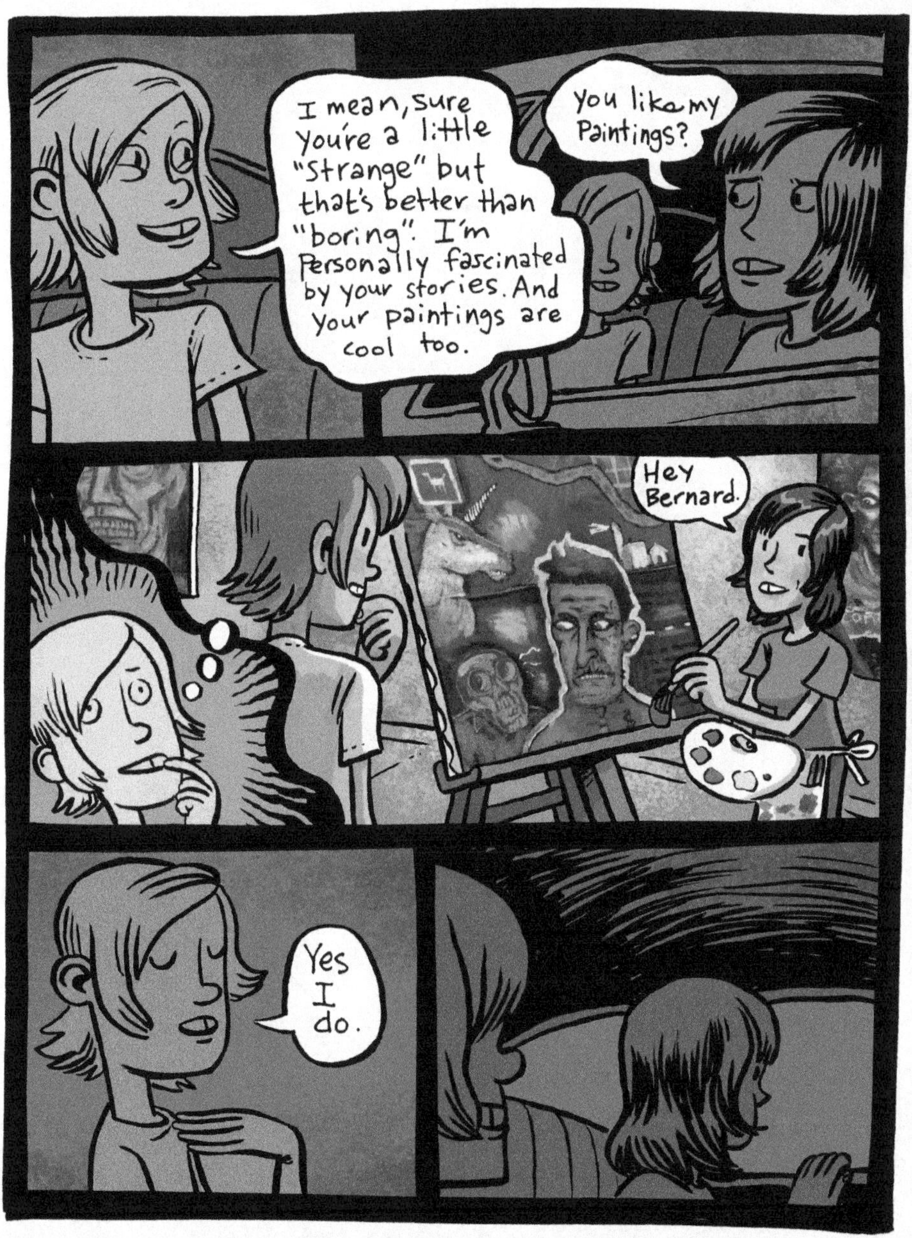
I mean, sure you're a little "strange" but that's better than "boring". I'm personally fascinated by your stories. And your paintings are cool too.
You like my Paintings?
Hey Bernard.
Yes I do.

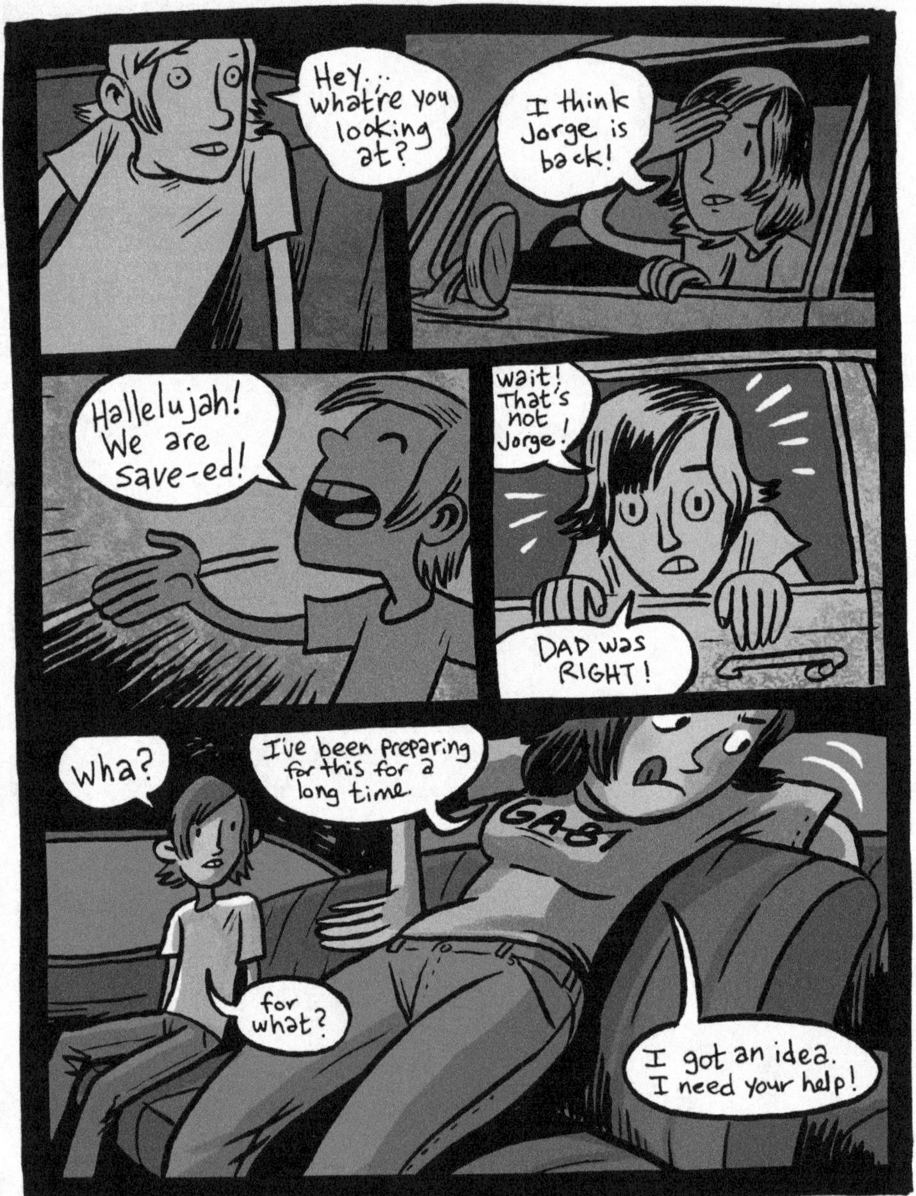
Hey... what're you looking at?
I think Jorge is back!
Hallelujah! We are save-ed!
wait! That's not Jorge!
DAD was RIGHT!
Wha?
I've been preparing for this for a long time.
GABI
for what?
I got an idea. I need your help!

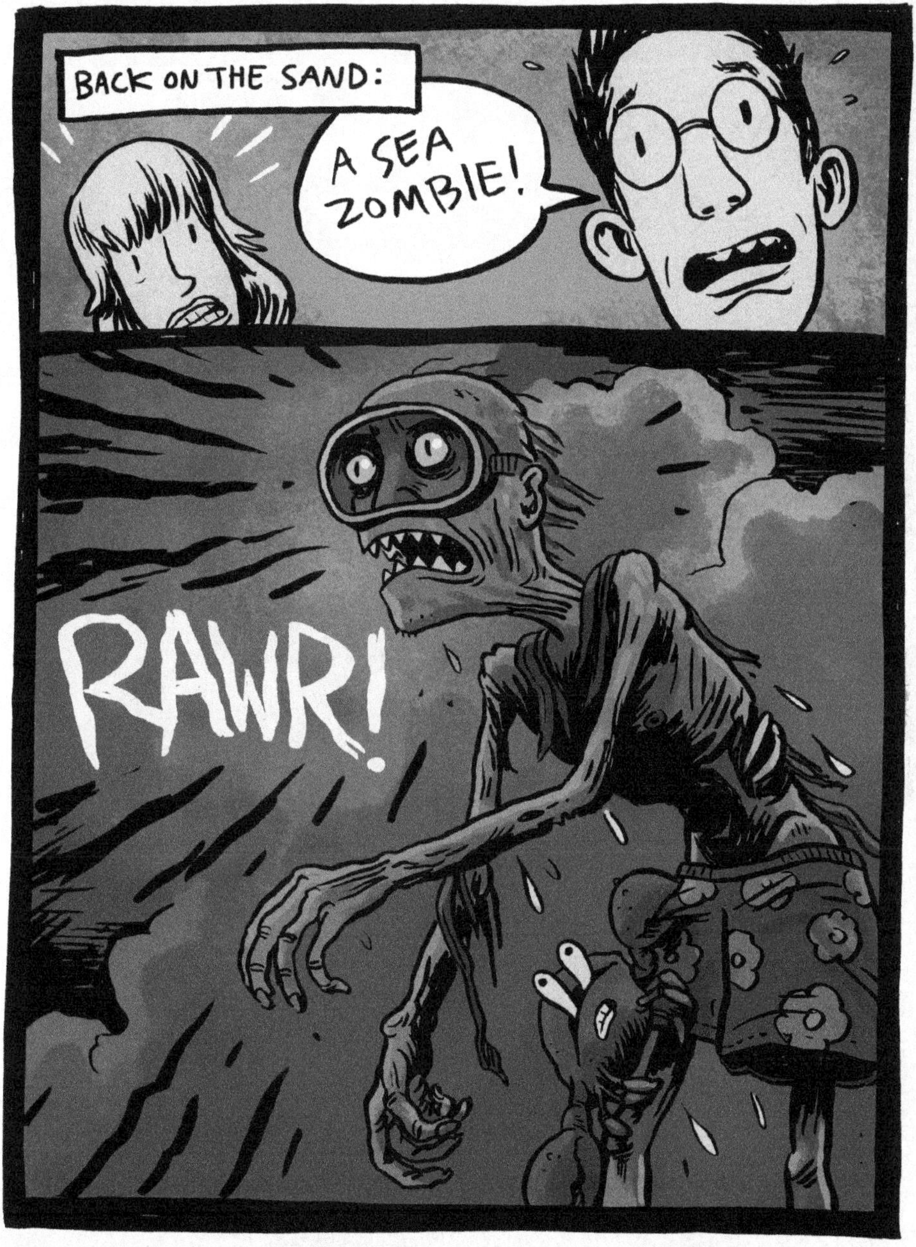
BACK ON THE SAND:
A SEA ZOMBIE!
RAWR!

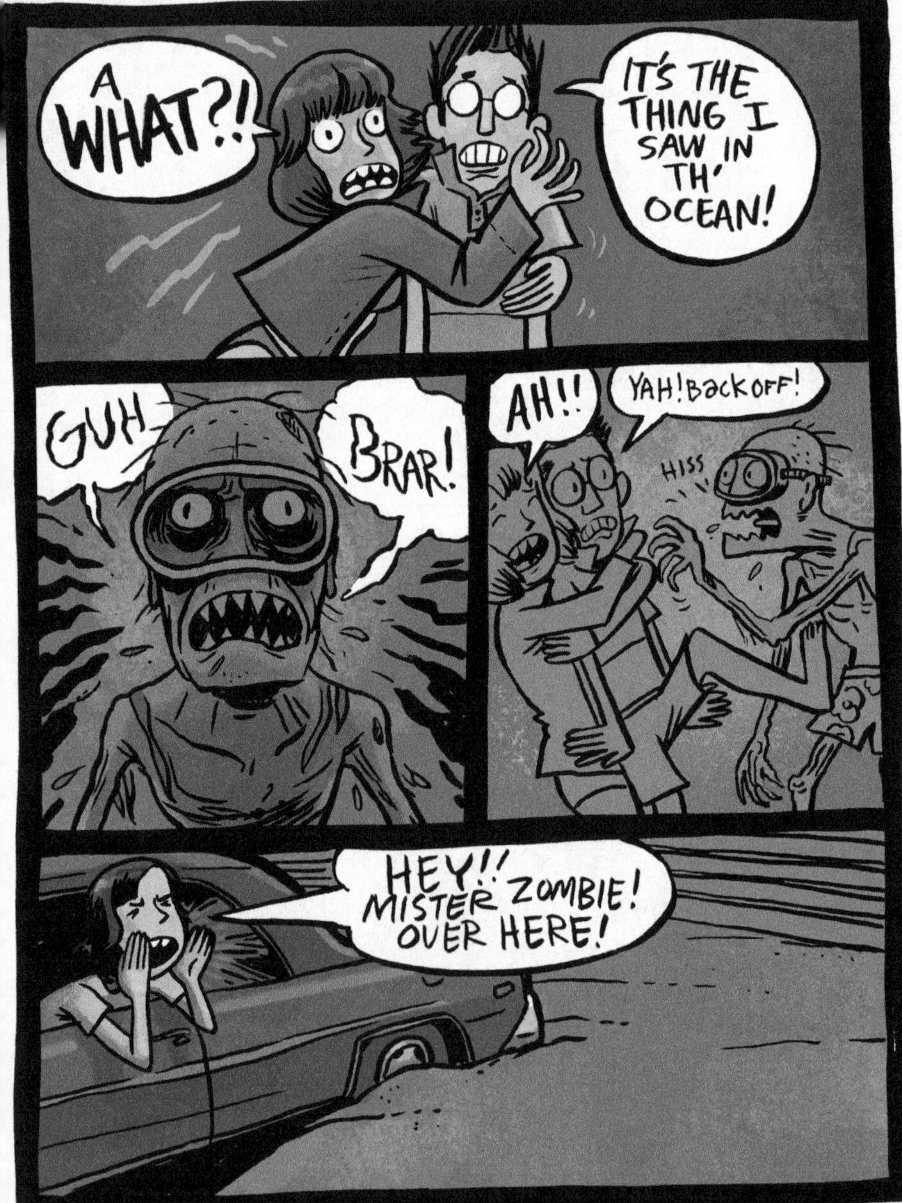
A WHAT?!
IT'S THE THING I SAW IN TH' OCEAN!
GUH
BRAR!
AH!!
YAH! BACK OFF!
HISS
HEY!! MISTER ZOMBIE! OVER HERE!

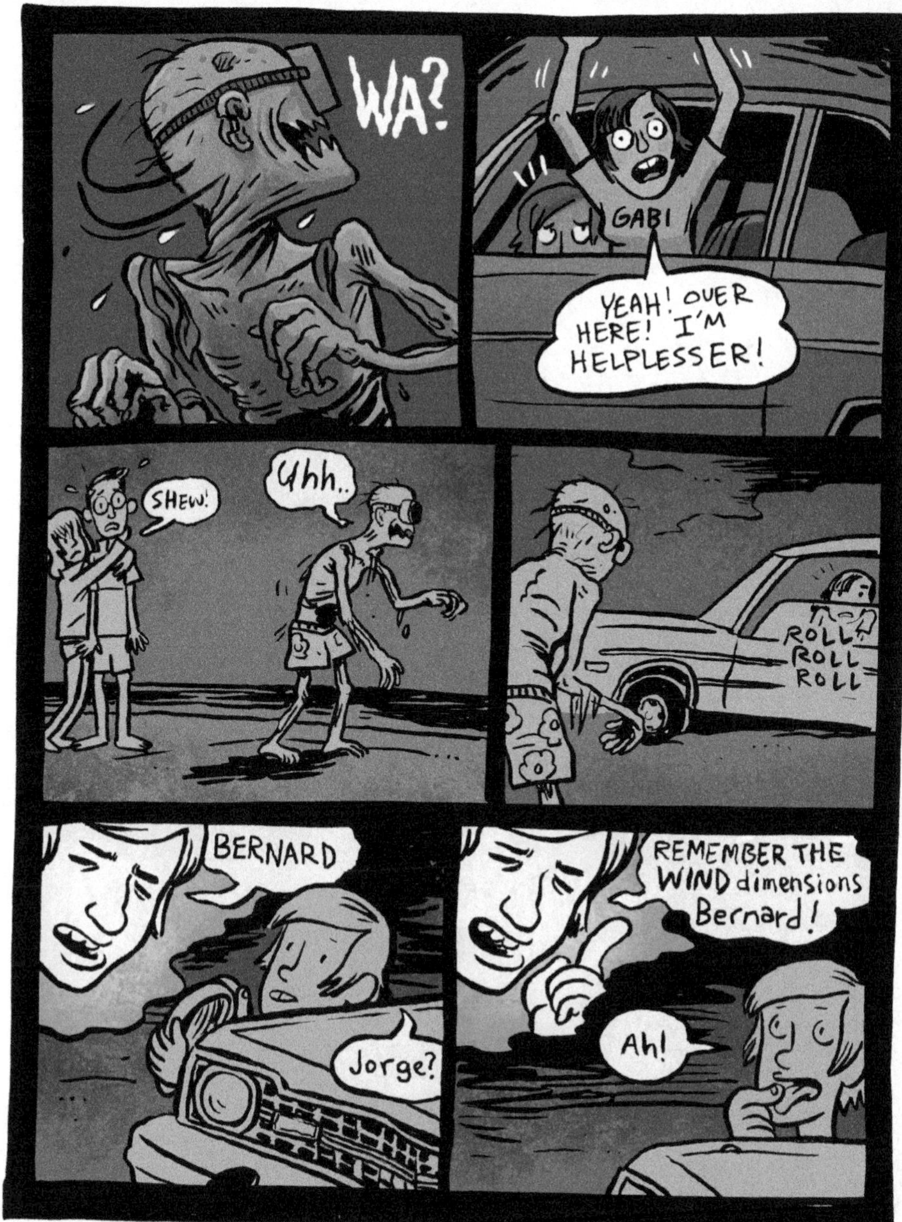
WA?
GABI
YEAH! OVER HERE! I'M HELPLESSER!
SHEW!
Uhh..
ROLL ROLL ROLL
BERNARD
Jorge?
REMEMBER THE WIND dimensions Bernard!
Ah!

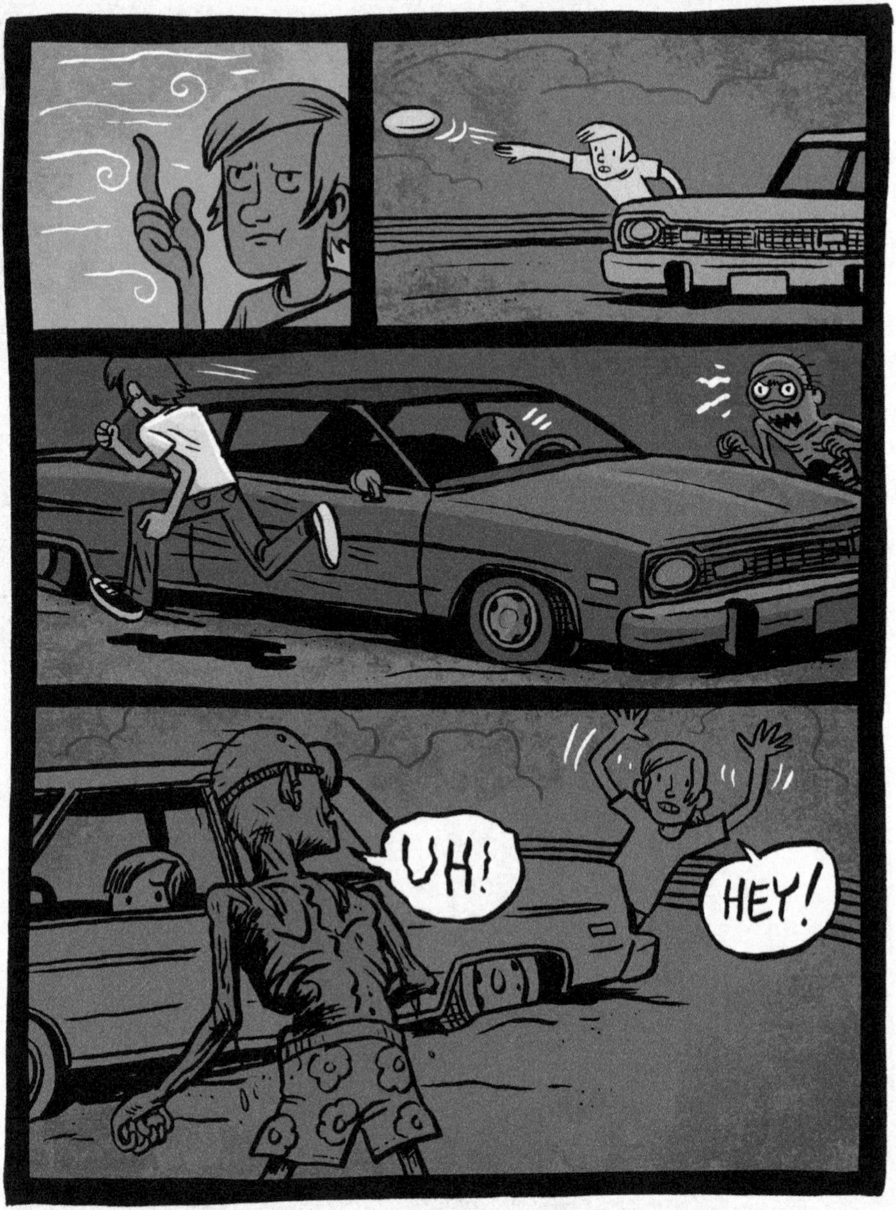
UH!
HEY!

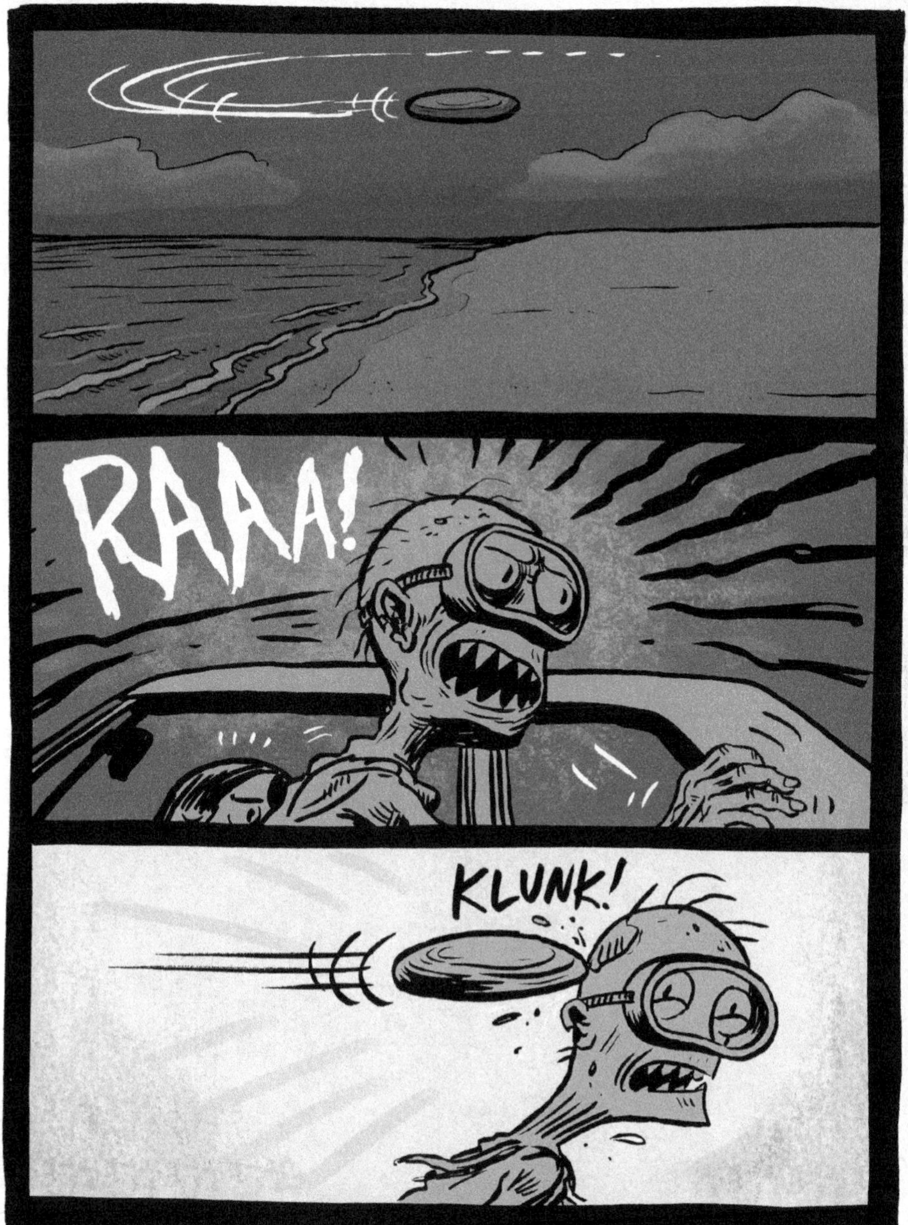
RAAA!
KLUNK!

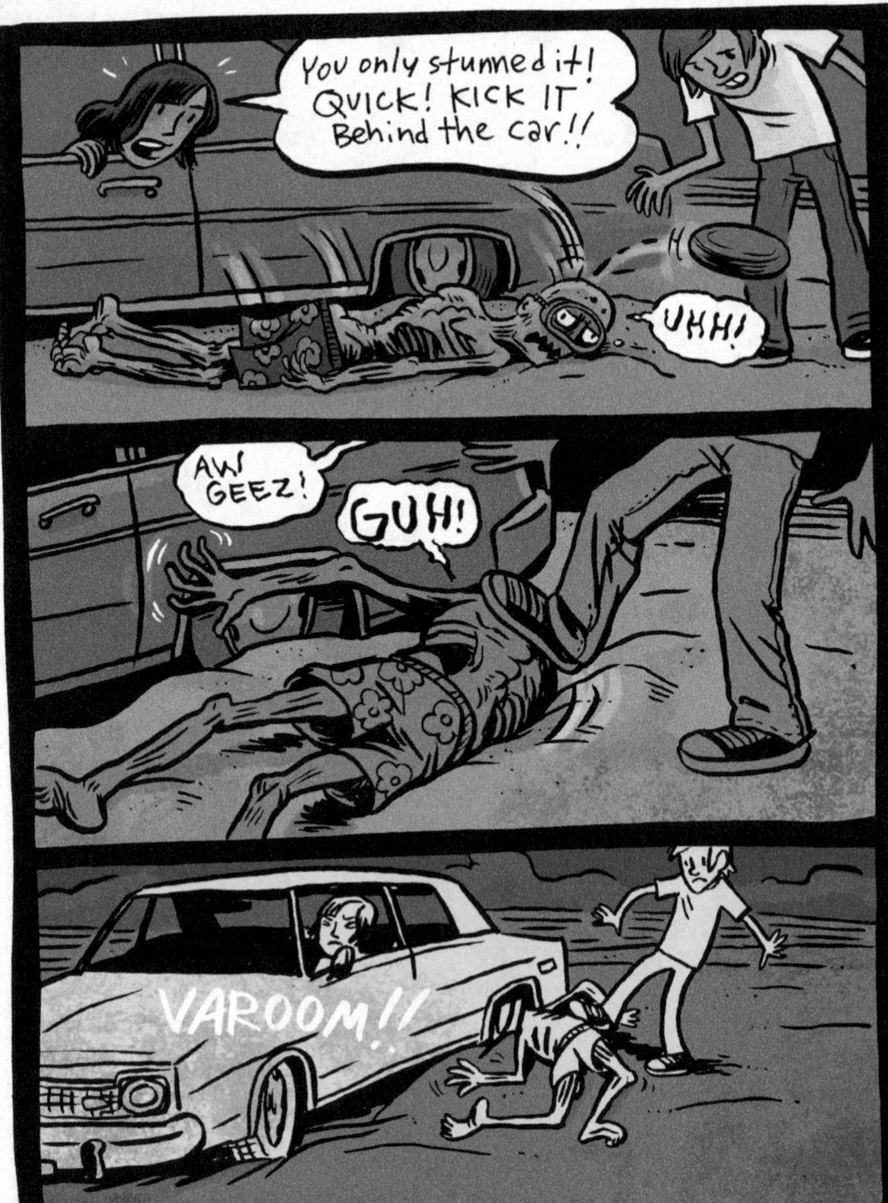
You only stunned it! QUICK! KICK IT Behind the car!!
UHH!
AW GEEZ!
GUH!
VAROOM!!

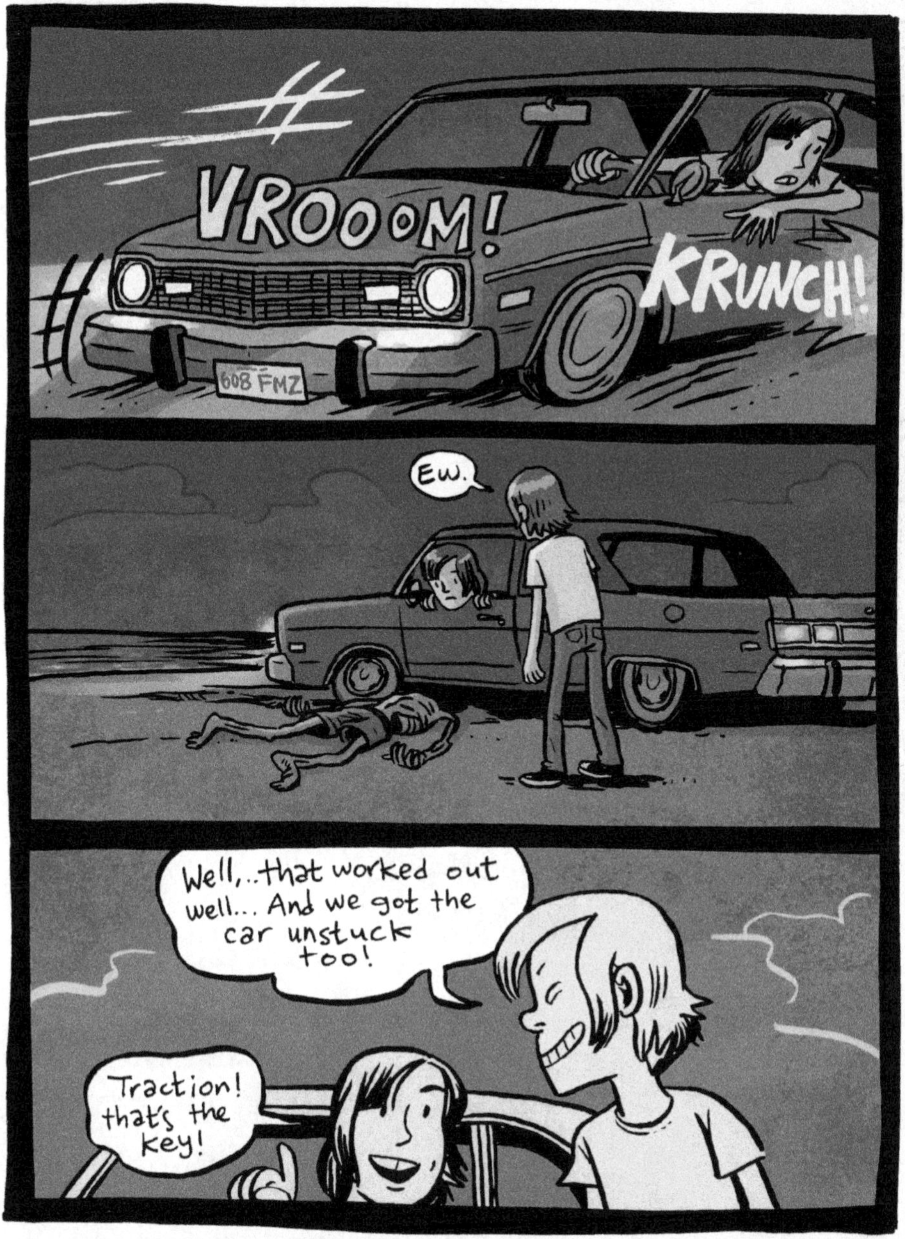
VROOOM!
KRUNCH!
608 FMZ
Ew.
Well,..that worked out well... And we got the car unstuck too!
Traction! that's the key!

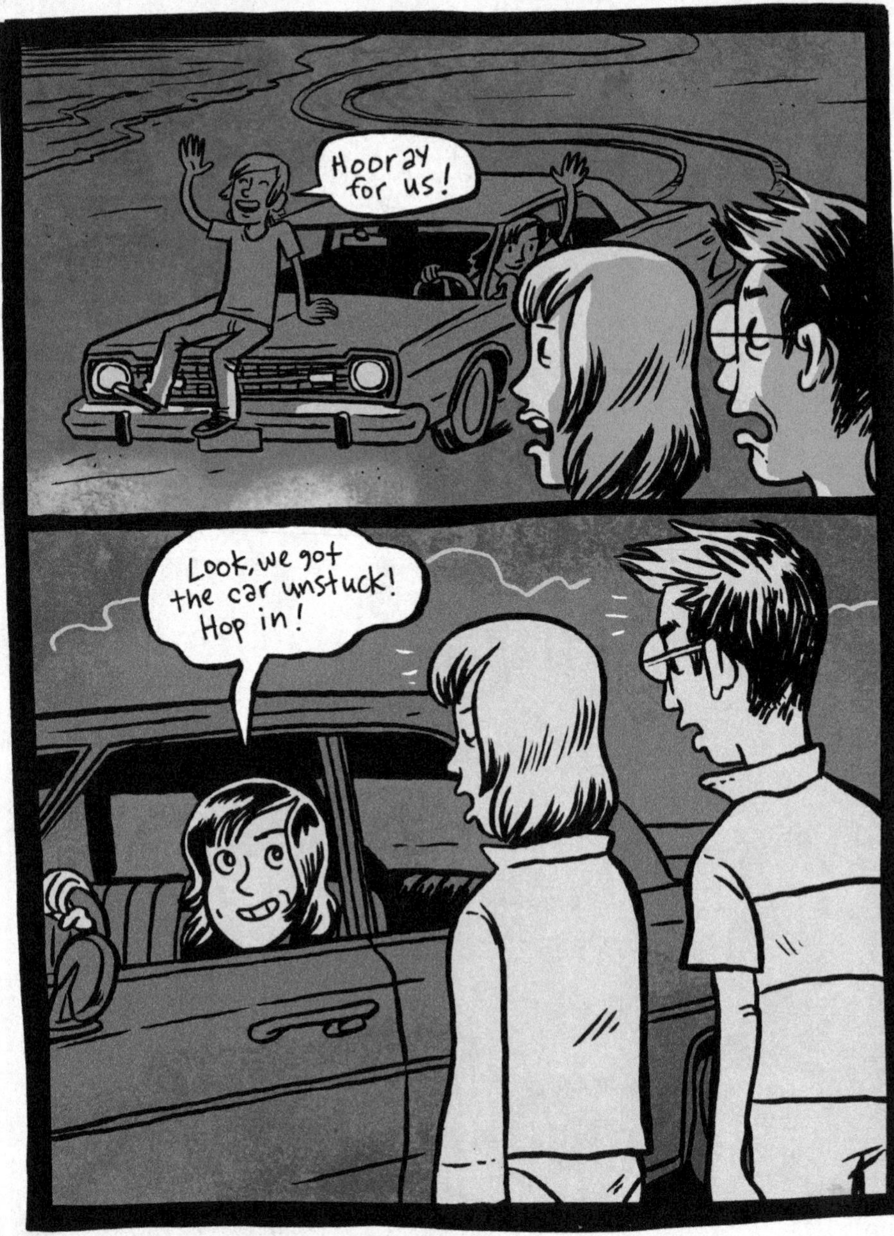
Hooray for us!
Look, we got the car unstuck! Hop in!

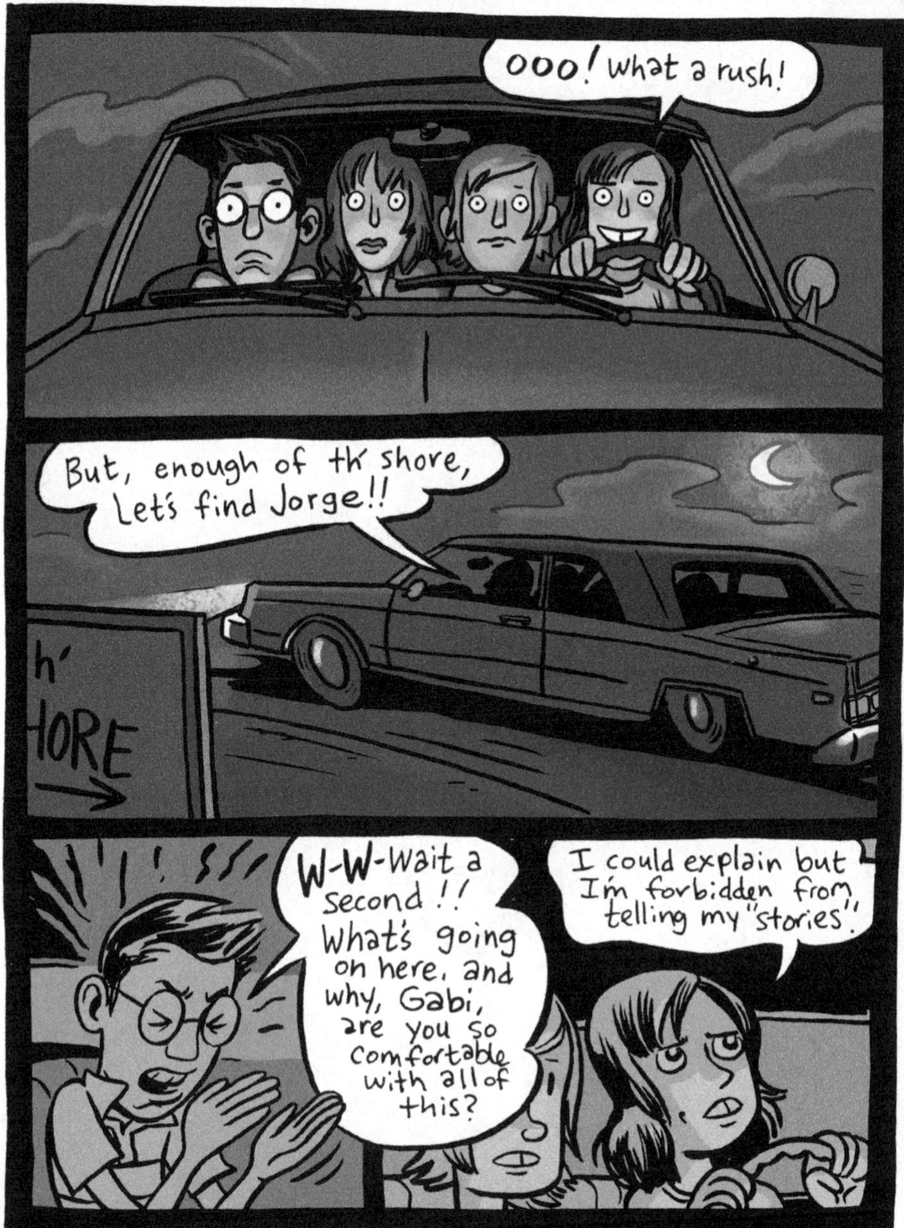
OOO! What a rush!
But, enough of th' shore, Let's find Jorge!!
h'
HORE
W-W-Wait a second!! What's going on here, and why, Gabi, are you so comfortable with all of this?
I could explain but I'm forbidden from telling my "stories".

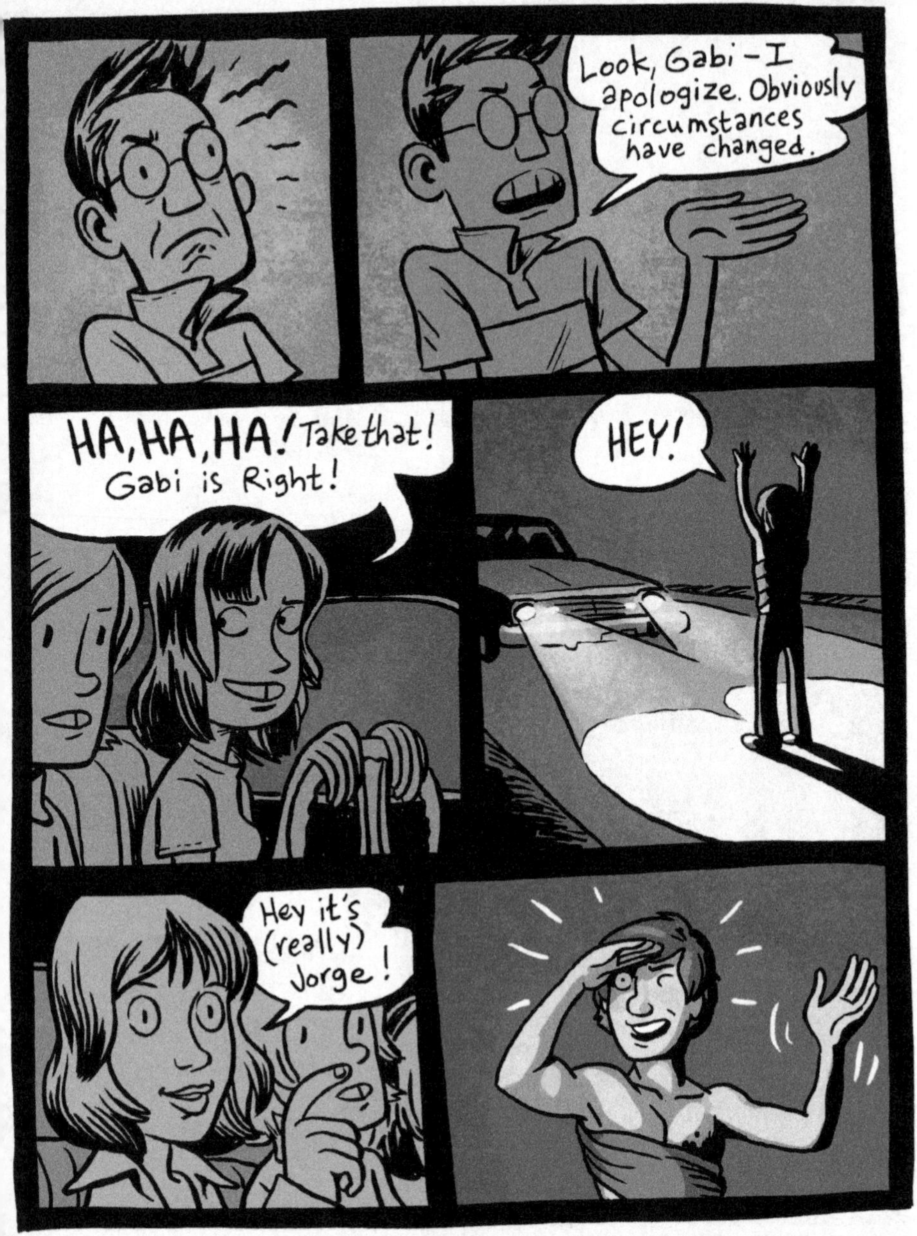
Look, Gabi – I apologize. Obviously circumstances have changed.
HA, HA, HA! Take that! Gabi is Right!
HEY!
Hey it's (really) Jorge!

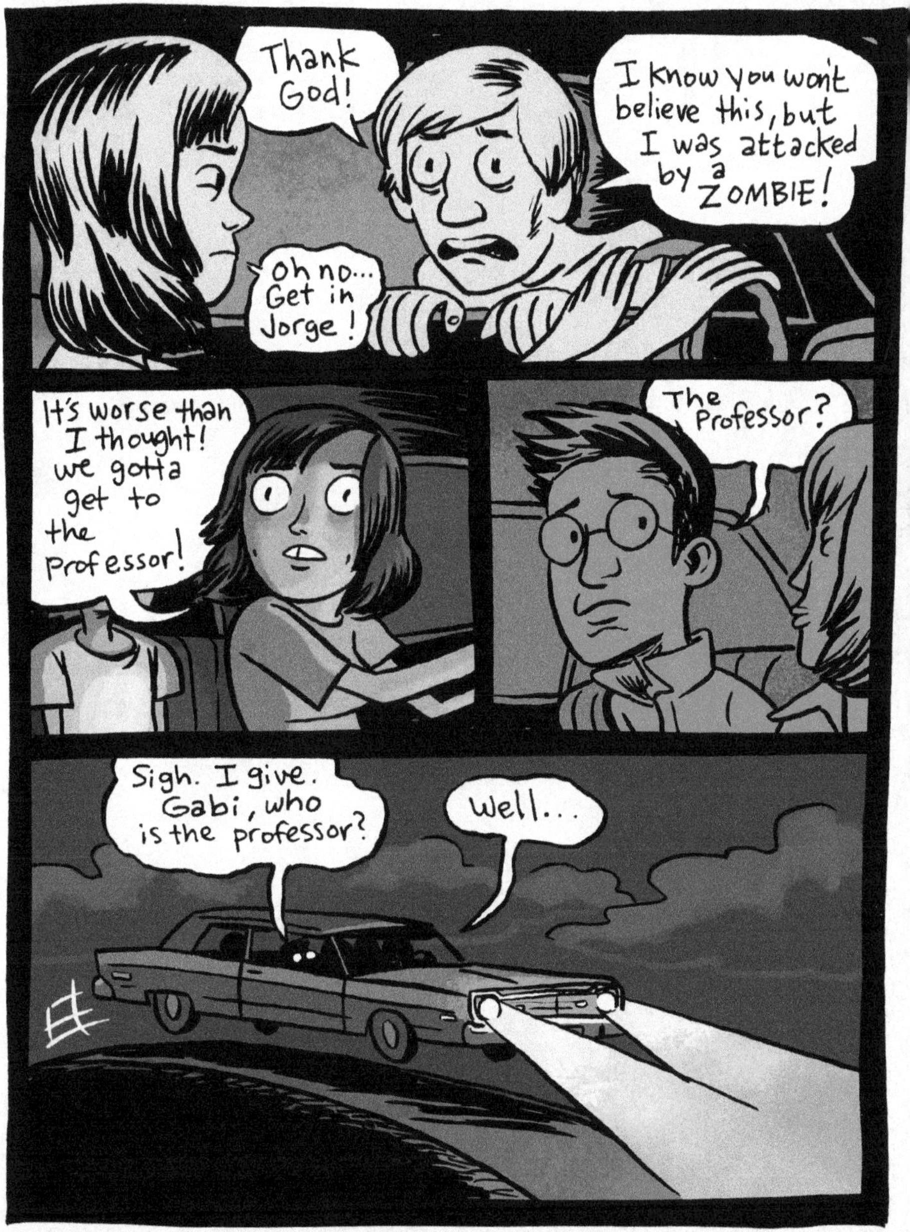
Thank God!
I know you won't believe this, but I was attacked by a ZOMBIE!
Oh no... Get in Jorge!
It's worse than I thought! we gotta get to the professor!
The Professor?
Sigh. I give. Gabi, who is the professor?
Well...

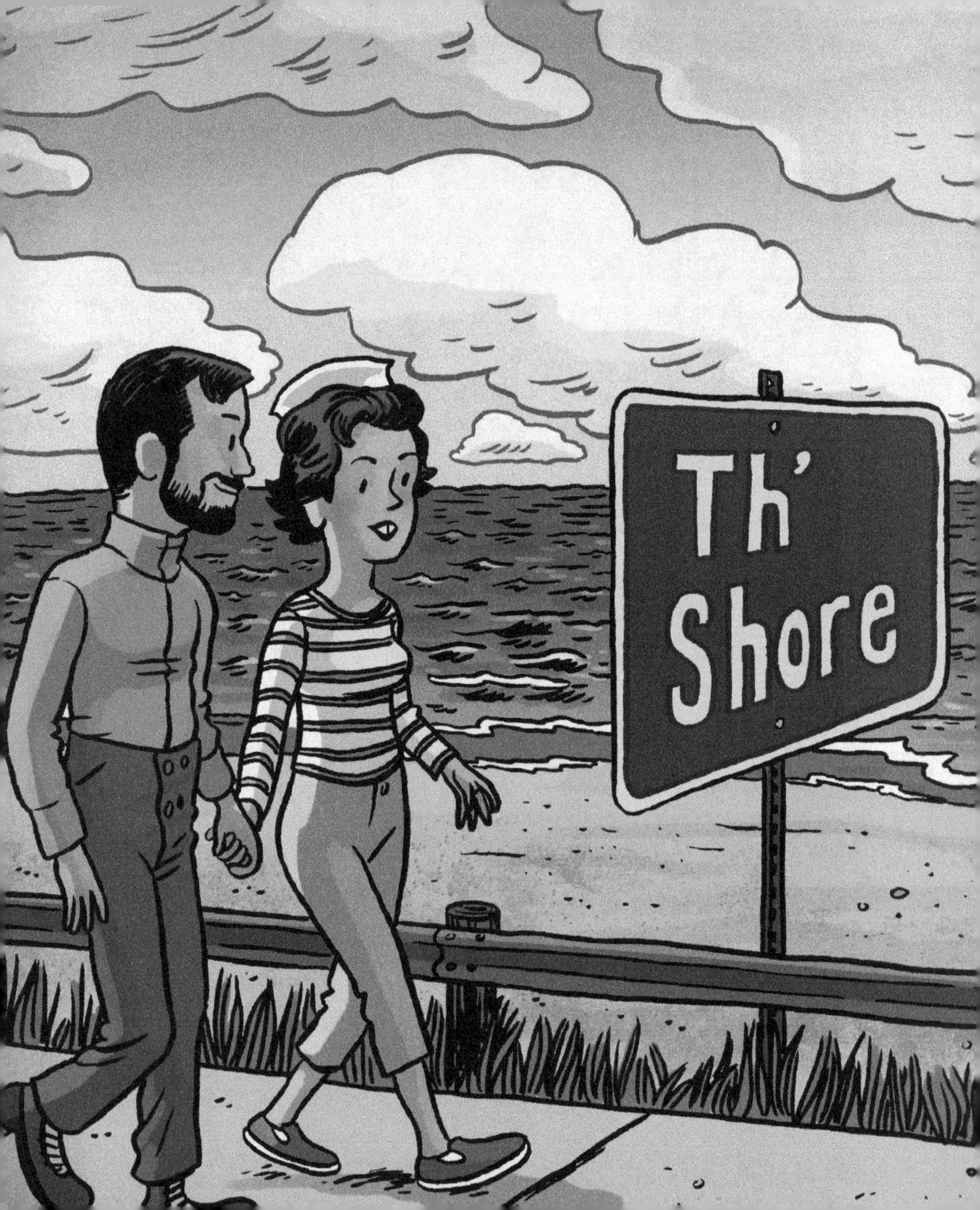
Th'
Shore

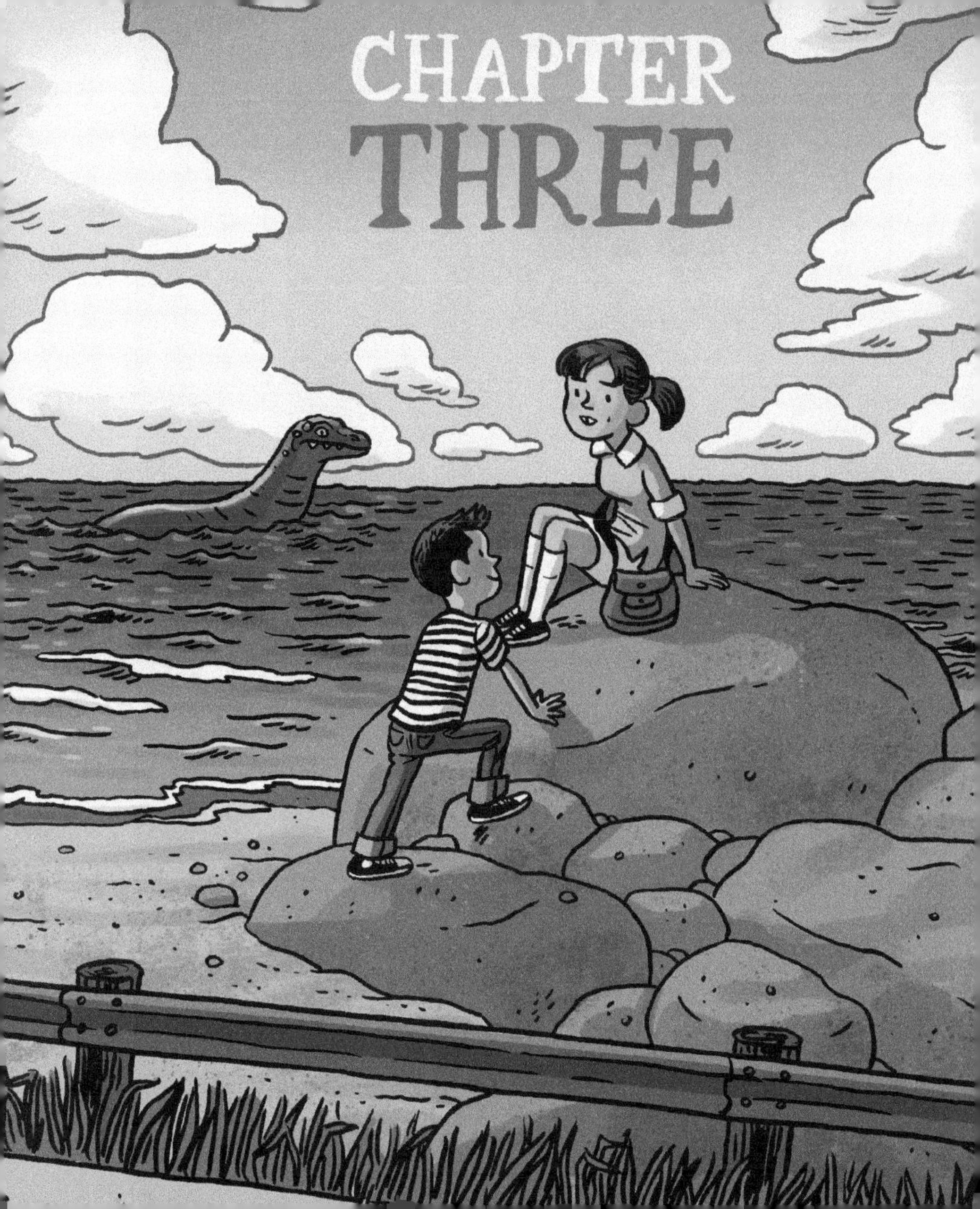
CHAPTER
THREE

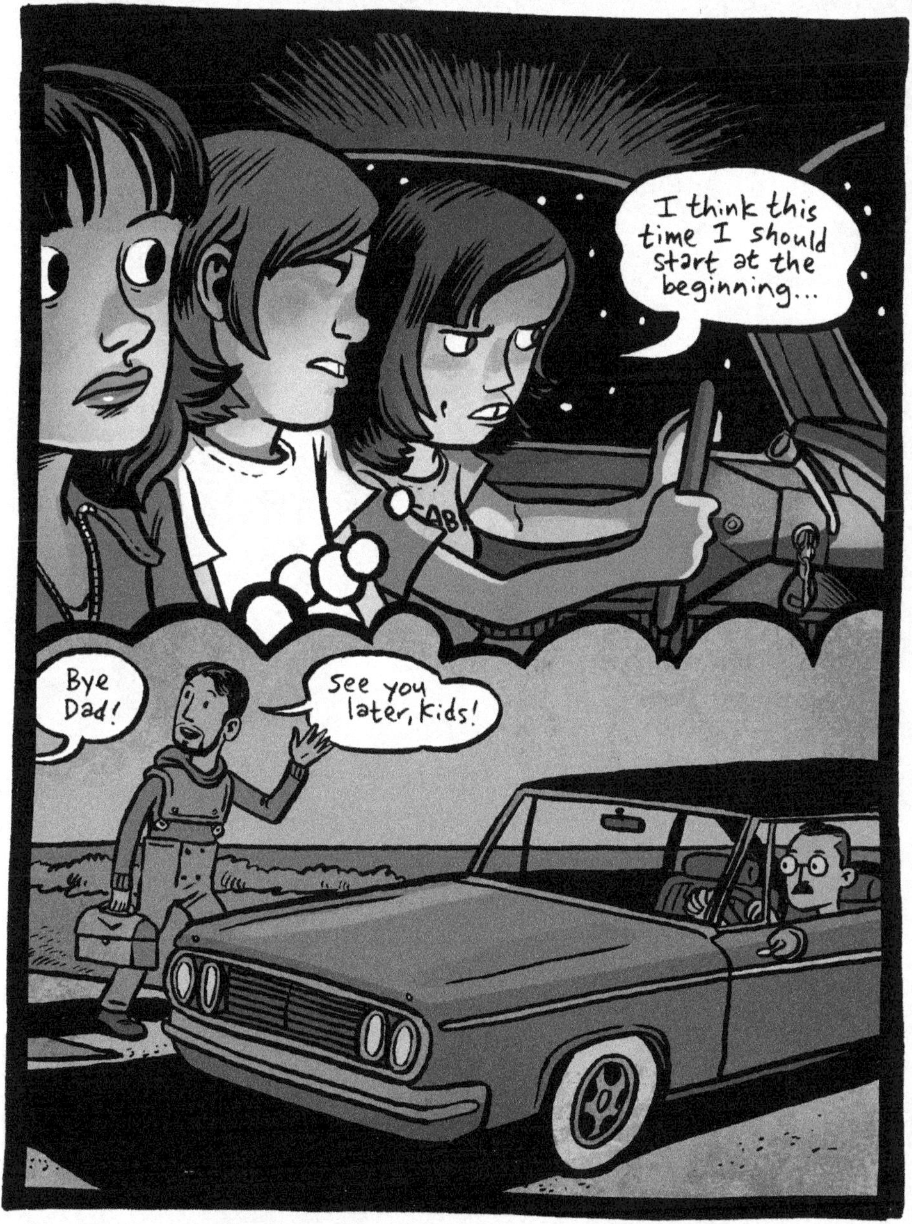
I think this time I should start at the beginning...
Bye Dad!
See you later, kids!

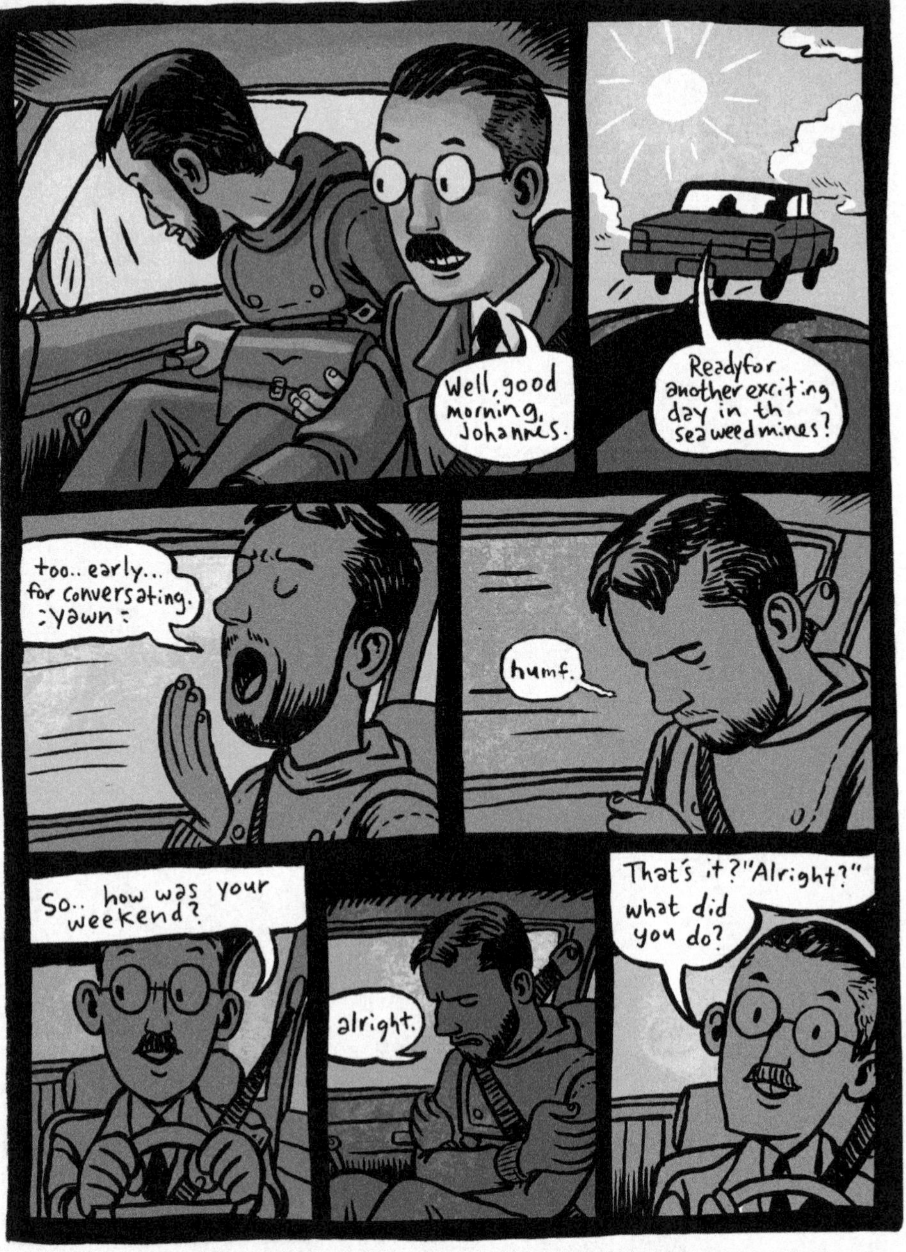
Well, good morning, Johannes.
Ready for another exciting day in th' seaweed mines?
too.. early... for conversating. :yawn:
humf.
So.. how was your weekend?
alright.
That's it? "Alright?" what did you do?

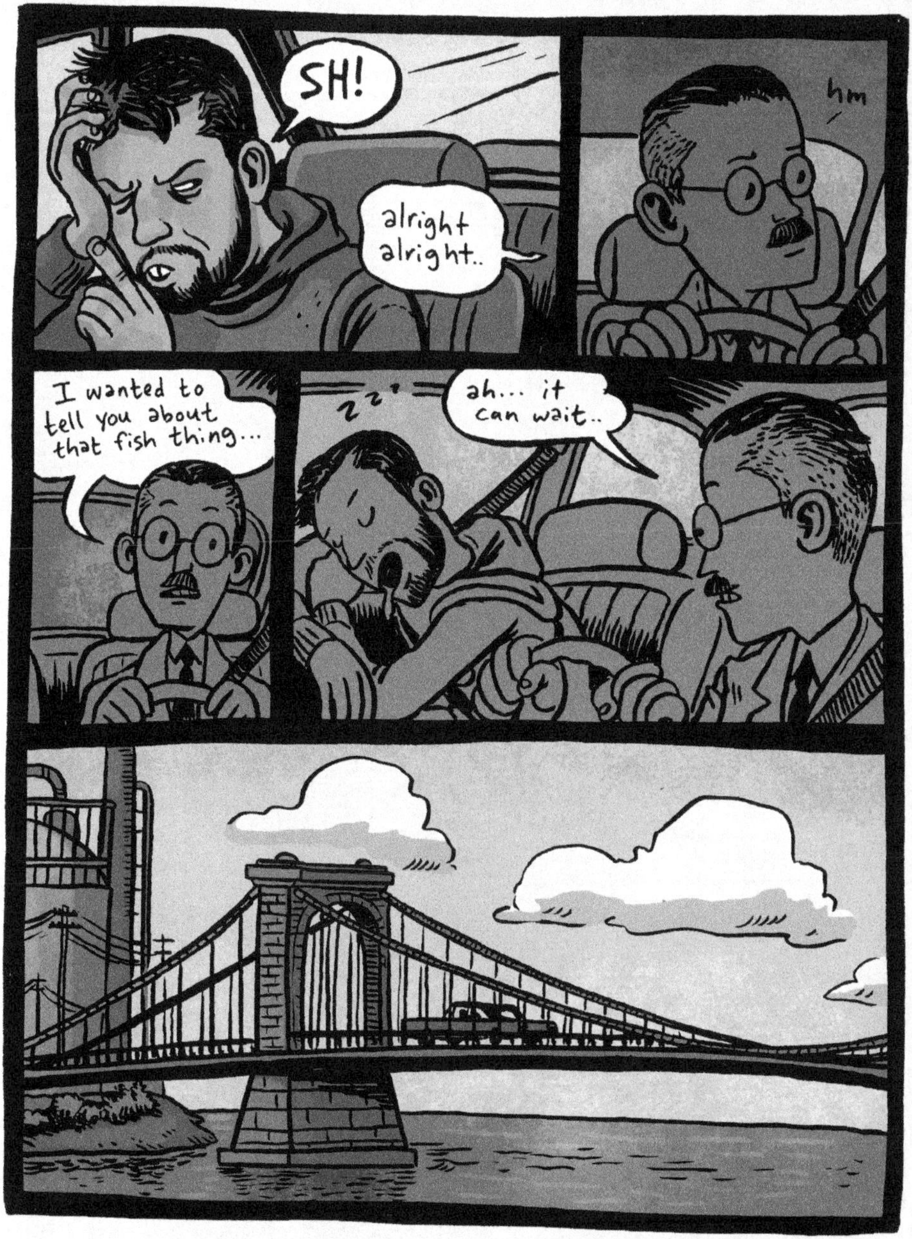
SH!
alright alright..
hm
I wanted to tell you about that fish thing...
z z z
ah... it can wait..

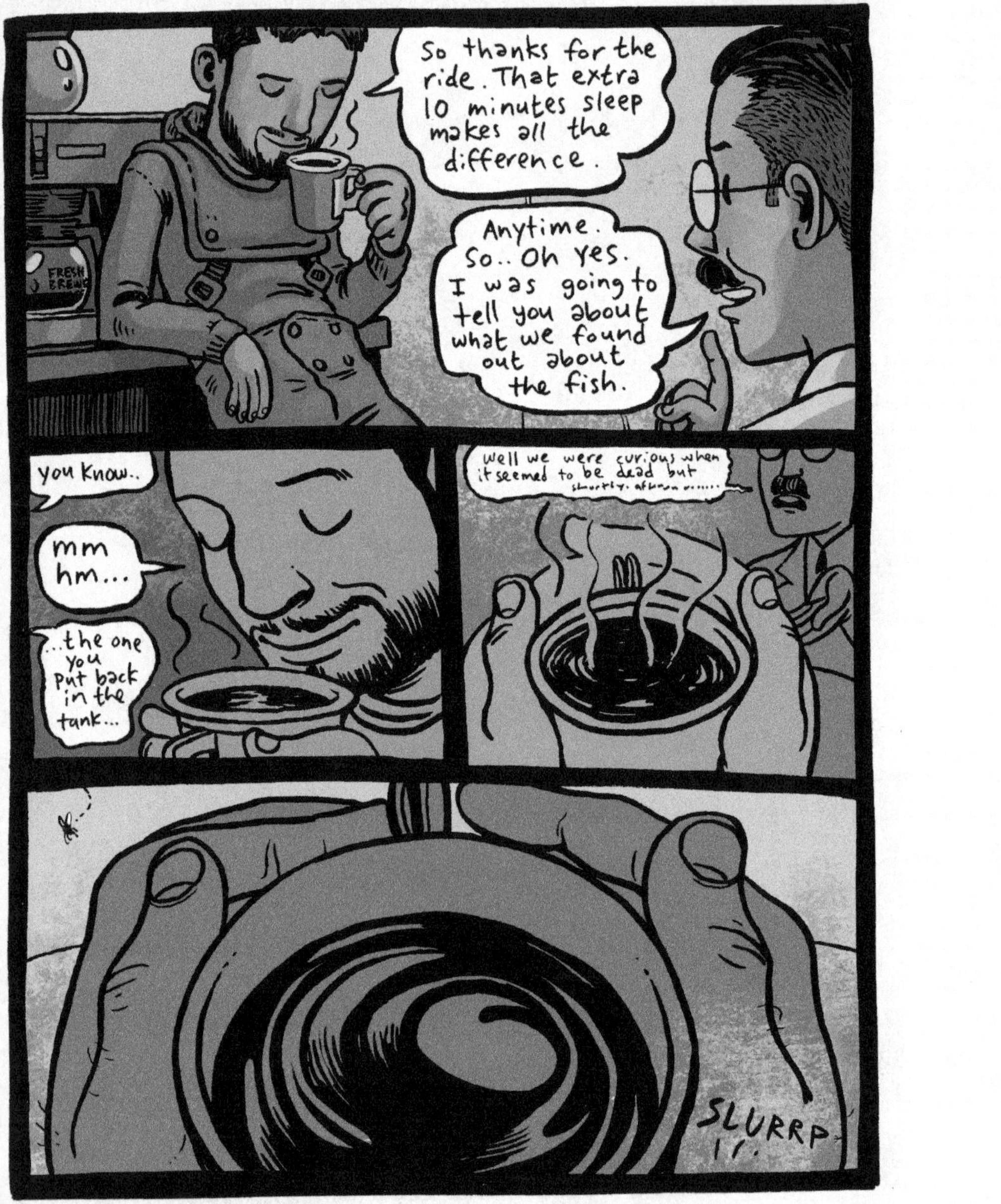

So thanks for the ride. That extra 10 minutes sleep makes all the difference.
Anytime. So... Oh yes. I was going to tell you about what we found out about the fish.
FRESH BREW
you know..
mm hm...
...the one you put back in the tank...
well we were curious when it seemed to be dead but
SLURRP

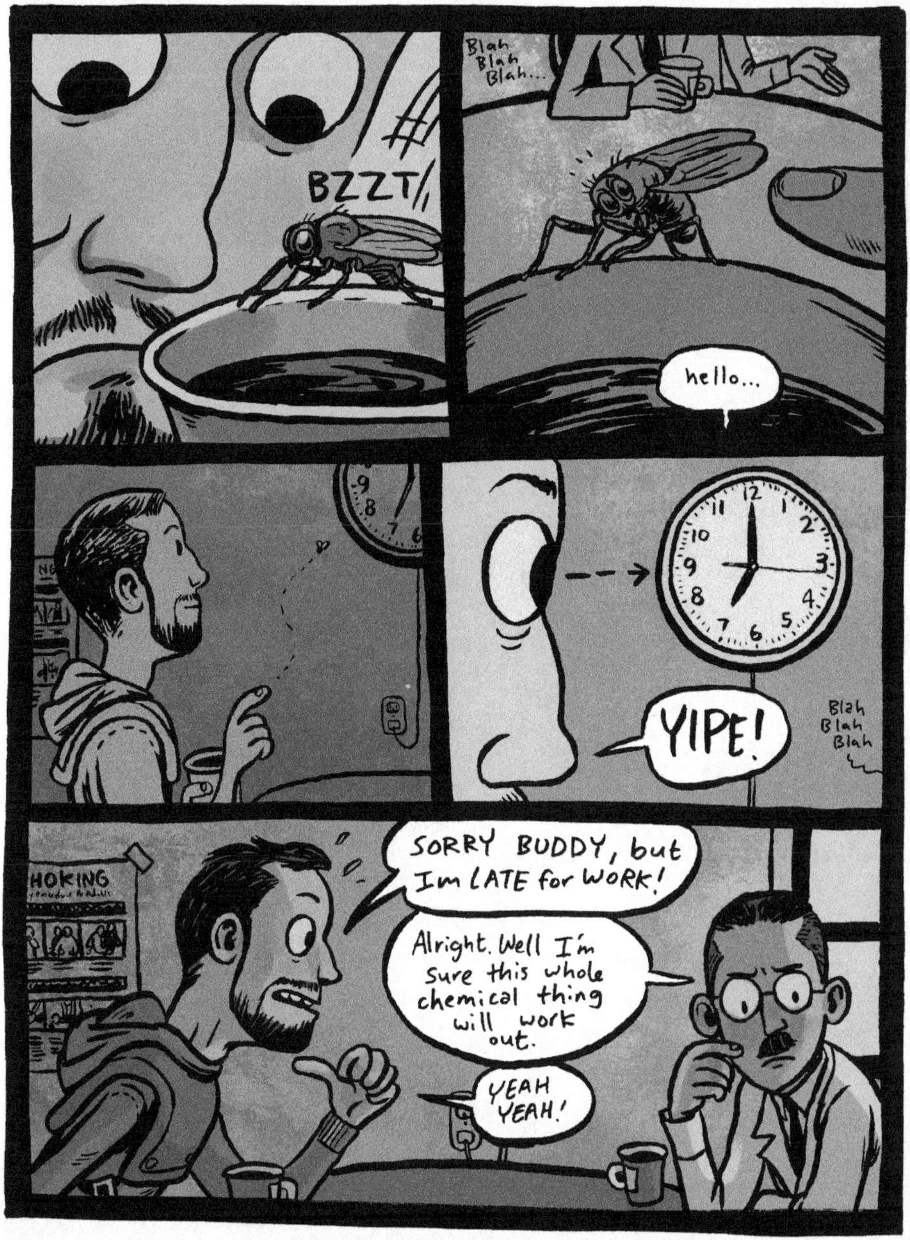
BZZZT
Blah
Blah
Blah...
hello...
YIPE!
Blah
Blah
Blah
SORRY BUDDY, but Im LATE for WORK!
Alright. Well I'm sure this whole chemical thing will work out.
YEAH YEAH!

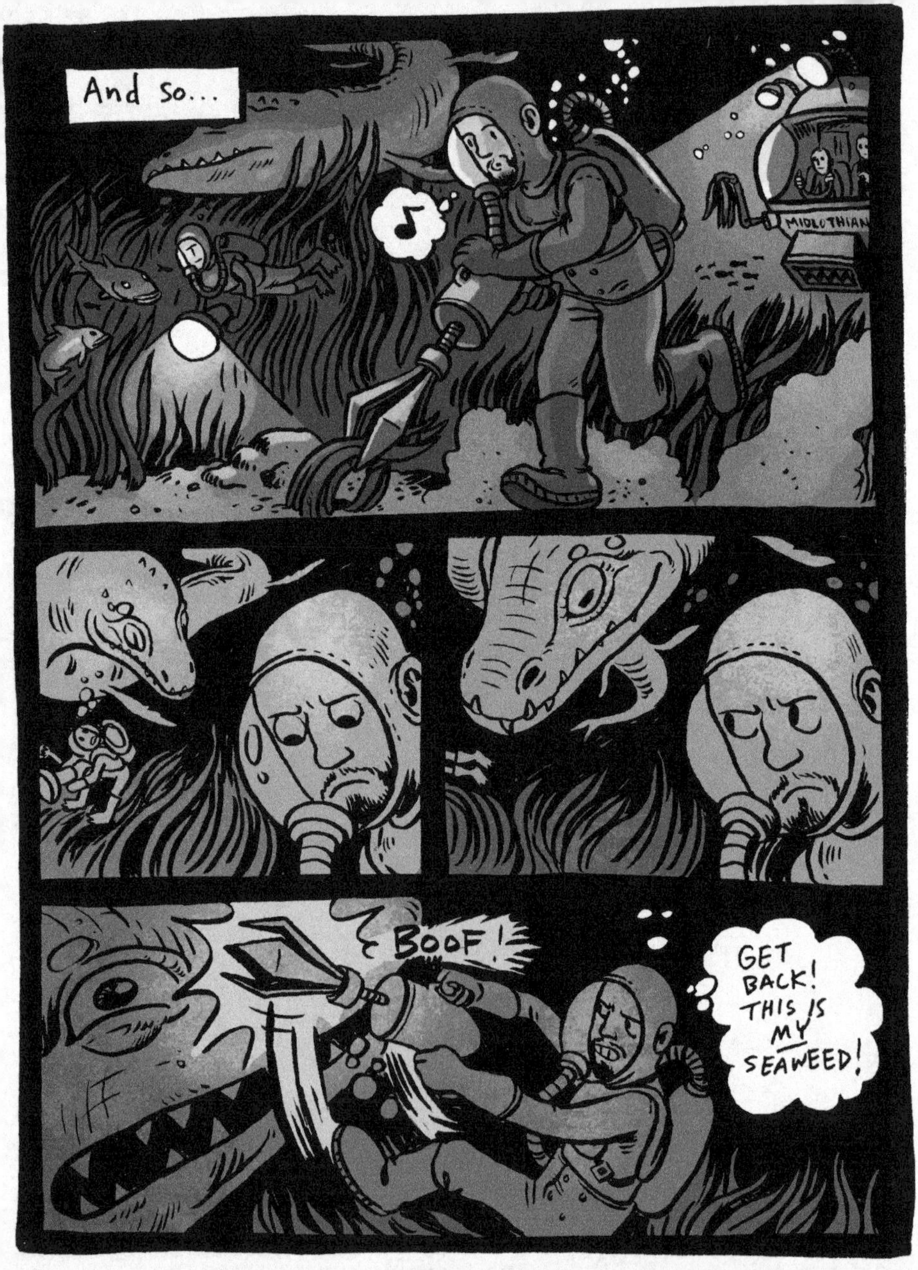
And so...
MIDLOTHIAN
BOOF!
GET BACK! THIS IS MY SEAWEED!

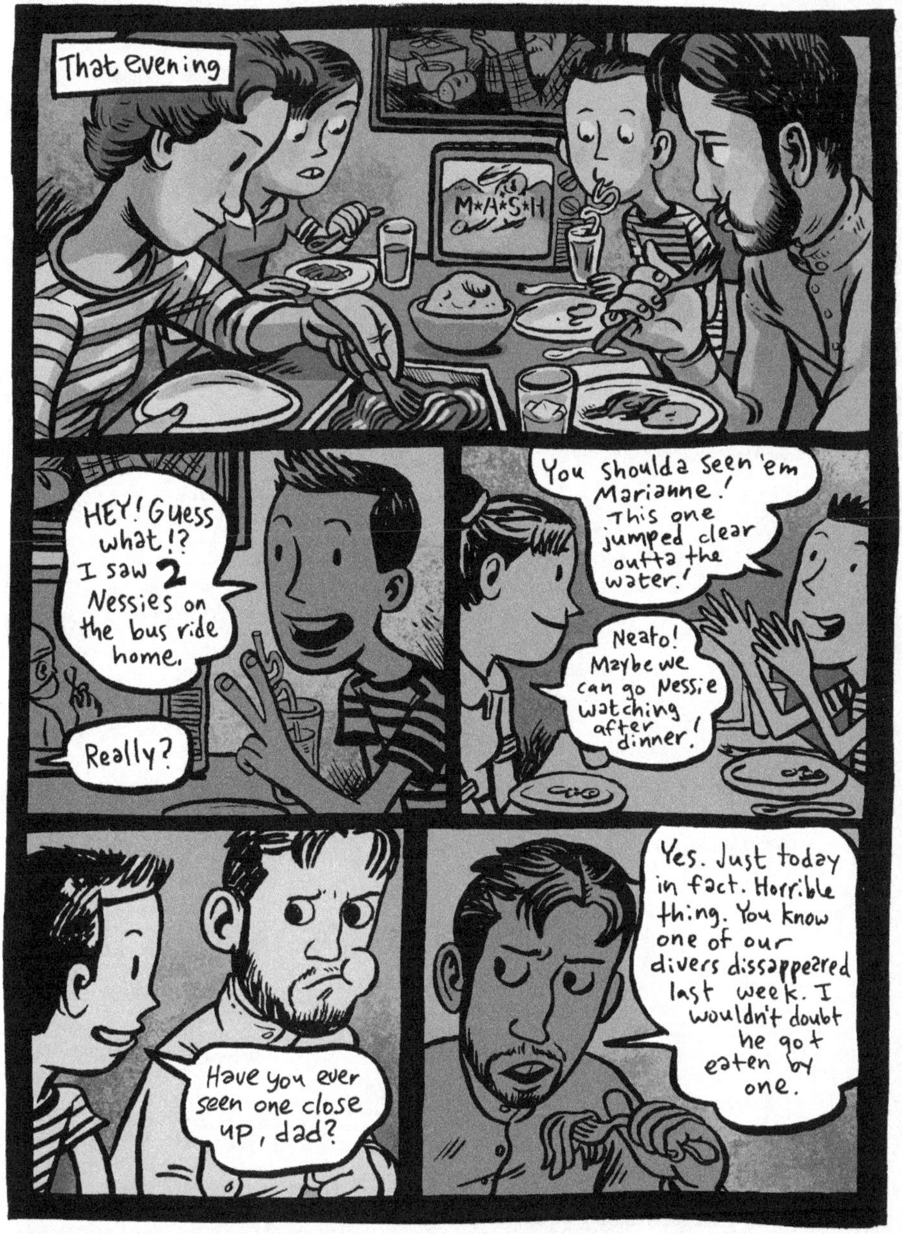
That evening
M*A*S*H
HEY! Guess what!? I saw 2 Nessies on the bus ride home.
Really?
You shoulda seen 'em Marianne! This one jumped clear outta the water!
Neato! Maybe we can go Nessie watching after dinner!
Have you ever seen one close up, dad?
Yes. Just today in fact. Horrible thing. You know one of our divers dissappeared last week. I wouldn't doubt he got eaten by one.

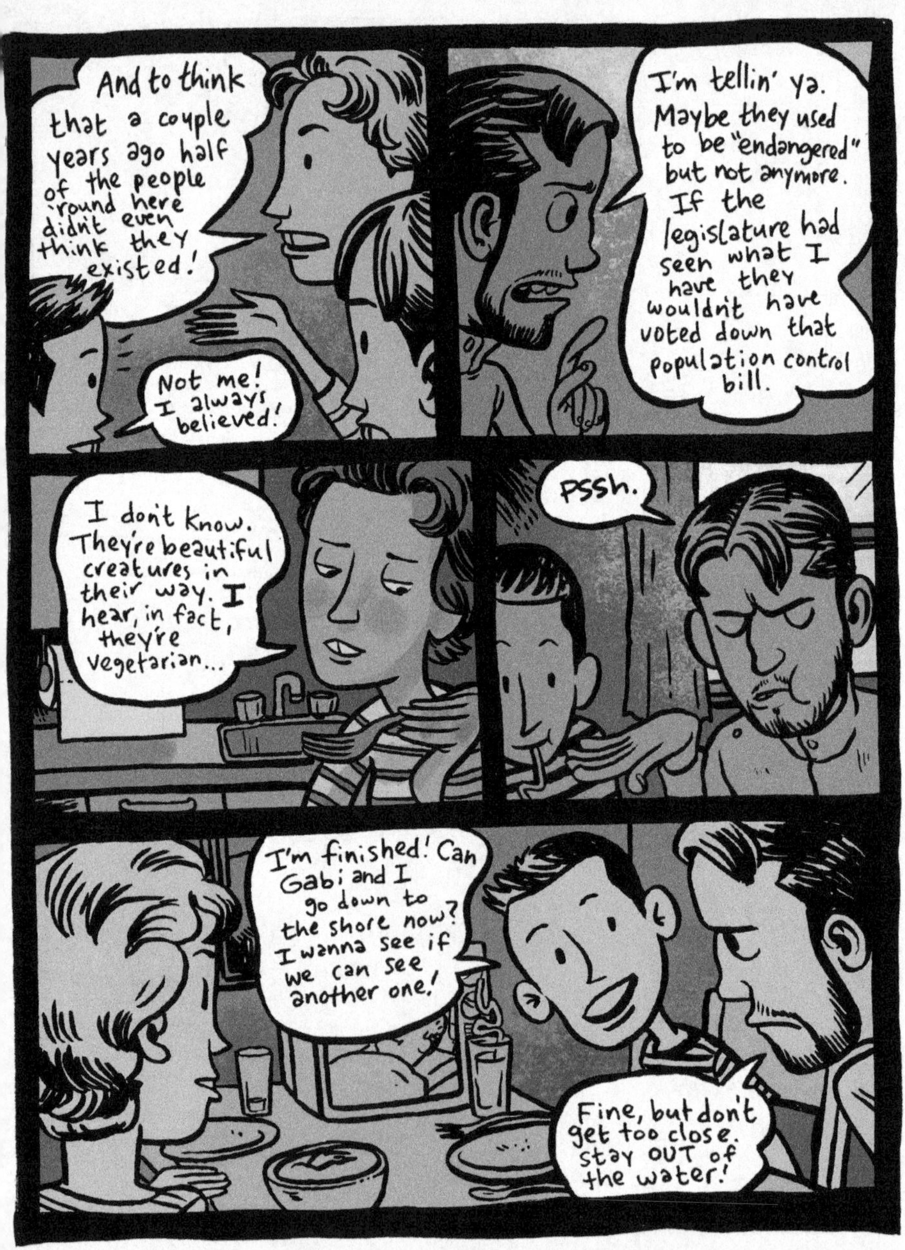
And to think that a couple years ago half of the people 'round here didn't even think they existed!
Not me! I always believed!
I'm tellin' ya. Maybe they used to be "endangered" but not anymore. If the legislature had seen what I have they wouldn't have voted down that population control bill.
I don't know. They're beautiful creatures in their way. I hear, in fact, they're vegetarian...
PSSH.
I'm finished! Can Gabi and I go down to the shore now? I wanna see if we can see another one!
Fine, but don't get too close. Stay OUT of the water!

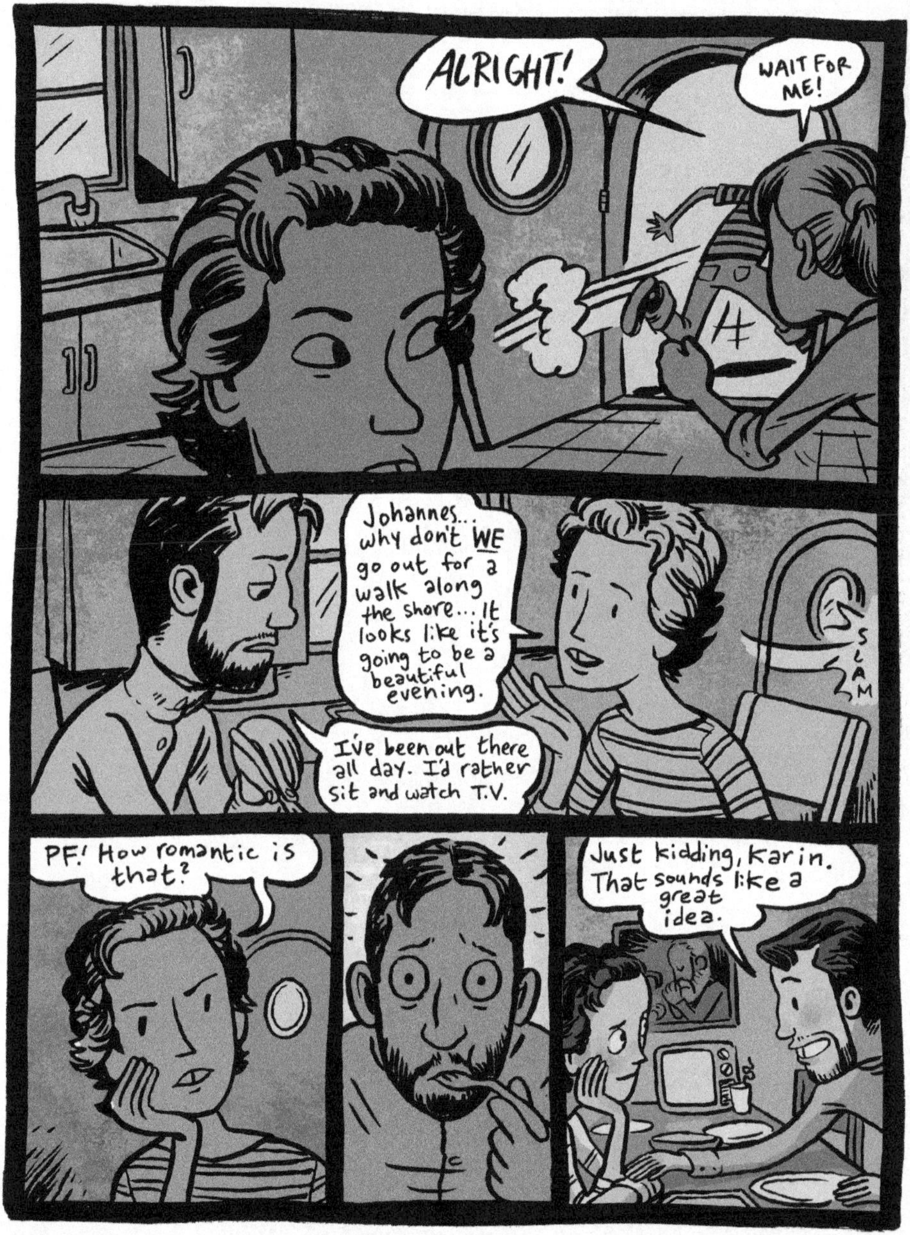
ALRIGHT!
WAIT FOR ME!
Johannes... why don't WE go out for a walk along the shore... It looks like it's going to be a beautiful evening.
SLAM
I've been out there all day. I'd rather sit and watch T.V.
PF! How romantic is that?
Just kidding, Karin. That sounds like a great idea.

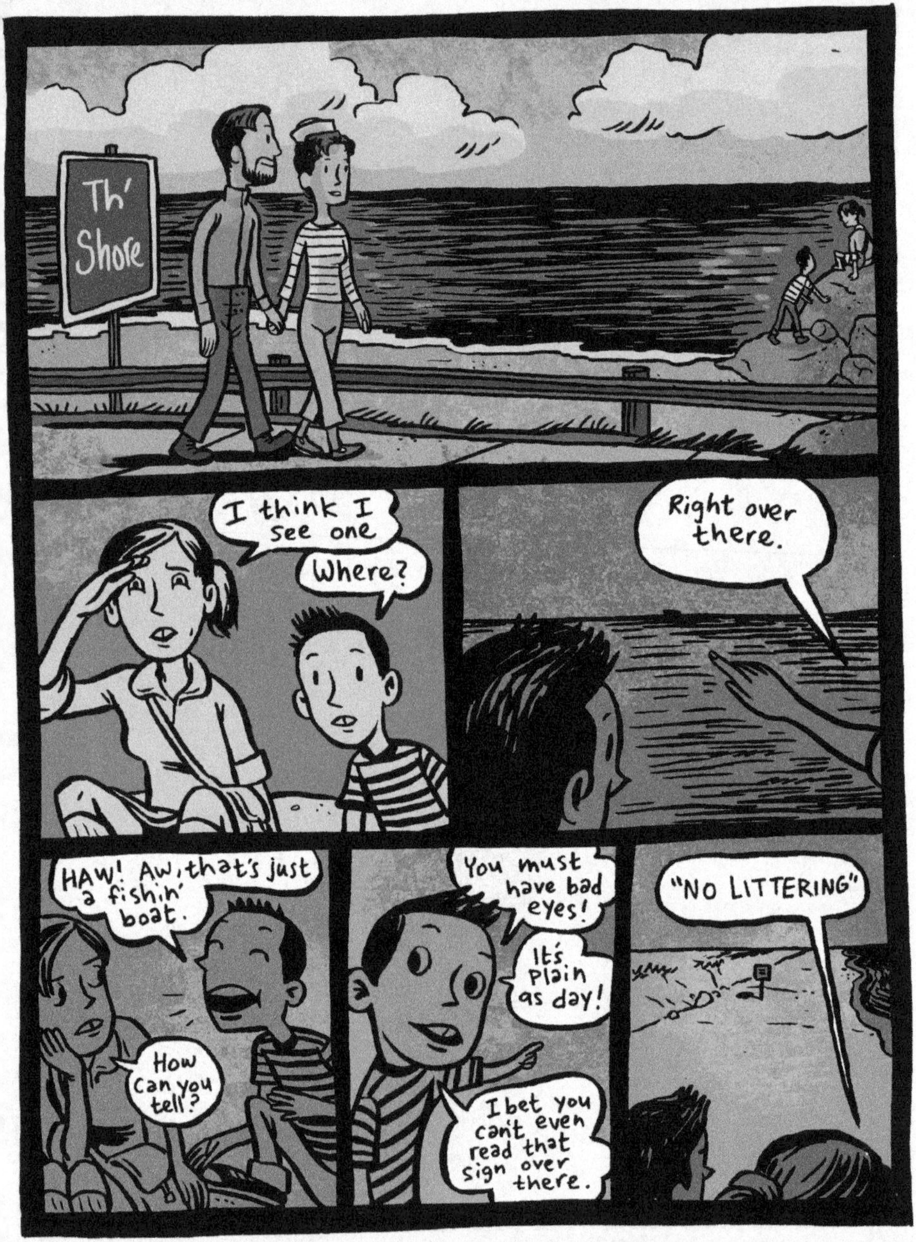
Th' Shore
I think I see one
Where?
Right over there.
HAW! Aw, that's just a fishin' boat.
How can you tell?
You must have bad eyes!
It's plain as day!
I bet you can't even read that sign over there.
"NO LITTERING"

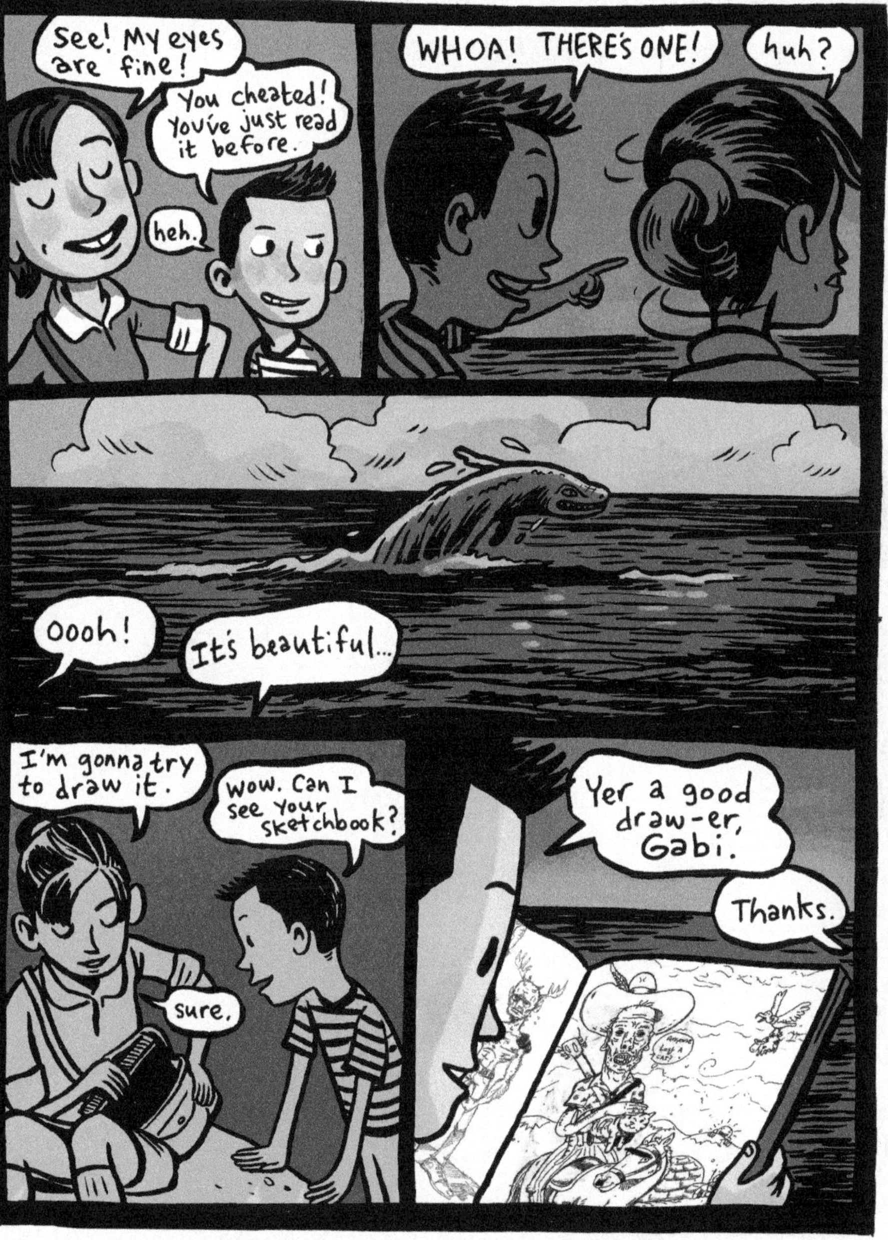
See! My eyes are fine!
You cheated! You've just read it before.
heh.
WHOA! THERE'S ONE!
huh?
Oooh!
It's beautiful...
I'm gonna try to draw it.
Wow. Can I see your sketchbook?
sure.
Yer a good draw-er, Gabi.
Thanks.

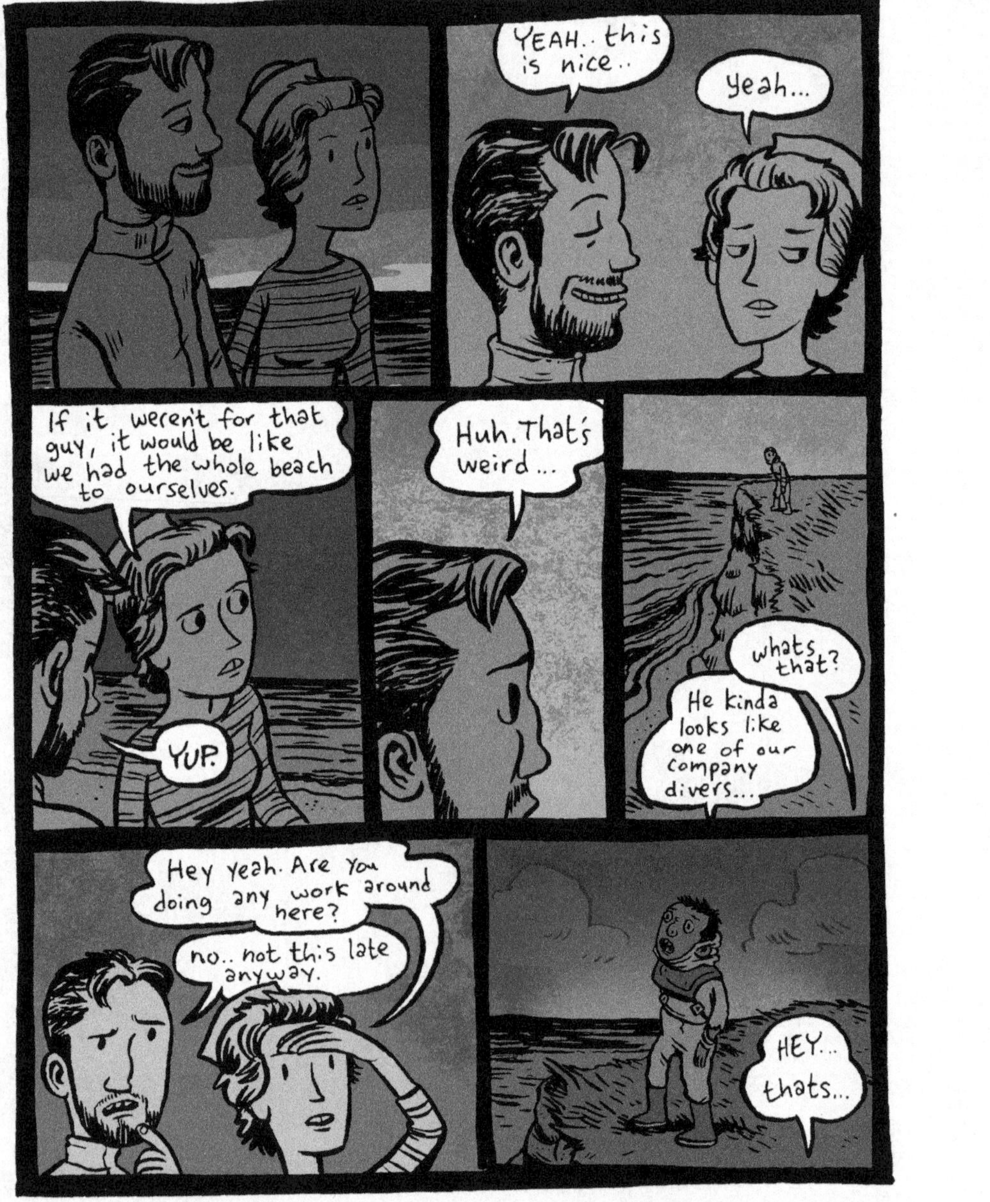
YEAH.. this is nice..
yeah...
If it weren't for that guy, it would be like we had the whole beach to ourselves.
YUP.
Huh. That's weird...
whats that?
He kinda looks like one of our company divers...
Hey yeah. Are You doing any work around here?
no.. not this late anyway.
HEY... thats...

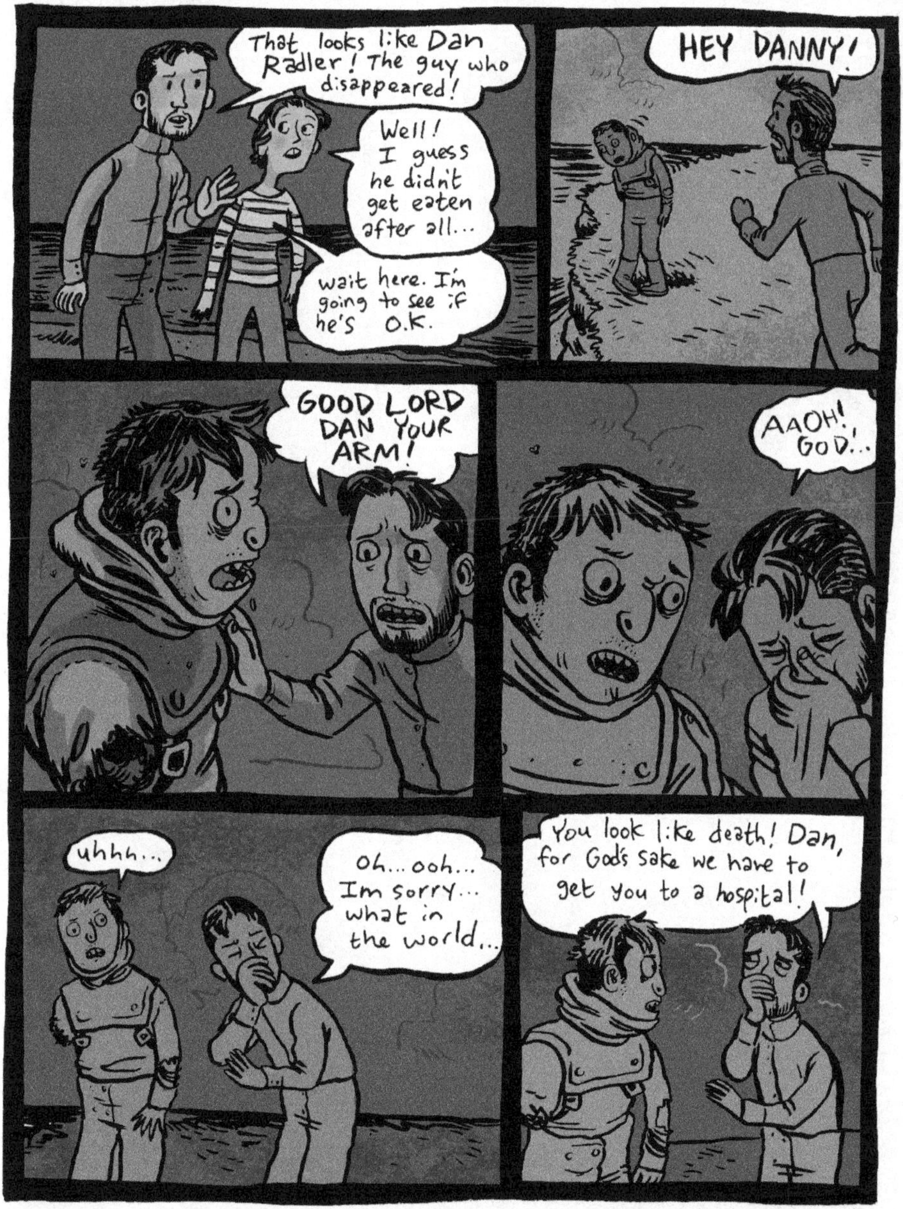

That looks like Dan Radler! The guy who disappeared!
Well! I guess he didn't get eaten after all...
wait here. I'm going to see if he's O.K.
HEY DANNY!
GOOD LORD DAN YOUR ARM!
AAOH! GOD!..
uhhh...
Oh... ooh... Im sorry... what in the world...
You look like death! Dan, for God's sake we have to get you to a hospital!

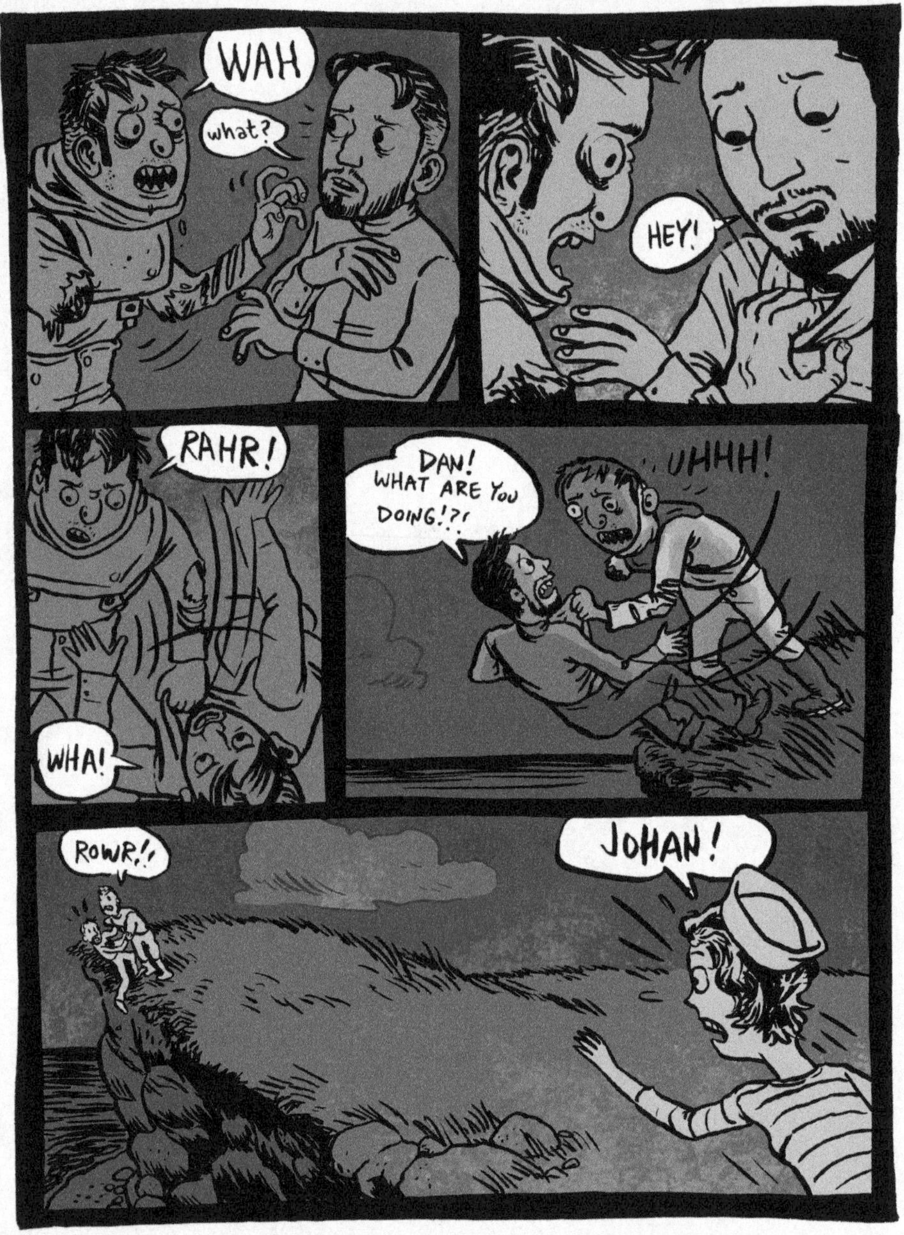
WAH
what?
HEY!
RAHR!
WHA!
DAN! WHAT ARE YOU DOING!?!
UHHH!
ROWR!!
JOHAN!

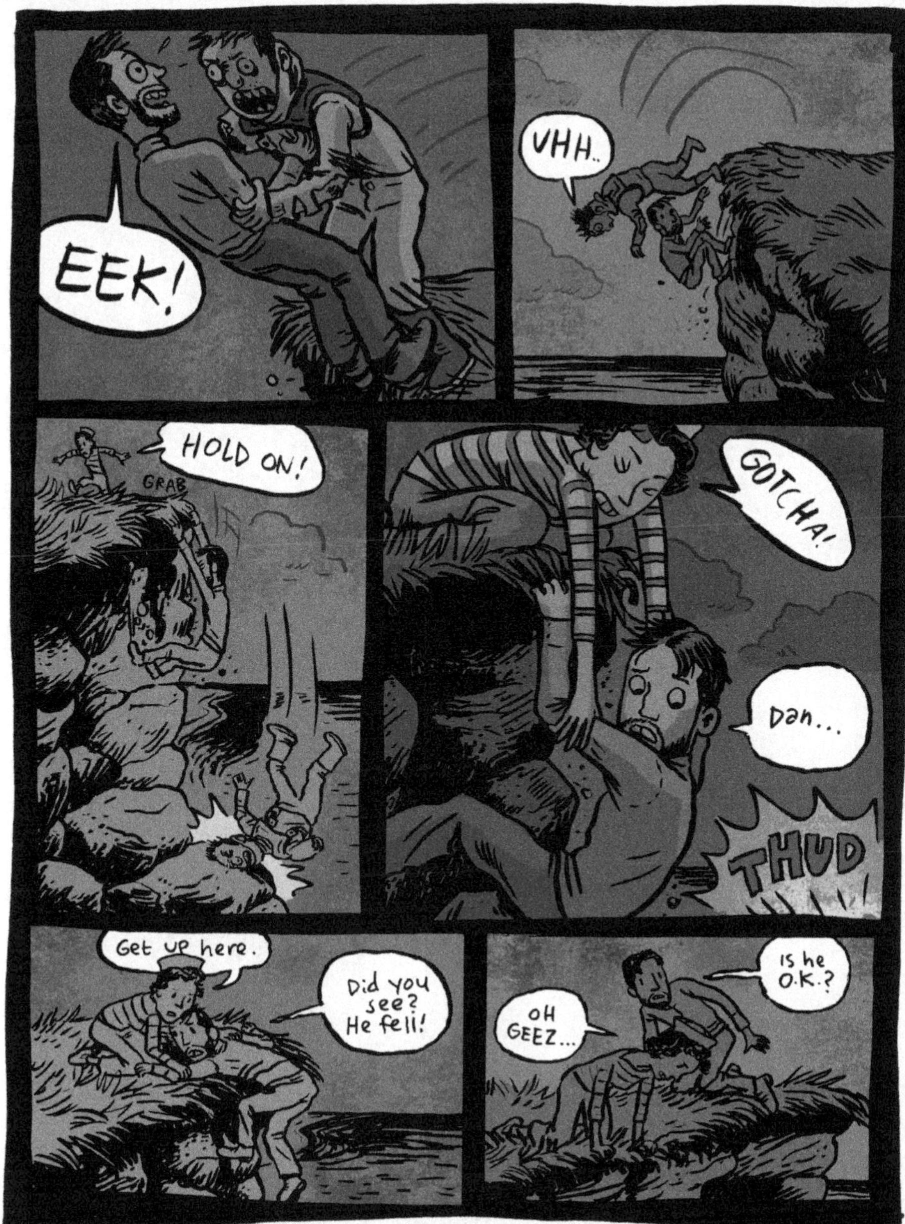
EEK!
VHH..
HOLD ON!
GRAB
GOTCHA!
Dan...
THUD
Get up here.
Did you see? He fell!
Is he O.K.?
OH GEEZ...

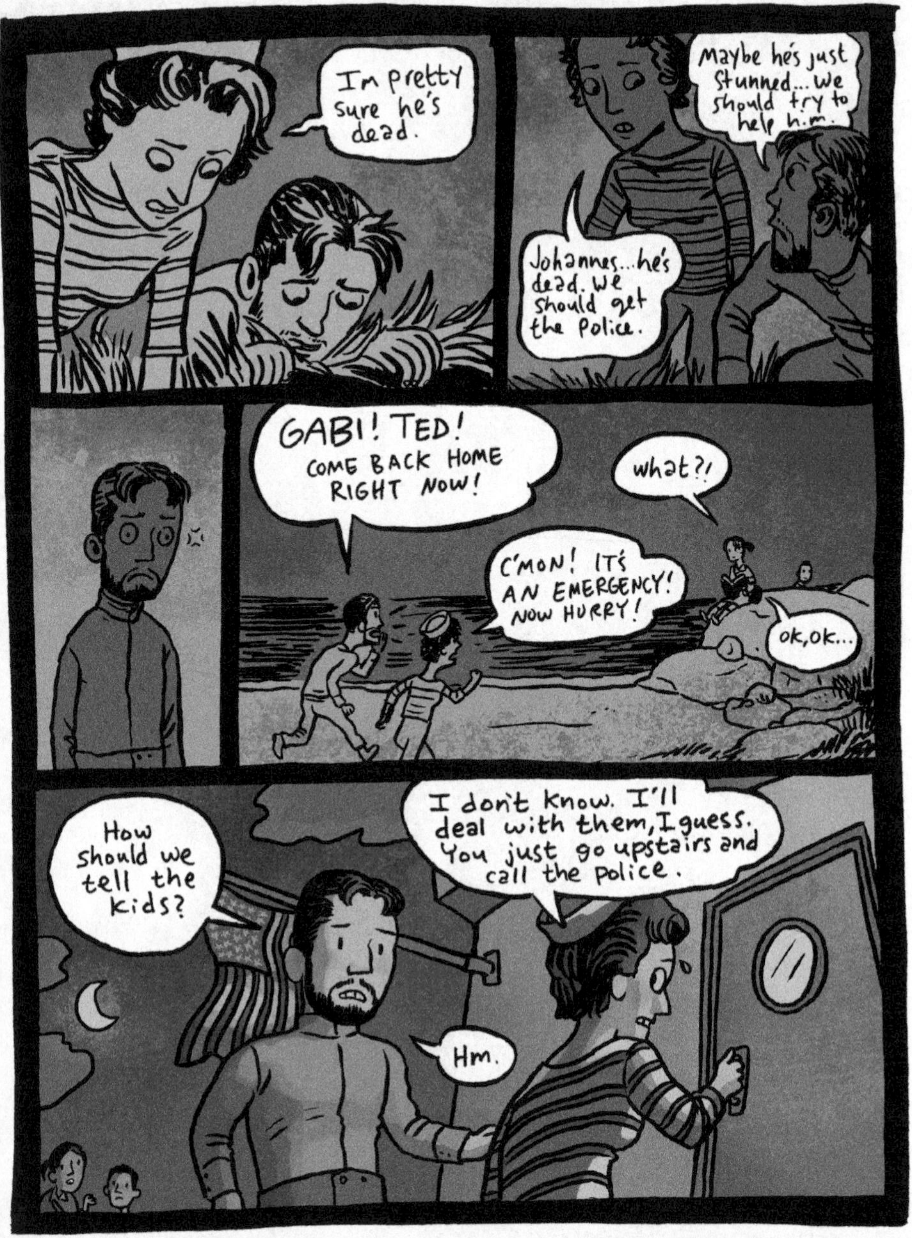

I'm pretty sure he's dead.
Maybe he's just stunned... we should try to help him.
Johannes...he's dead. We should get the police.
GABI! TED! COME BACK HOME RIGHT NOW!
what?!
C'MON! IT'S AN EMERGENCY! NOW HURRY!
ok,ok...
How should we tell the kids?
I don't know. I'll deal with them, I guess. You just go upstairs and call the police.
Hm.

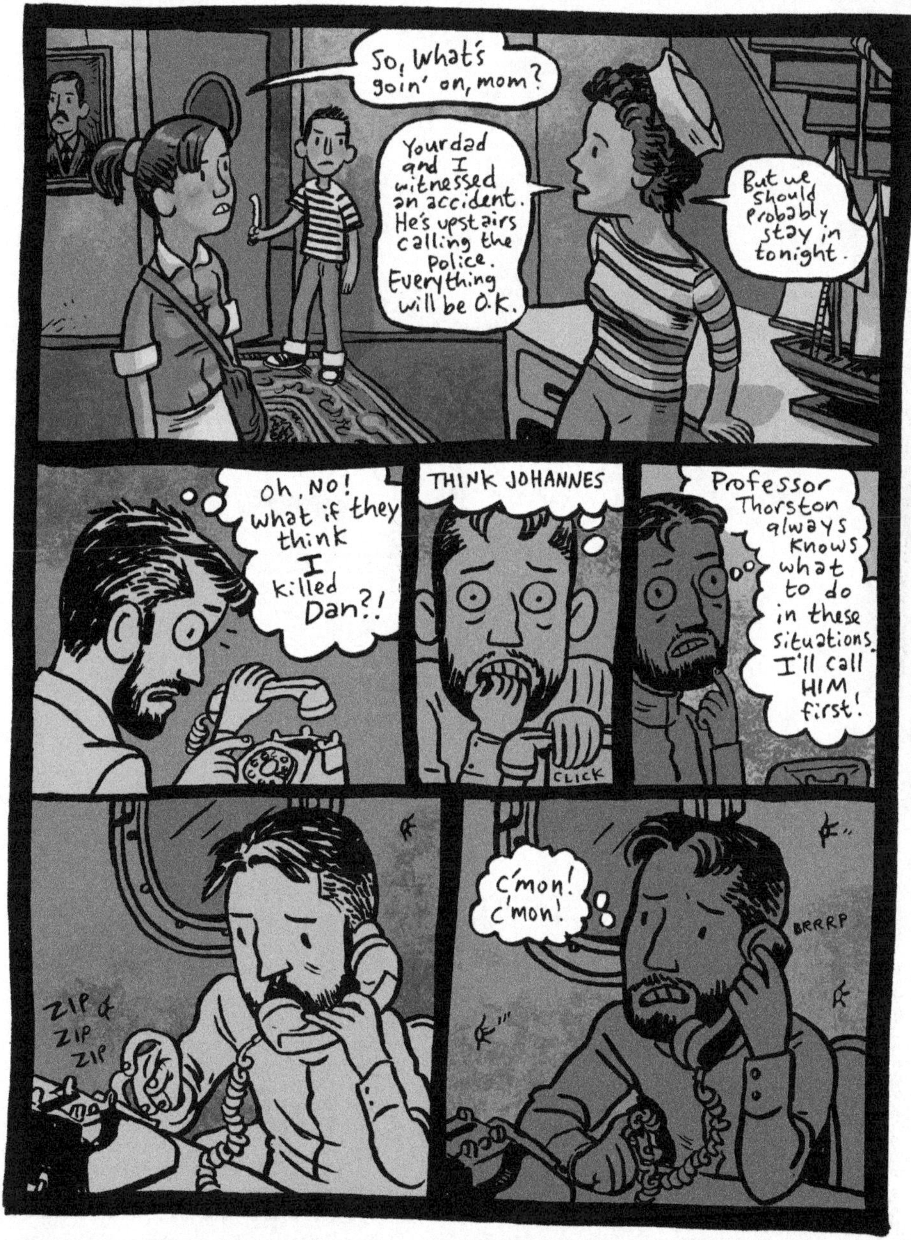
So, what's goin' on, mom?
Your dad and I witnessed an accident. He's upstairs calling the police. Everything will be O.K.
But we should probably stay in tonight.
Oh, NO! what if they think I killed Dan?!
THINK JOHANNES
CLICK
Professor Thorston always knows what to do in these situations. I'll call HIM first!
ZIP ZIP ZIP
C'mon! C'mon!
BRRRP

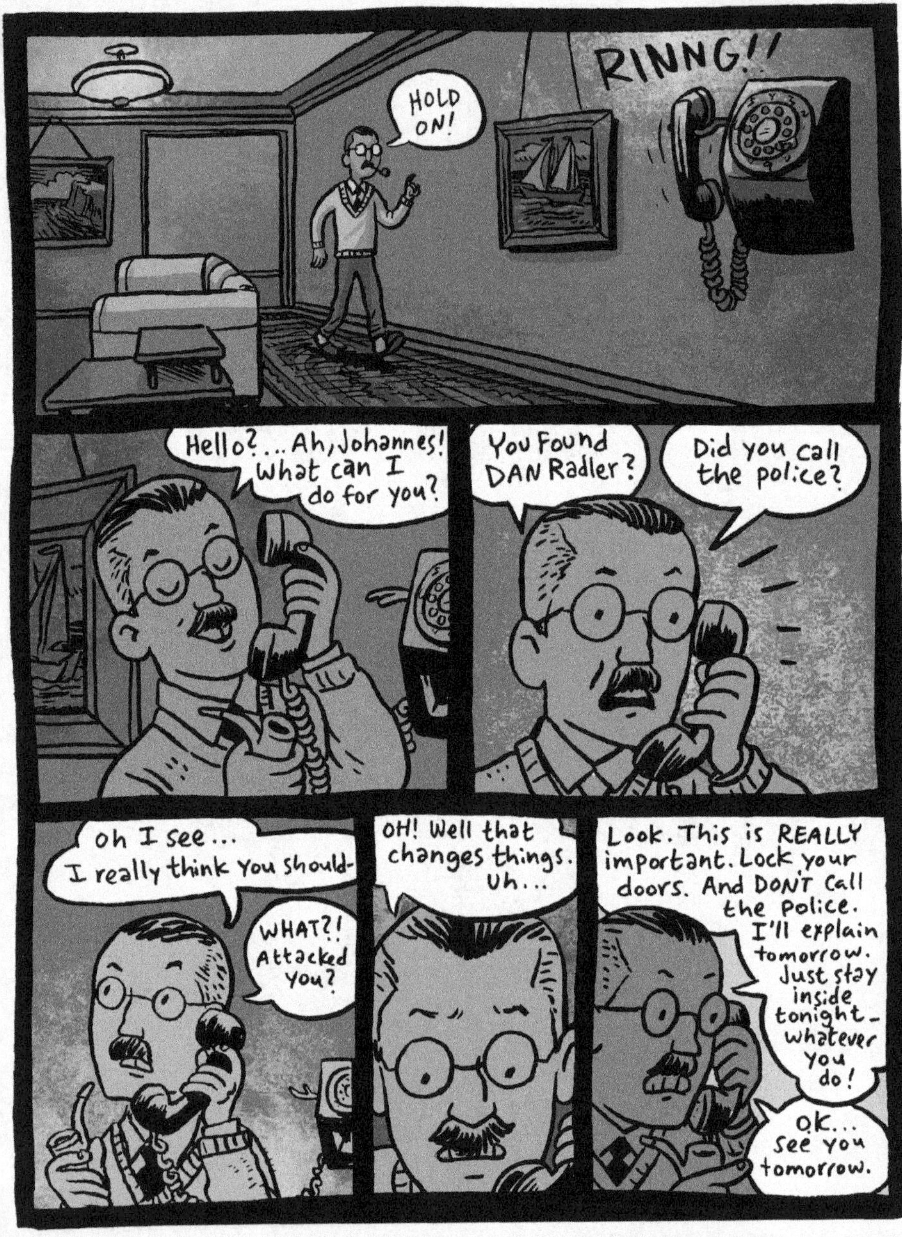
RINNG!!
HOLD ON!
Hello? ... Ah, Johannes! What can I do for you?
You Found DAN Radler?
Did you call the police?
Oh I see... I really think you should-
WHAT?! Attacked you?
OH! Well that changes things. Uh...
Look. This is REALLY important. Lock your doors. And DON'T call the Police. I'll explain tomorrow. Just stay inside tonight - whatever you do!
OK... see you tomorrow.

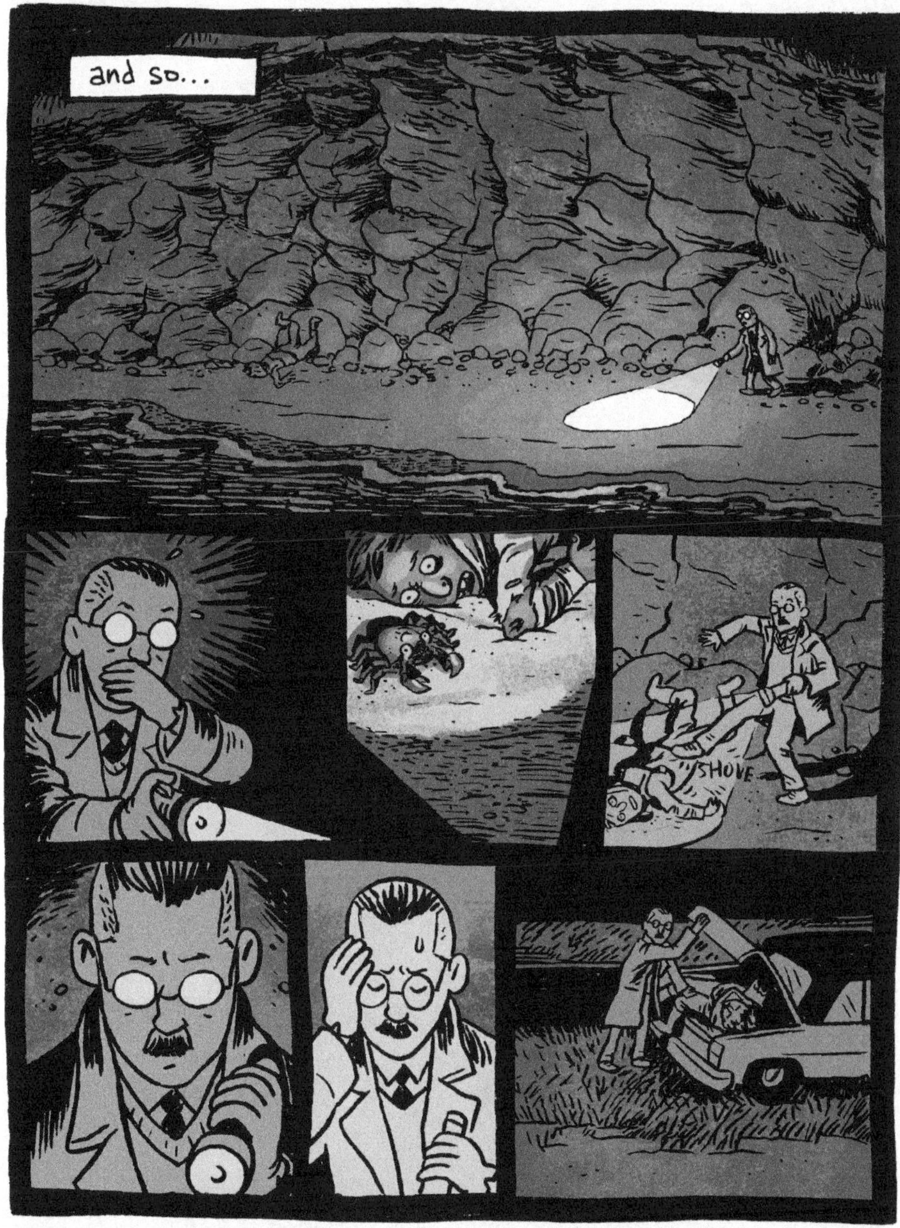
and so...
SHOVE

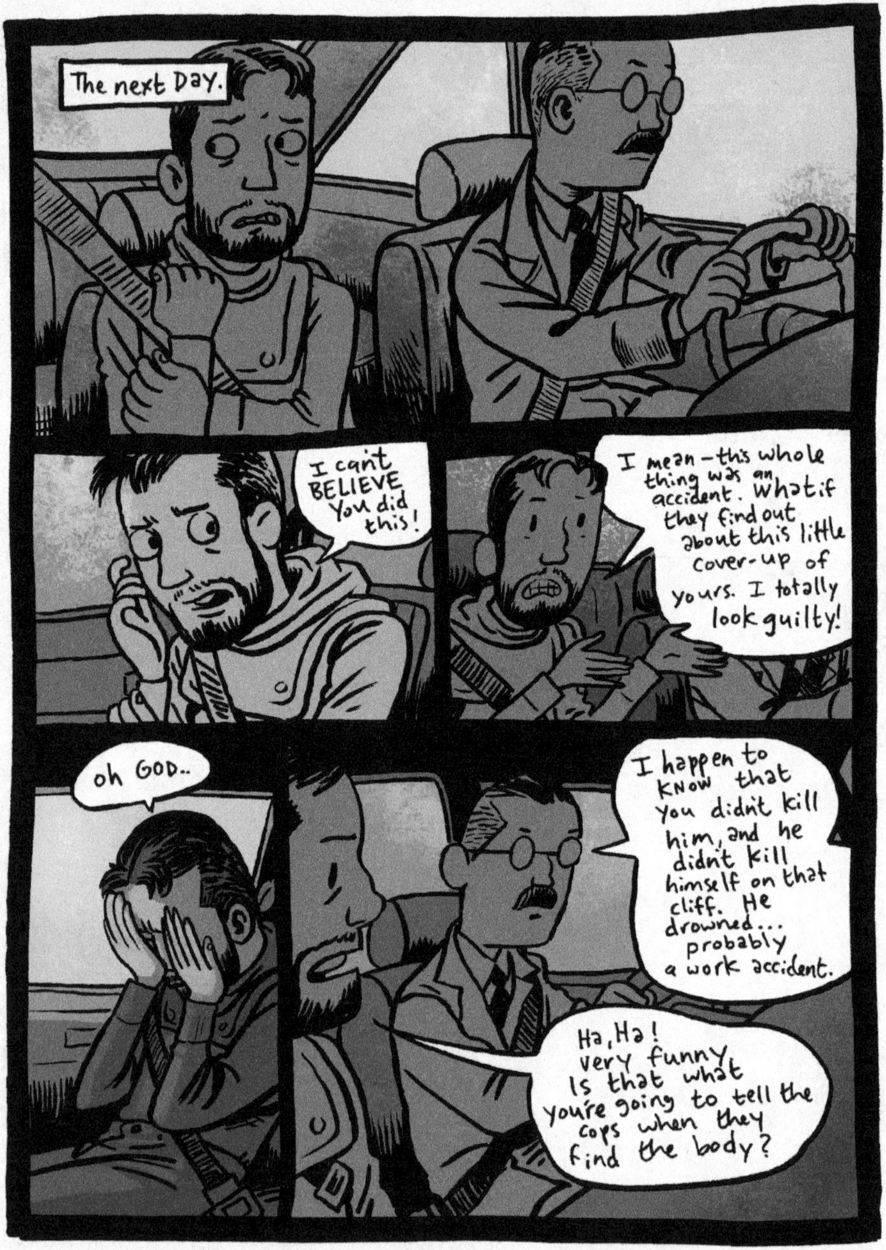
The next Day.
I can't BELIEVE You did this!
I mean—this whole thing was an accident. What if they find out about this little cover-up of yours. I totally look guilty!
oh GOD..
I happen to KNOW that You didn't kill him, and he didn't kill himself on that cliff. He drowned... probably a work accident.
Ha, Ha! very funny. Is that what you're going to tell the cops when they find the body?

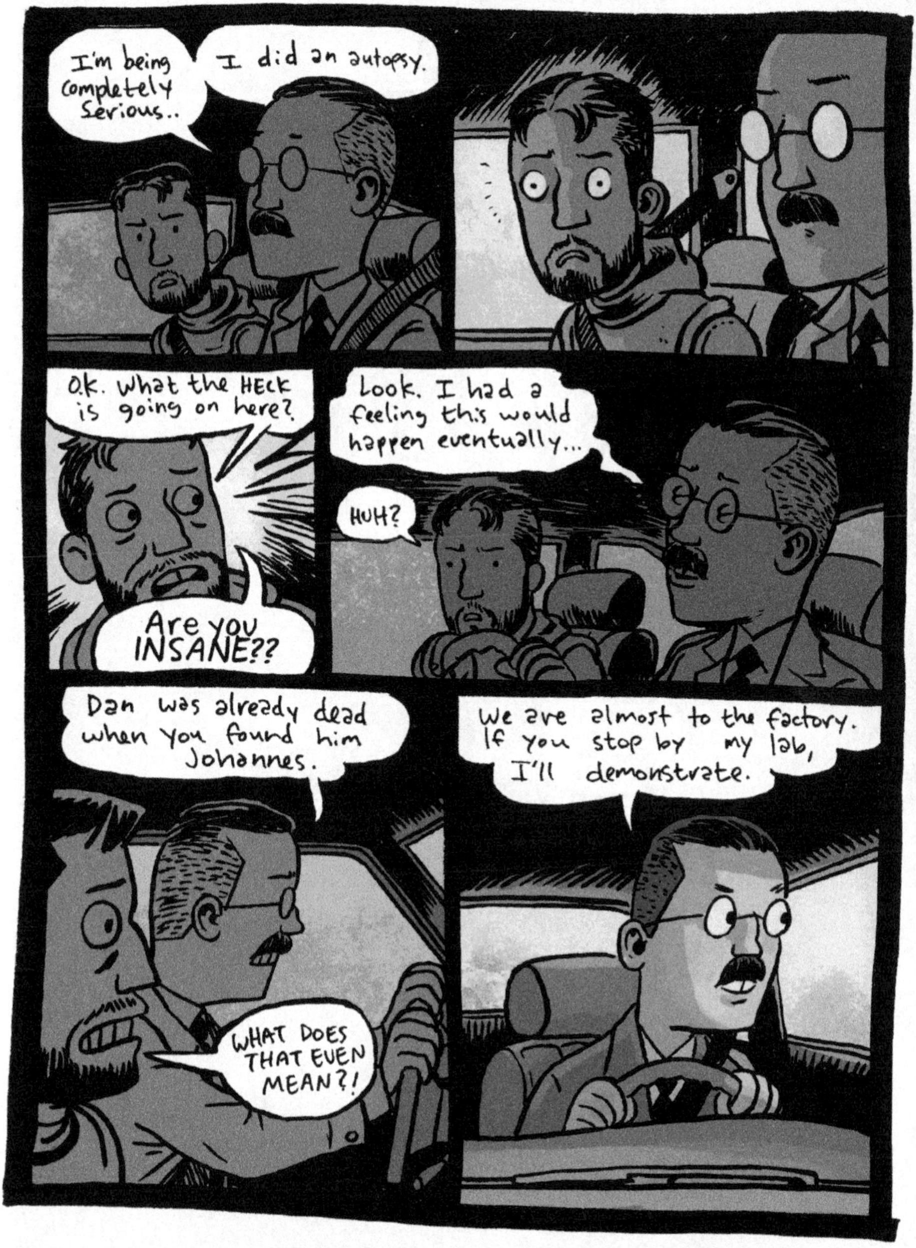
I'm being completely serious..
I did an autopsy.
O.K. What the HECK is going on here?
Are you INSANE??
Look. I had a feeling this would happen eventually...
HUH?
Dan was already dead when you found him Johannes.
WHAT DOES THAT EVEN MEAN?!
We are almost to the factory. If you stop by my lab, I'll demonstrate.

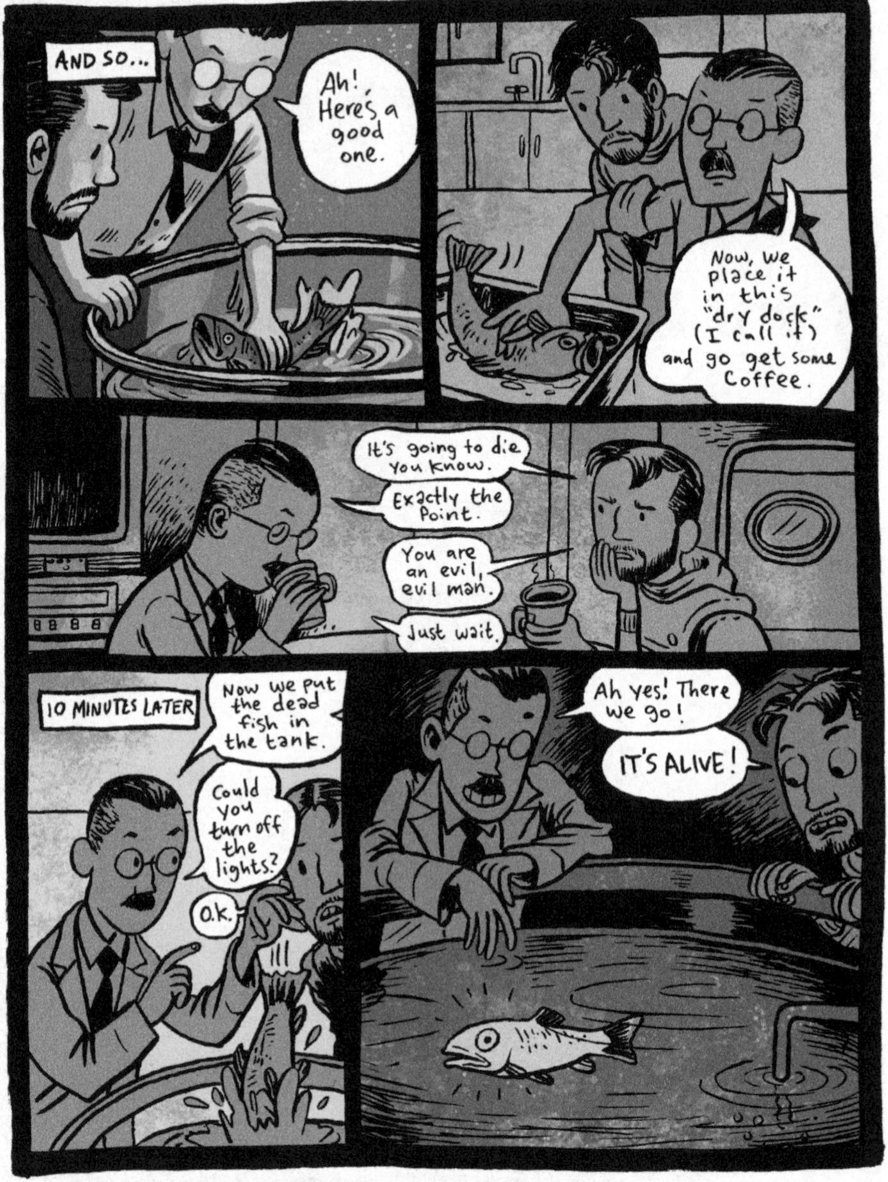
AND SO...
Ah! Here's a good one.
Now, we place it in this "dry dock" (I call it) and go get some Coffee.
It's going to die you know.
Exactly the Point.
You are an evil, evil man.
Just wait.
10 MINUTES LATER
Now we put the dead fish in the tank.
Could you turn off the lights?
O.K.
Ah yes! There we go!
IT'S ALIVE!

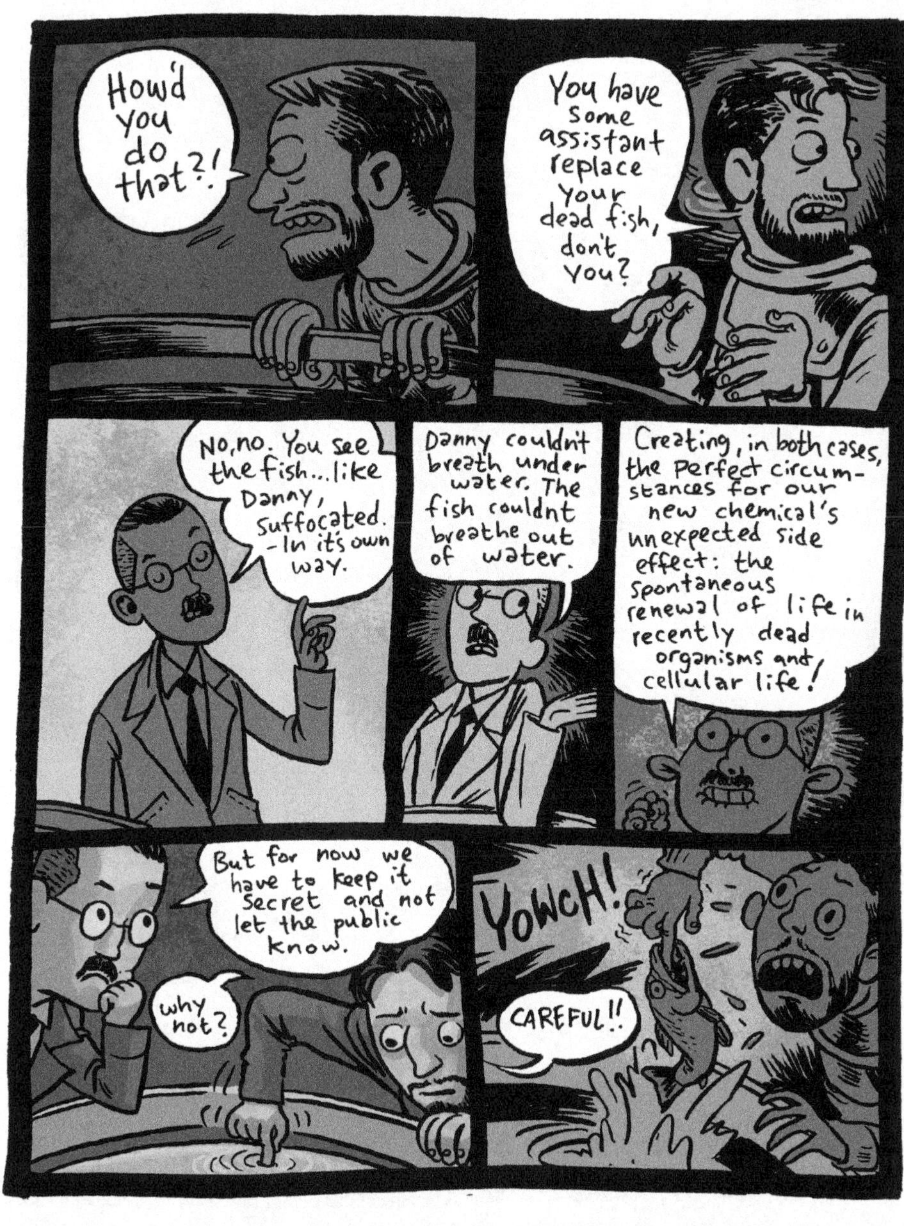
How'd you do that?!
You have some assistant replace your dead fish, don't you?
No, no. You see the fish... like Danny, suffocated. -In it's own way.
Danny couldn't breath under water. The fish couldnt breathe out of water.
Creating, in both cases, the perfect circumstances for our new chemical's unexpected side effect: the spontaneous renewal of life in recently dead organisms and cellular life!
But for now we have to keep it secret and not let the public know.
why not?
YOWCH!
CAREFUL!!

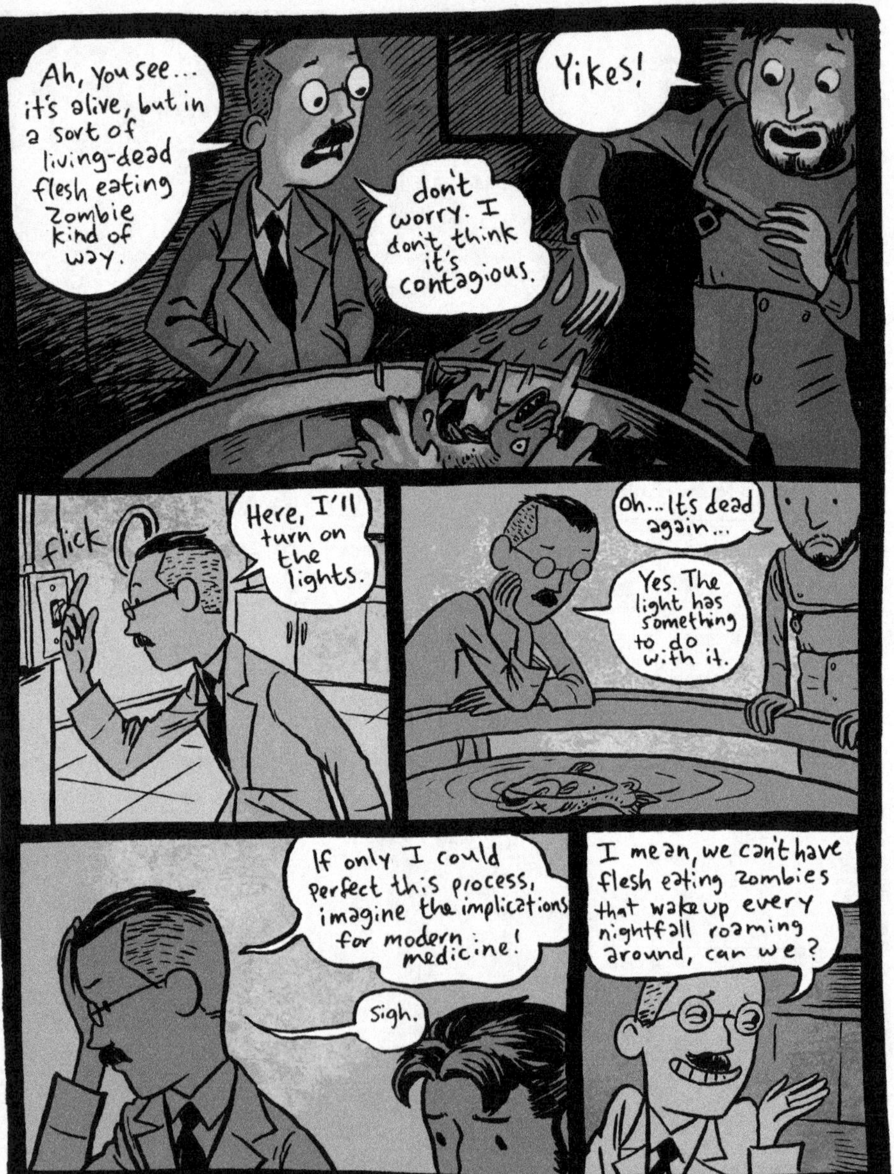
Ah, you see... it's alive, but in a sort of living-dead flesh eating zombie kind of way.
Yikes!
don't worry. I don't think it's contagious.
flick
Here, I'll turn on the lights.
Oh... It's dead again...
Yes. The light has something to do with it.
If only I could perfect this process, imagine the implications for modern medicine!
Sigh.
I mean, we can't have flesh eating zombies that wake up every nightfall roaming around, can we?

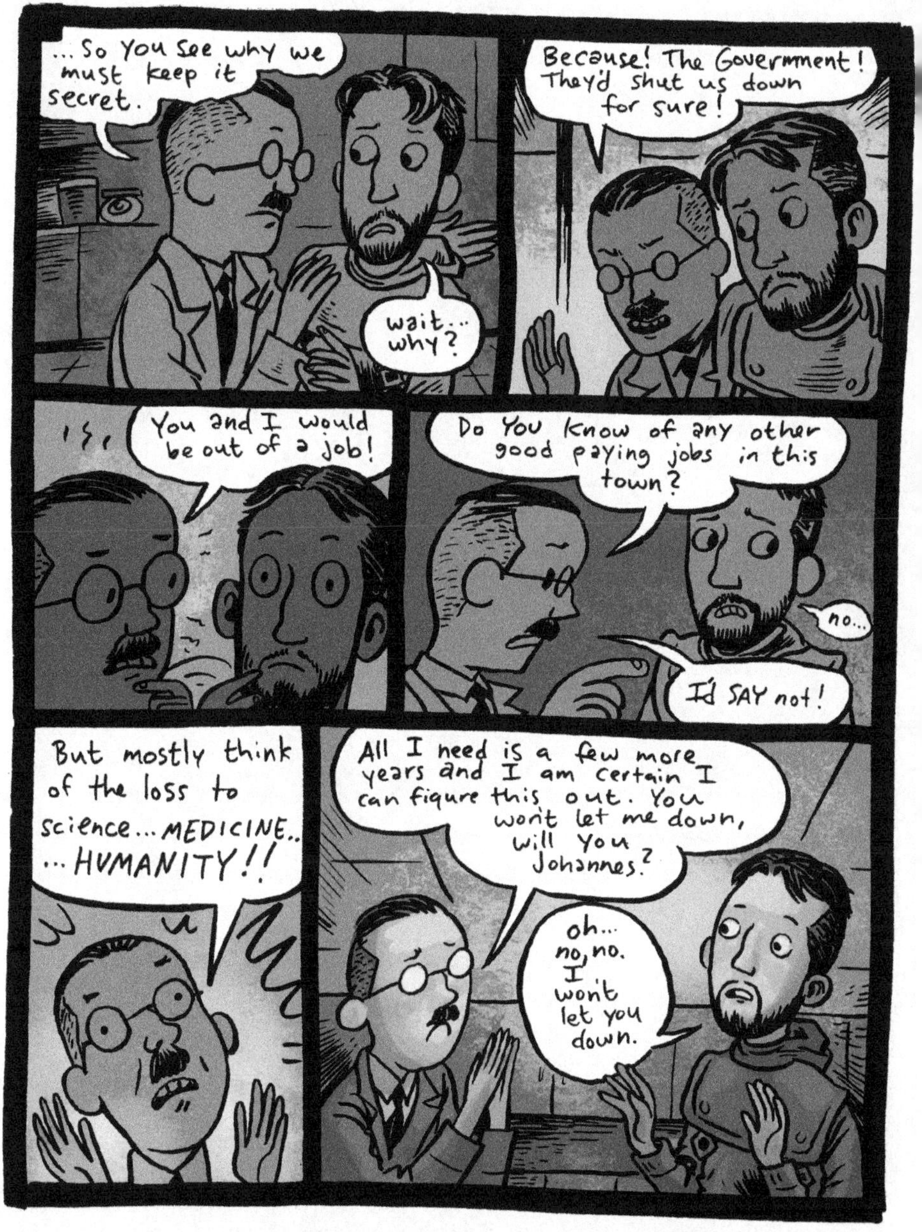
...So You see why we must keep it secret.
wait... why?
Because! The Government! They'd shut us down for sure!
You and I would be out of a job!
Do You know of any other good paying jobs in this town?
no...
I'd SAY not!
But mostly think of the loss to science... MEDICINE.. ...HUMANITY!!
All I need is a few more years and I am certain I can figure this out. You won't let me down, will You Johannes?
oh... no, no. I won't let you down.

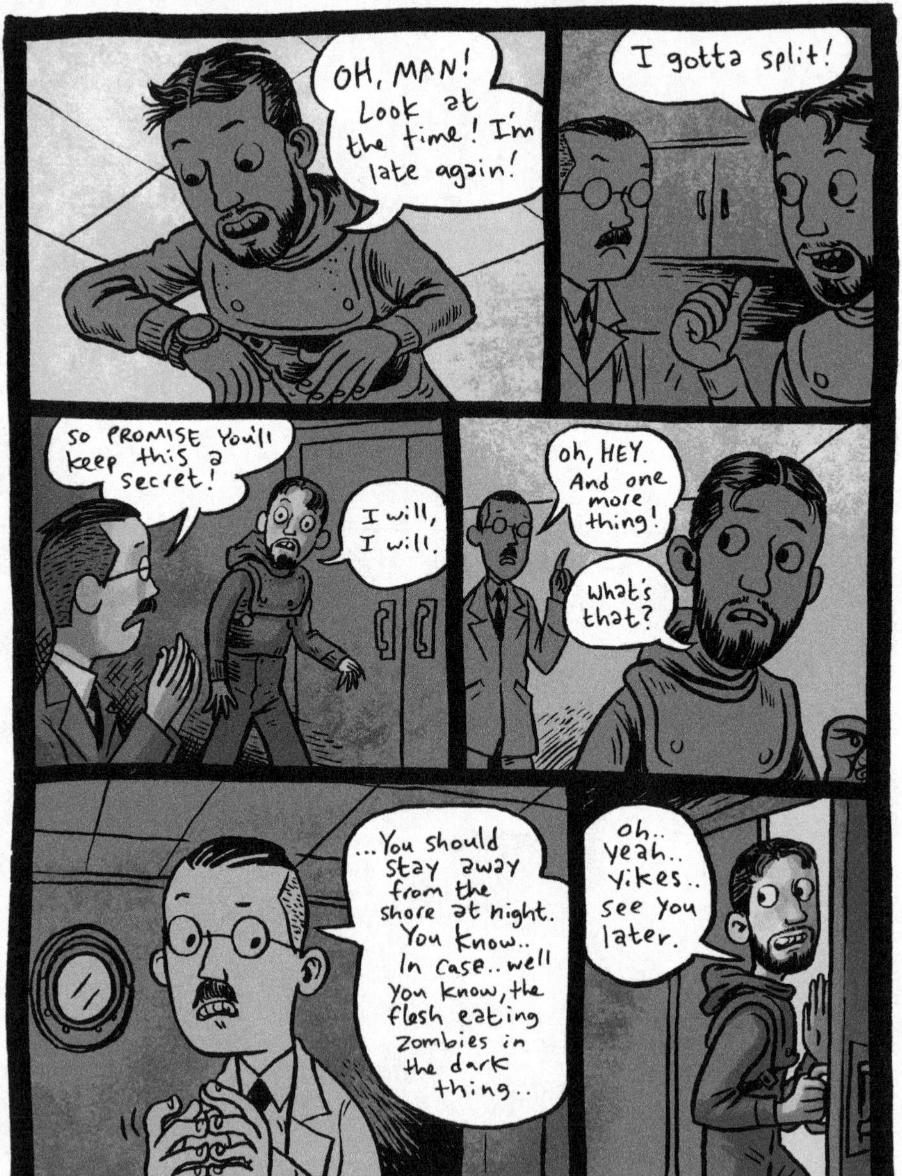
OH, MAN! Look at the time! I'm late again!
I gotta split!
SO PROMISE You'll keep this a secret!
I will, I will.
oh, HEY. And one more thing!
What's that?
...You should stay away from the shore at night. You know.. In case.. well You know, the flesh eating zombies in the dark thing..
oh.. yeah.. Yikes.. see you later.

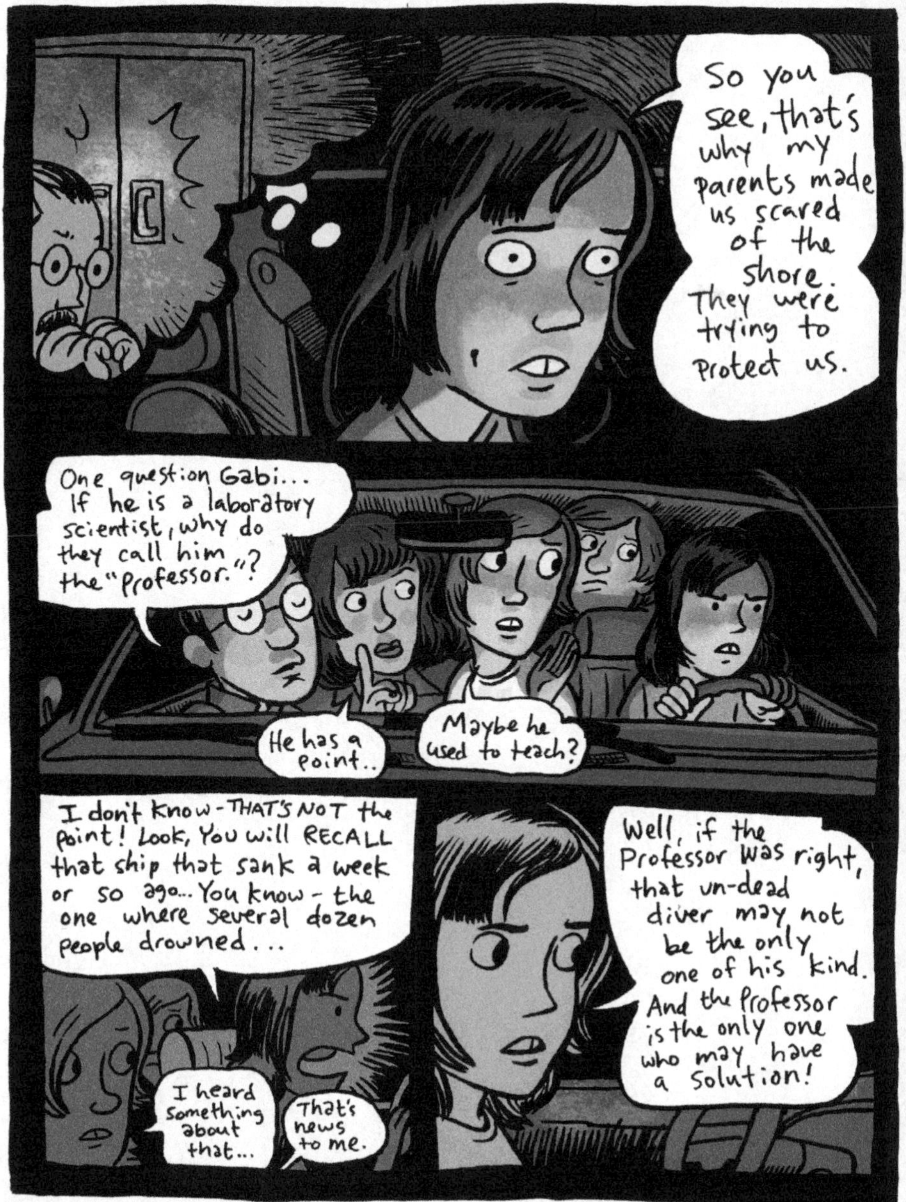
So you see, that's why my parents made us scared of the shore. They were trying to protect us.
One question Gabi... If he is a laboratory scientist, why do they call him the "Professor."?
He has a point..
Maybe he used to teach?
I don't know - THAT'S NOT the point! Look, You will RECALL that ship that sank a week or so ago... You know - the one where several dozen people drowned...
I heard something about that...
That's news to me.
Well, if the Professor was right, that un-dead diver may not be the only one of his kind. And the Professor is the only one who may have a solution!

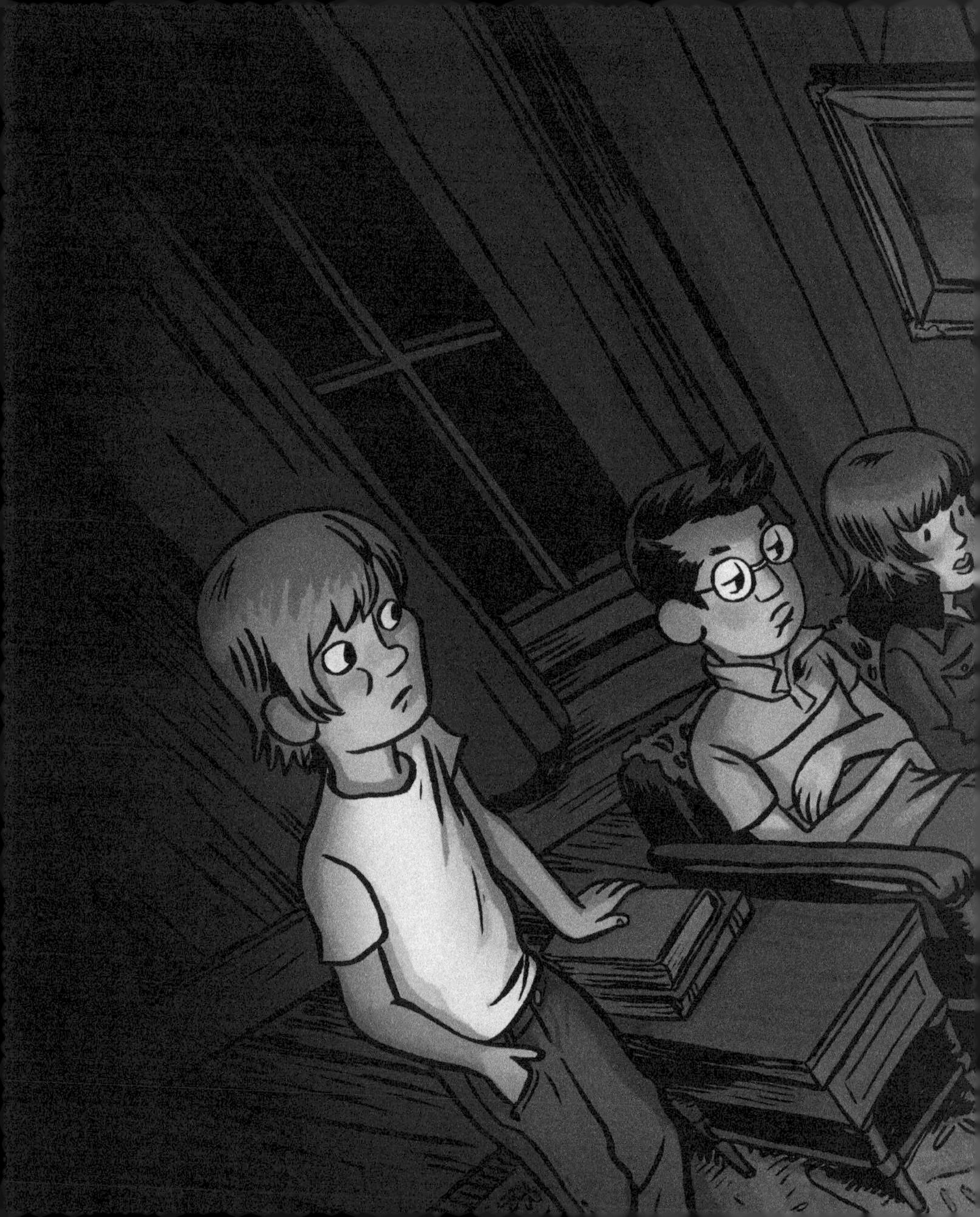

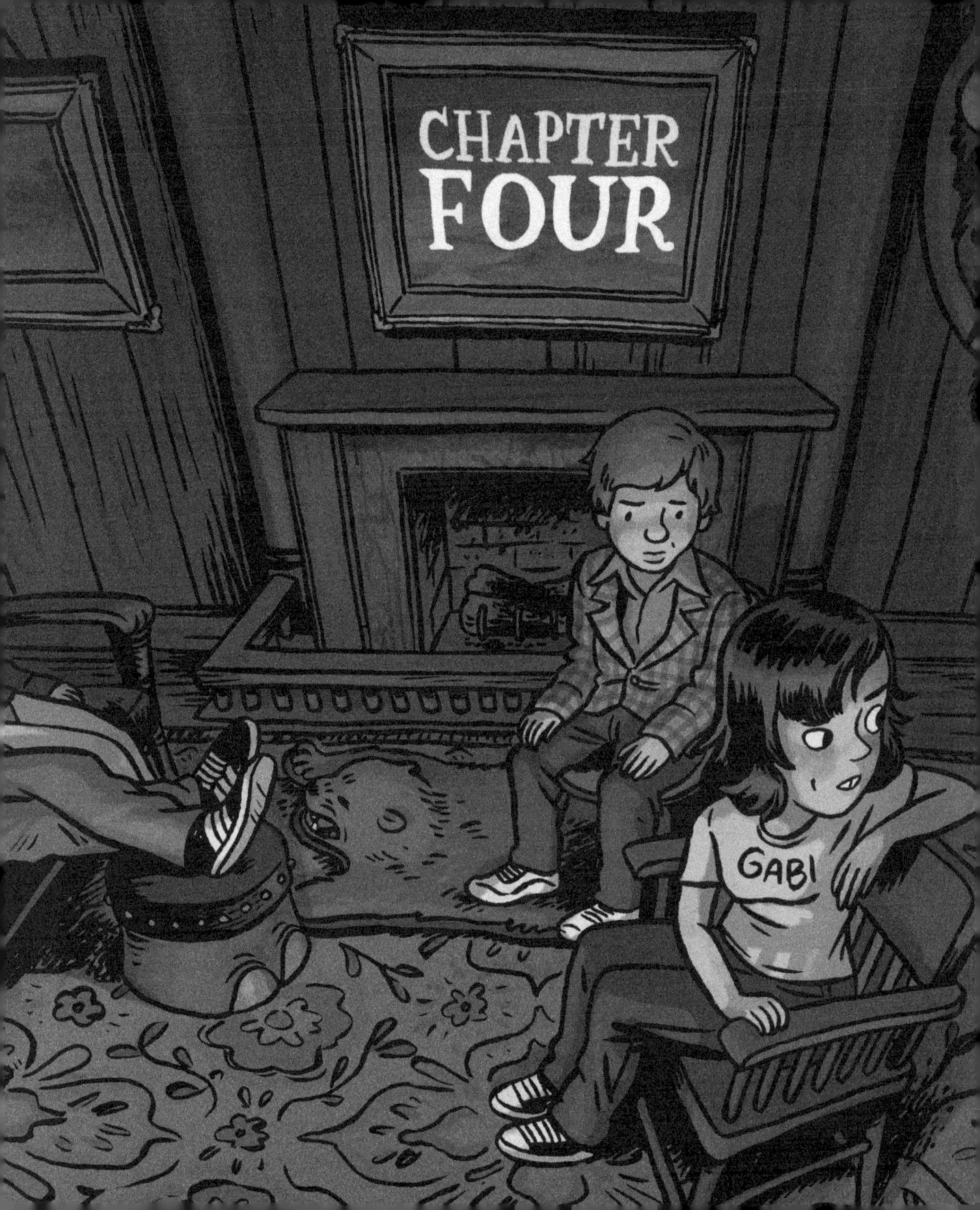
CHAPTER
FOUR
GABI

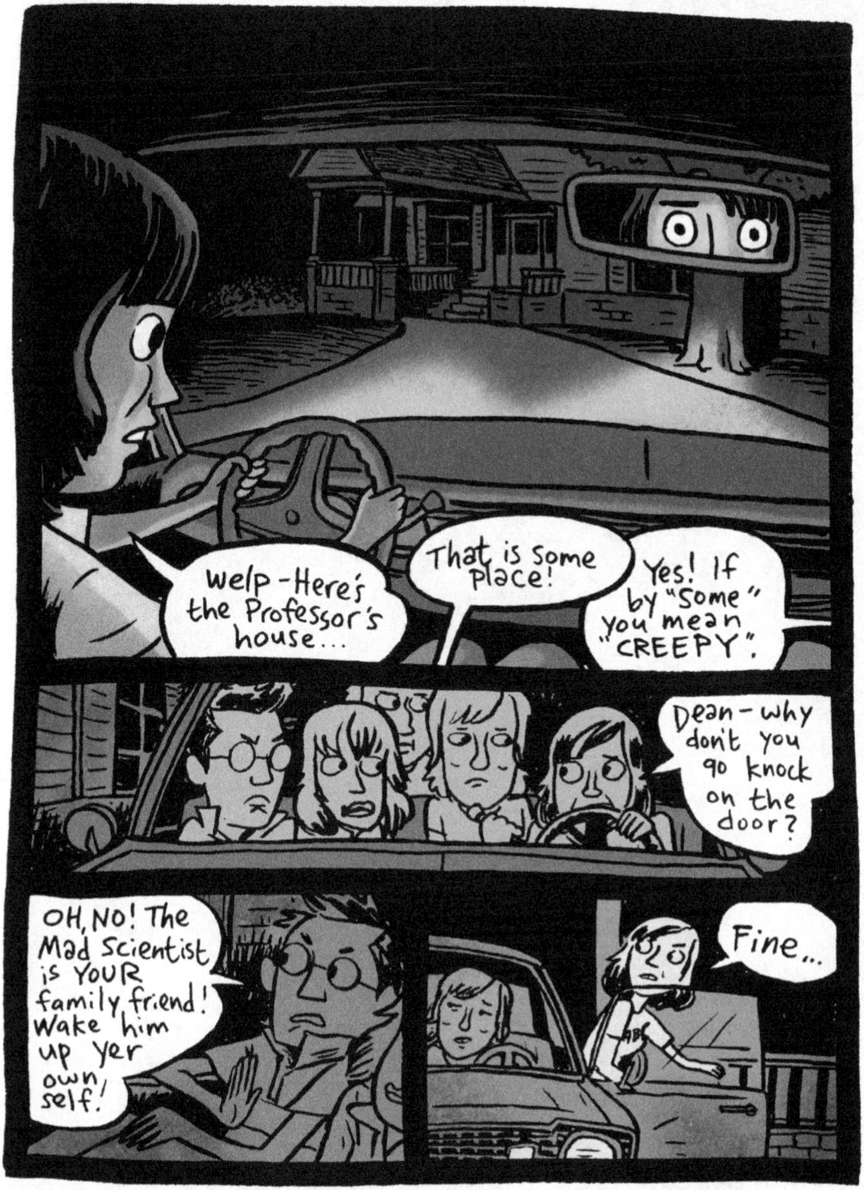
Welp-Here's the Professor's house...
That is some place!
Yes! If by "some" you mean "CREEPY".
Dean-why don't you go knock on the door?
OH, NO! The Mad Scientist is YOUR family friend! Wake him up yer own self!
Fine...

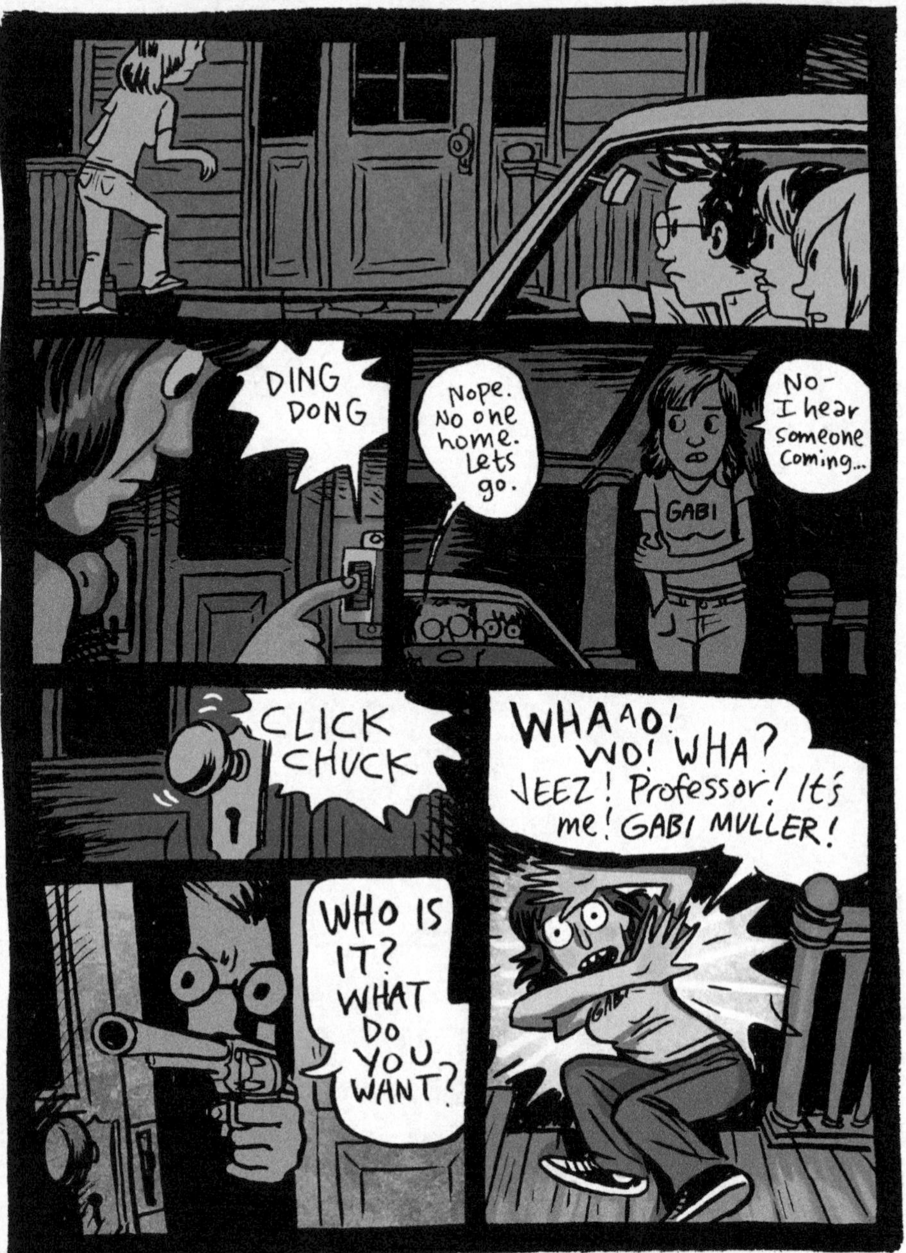
DING DONG
Nope. No one home. Lets go.
No- I hear someone coming...
GABI
CLICK CHUCK
WHO IS IT? WHAT DO YOU WANT?
WHAAO! WO! WHA? JEEZ! Professor! It's me! GABI MULLER!

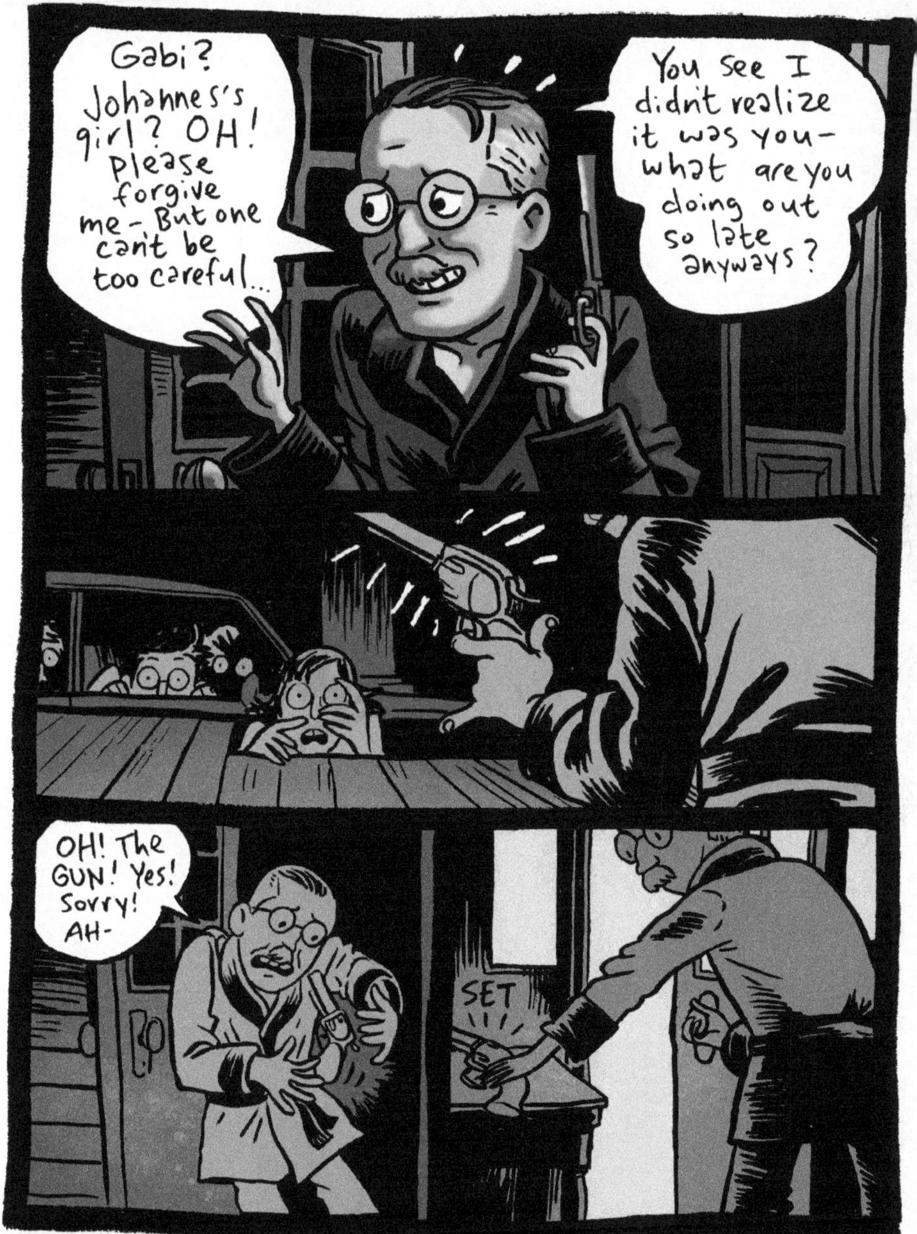
Gabi? Johannes's girl? OH! Please forgive me- But one can't be too careful...
You see I didnt realize it was you- what are you doing out so late anyways?
OH! The GUN! Yes! Sorry! AH-
SET

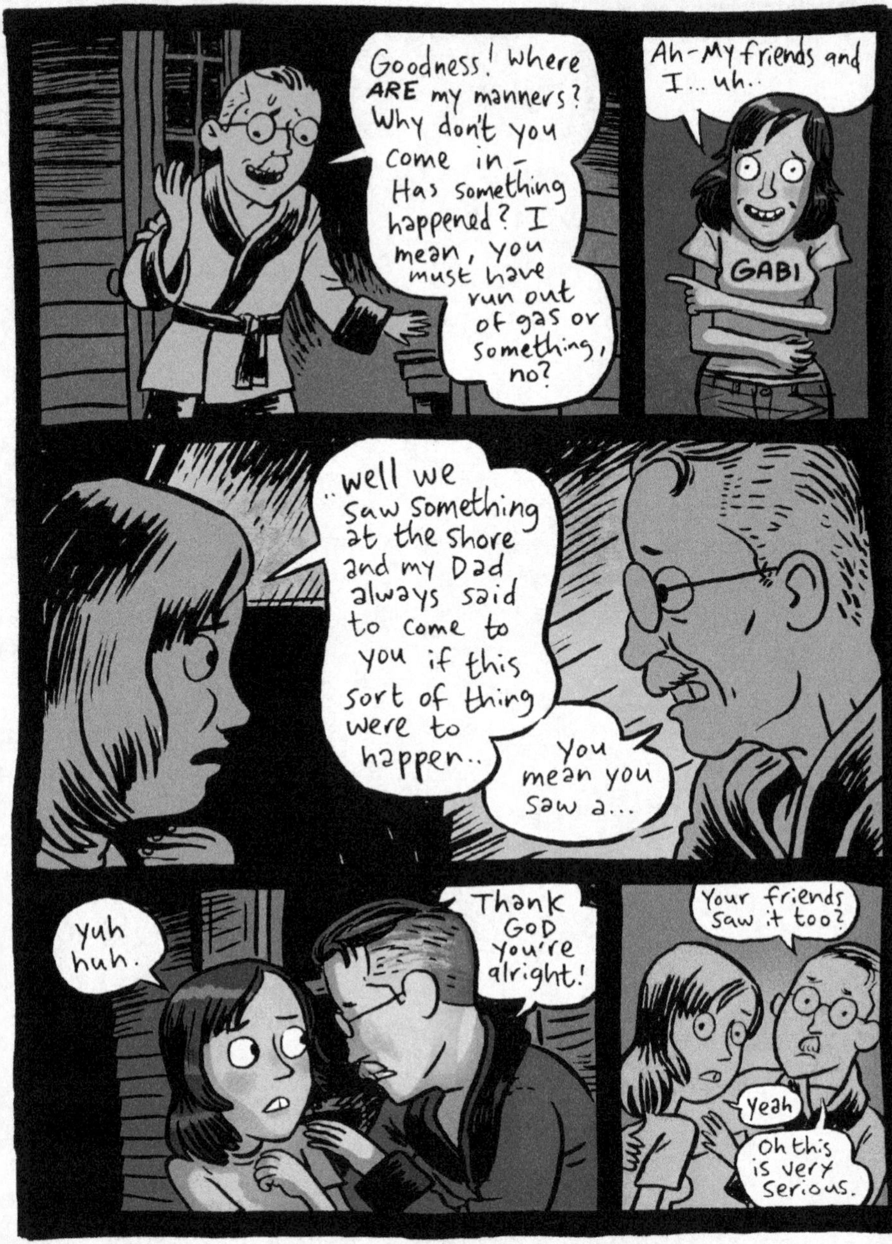
Goodness! Where ARE my manners? Why don't you come in- Has something happened? I mean, you must have run out of gas or something, no?
Ah-My friends and I... uh..
..well we saw something at the shore and my Dad always said to come to you if this sort of thing were to happen..
You mean you saw a...
yuh huh.
Thank GOD you're alright!
Your friends saw it too?
Yeah
Oh this is very serious.

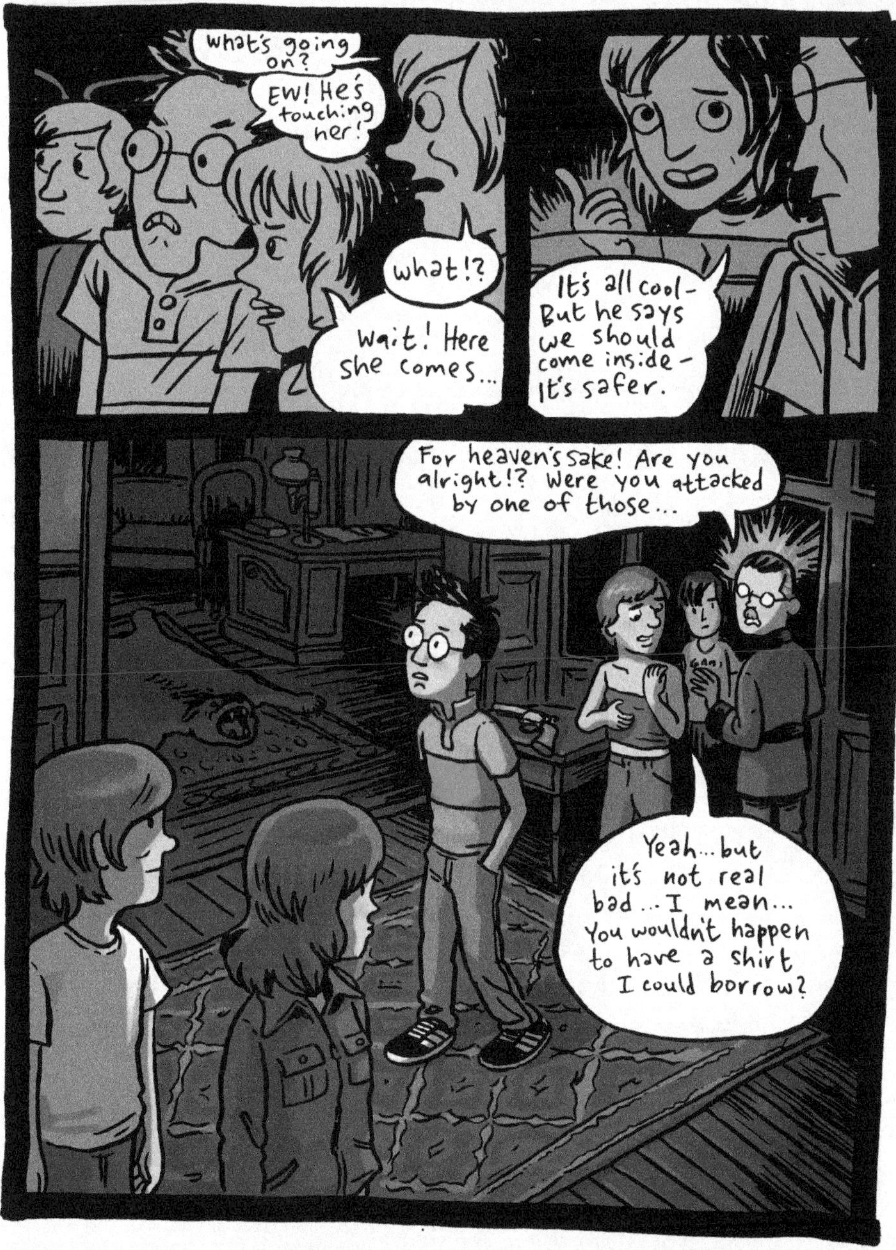
what's going on?
EW! He's touching her!
what!?
Wait! Here she comes...
It's all cool- But he says we should come inside- It's safer.
For heaven's sake! Are you alright!? Were you attacked by one of those...
Yeah... but it's not real bad... I mean... You wouldn't happen to have a shirt I could borrow?

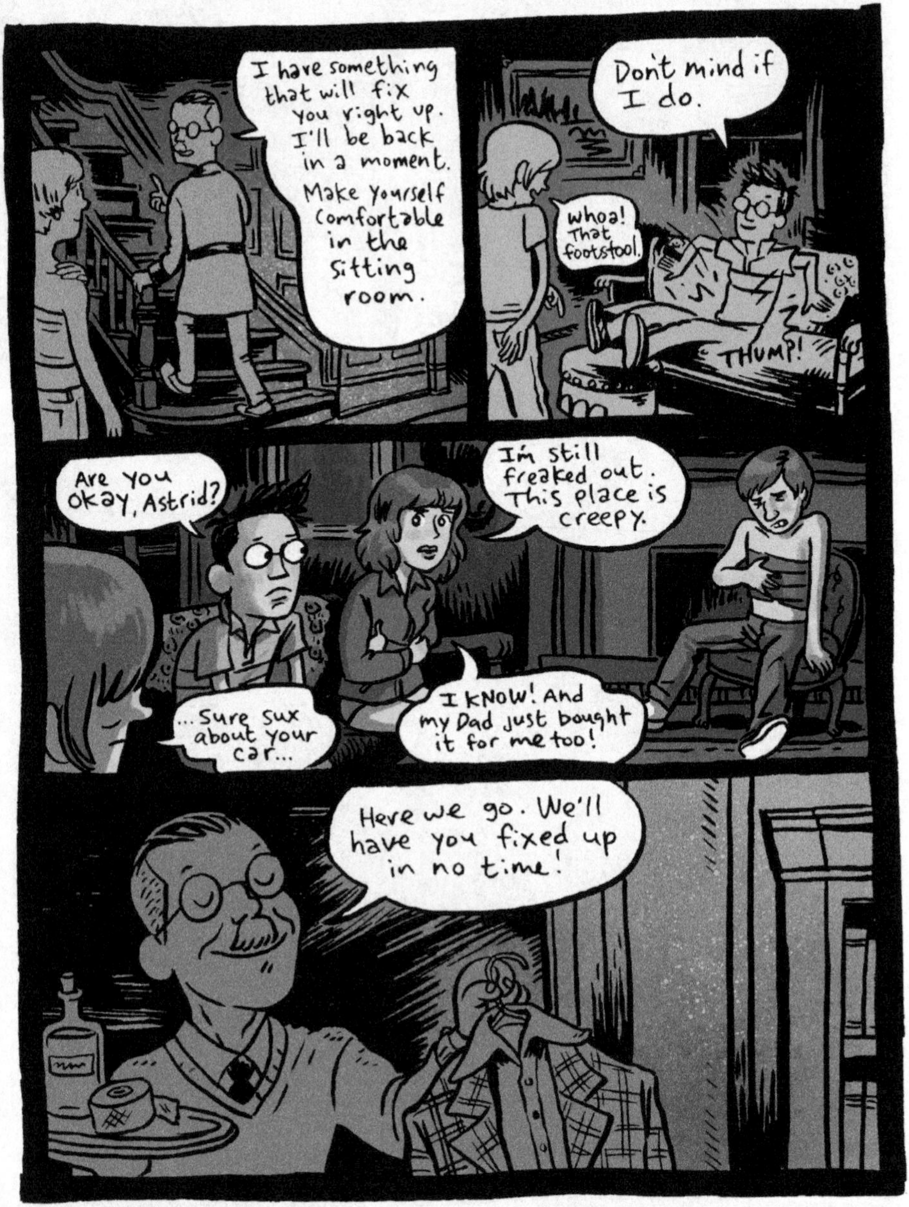
I have something that will fix you right up. I'll be back in a moment.
Make yourself comfortable in the sitting room.
Don't mind if I do.
Whoa! That footstool.
THUMP!
Are you okay, Astrid?
I'm still freaked out. This place is creepy.
...Sure sux about your car...
I KNOW! And my Dad just bought it for me too!
Here we go. We'll have you fixed up in no time!

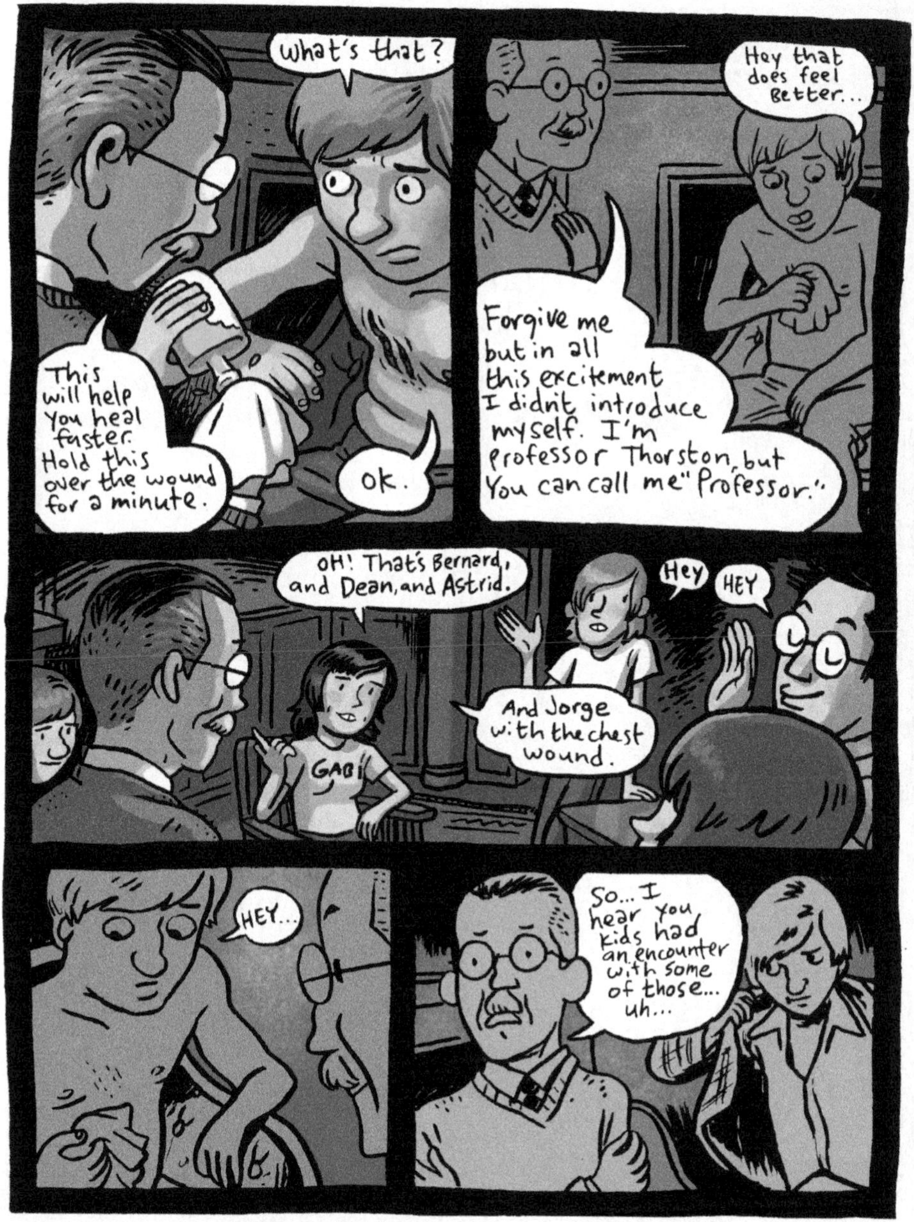
What's that?
This will help you heal faster. Hold this over the wound for a minute.
OK.
Forgive me but in all this excitement I didn't introduce myself. I'm Professor Thorston, but you can call me "Professor."
Hey that does feel better...
OH! That's Bernard, and Dean, and Astrid.
Hey
HEY
And Jorge with the chest wound.
GABI
HEY...
So... I hear you kids had an encounter with some of those... uh...

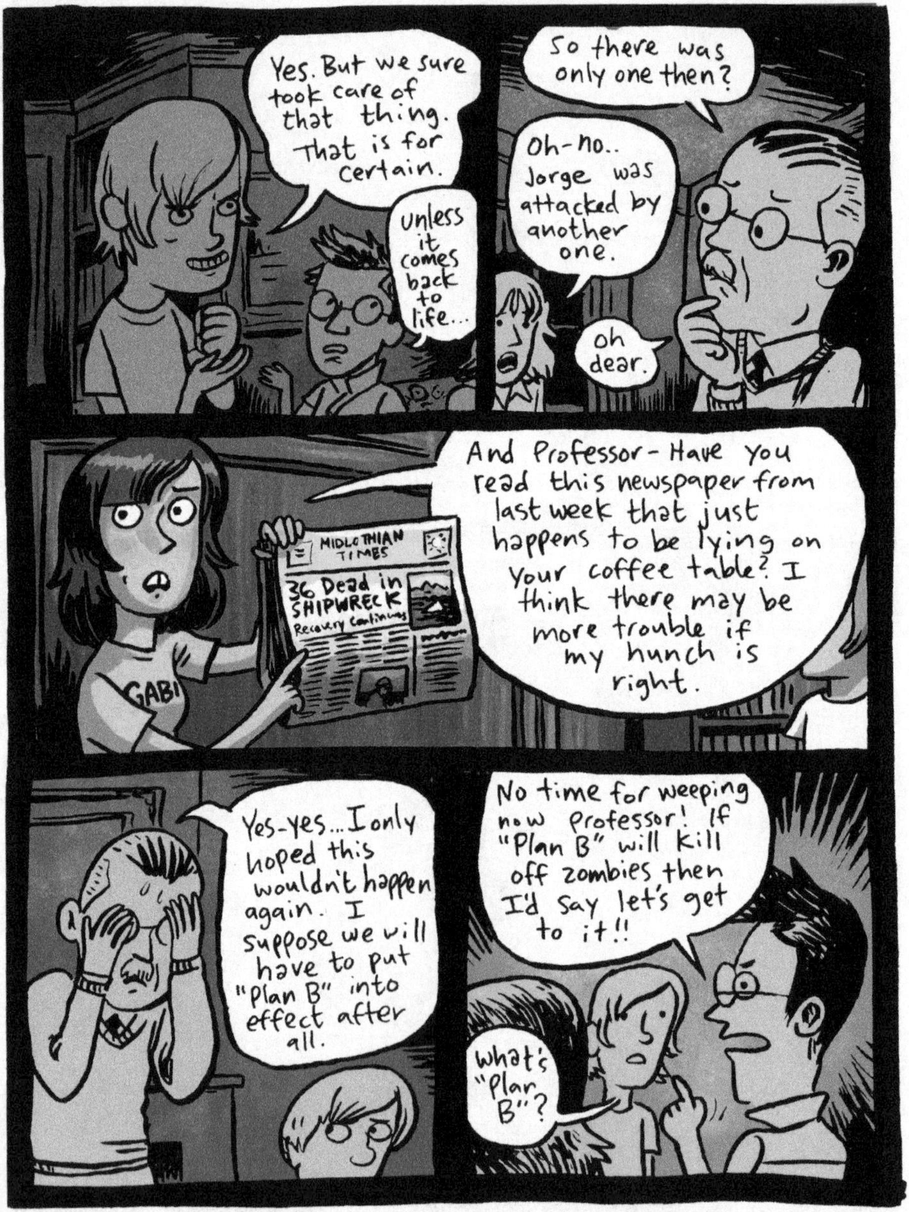
Yes. But we sure took care of that thing. That is for certain.
Unless it comes back to life...
So there was only one then?
Oh-no.. Jorge was attacked by another one.
oh dear.
And Professor- Have you read this newspaper from last week that just happens to be lying on your coffee table? I think there may be more trouble if my hunch is right.
MIDLOTHIAN TIMES
36 Dead in SHIPWRECK
Recovery Continues
GABI
Yes-yes... I only hoped this wouldn't happen again. I suppose we will have to put "Plan B" into effect after all.
No time for weeping now professor! If "Plan B" will kill off zombies then I'd say let's get to it!!
What's "Plan B"?

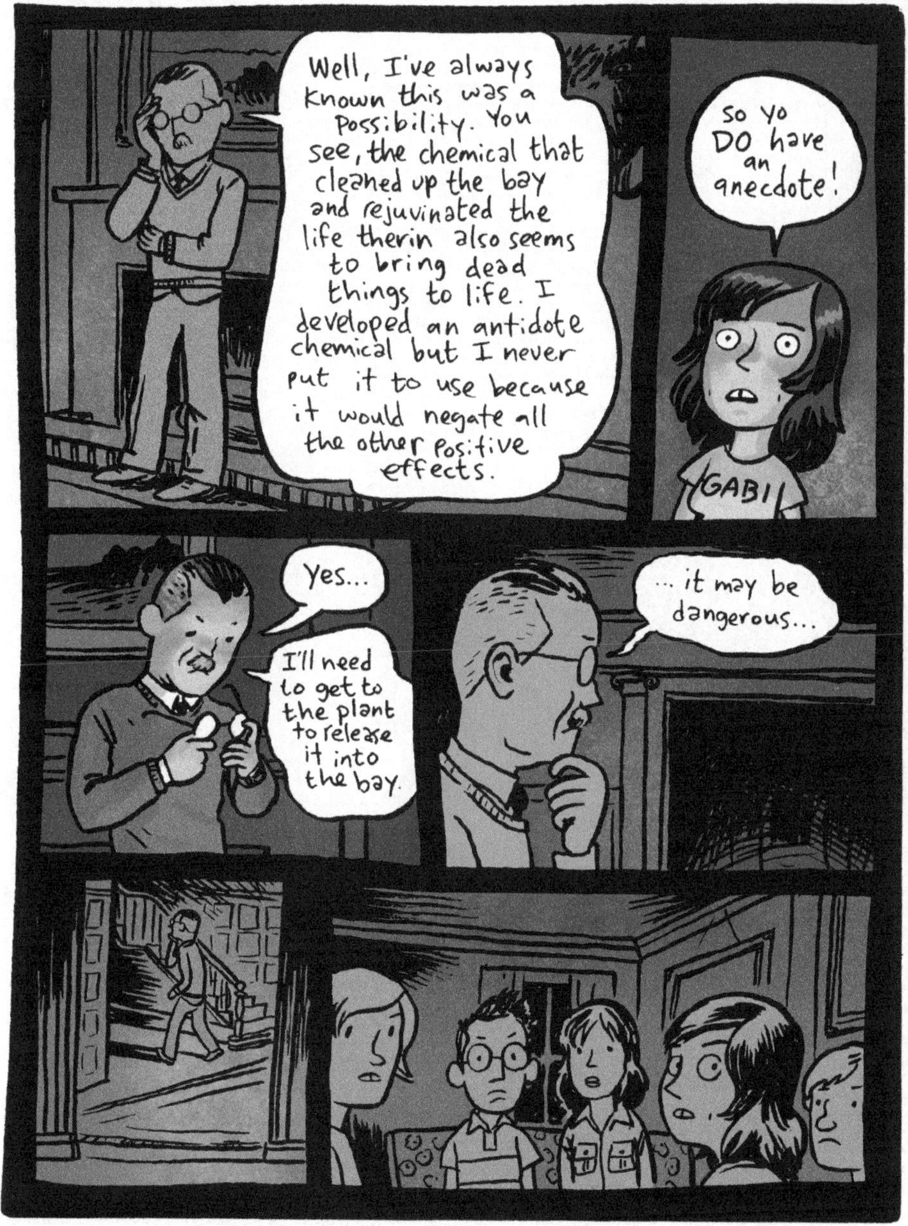

Well, I've always known this was a possibility. You see, the chemical that cleaned up the bay and rejuvinated the life therin also seems to bring dead things to life. I developed an antidote chemical but I never put it to use because it would negate all the other positive effects.
So yo DO have an anecdote!
Yes...
I'll need to get to the plant to release it into the bay.
... it may be dangerous...
GABI

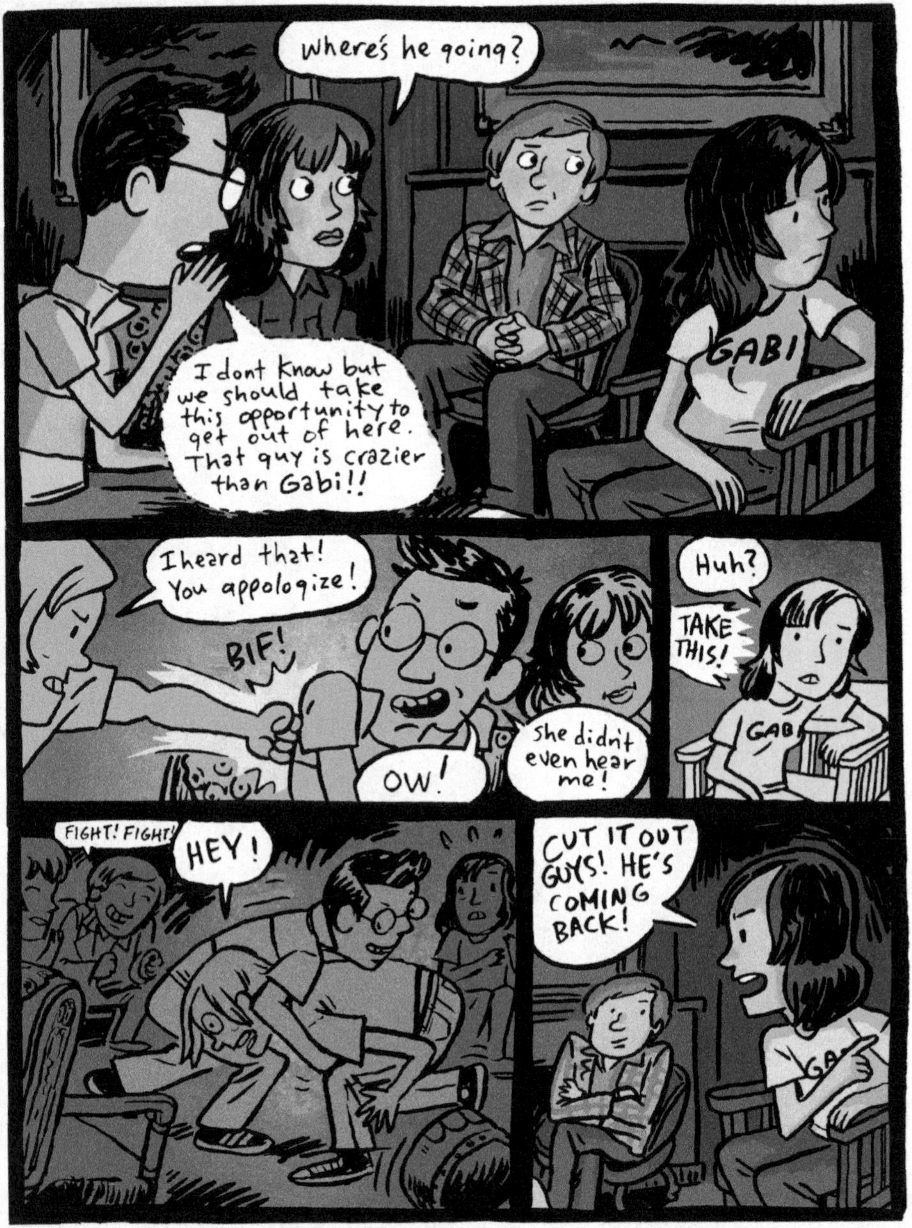
where's he going?
I dont know but we should take this opportunity to get out of here. That guy is crazier than Gabi!!
GABI
I heard that! You appologize!
BIF!
OW!
She didn't even hear me!
Huh?
TAKE THIS!
GABI
FIGHT! FIGHT!
HEY!
CUT IT OUT GUYS! HE'S COMING BACK!

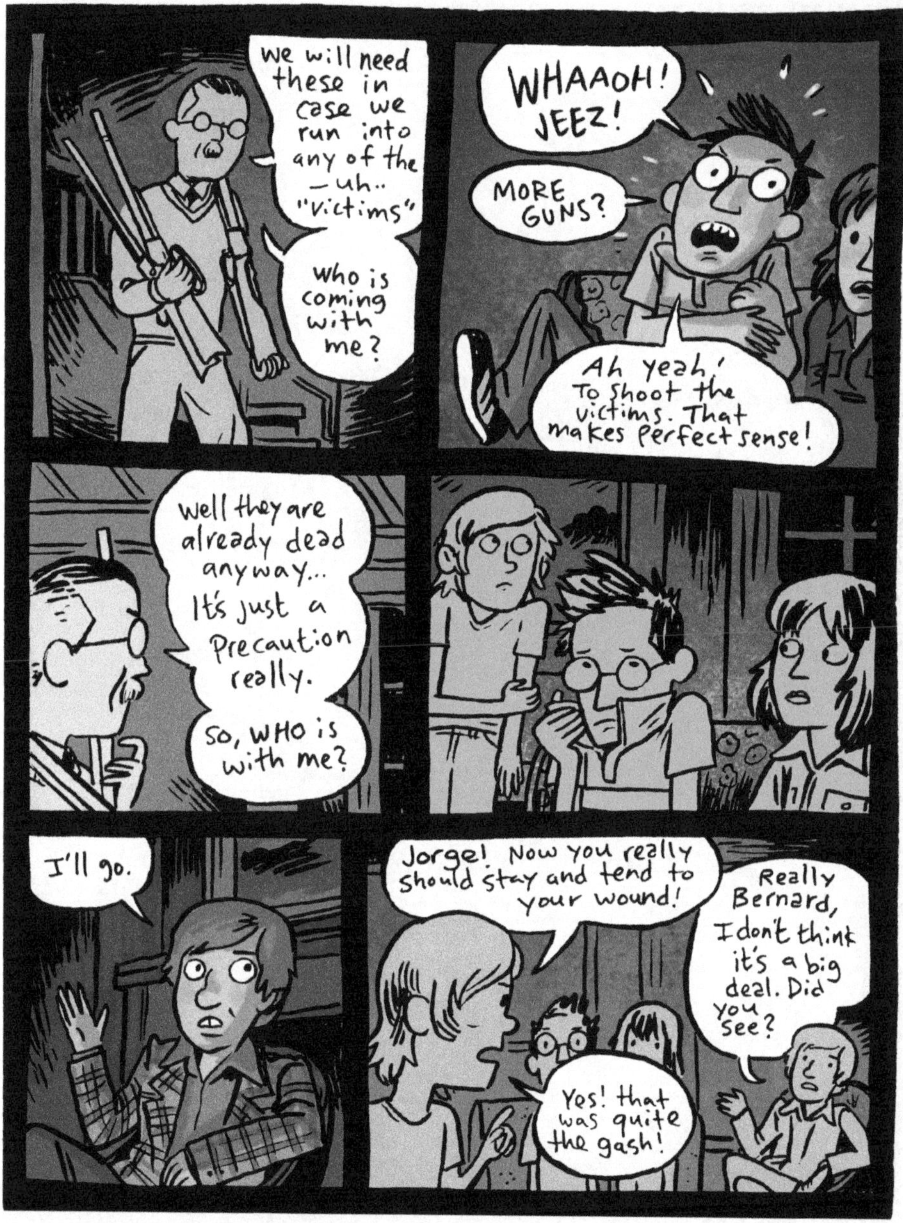

We will need these in case we run into any of the —uh.. "victims"
Who is coming with me?
WHAAOH! JEEZ!
MORE GUNS?
Ah yeah! To shoot the victims. That makes perfect sense!
Well they are already dead anyway... It's just a precaution really.
So, WHO is with me?
I'll go.
Jorge! Now you really should stay and tend to your wound!
Really Bernard, I don't think it's a big deal. Did you see?
Yes! that was quite the gash!

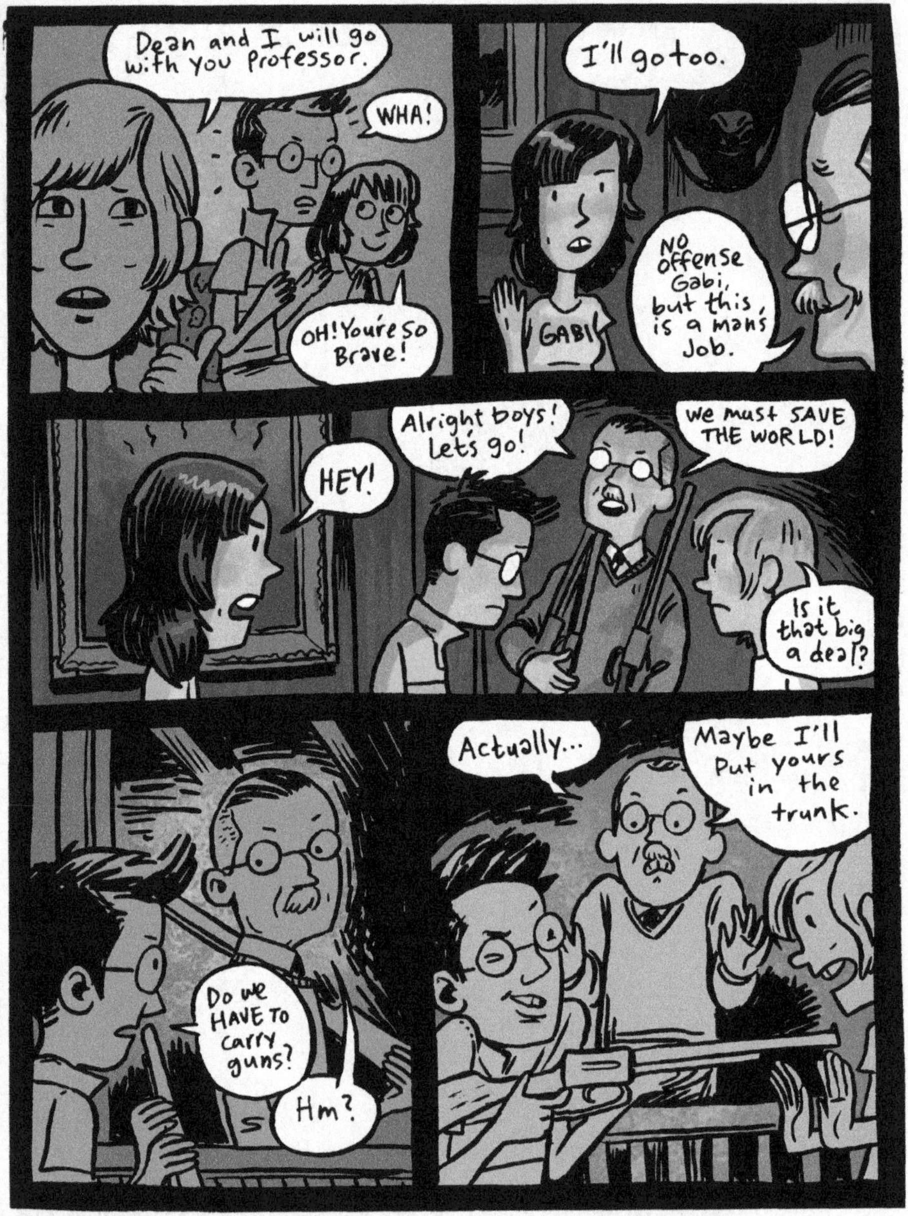
Dean and I will go with you Professor.
WHA!
OH! You're So Brave!
I'll go too.
NO offense Gabi, but this, is a man's Job.
GABI
HEY!
Alright boys! Let's go!
we must SAVE THE WORLD!
Is it that big a deal?
Do we HAVE TO carry guns?
Hm?
Actually...
Maybe I'll Put yours in the trunk.

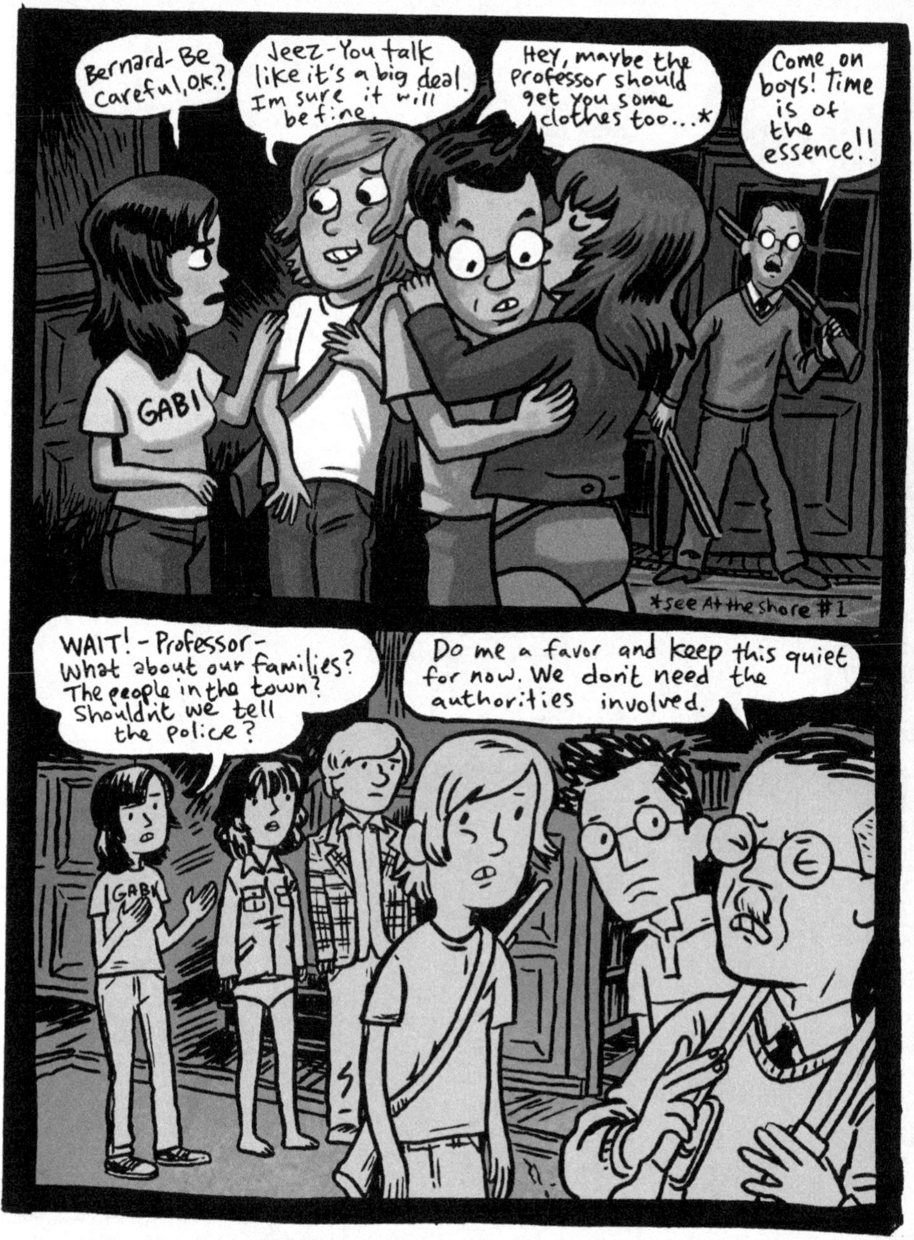
Bernard- Be careful, O.K.?
Jeez- You talk like it's a big deal. I'm sure it will be fine.
Hey, maybe the professor should get you some clothes too...*
Come on boys! Time is of the essence!!
GABI
*see At the Shore #1
WAIT! - Professor- What about our families? The people in the town? Shouldn't we tell the police?
Do me a favor and keep this quiet for now. We don't need the authorities involved.
GABI

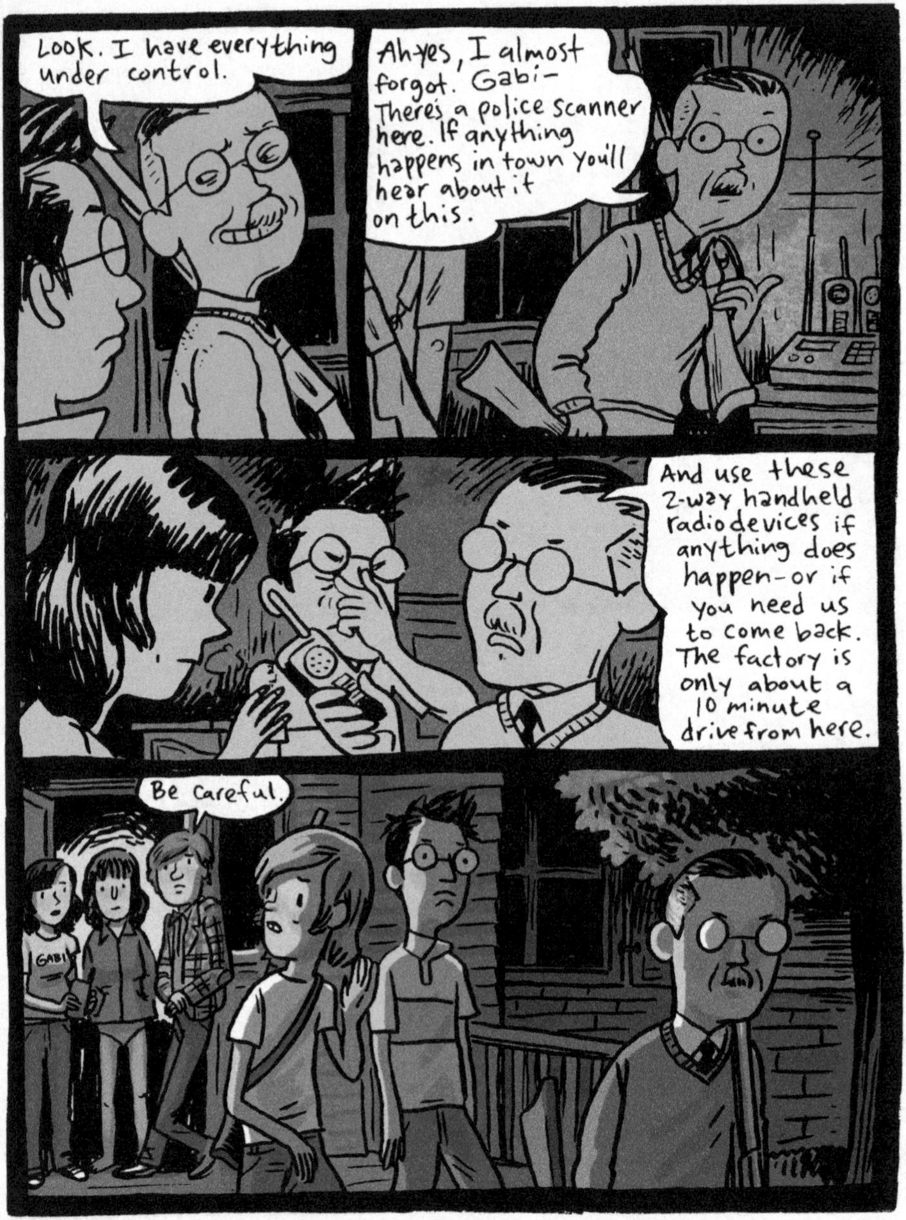
Look. I have everything under control.
Ah-yes, I almost forgot. Gabi- There's a police scanner here. If anything happens in town you'll hear about it on this.
And use these 2-way handheld radio devices if anything does happen-or if you need us to come back. The factory is only about a 10 minute drive from here.
Be careful.
GABI

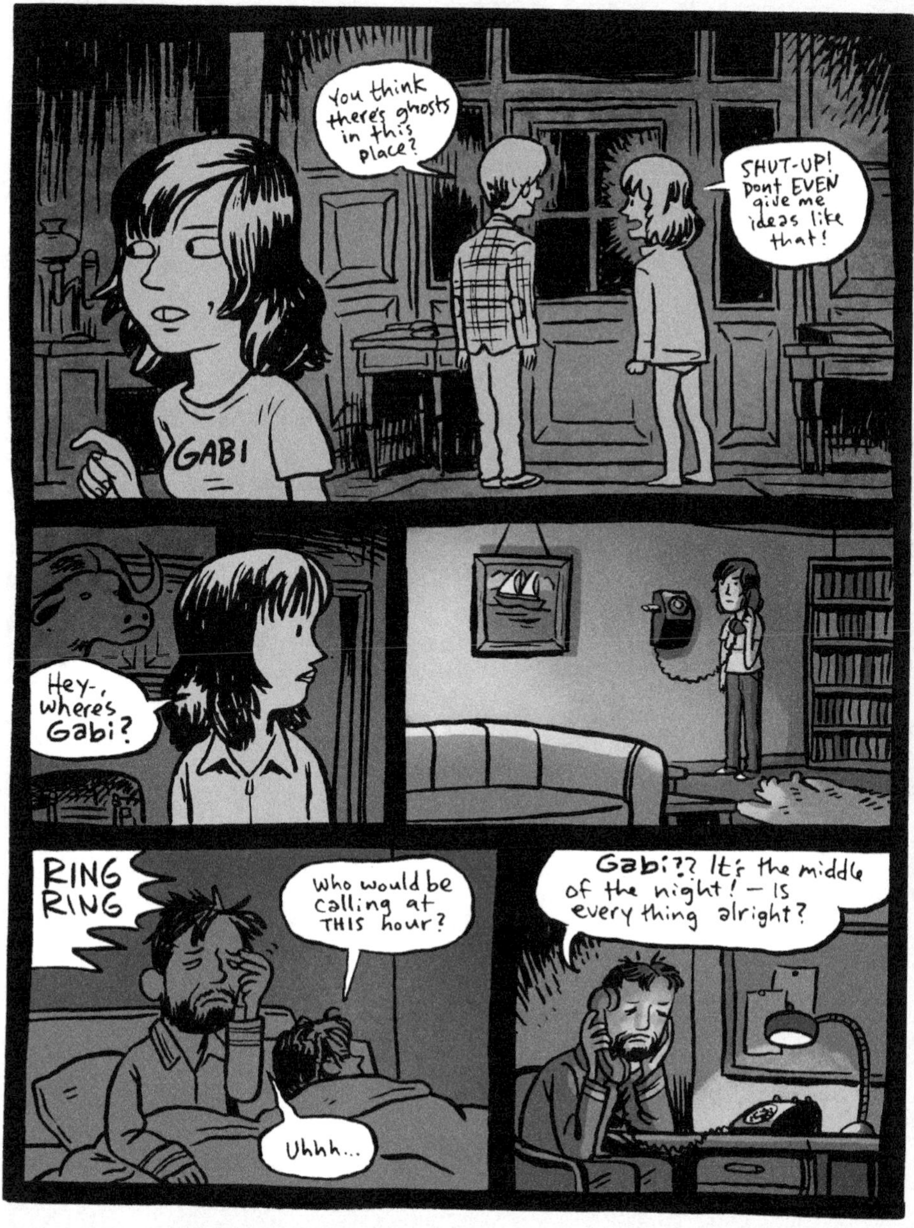
You think there's ghosts in this place?
SHUT-UP! Dont EVEN give me ideas like that!
GABI
Hey-, where's Gabi?
RING RING
Who would be calling at THIS hour?
Uhhh...
Gabi?? It's the middle of the night! — Is every thing alright?

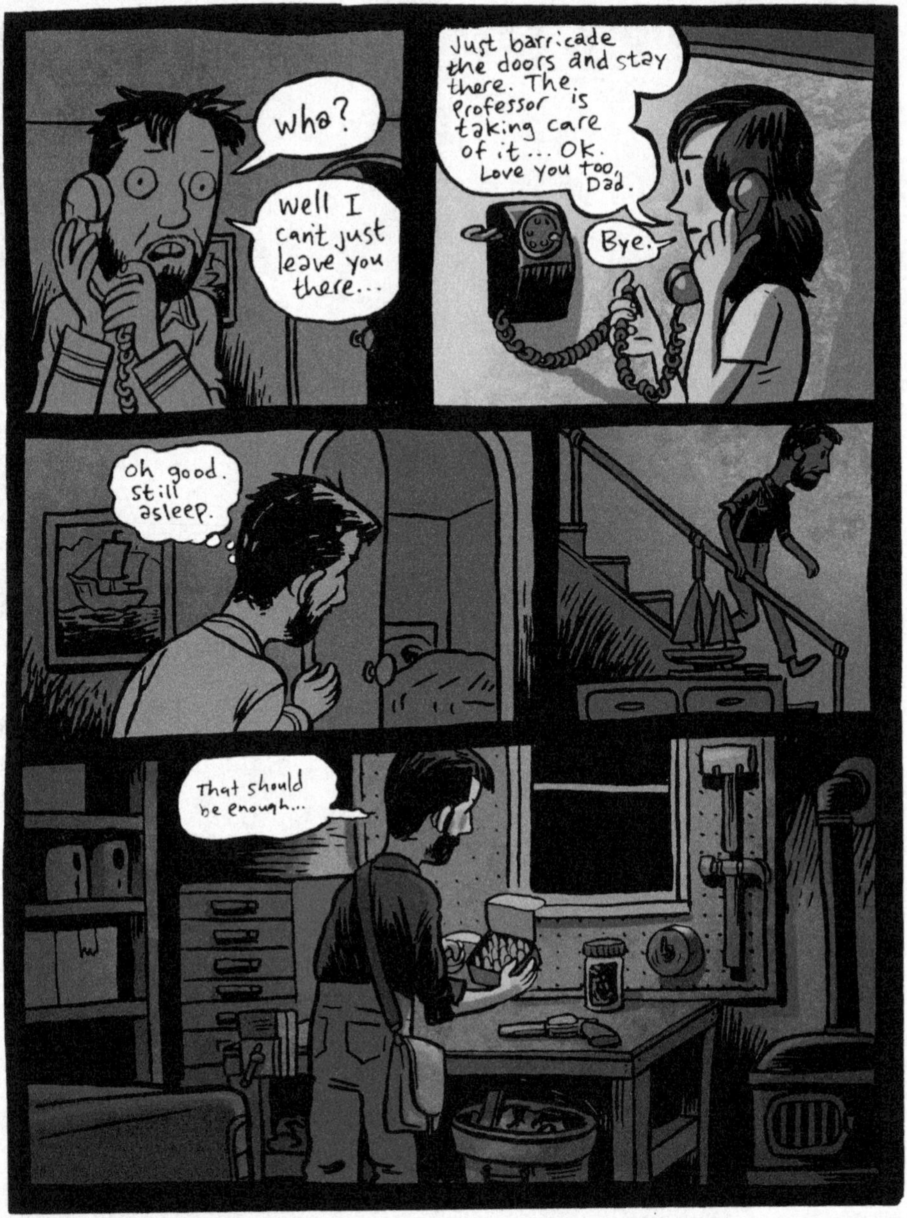

wha?
Just barricade the doors and stay there. The professor is taking care of it... Ok. Love you too, Dad.
well I can't just leave you there...
Bye.
oh good. still asleep.
That should be enough...

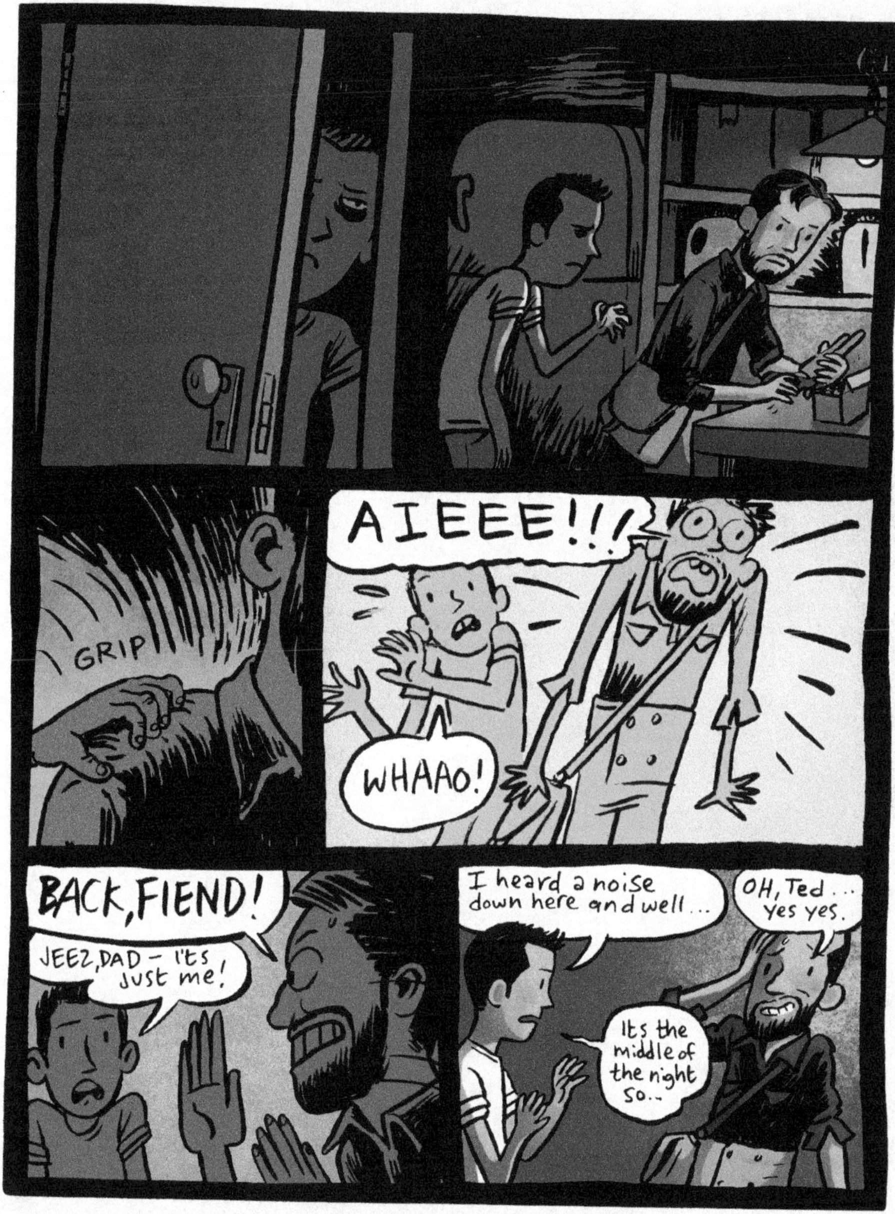
GRIP
AIEEE!!!
WHAAO!
BACK, FIEND!
JEEZ, DAD - It's just me!
I heard a noise down here and well...
OH, Ted... yes yes.
It's the middle of the night so..

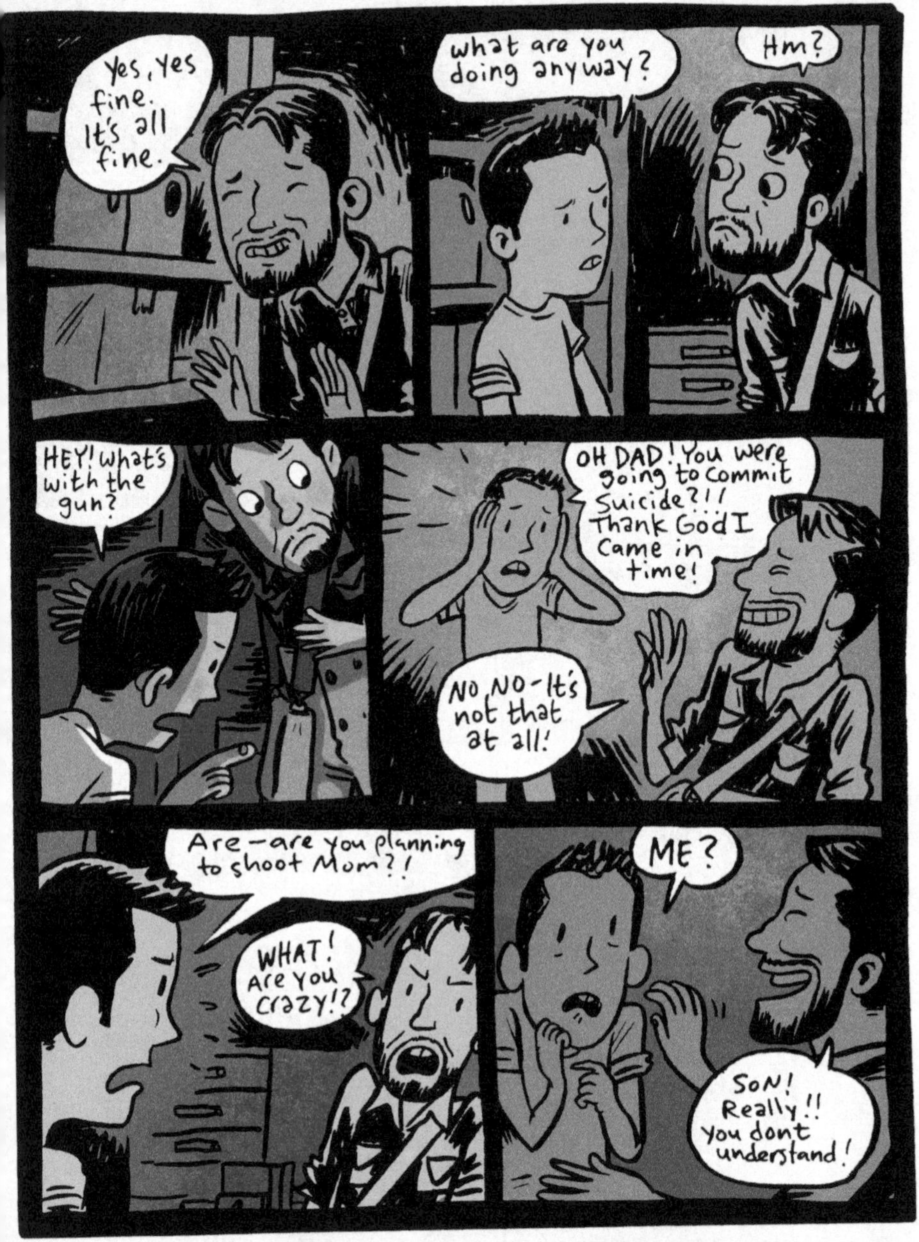
Yes, yes fine. It's all fine.
what are you doing anyway?
Hm?
HEY! what's with the gun?
OH DAD! You were going to commit suicide?!! Thank God I came in time!
NO NO- It's not that at all!
Are-are you planning to shoot Mom?!
WHAT! Are you crazy!?
ME?
SON! Really!! You dont understand!

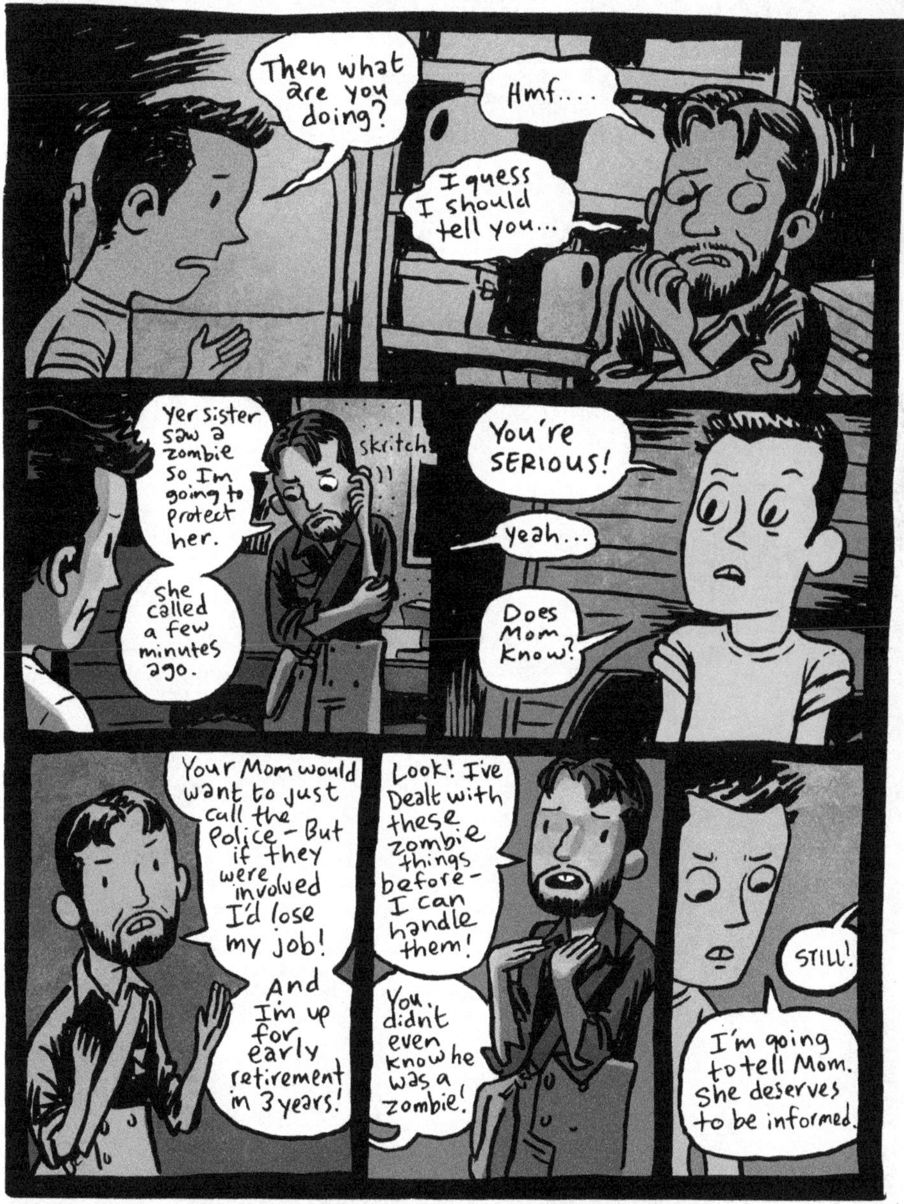
Then what are you doing?
Hmf....
I guess I should tell you...
Yer sister saw a zombie so I'm going to protect her.
skritch
she called a few minutes ago.
You're SERIOUS!
yeah...
Does Mom know?
Your Mom would want to just call the Police - But if they were involved I'd lose my job!
And I'm up for early retirement in 3 years!
Look! I've Dealt with these zombie things before - I can handle them!
You didn't even know he was a zombie!
STILL!
I'm going to tell Mom. She deserves to be informed.

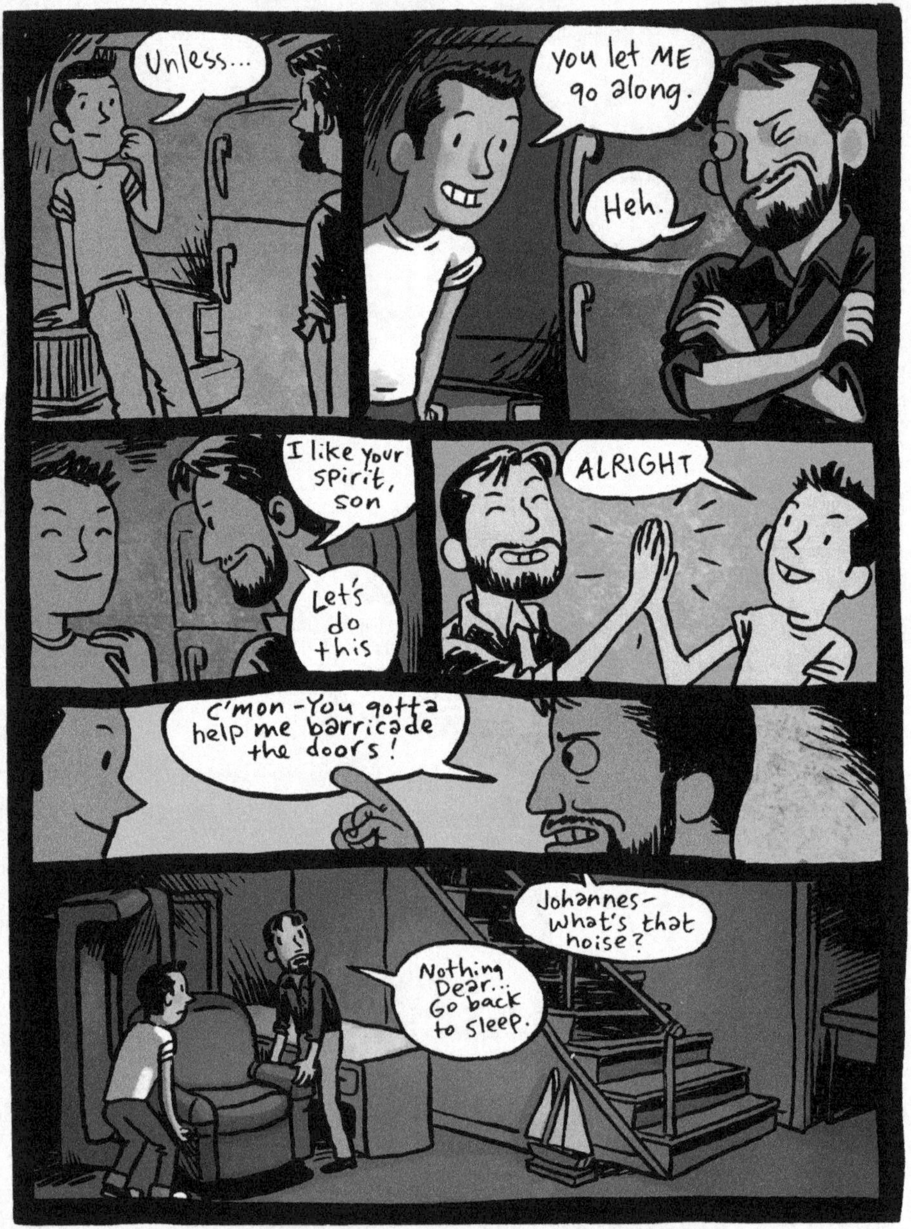
Unless...
you let ME go along.
Heh.
I like your spirit, son
Let's do this
ALRIGHT
C'mon-You gotta help me barricade the doors!
Johannes-what's that noise?
Nothing Dear... Go back to sleep.

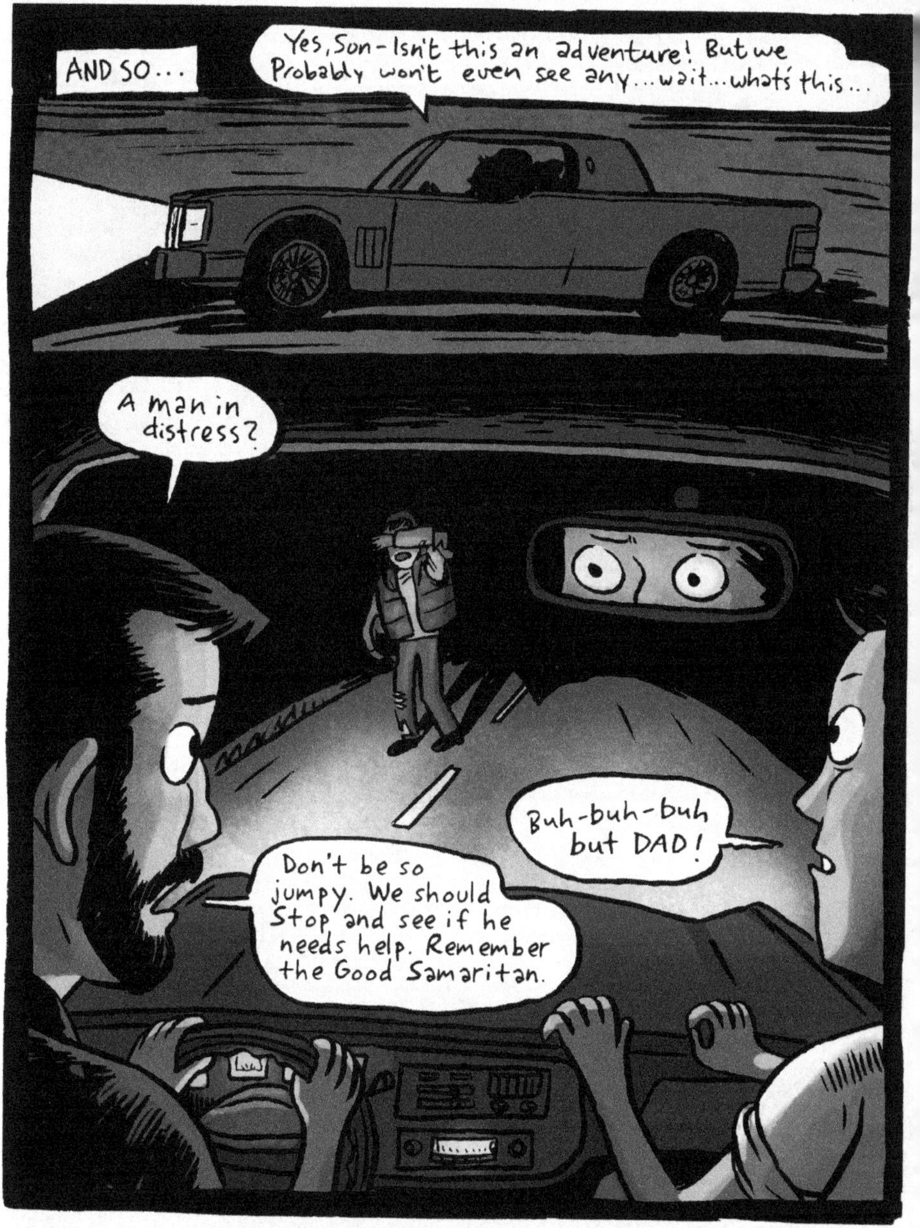
AND SO...
Yes, Son- Isn't this an adventure! But we Probably won't even see any... wait... what's this...
A man in distress?
Buh-buh-buh but DAD!
Don't be so jumpy. We should Stop and see if he needs help. Remember the Good Samaritan.

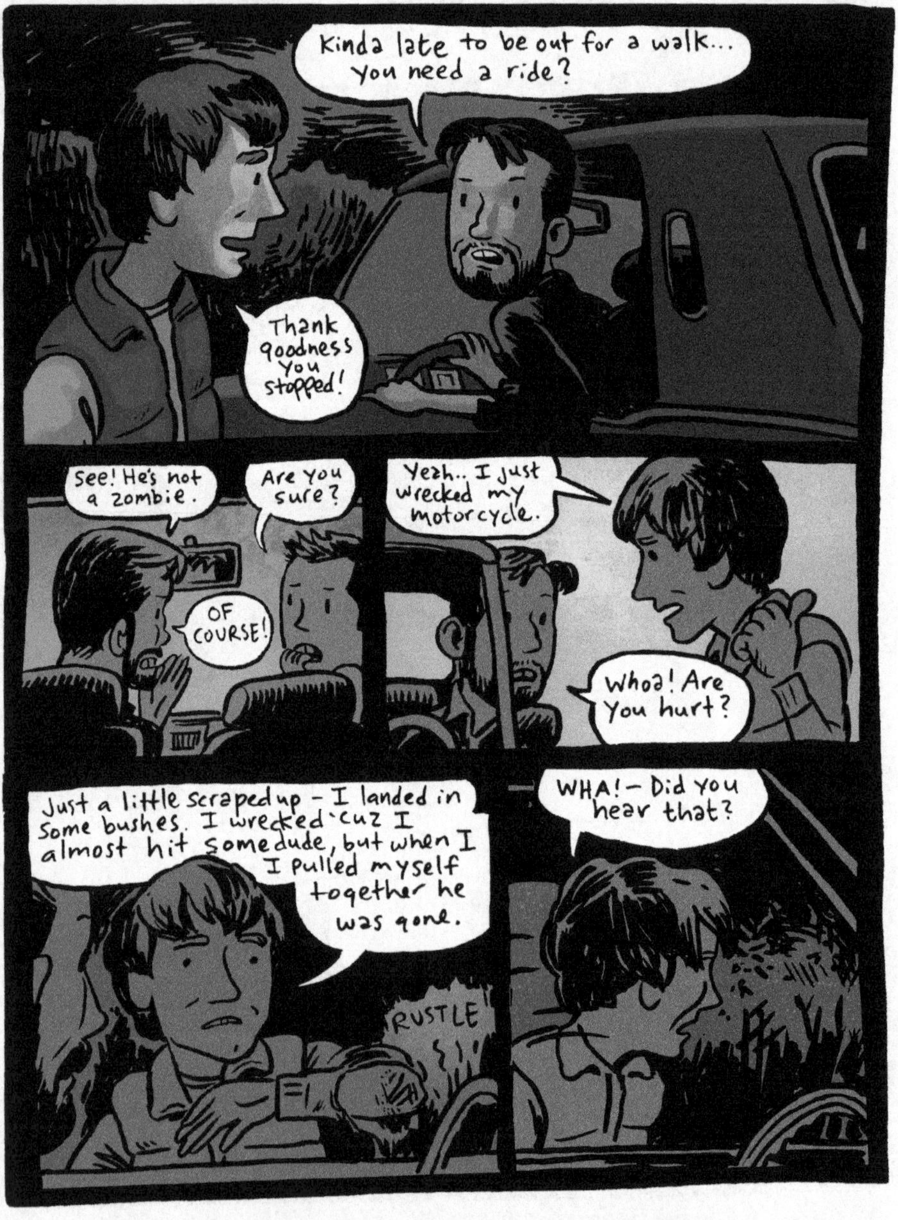
Kinda late to be out for a walk... you need a ride?
Thank goodness you stopped!
See! He's not a zombie.
Are you sure?
OF COURSE!
Yeah.. I just wrecked my motorcycle.
Whoa! Are you hurt?
Just a little scraped up - I landed in some bushes. I wrecked 'cuz I almost hit some dude, but when I I pulled myself together he was gone.
RUSTLE
WHA! - Did you hear that?

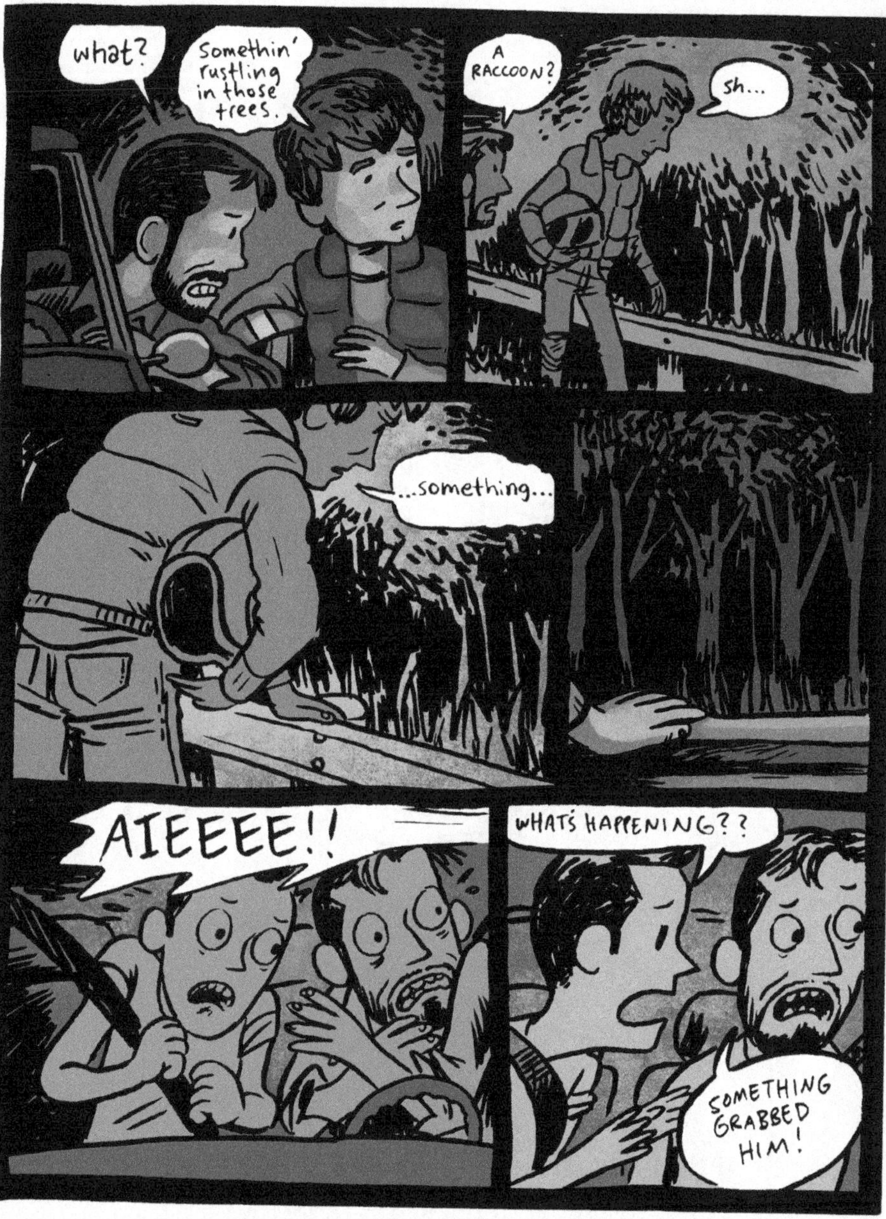
what?
Somethin' rustling in those trees.
A RACCOON?
Sh...
...something...
AIEEEE!!
WHAT'S HAPPENING??
SOMETHING GRABBED HIM!

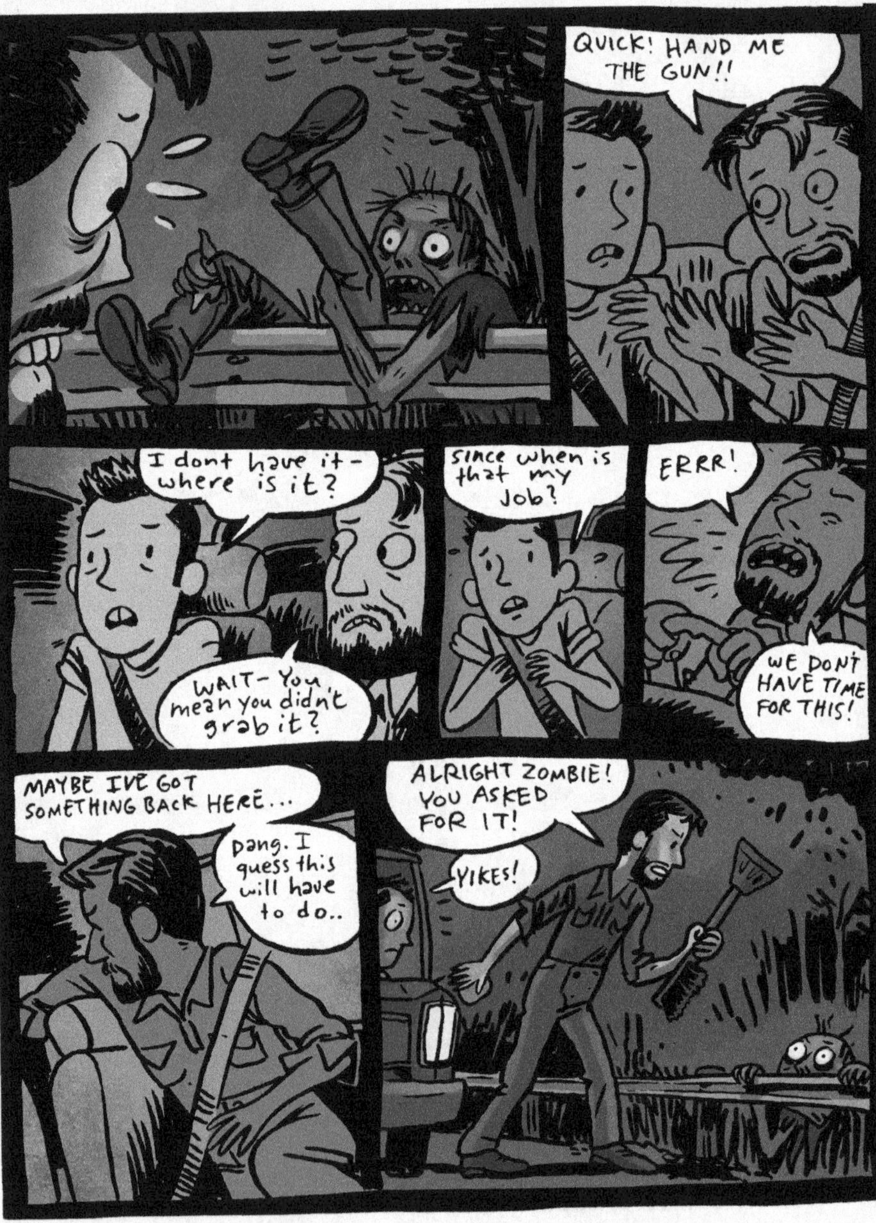
QUICK! HAND ME THE GUN!!
I dont have it- where is it?
WAIT- You mean you didn't grab it?
since when is that my job?
ERRR!
WE DON'T HAVE TIME FOR THIS!
MAYBE I'VE GOT SOMETHING BACK HERE...
Dang. I guess this will have to do..
ALRIGHT ZOMBIE! YOU ASKED FOR IT!
YIKES!

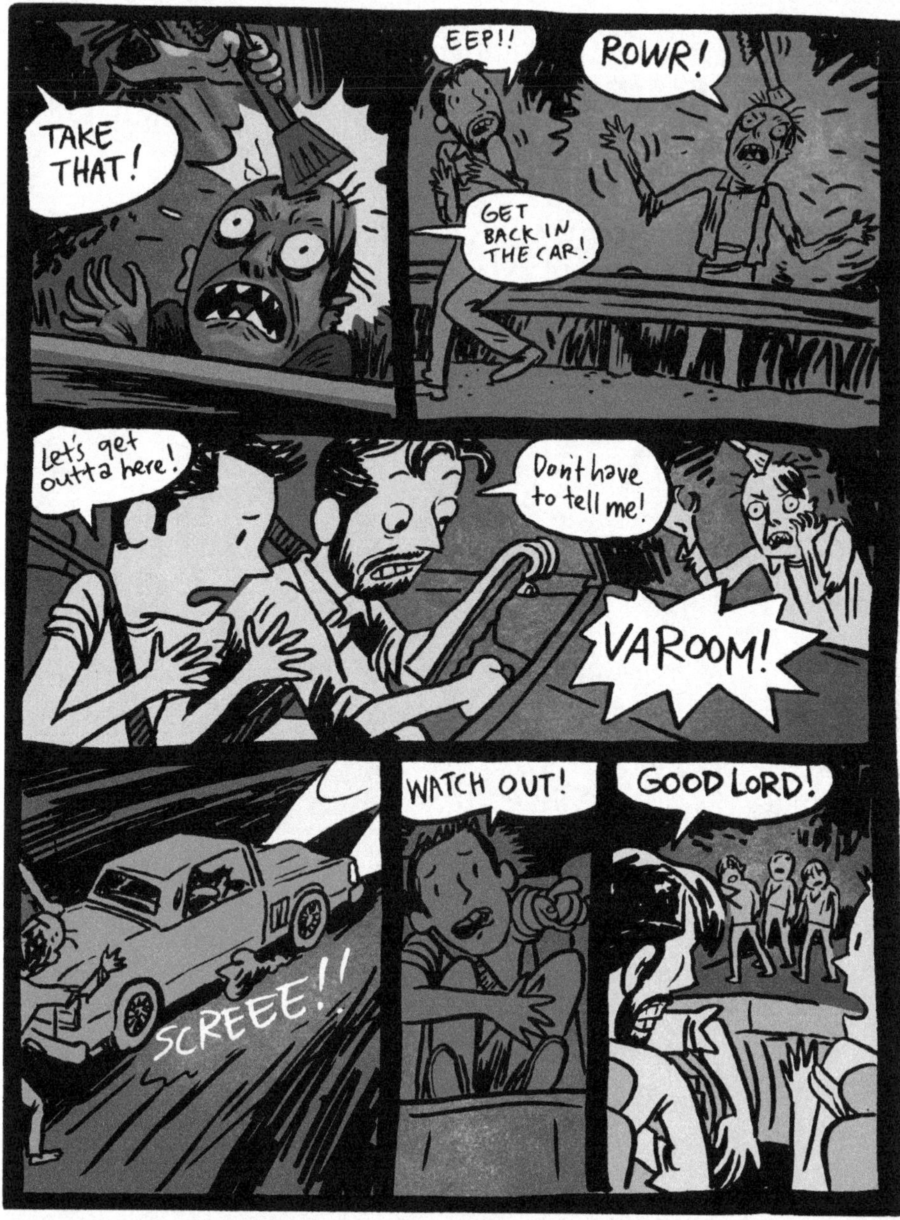
TAKE THAT!
EEP!!
ROWR!
GET BACK IN THE CAR!
Let's get outta here!
Don't have to tell me!
VAROOM!
SCREEE!!
WATCH OUT!
GOOD LORD!

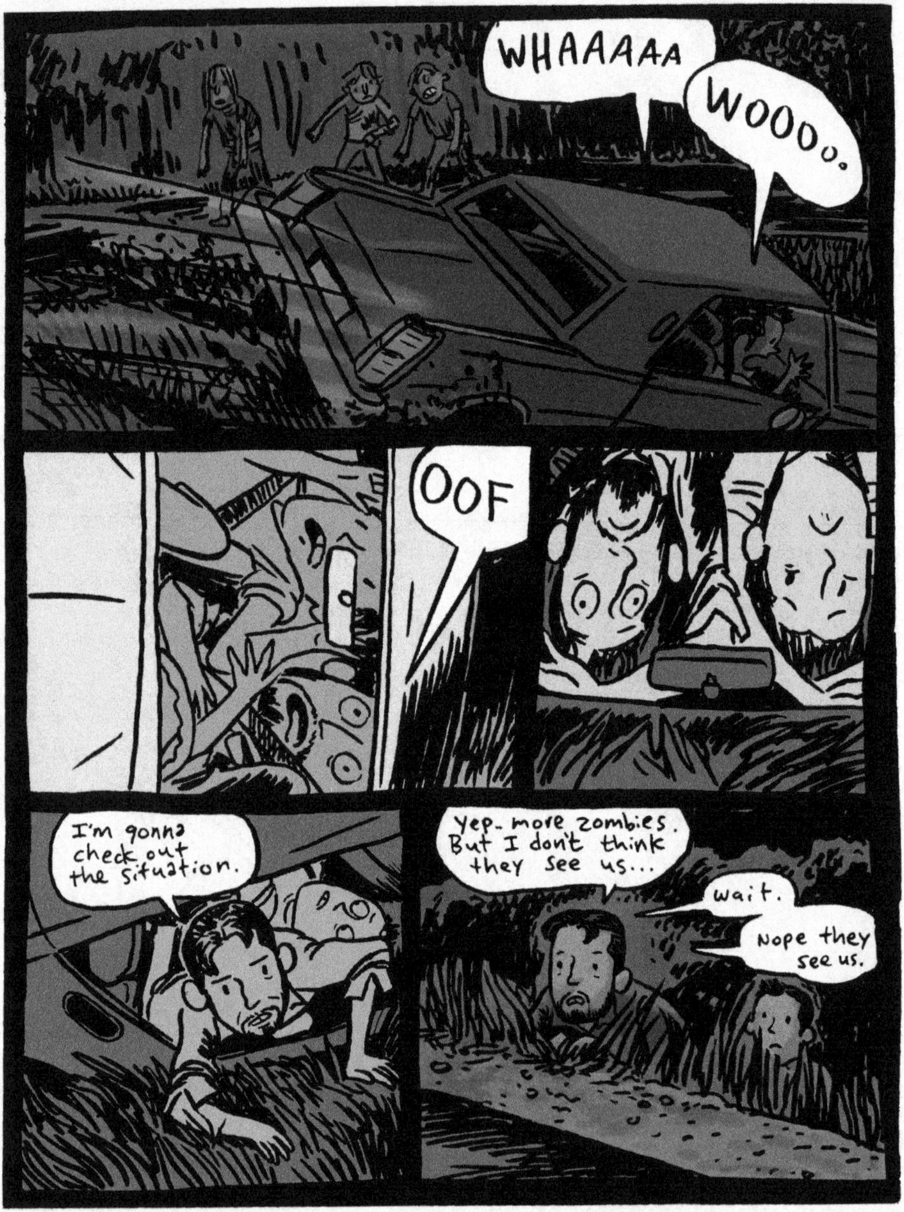
WHAAAAA
WOOOo.
OOF
I'm gonna check out the situation.
yep- more zombies. But I don't think they see us...
wait.
Nope they see us.

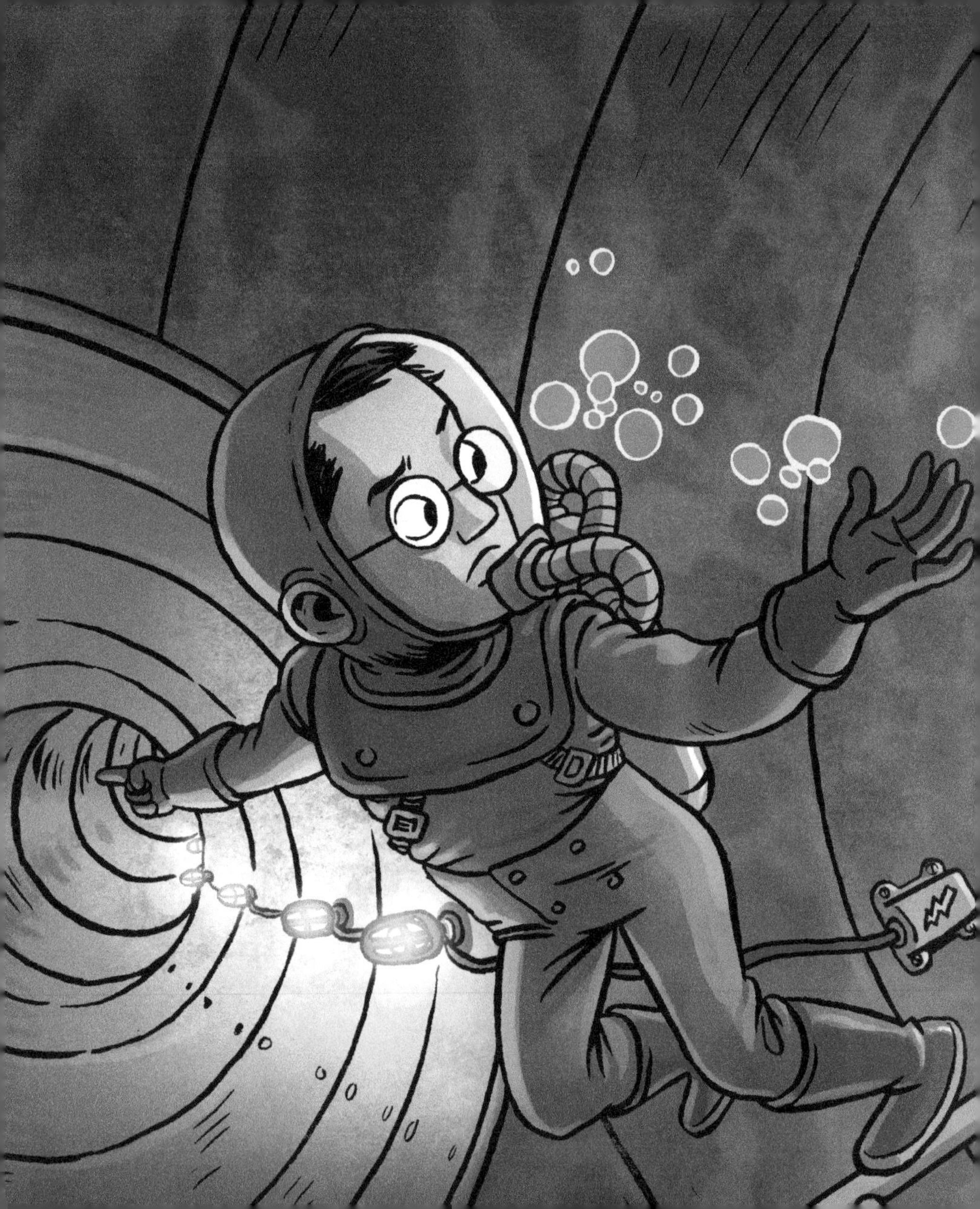

CHAPTER FIVE

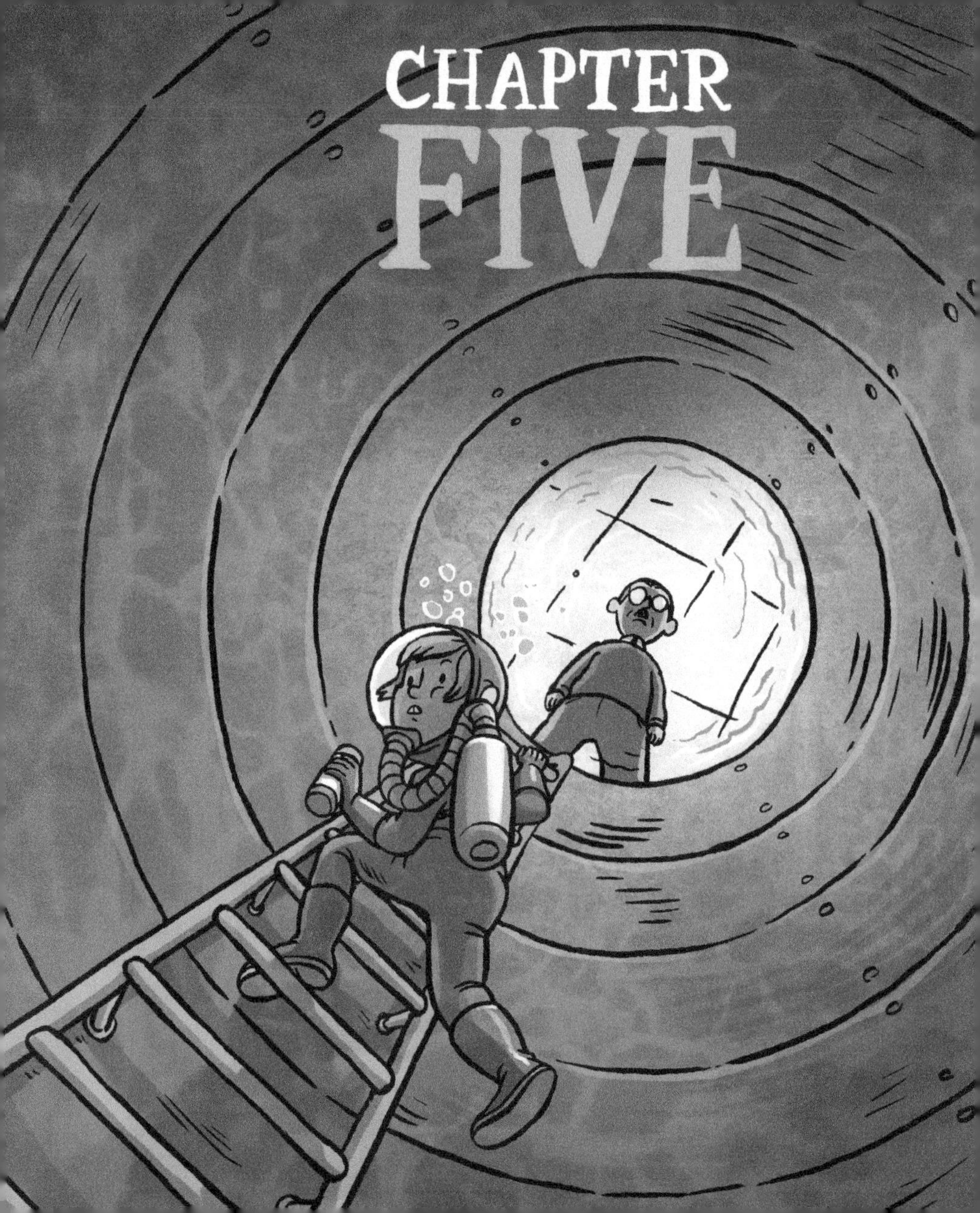

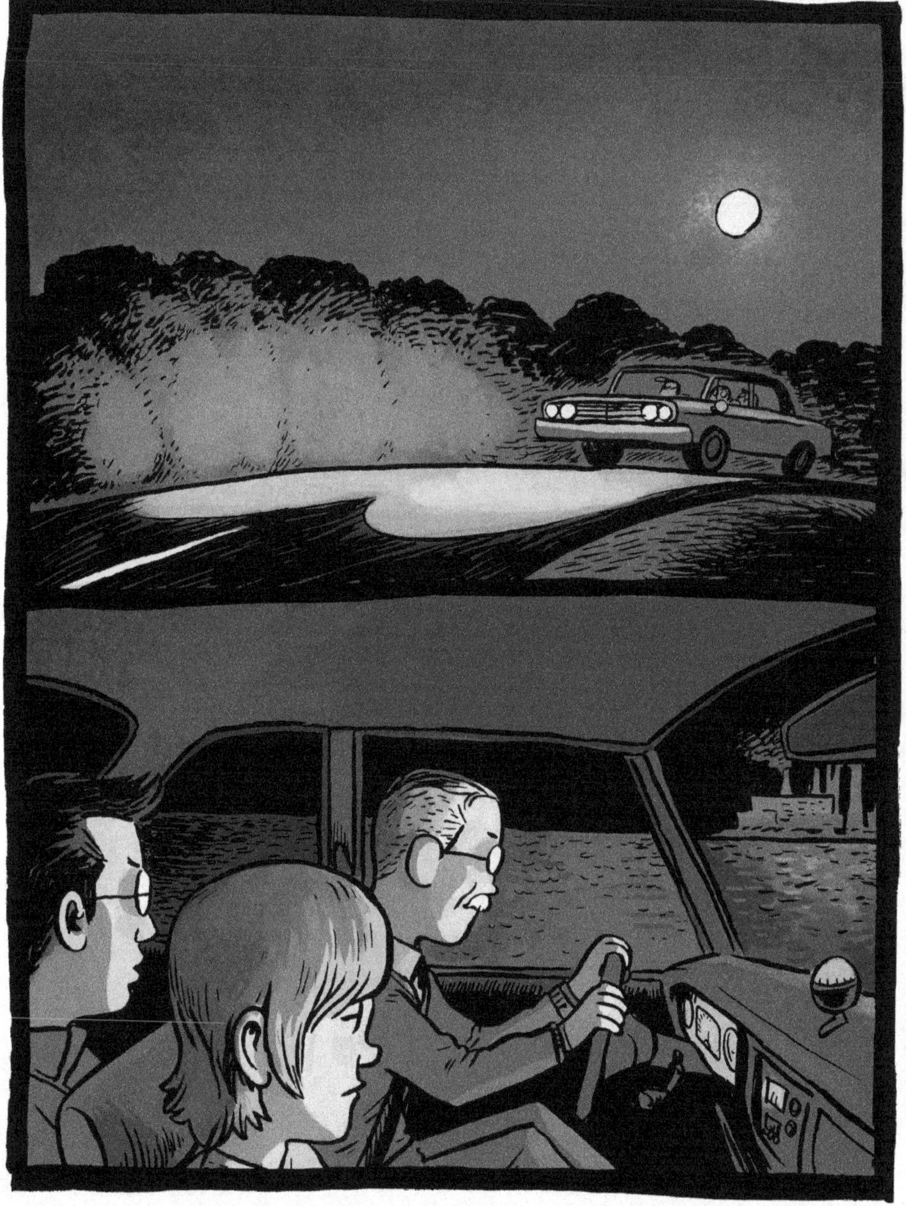

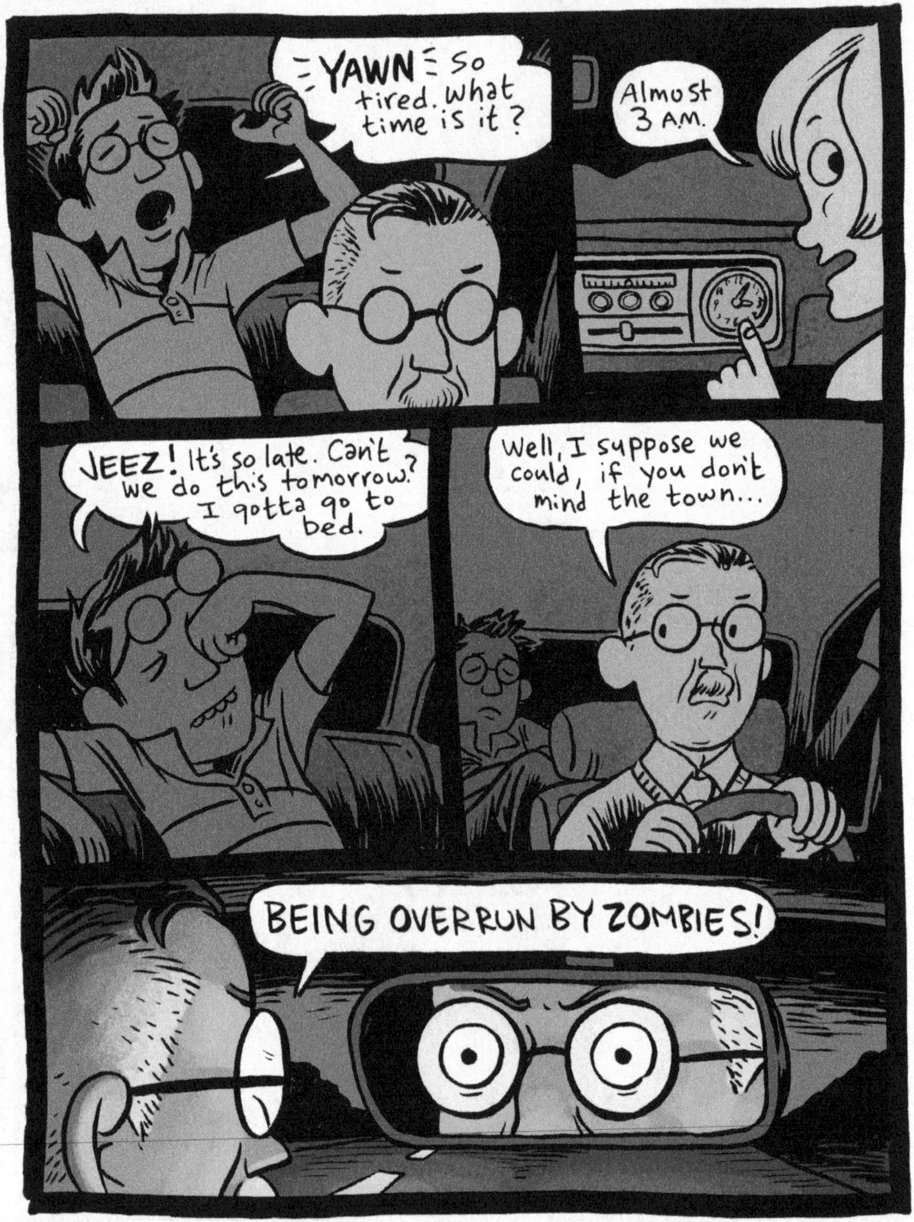
YAWN So tired. what time is it?
Almost 3 A.M.
JEEZ! It's so late. Can't we do this tomorrow? I gotta go to bed.
Well, I suppose we could, if you don't mind the town...
BEING OVERRUN BY ZOMBIES!

MEANWHILE...
Oh, great. What do we do now?
RUN!
MIDLOTHIAN BAY TOWNSHIP 2 MILES

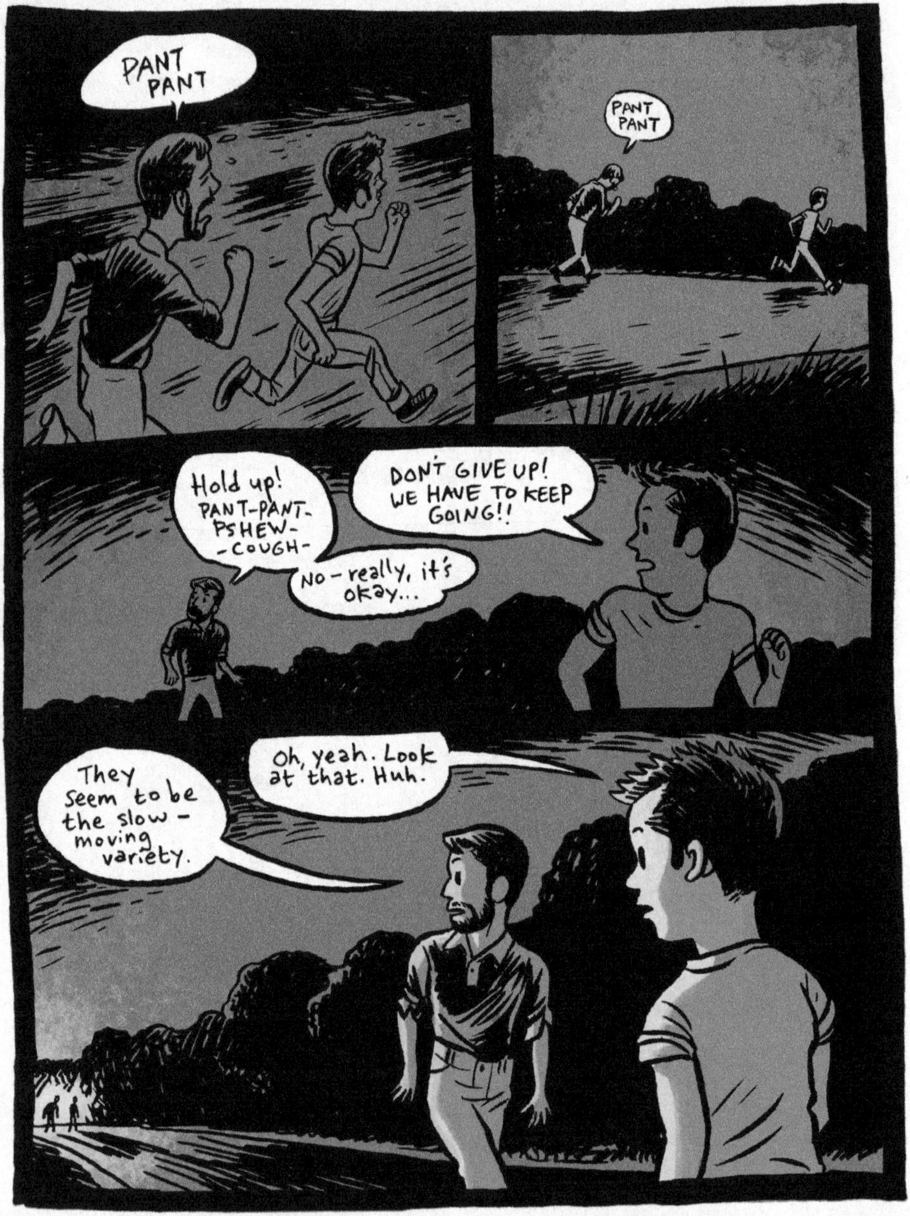
PANT PANT
PANT PANT
Hold up! PANT-PANT- PSHEW- -COUGH-
DON'T GIVE UP! WE HAVE TO KEEP GOING!!
No-really, it's okay...
They seem to be the slow-moving variety.
Oh, yeah. Look at that. Huh.

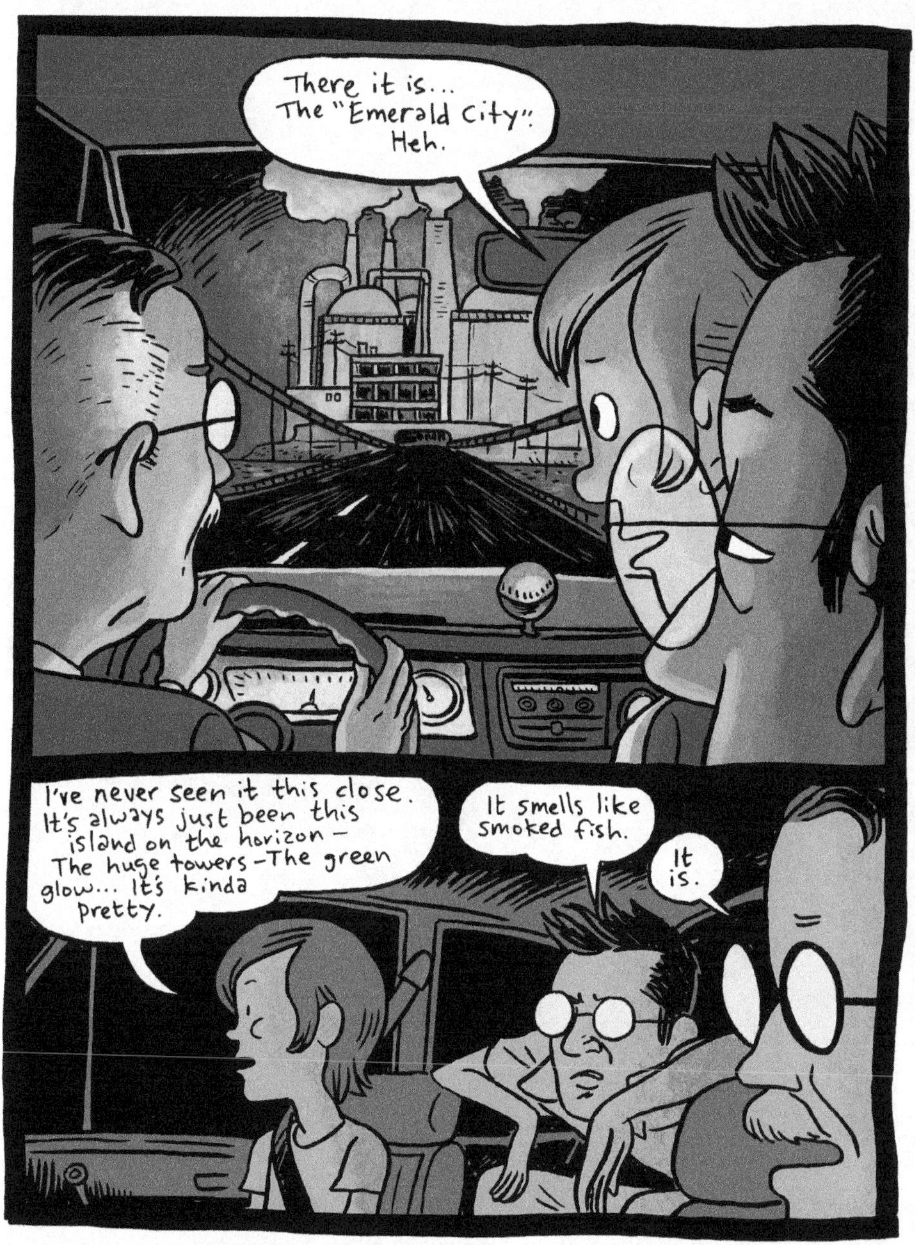
There it is... The "Emerald City". Heh.
I've never seen it this close. It's always just been this island on the horizon— The huge towers—The green glow... It's kinda pretty.
It smells like smoked fish.
It is.

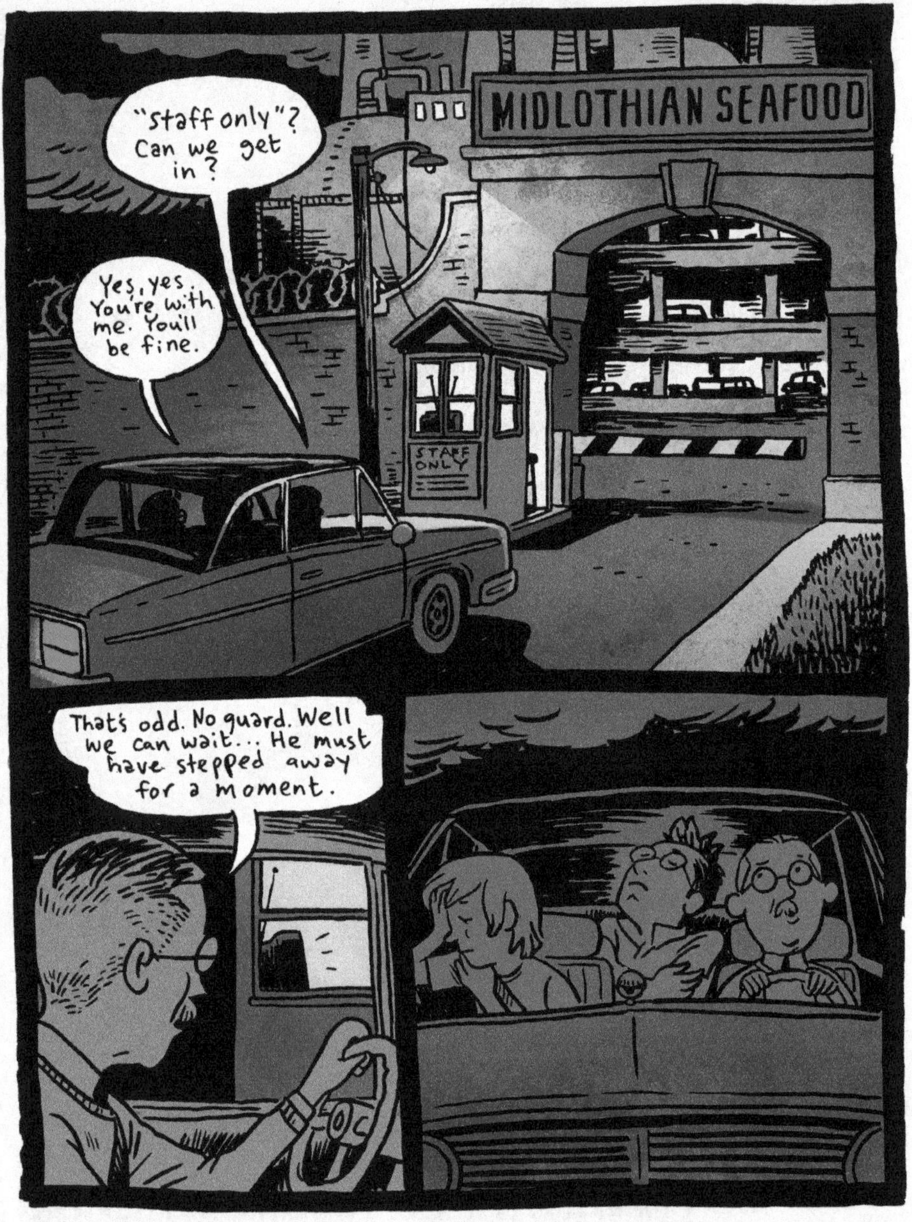

MIDLOTHIAN SEAFOOD
"staff only"? Can we get in?
Yes, yes. You're with me. You'll be fine.
STAFF ONLY
That's odd. No guard. Well we can wait... He must have stepped away for a moment.

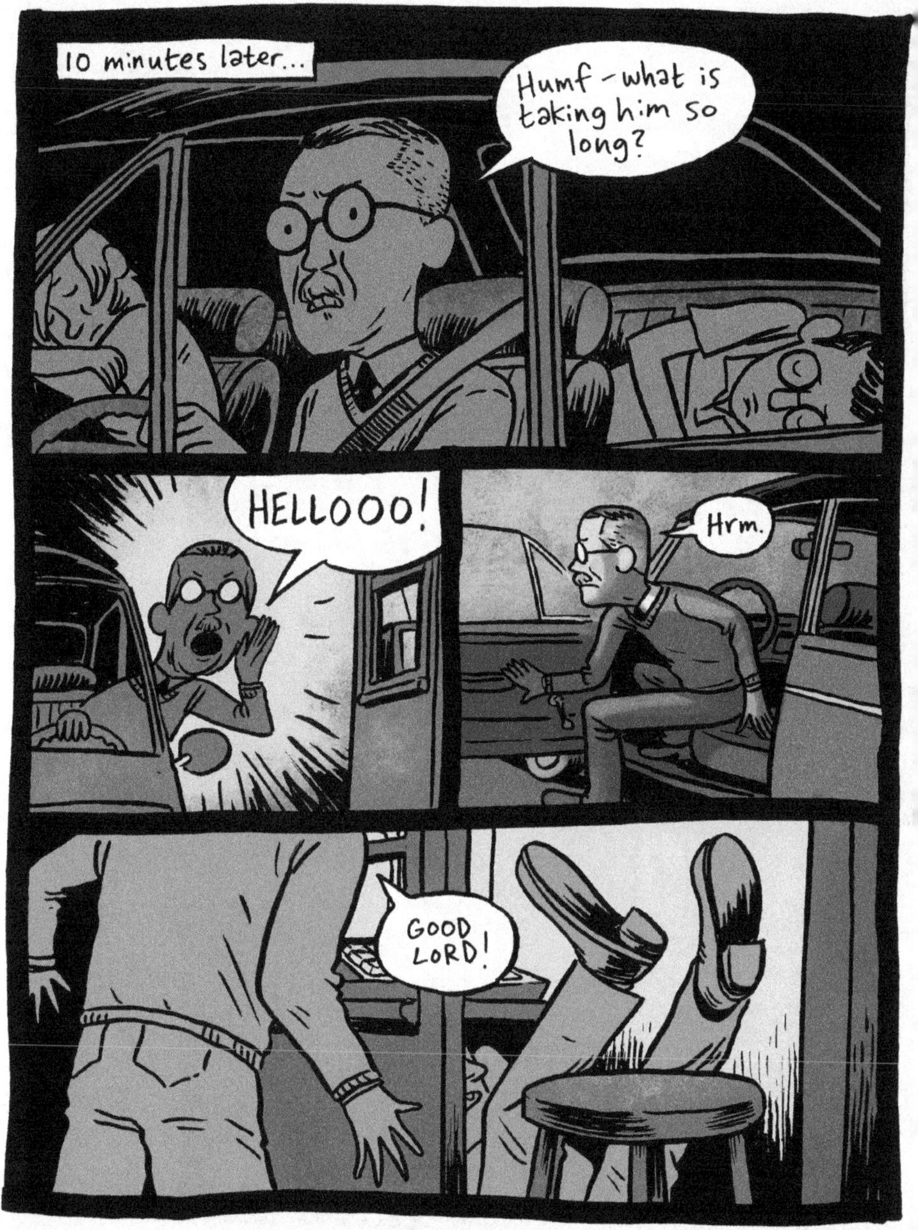
10 minutes later...
Humf - what is taking him so long?
HELLOOO!
Hrm.
GOOD LORD!

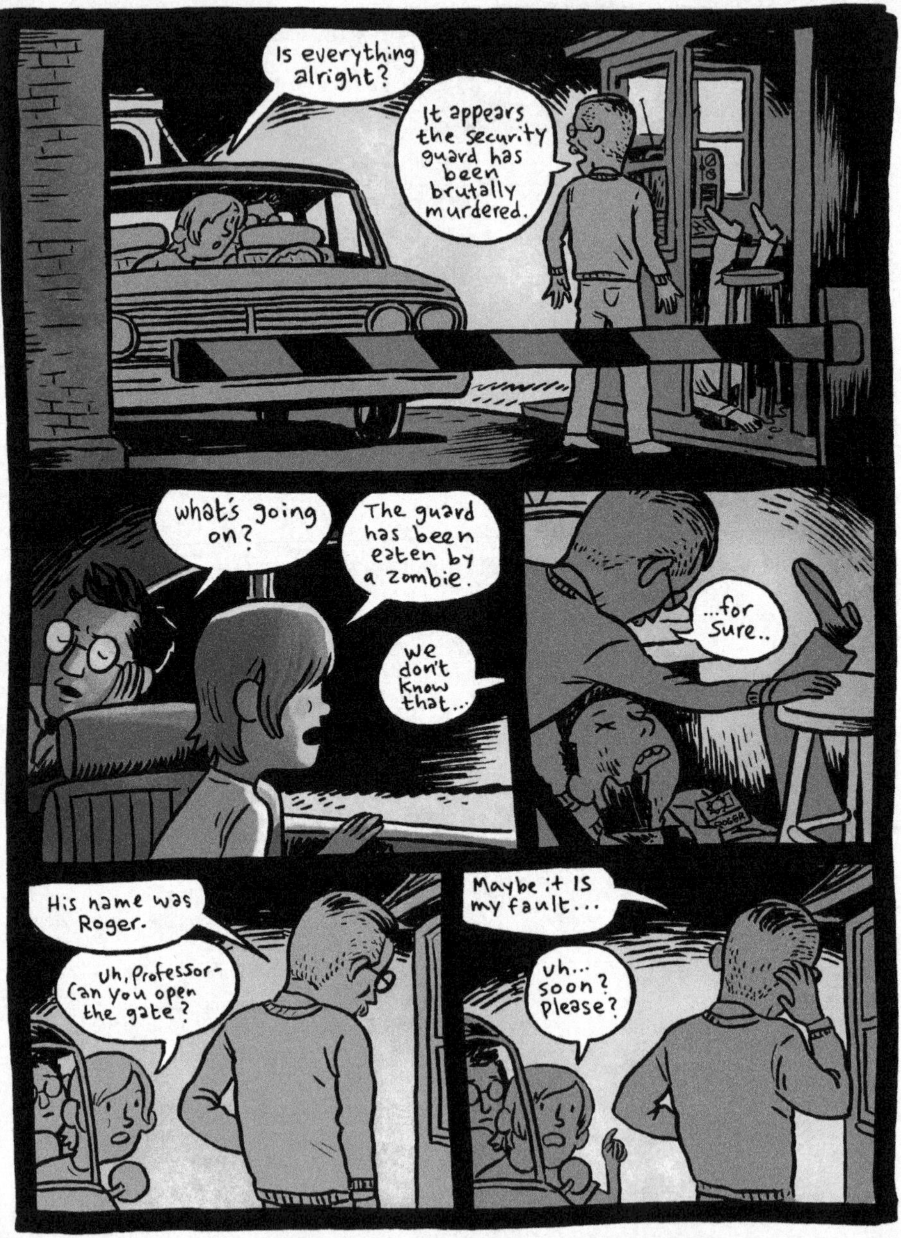

Is everything alright?
It appears the security guard has been brutally murdered.
what's going on?
The guard has been eaten by a zombie.
we don't know that...
...for sure..
ROGER
His name was Roger.
Uh, Professor- Can you open the gate?
Maybe it IS my fault...
uh... soon? Please?

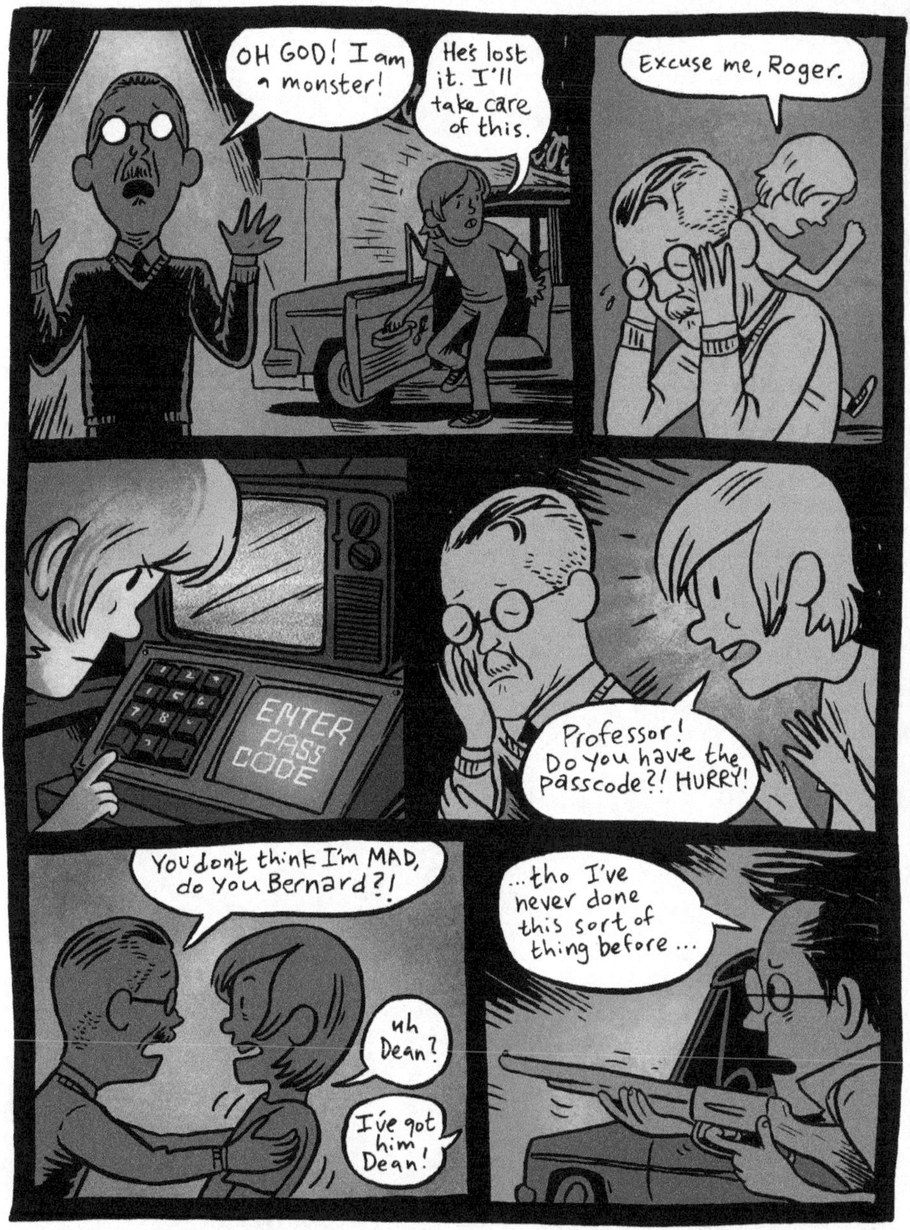
OH GOD! I am a monster!
He's lost it. I'll take care of this.
Excuse me, Roger.
ENTER PASS CODE
Professor! Do you have the passcode?! HURRY!
You don't think I'm MAD, do you Bernard?!
uh Dean?
I've got him! Dean!
...tho I've never done this sort of thing before...

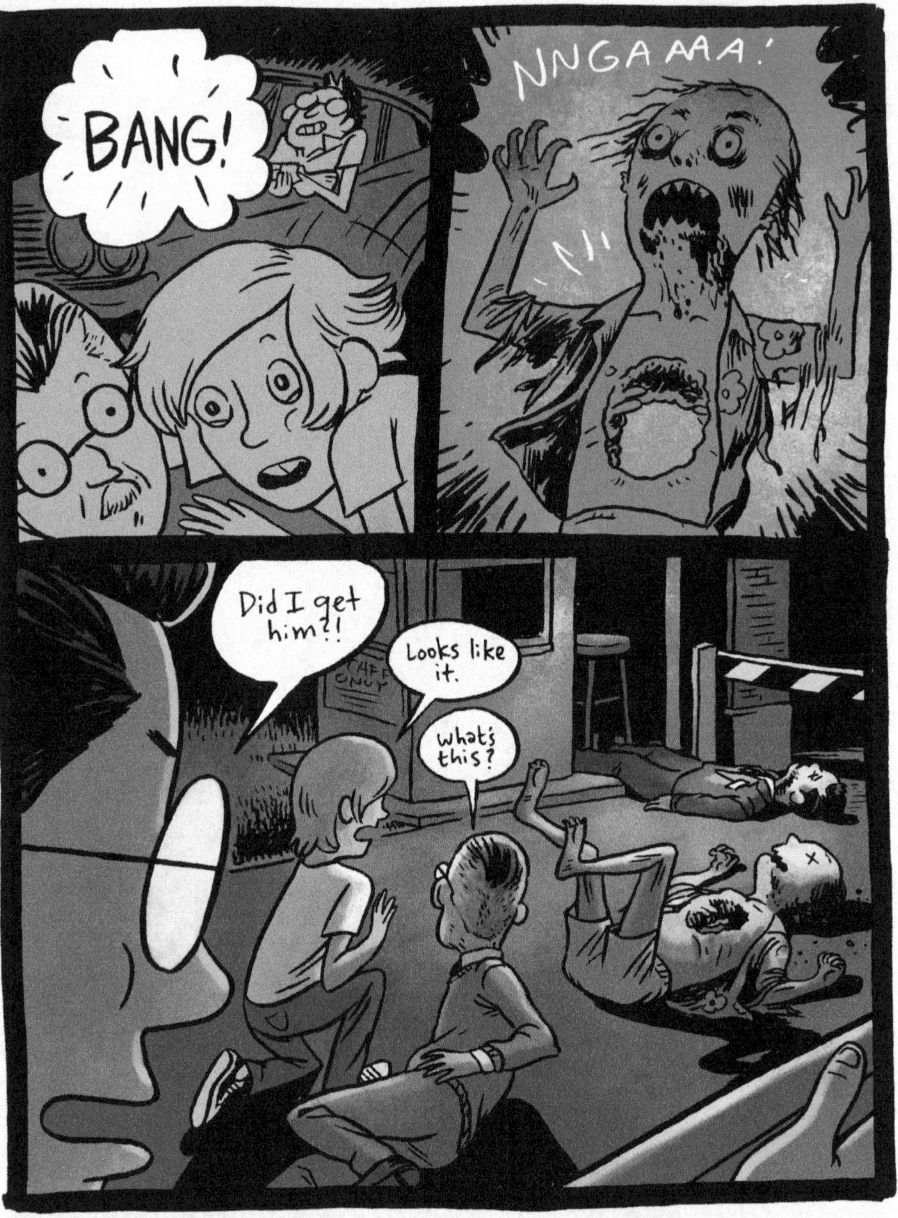
BANG!
NNGAAAA!
Did I get him?!
Looks like it.
what's this?

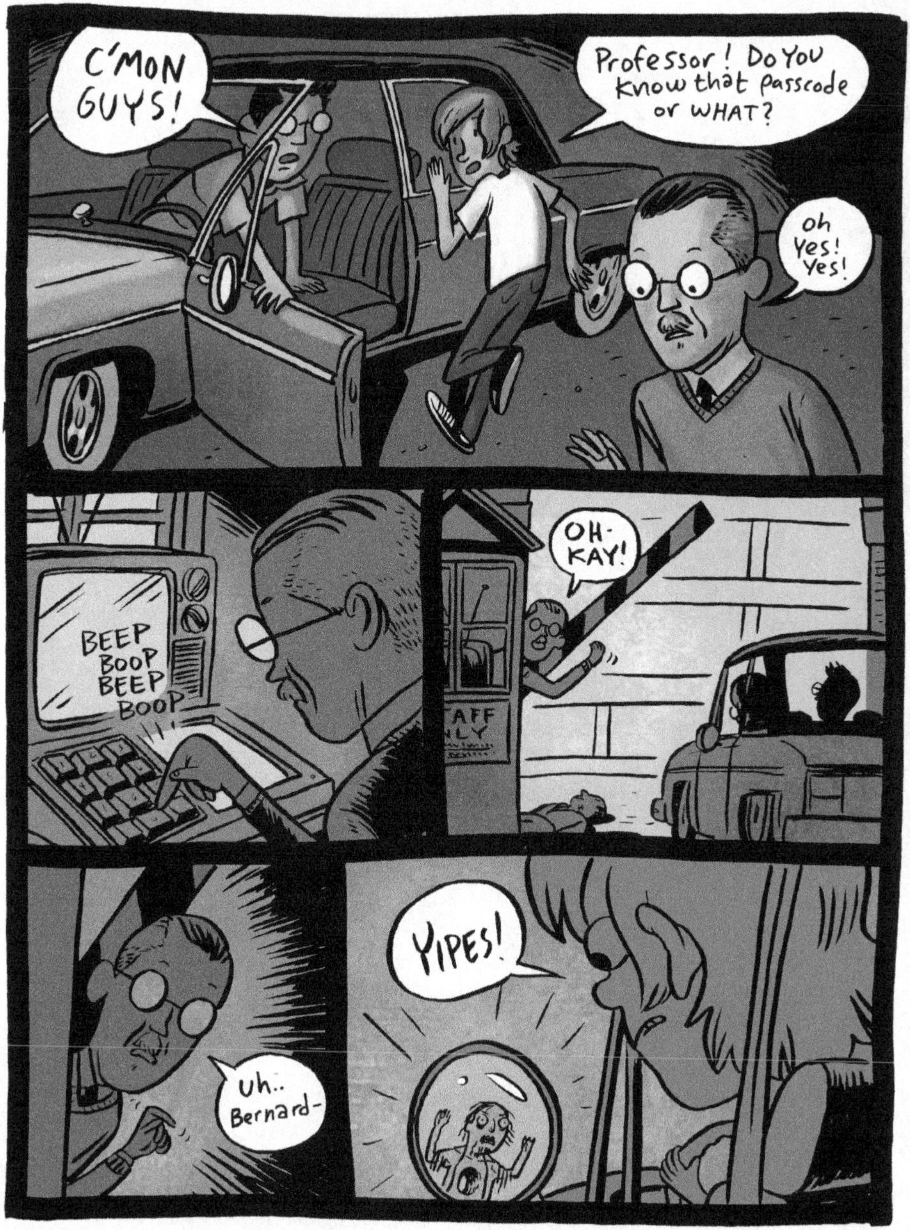
C'MON GUYS!
Professor! Do You know that passcode or WHAT?
oh yes! yes!
BEEP BOOP BEEP BOOP
OH-KAY!
STAFF ONLY
Uh.. Bernard-
YIPES!

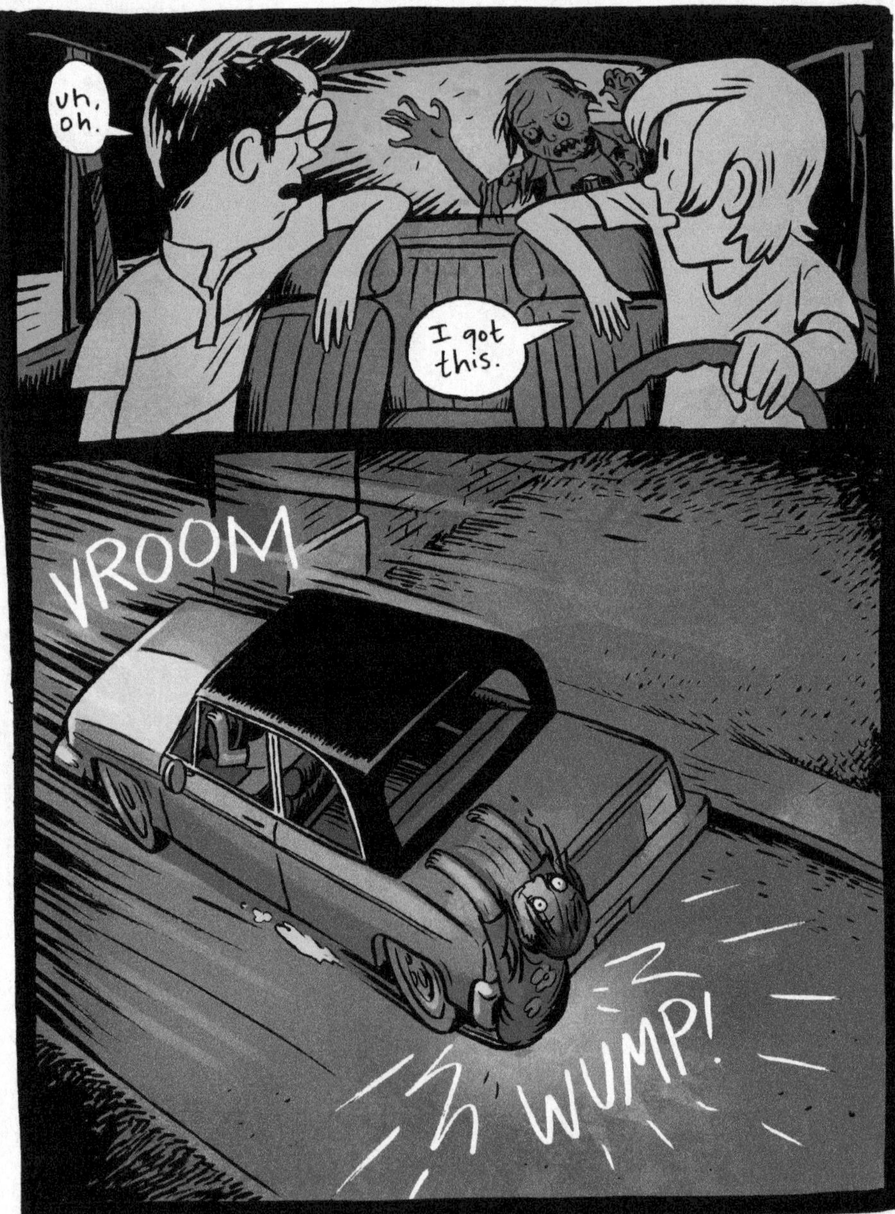
uh, oh.
I got this.
VROOM
WUMP!

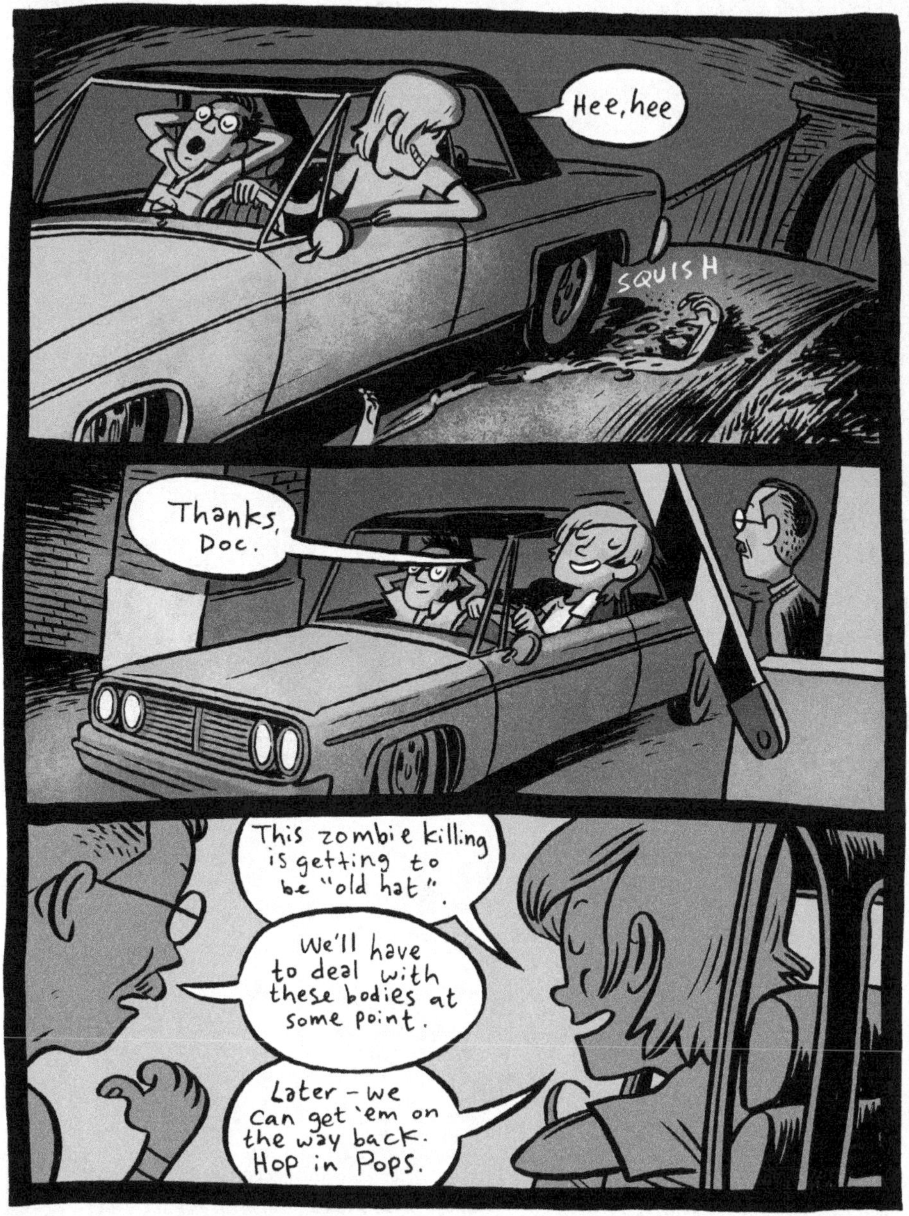
Hee, hee
SQUISH
Thanks, Doc.
This zombie killing is getting to be "old hat".
We'll have to deal with these bodies at some point.
Later - we can get 'em on the way back. Hop in Pops.

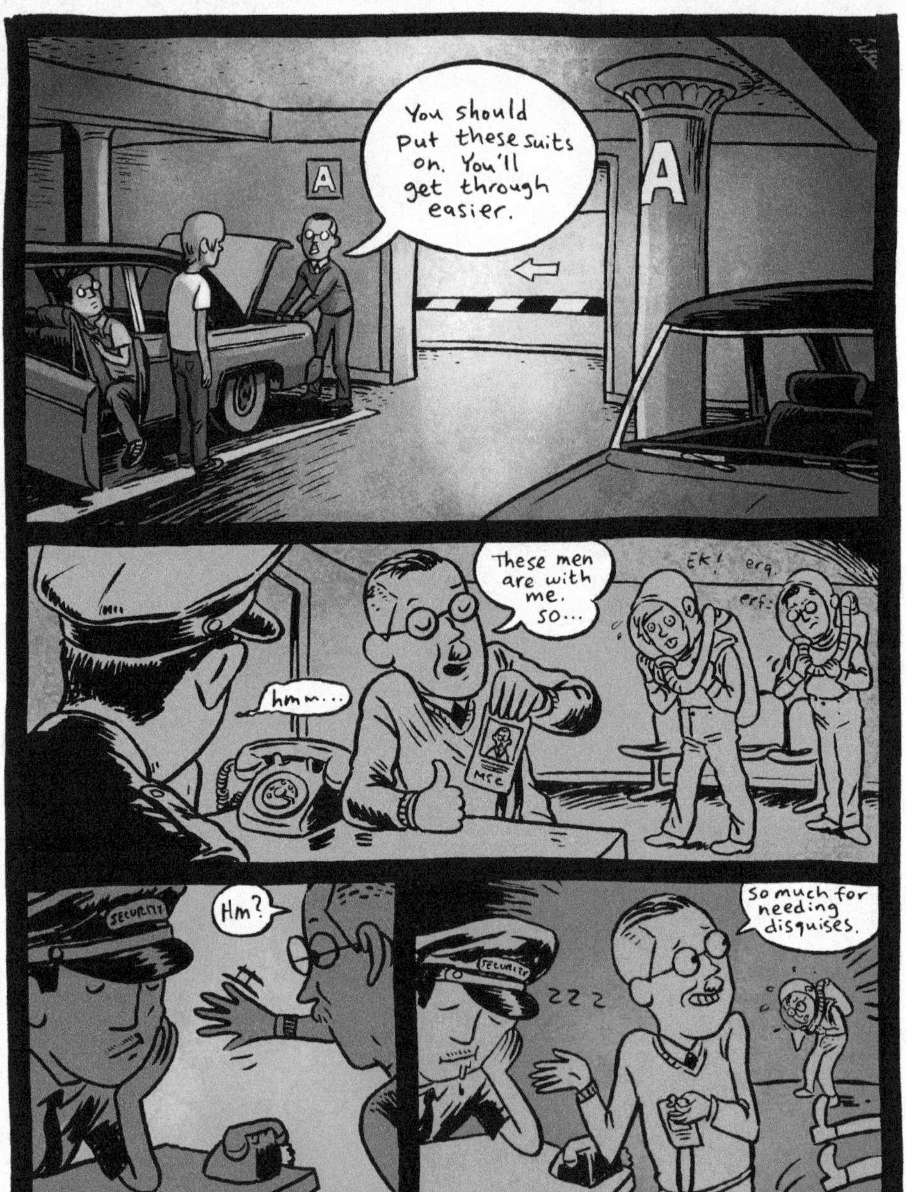

A
A
You should put these suits on. You'll get through easier.
These men are with me. So...
Ek! erg.
erf!
hmm...
MCC
SECURITY
Hm?
SECURITY
zzz
So much for needing disguises.

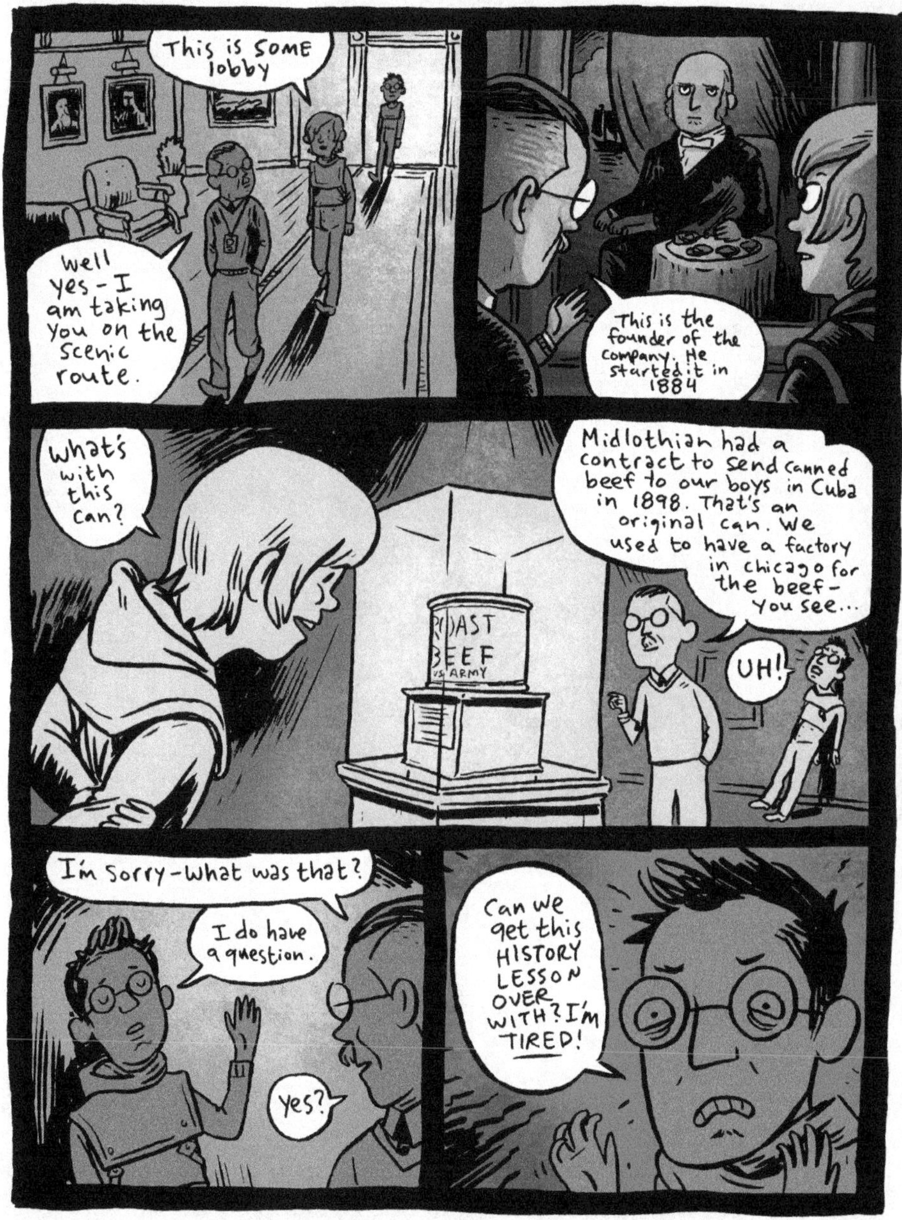
This is SOME lobby
well yes - I am taking you on the scenic route.
This is the founder of the company. He started it in 1884
What's with this can?
Midlothian had a contract to send canned beef to our boys in Cuba in 1898. That's an original can. We used to have a factory in chicago for the beef- You see...
ROAST BEEF US ARMY
UH!
I'm sorry-what was that?
I do have a question.
Yes?
Can we get this HISTORY LESSON OVER WITH? I'M TIRED!

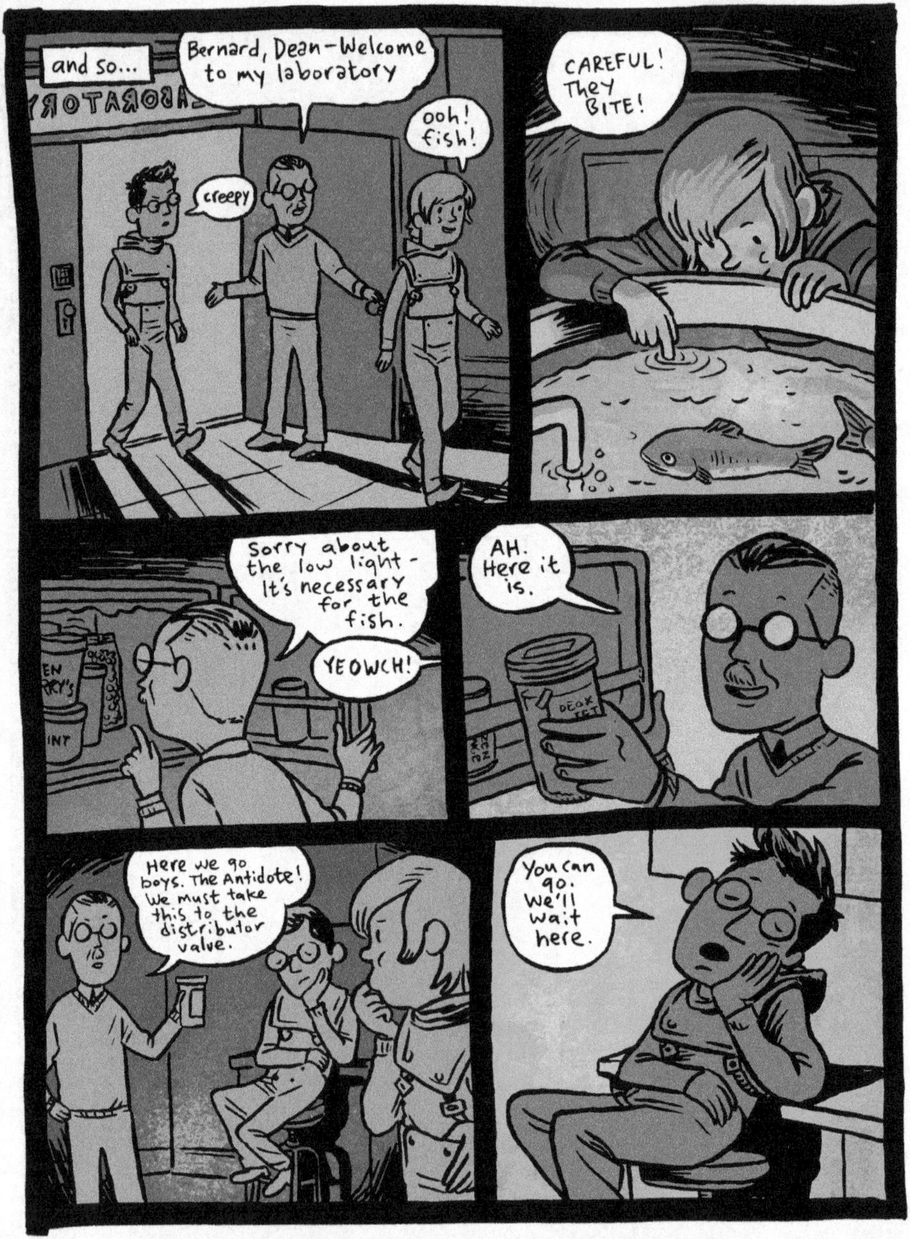
and so...
Bernard, Dean-Welcome to my laboratory
ooh! fish!
creepy
CAREFUL! They BITE!
Sorry about the low light - It's necessary for the fish.
YEOWCH!
AH. Here it is.
Here we go boys. The Antidote! We must take this to the distributor valve.
You can go. We'll wait here.

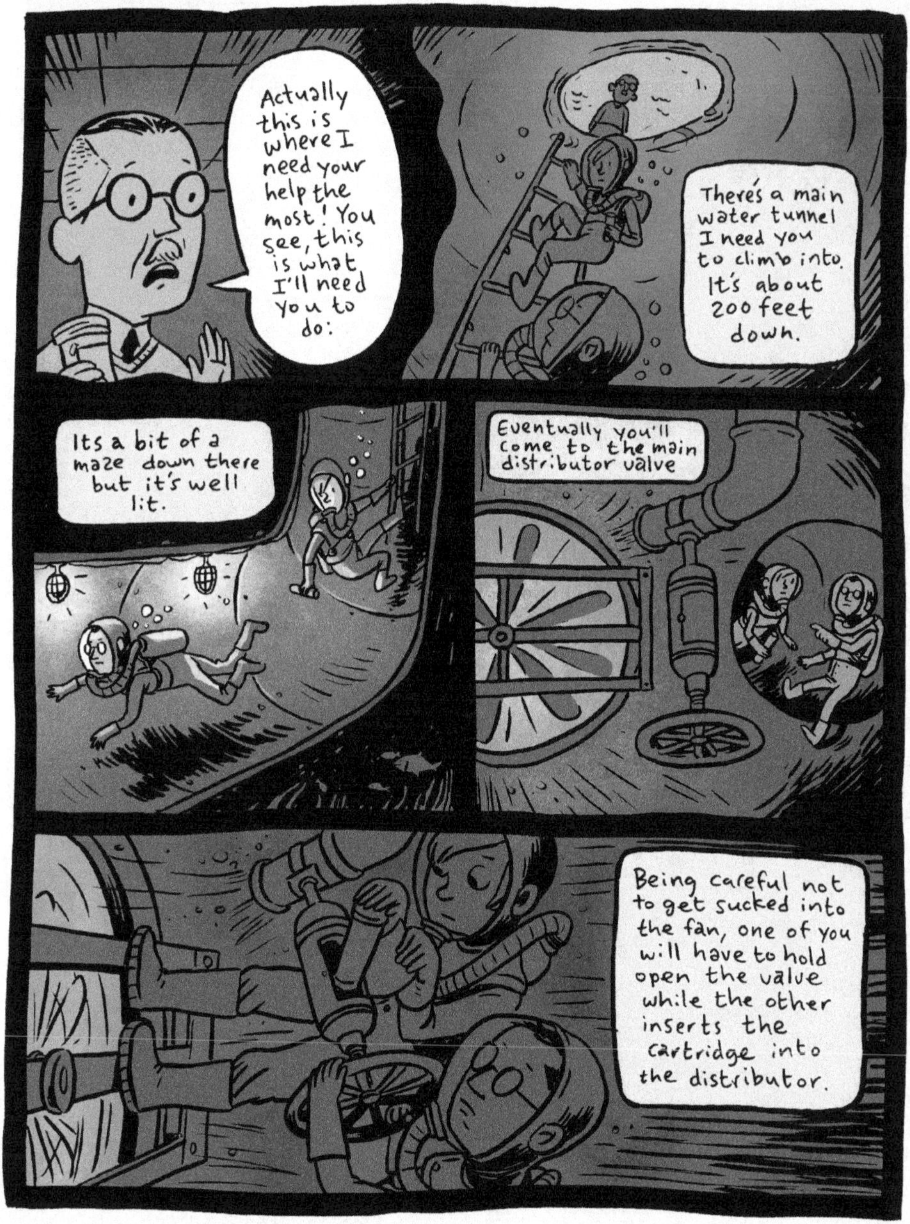
Actually this is where I need your help the most! You see, this is what I'll need you to do:
There's a main water tunnel I need you to climb into. It's about 200 feet down.
Its a bit of a maze down there but it's well lit.
Eventually you'll come to the main distributor valve
Being careful not to get sucked into the fan, one of you will have to hold open the valve while the other inserts the cartridge into the distributor.

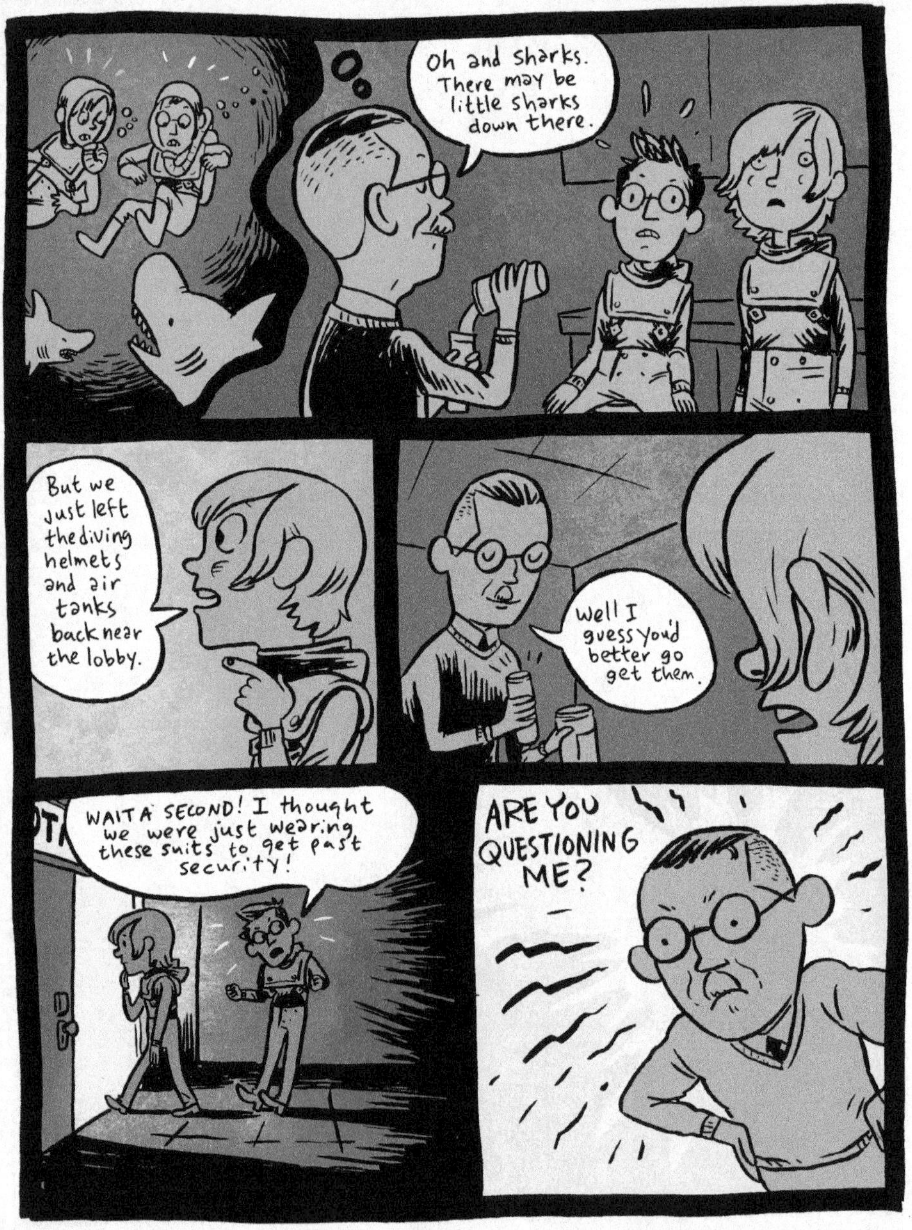
Oh and sharks. There may be little sharks down there.
But we just left the diving helmets and air tanks back near the lobby.
Well I guess you'd better go get them.
WAIT A SECOND! I thought we were just wearing these suits to get past security!
ARE YOU QUESTIONING ME?

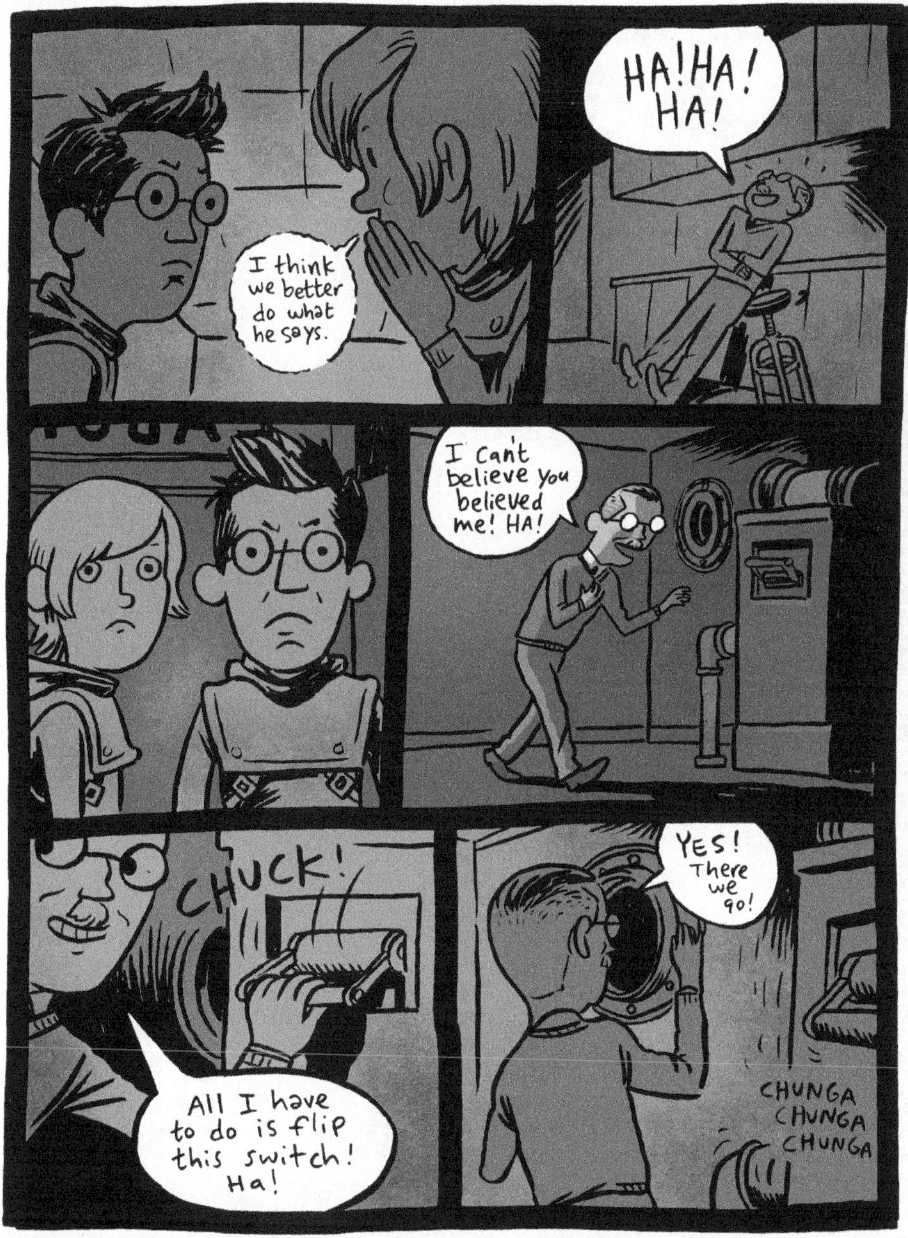
I think we better do what he says.
HA!HA! HA!
I can't believe you believed me! HA!
CHUCK!
All I have to do is flip this switch! Ha!
YES! There we go!
CHUNGA CHUNGA CHUNGA

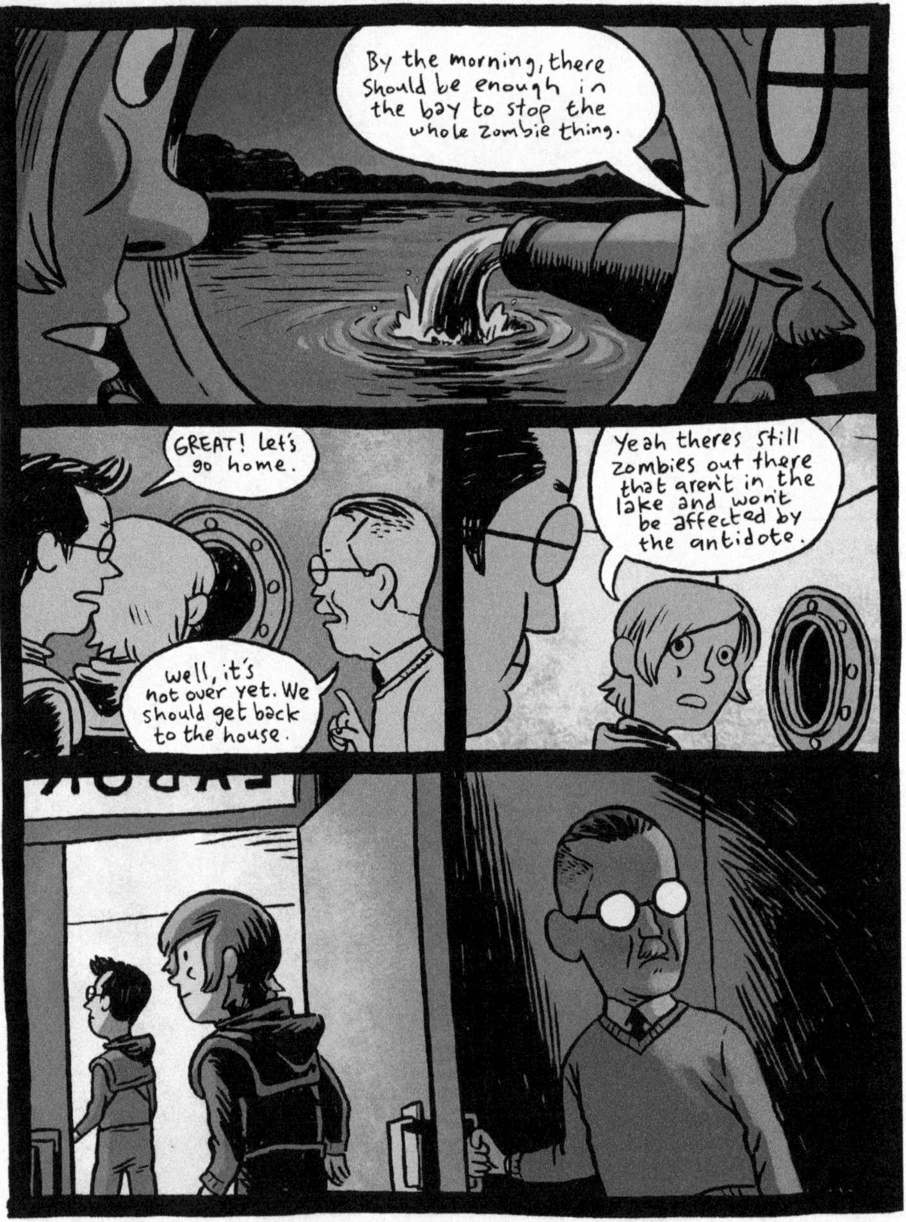

By the morning, there should be enough in the bay to stop the whole zombie thing.
GREAT! Let's go home.
Well, it's not over yet. We should get back to the house.
Yeah theres still zombies out there that aren't in the lake and won't be affected by the antidote.

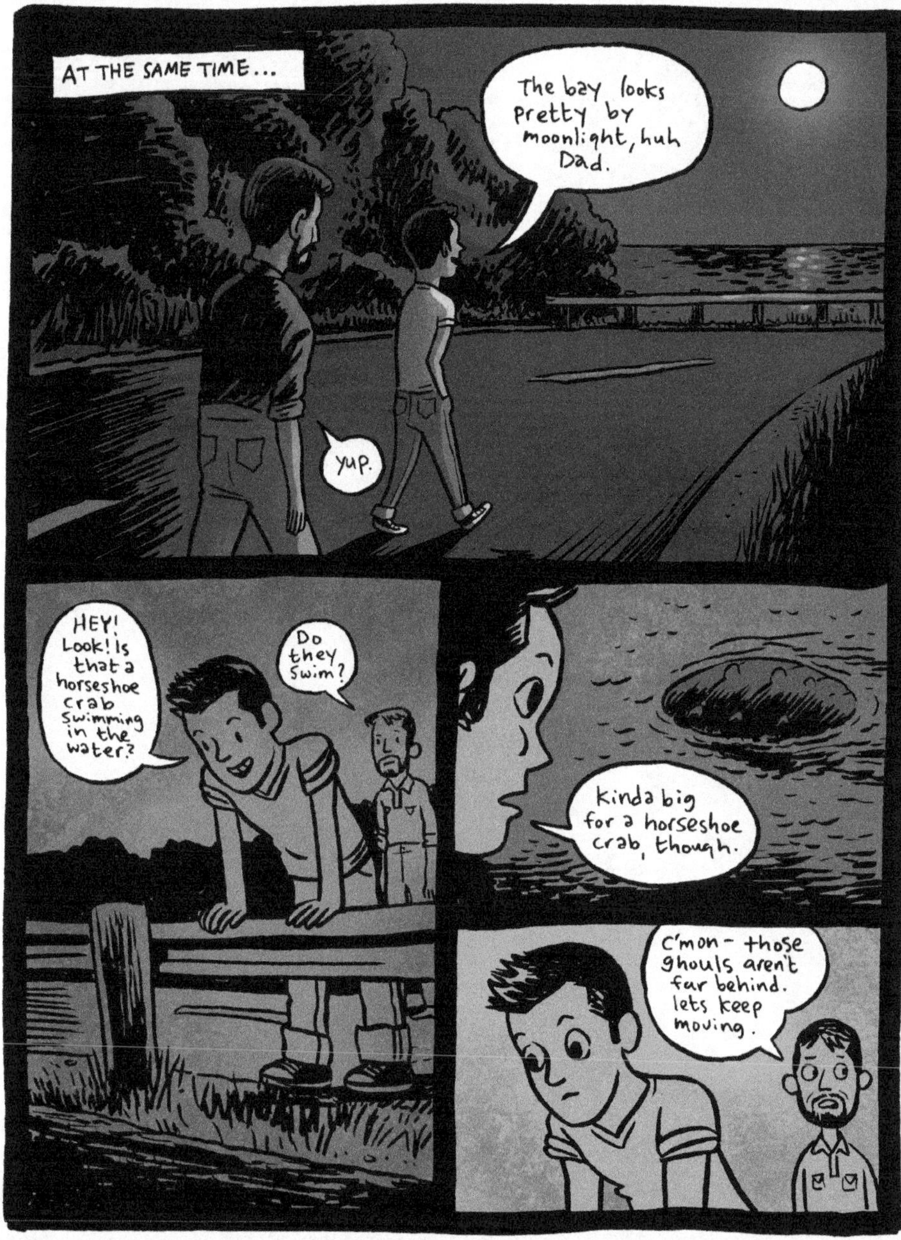
AT THE SAME TIME...
The bay looks pretty by moonlight, huh Dad.
yup.
HEY! Look! Is that a horseshoe crab swimming in the water?
Do they swim?
Kinda big for a horseshoe crab, though.
C'mon - those ghouls aren't far behind. lets keep moving.

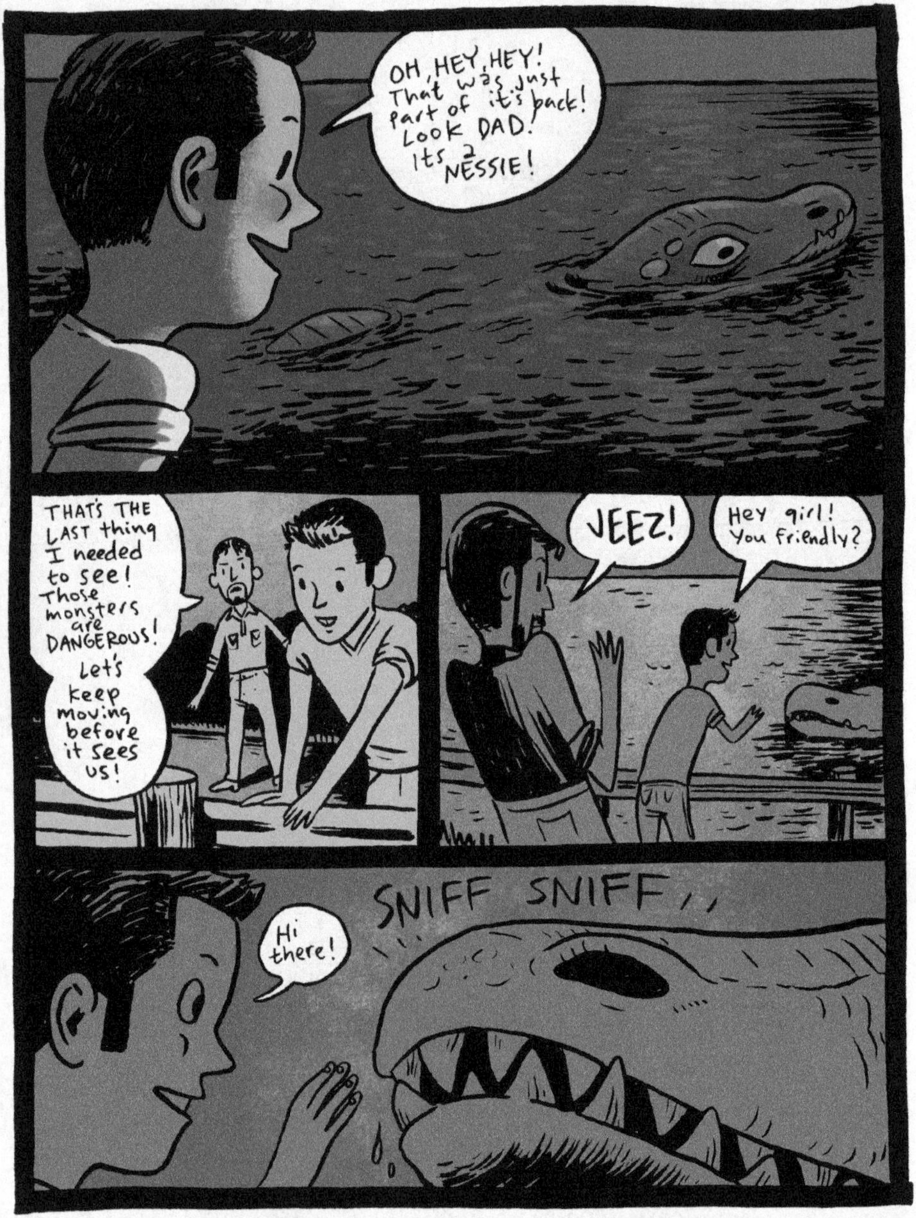
OH, HEY, HEY! That was just part of it's back! LOOK DAD! Its a NESSIE!
THAT'S THE LAST thing I needed to see! Those monsters are DANGEROUS! Let's keep moving before it sees us!
JEEZ!
Hey girl! You friendly?
SNIFF SNIFF
Hi there!

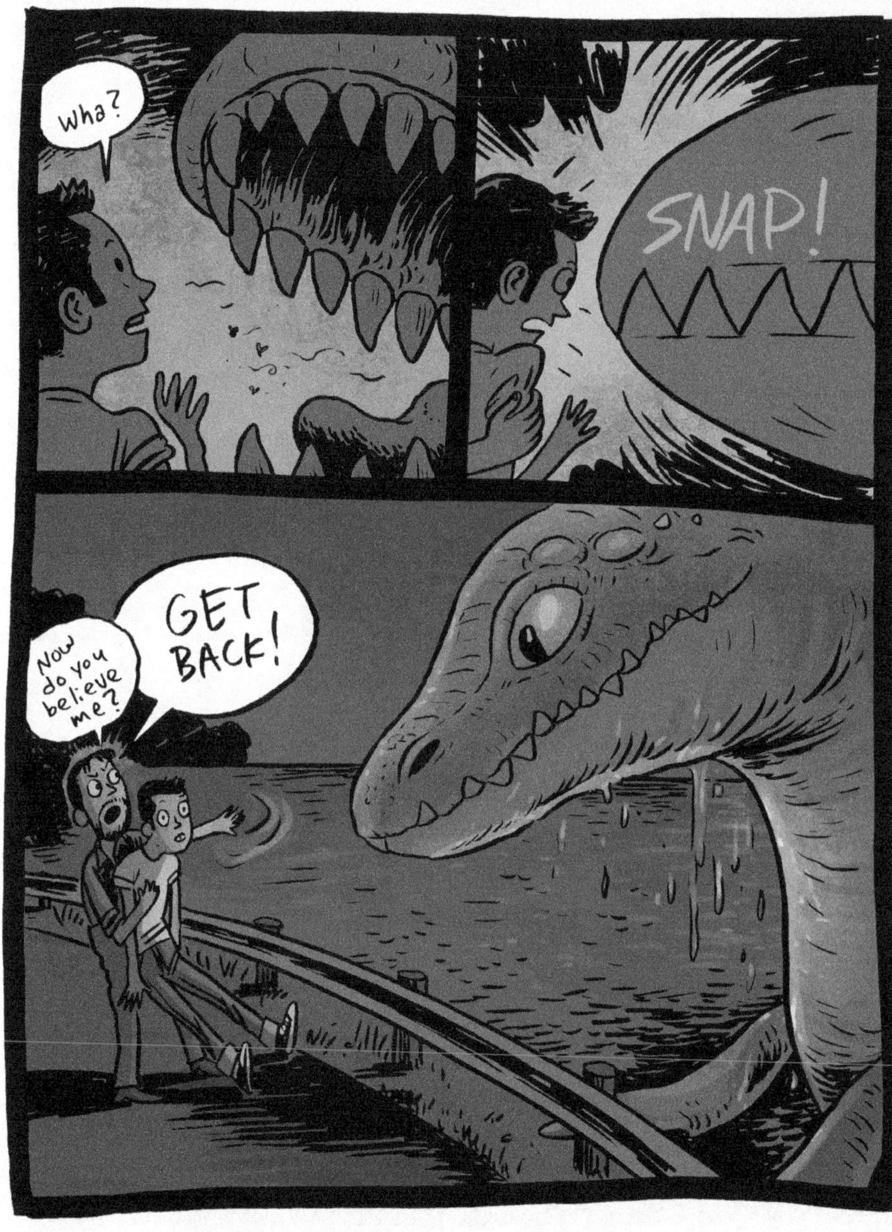
wha?
SNAP!
Now do you believe me?
GET BACK!

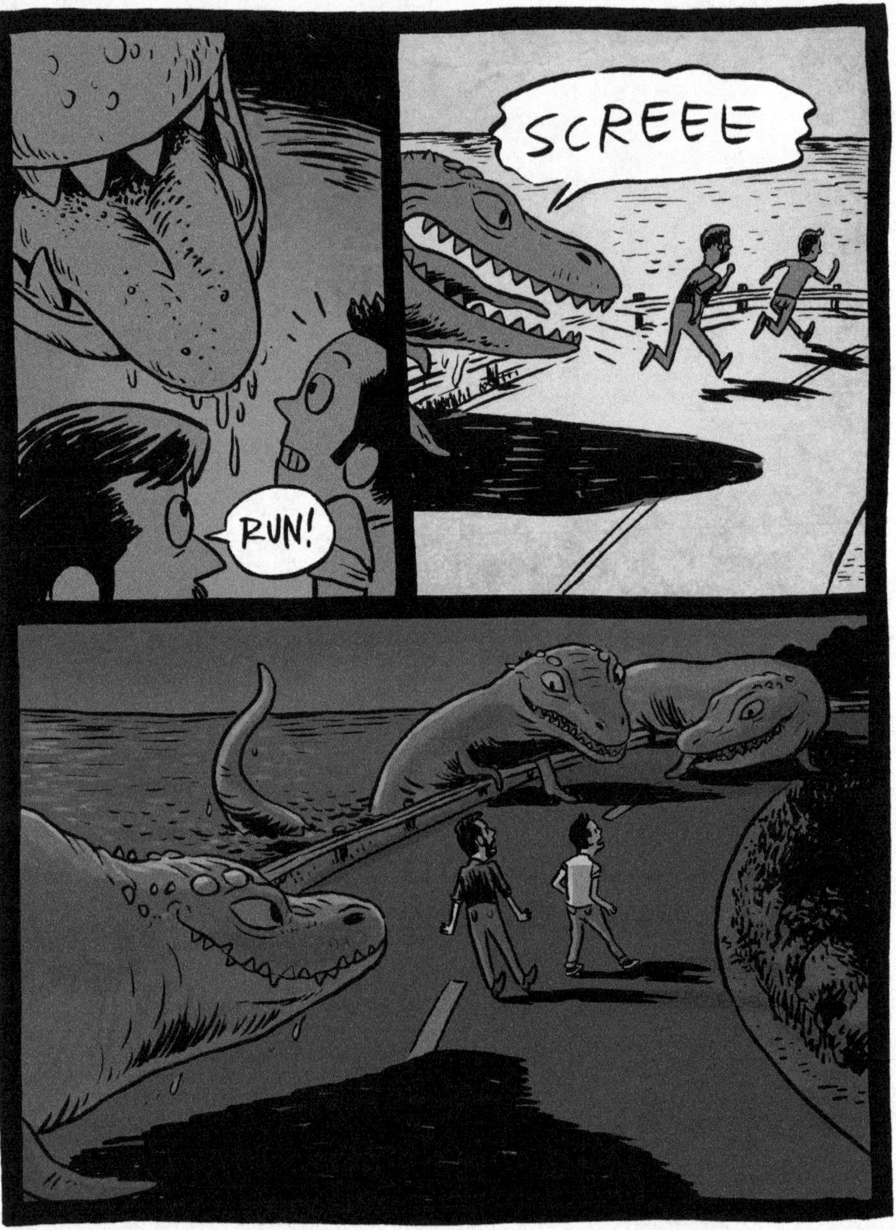
RUN!
SCREEE

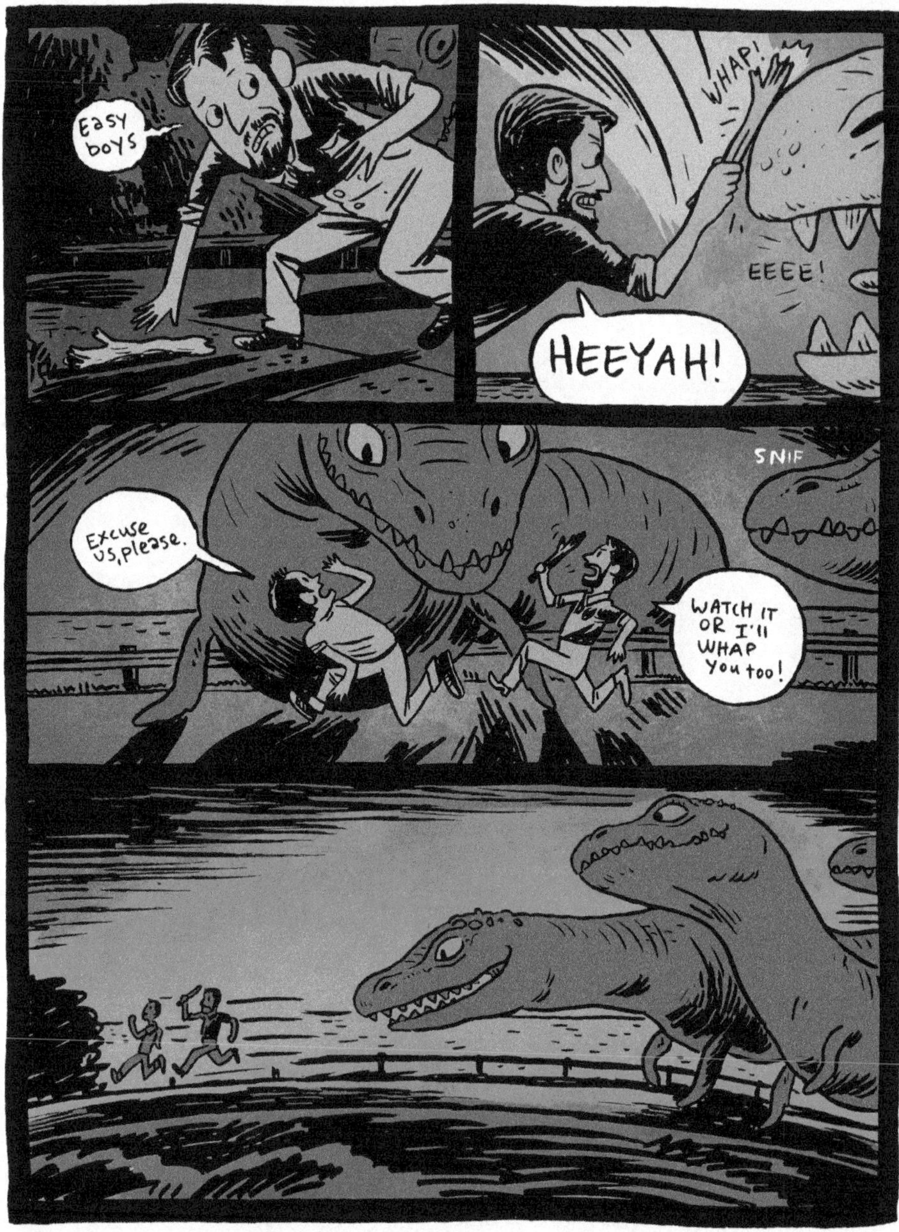
Easy boys
WHAP!
EEEE!
HEEYAH!
SNIF
Excuse us, please.
WATCH IT OR I'll WHAP you too!

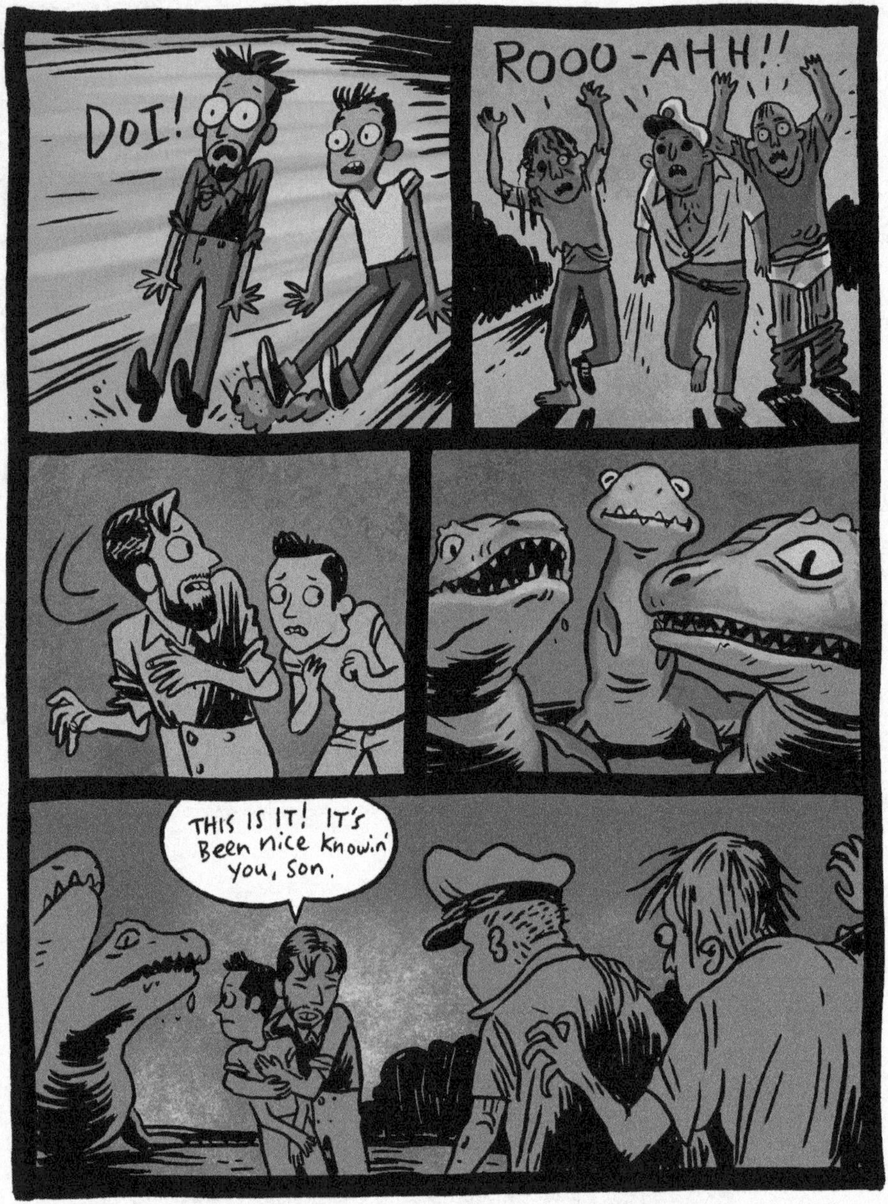
DOI!
ROOO-AHH!!
THIS IS IT! IT'S Been nice knowin' you, son.

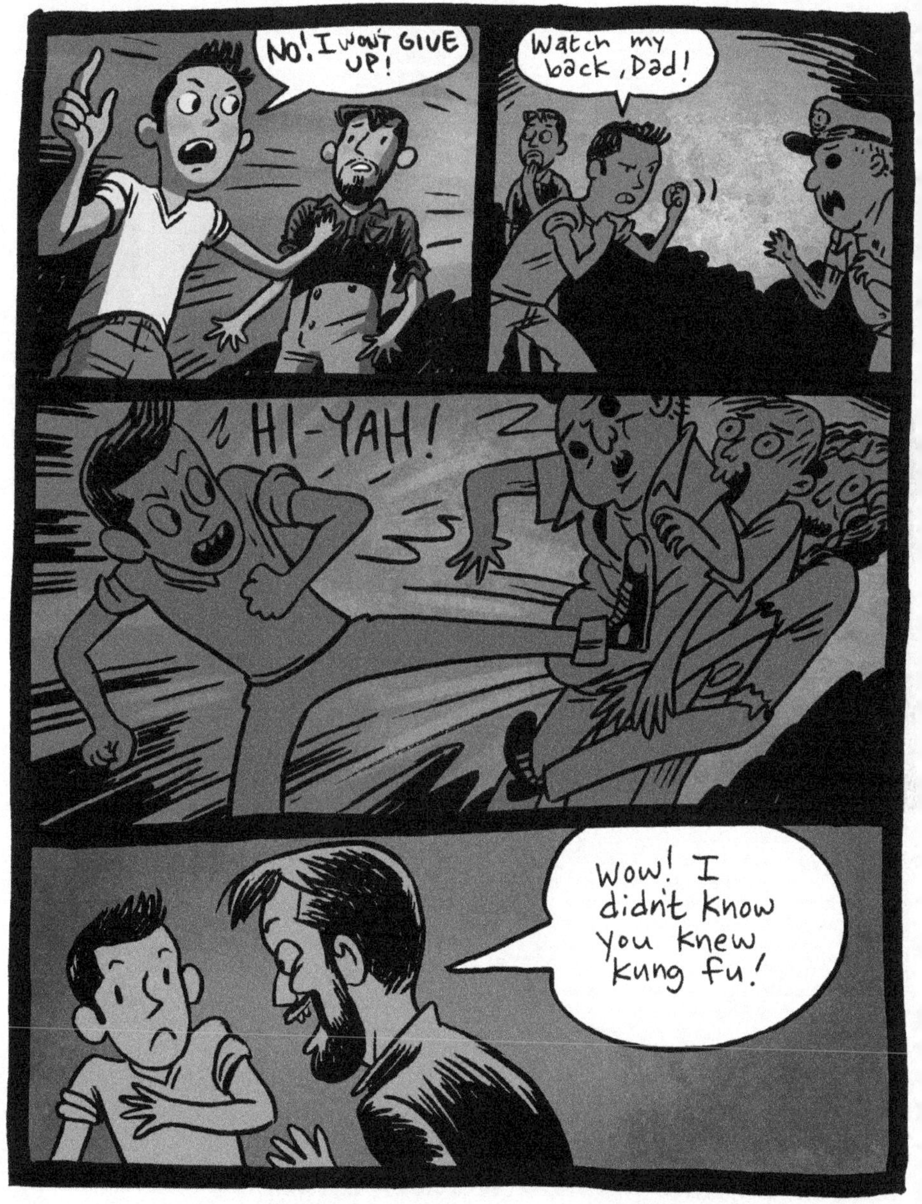
NO! I WON'T GIVE UP!
Watch my back, Dad!
HI-YAH!
Wow! I didn't know you knew kung fu!

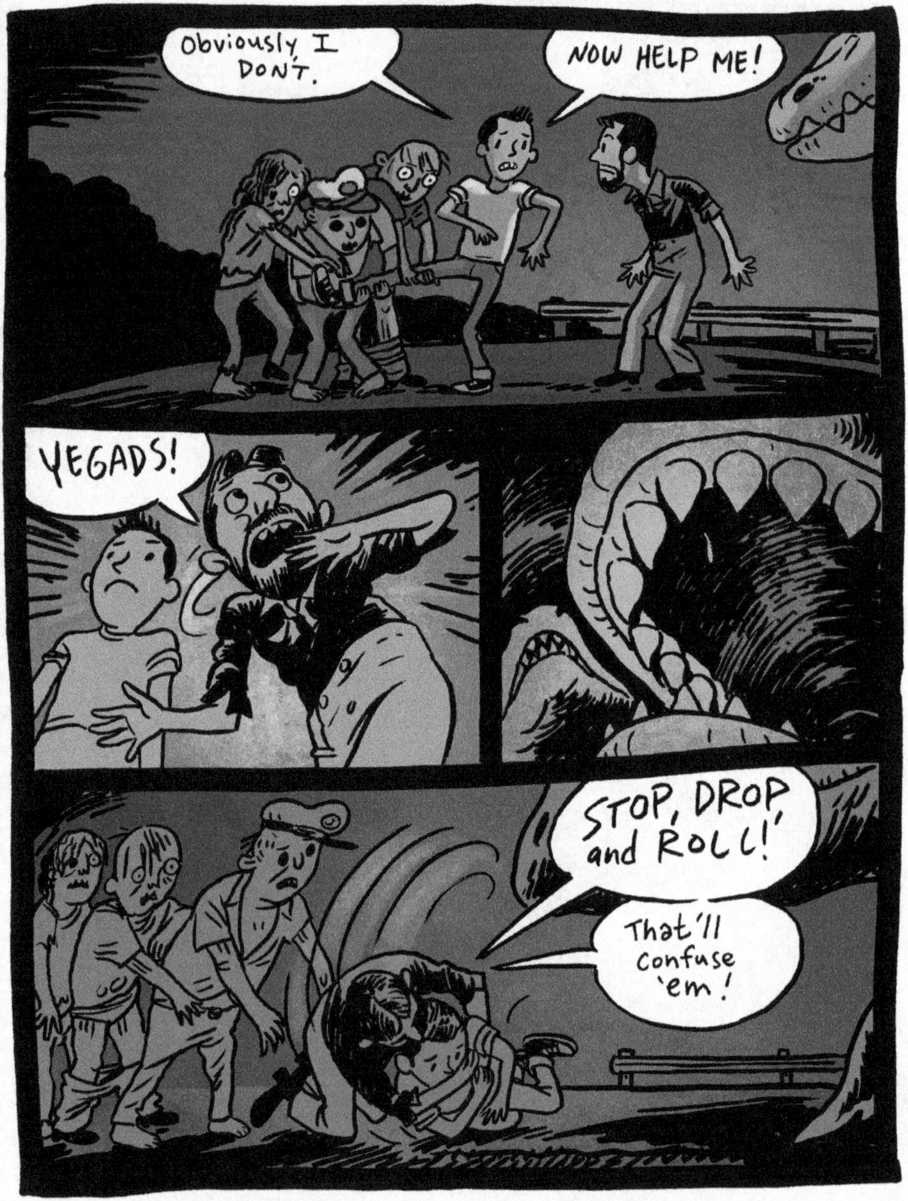
Obviously I DON'T.
NOW HELP ME!
YEGADS!
STOP, DROP, and ROLL!
That'll confuse 'em!

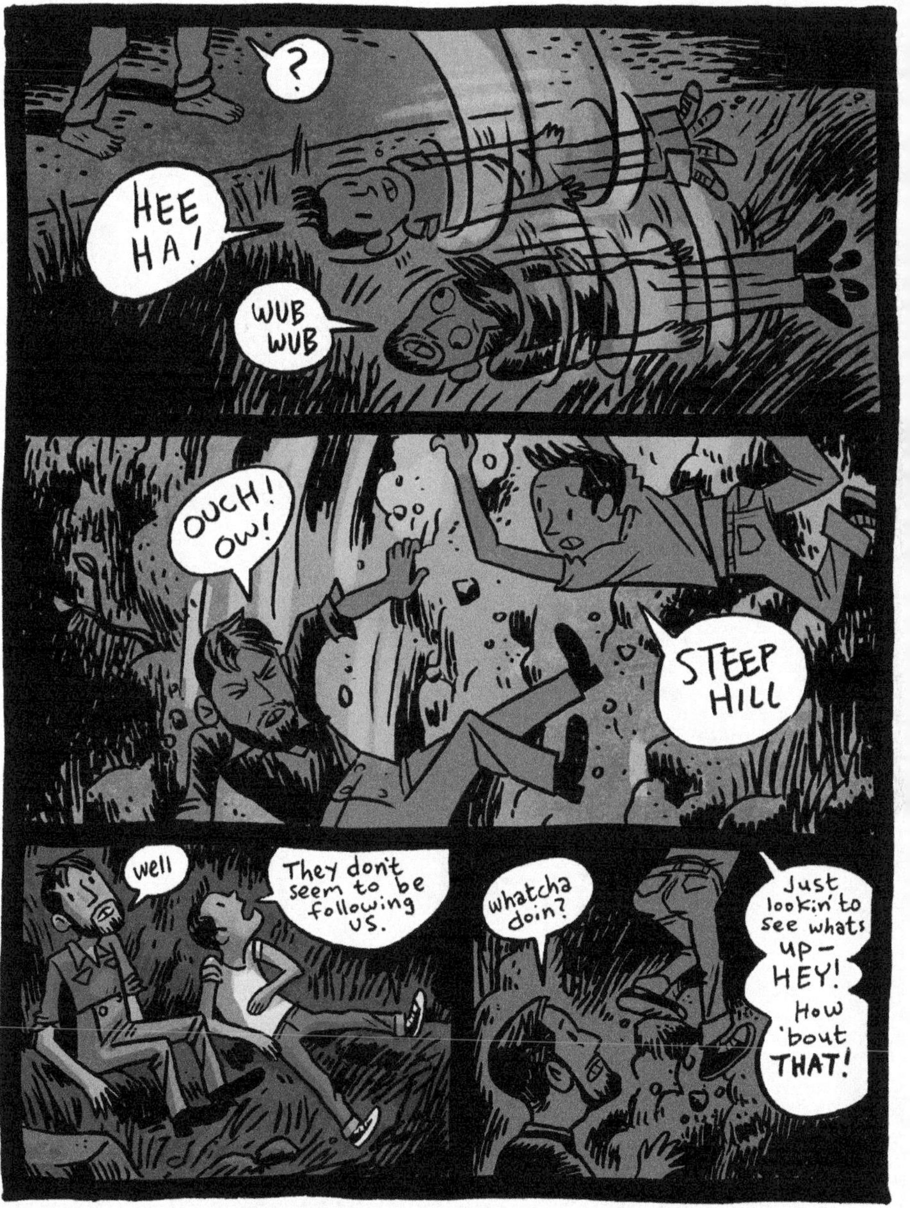
?
HEE HA!
WUB WUB
OUCH! OW!
STEEP HILL
well
They don't seem to be following us.
whatcha doin?
Just lookin' to see whats up— HEY! How 'bout THAT!

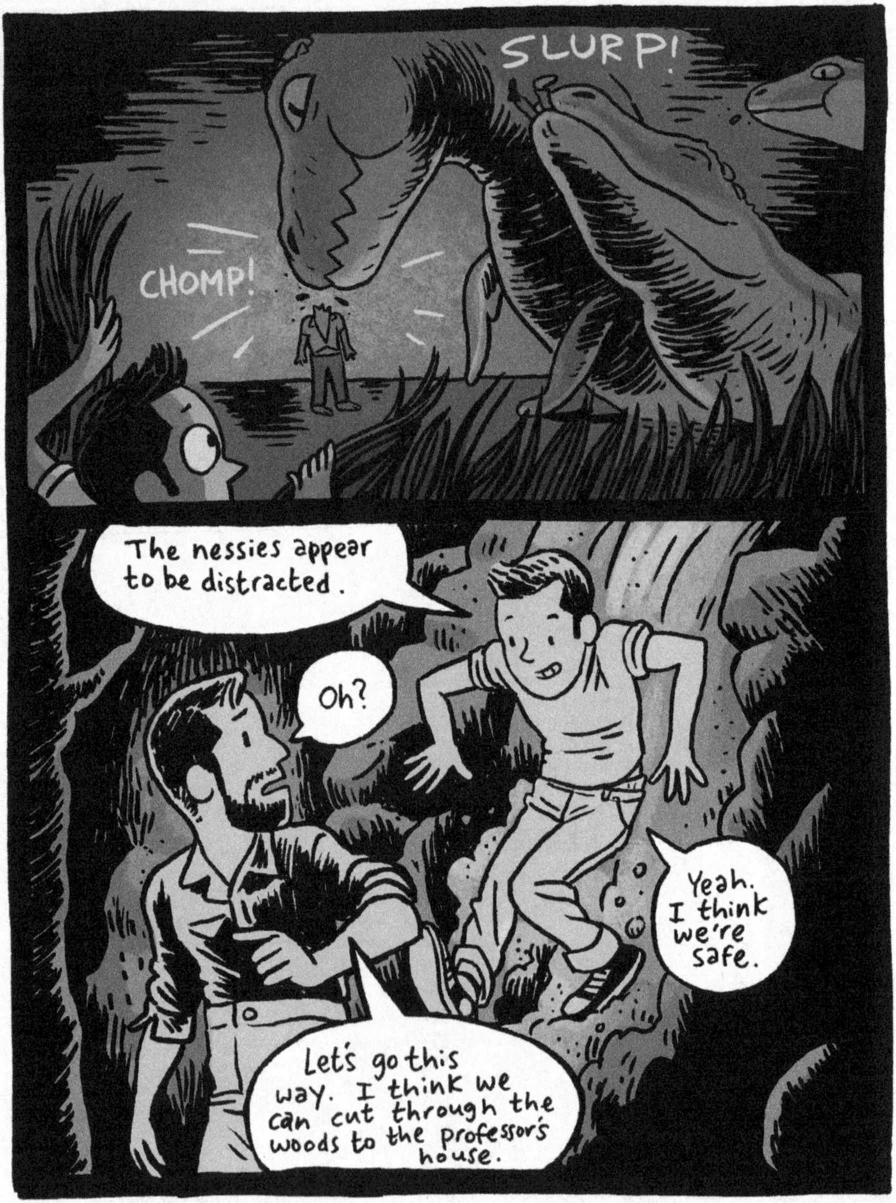
SLURP!
CHOMP!
The nessies appear to be distracted.
Oh?
Yeah. I think we're safe.
Let's go this way. I think we can cut through the woods to the professor's house.

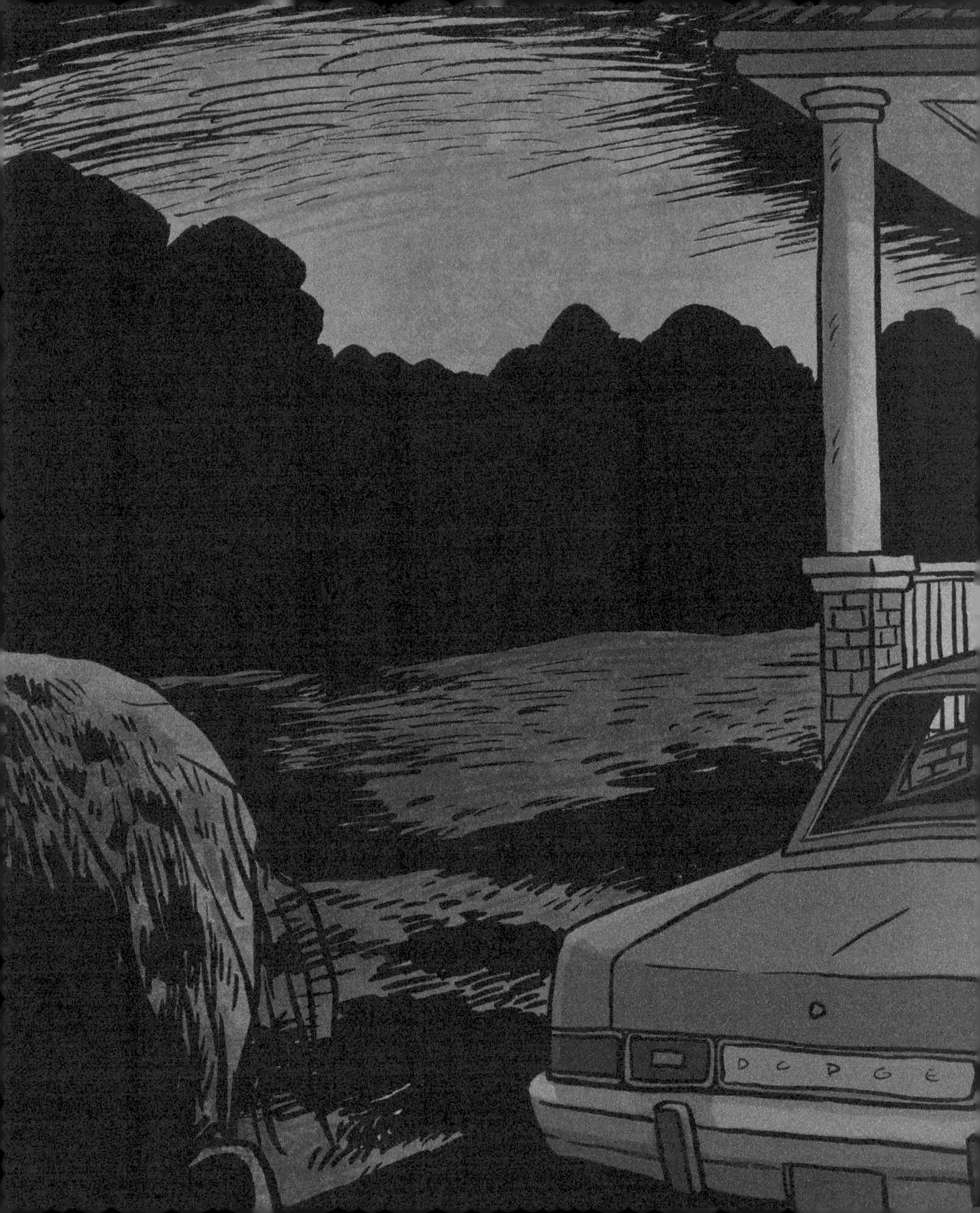
DODGE

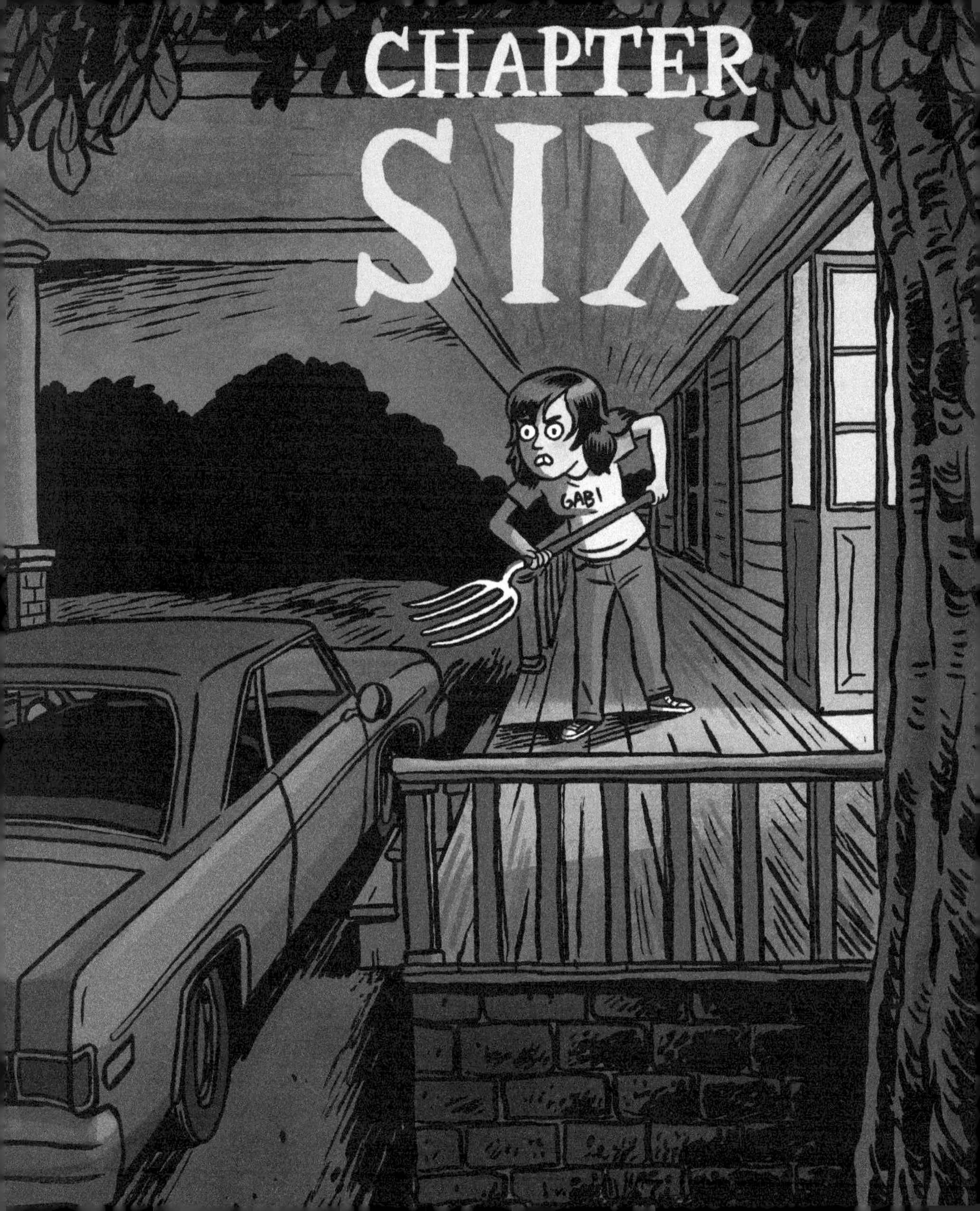
CHAPTER
SIX
GABI

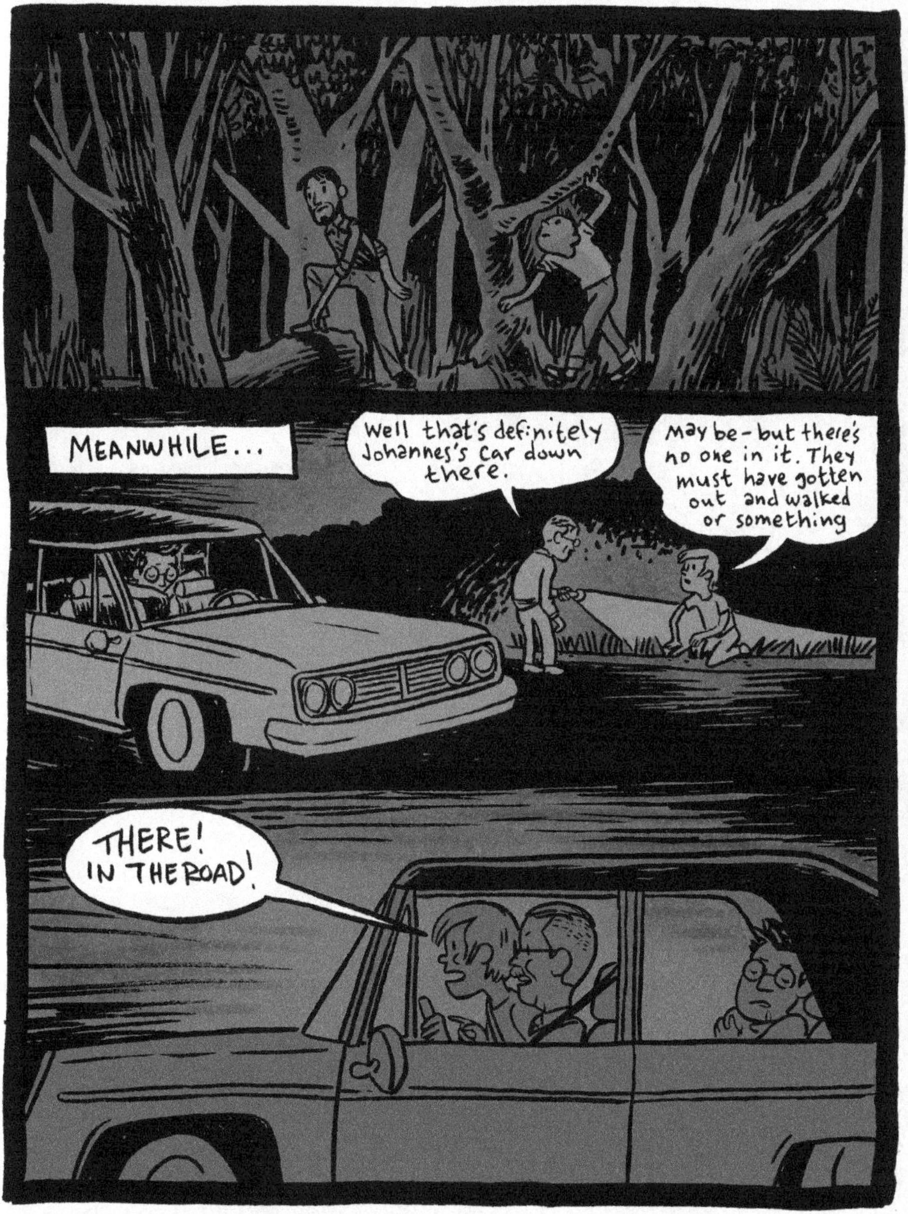
MEANWHILE...
Well that's definitely Johannes's car down there.
Maybe - but there's no one in it. They must have gotten out and walked or something
THERE! IN THE ROAD!

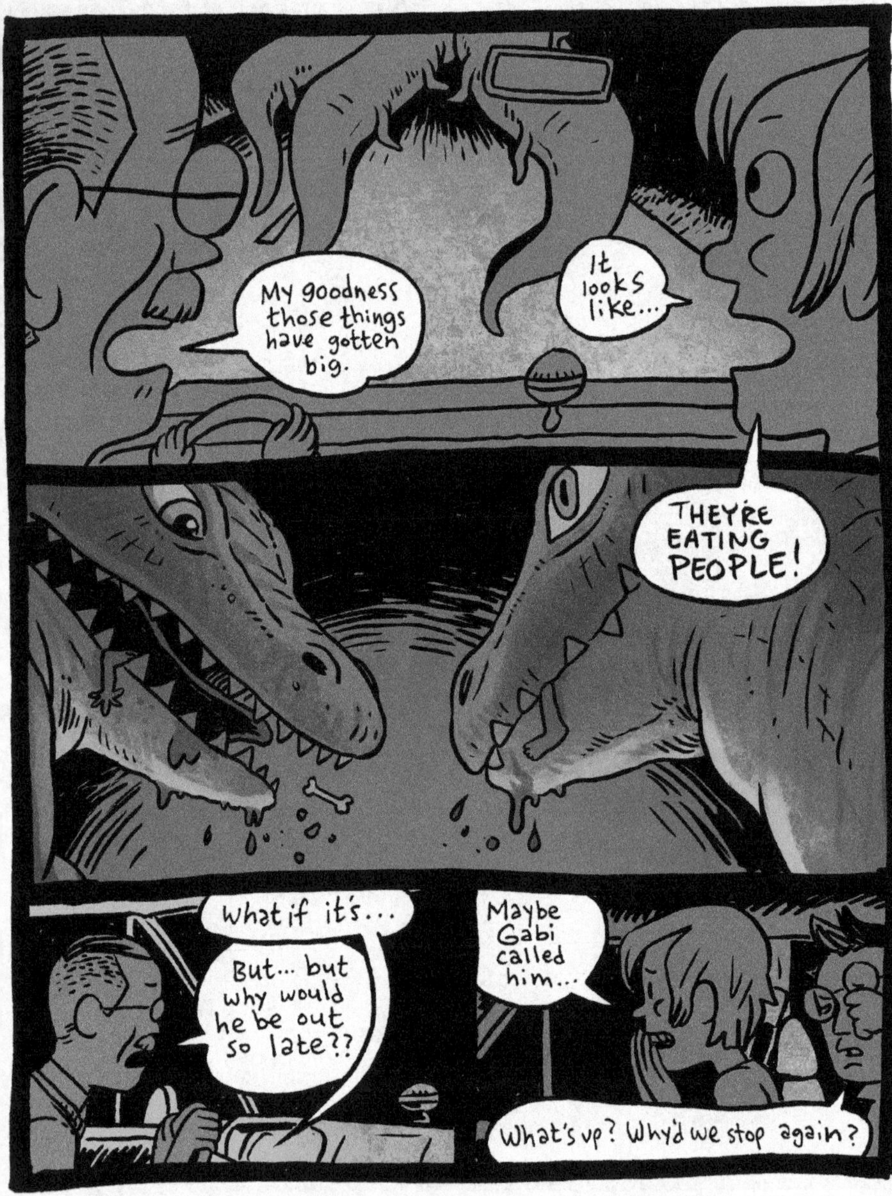
My goodness those things have gotten big.
It looks like...
THEY'RE EATING PEOPLE!
What if it's...
But... but why would he be out so late??
Maybe Gabi called him...
What's up? Why'd we stop again?

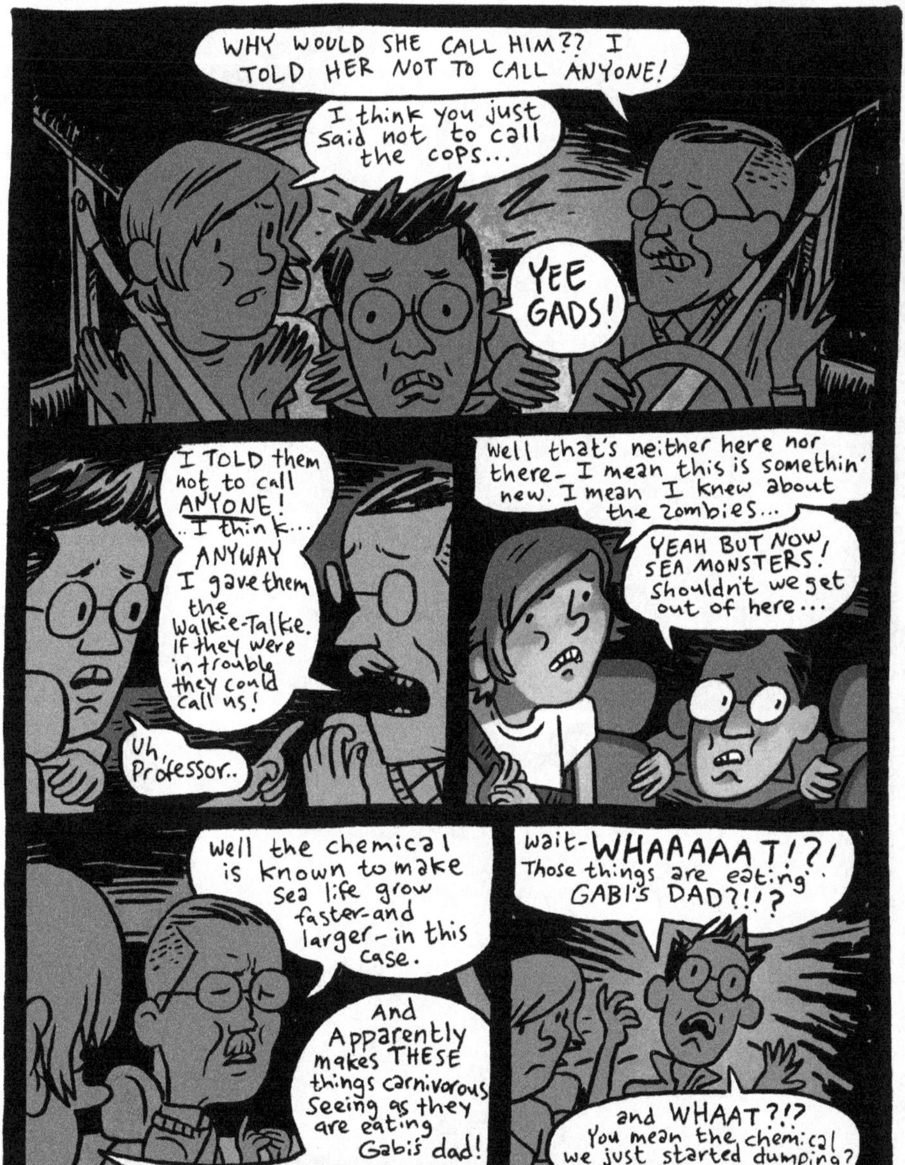
WHY WOULD SHE CALL HIM?? I TOLD HER NOT TO CALL ANYONE!
I think you just said not to call the cops...
YEE GADS!
I TOLD them not to call ANYONE! ..I think... ANYWAY I gave them the Walkie-Talkie. If they were in trouble they could call us!
Uh, Professor..
Well that's neither here nor there- I mean this is somethin' new. I mean I knew about the zombies...
YEAH BUT NOW, SEA MONSTERS! Shouldn't we get out of here...
Well the chemical is known to make sea life grow faster-and larger- in this case.
And Apparently makes THESE things carnivorous seeing as they are eating Gabi's dad!
wait-WHAAAAAT!?! Those things are eating GABI'S DAD?!!?
and WHAAT?!? You mean the chemical we just started dumping?

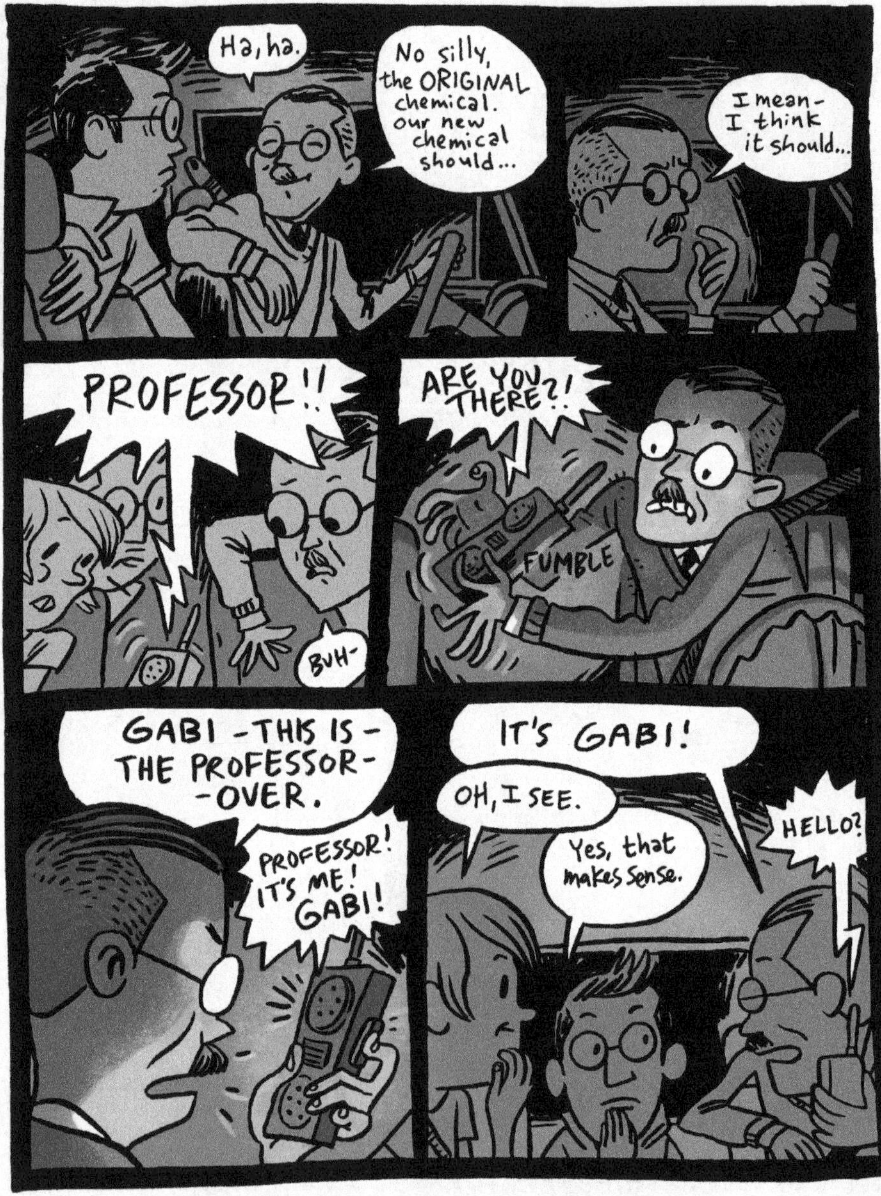

Ha, ha.
No silly, the ORIGINAL chemical. our new chemical should...
I mean- I think it should...
PROFESSOR!!
BUH-
ARE YOU THERE?!
FUMBLE
GABI -THIS IS- THE PROFESSOR- -OVER.
PROFESSOR! IT'S ME! GABI!
IT'S GABI!
OH, I SEE.
Yes, that makes Sense.
HELLO?

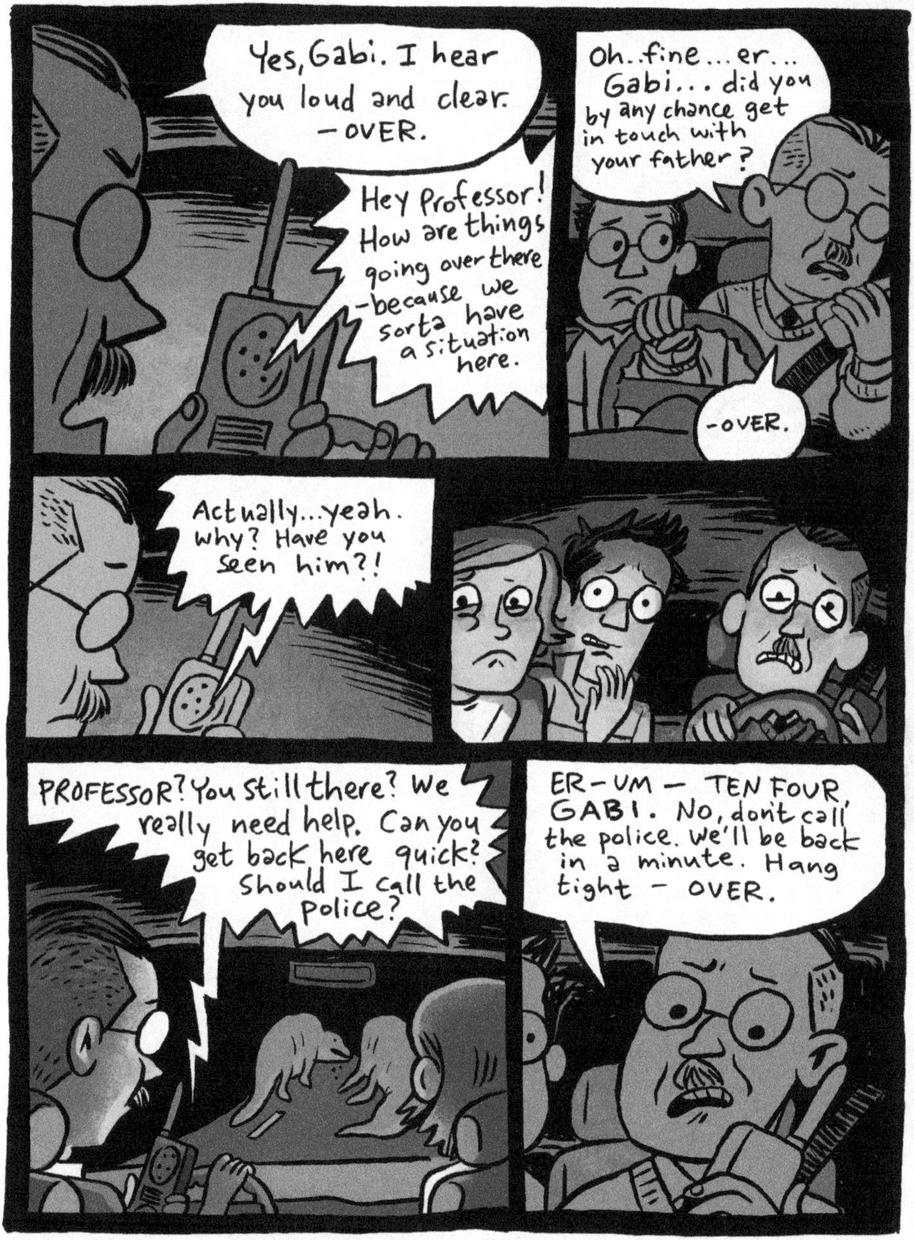
Yes, Gabi. I hear you loud and clear. —OVER.
Hey Professor! How are things going over there —because we sorta have a situation here.
Oh..fine... er... Gabi... did you by any chance get in touch with your father?
—OVER.
Actually...yeah. Why? Have you seen him?!
PROFESSOR? You still there? We really need help. Can you get back here quick? Should I call the police?
ER—UM — TEN FOUR, GABI. No, don't call the police. We'll be back in a minute. Hang tight — OVER.

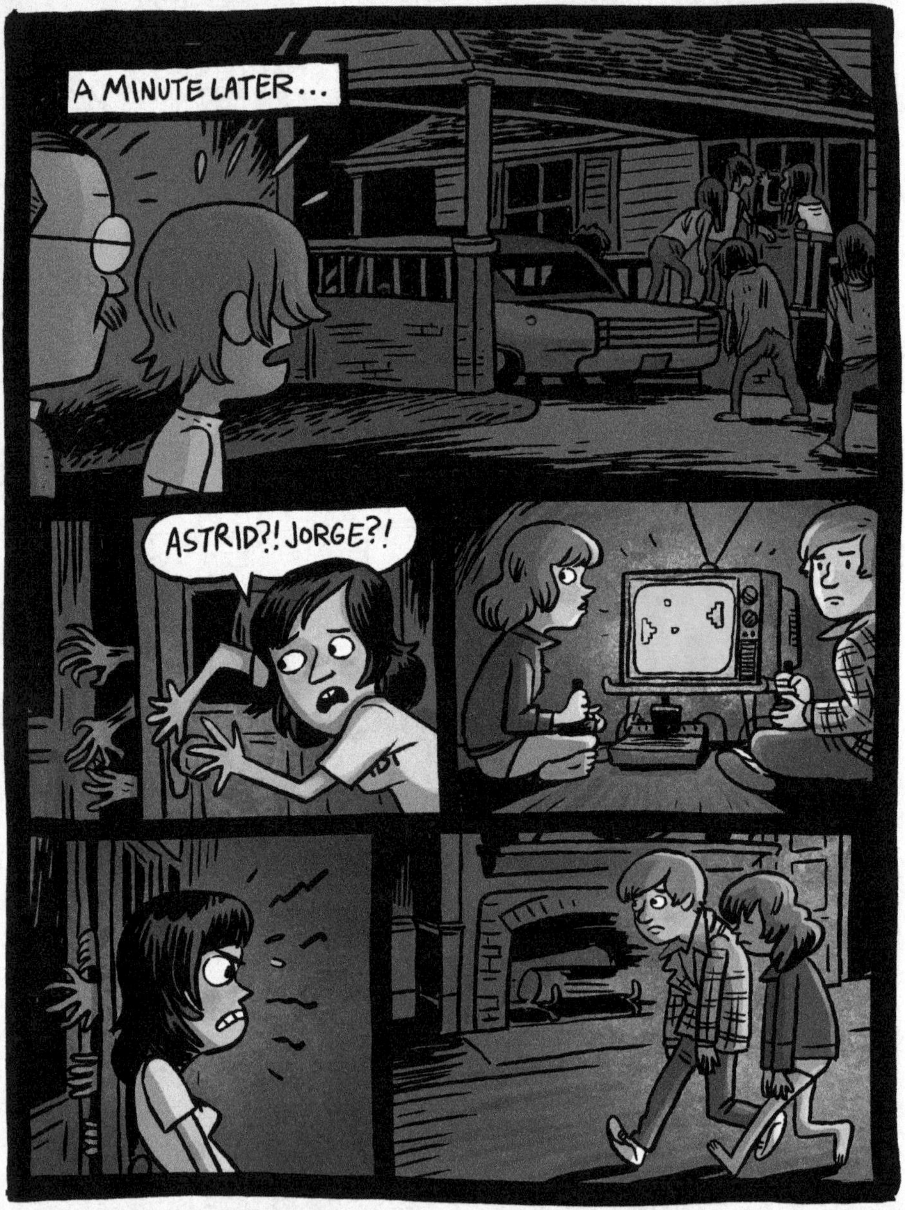
A MINUTE LATER...
ASTRID?! JORGE?!

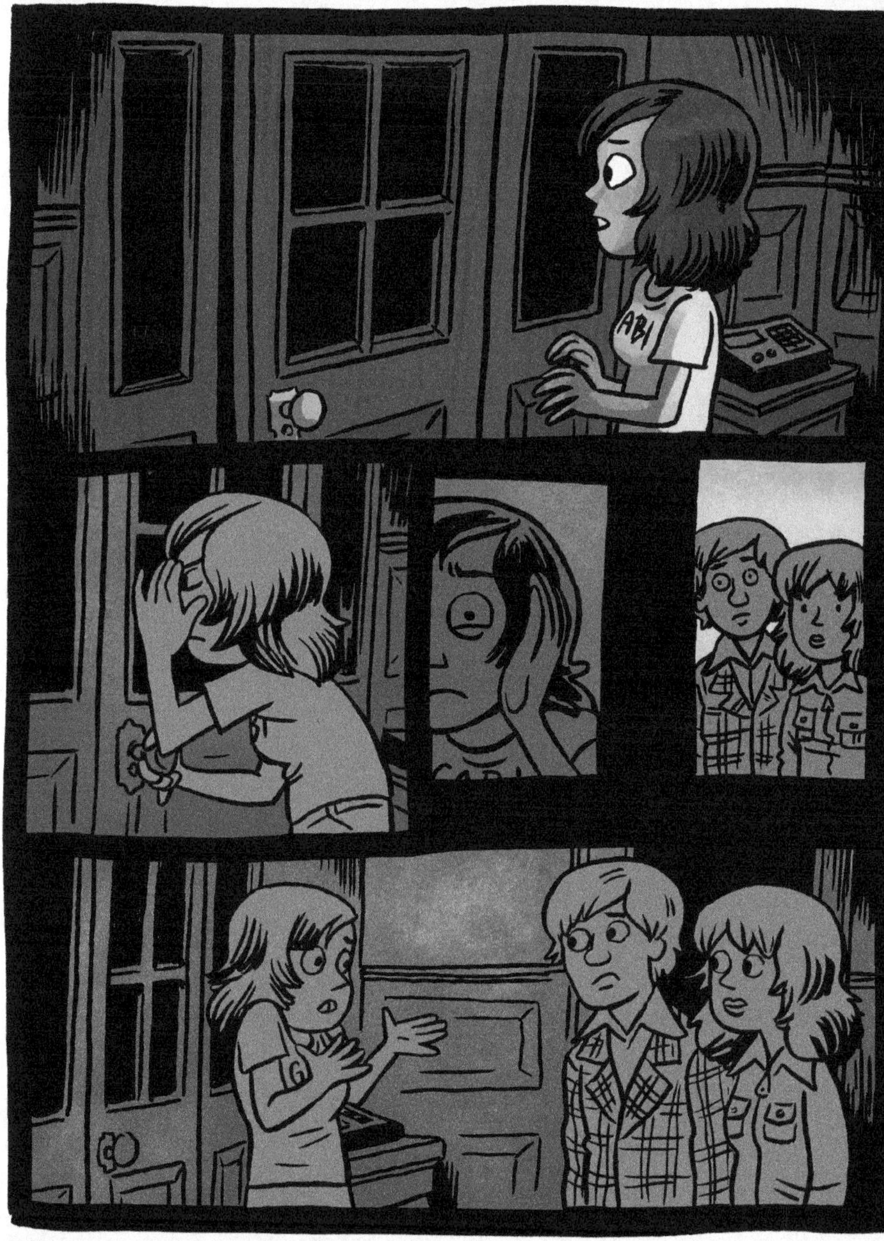
ABI

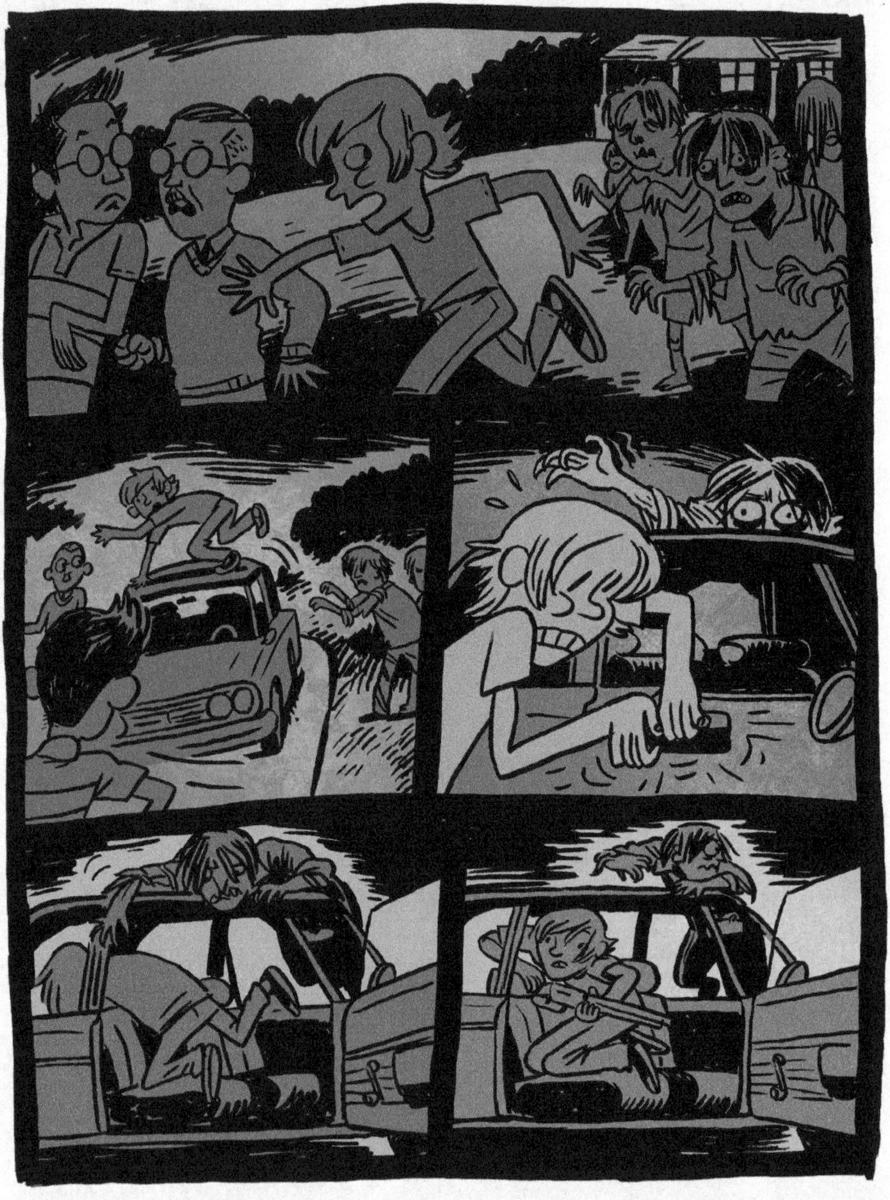

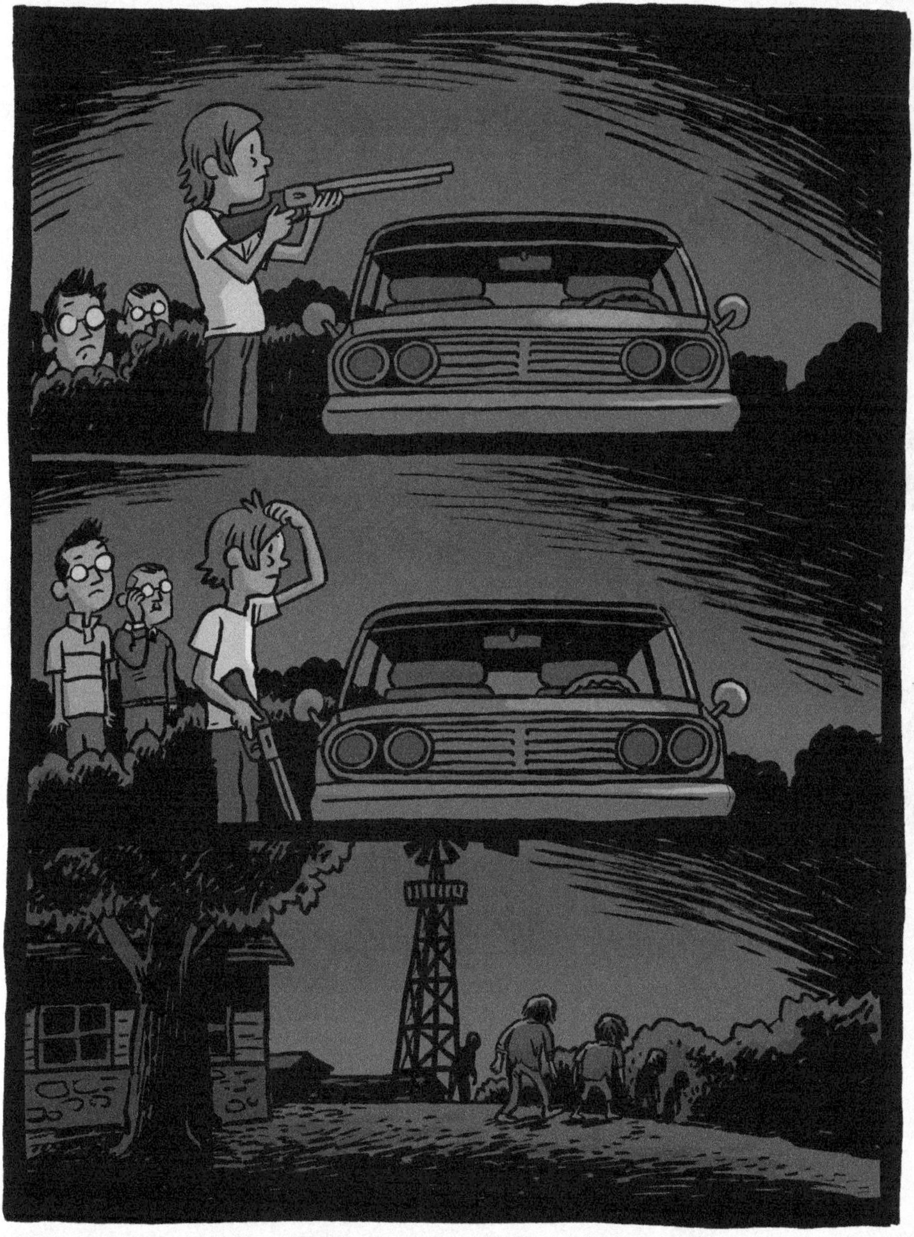

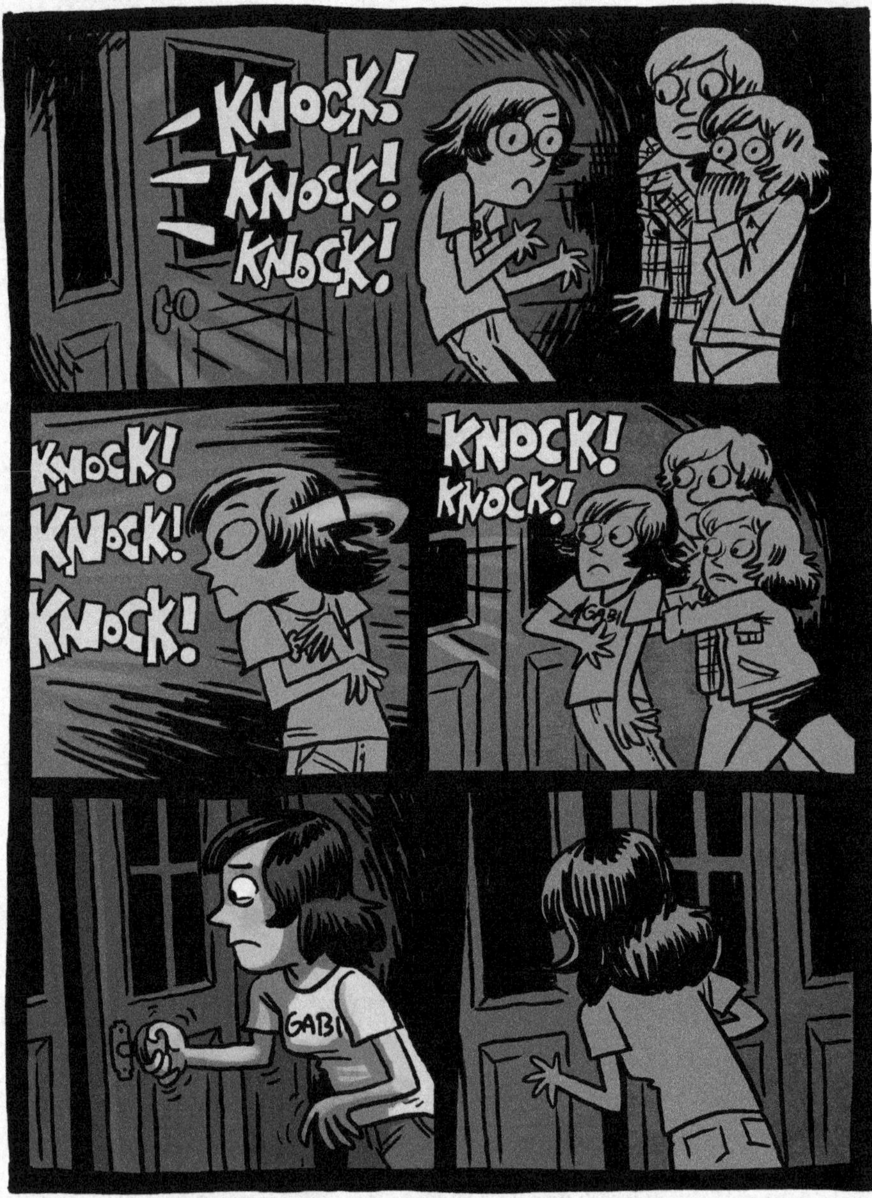
KNOCK!
KNOCK!
KNOCK!
KNOCK!
KNOCK!
KNOCK!
KNOCK!
KNOCK!
GABI
GABI

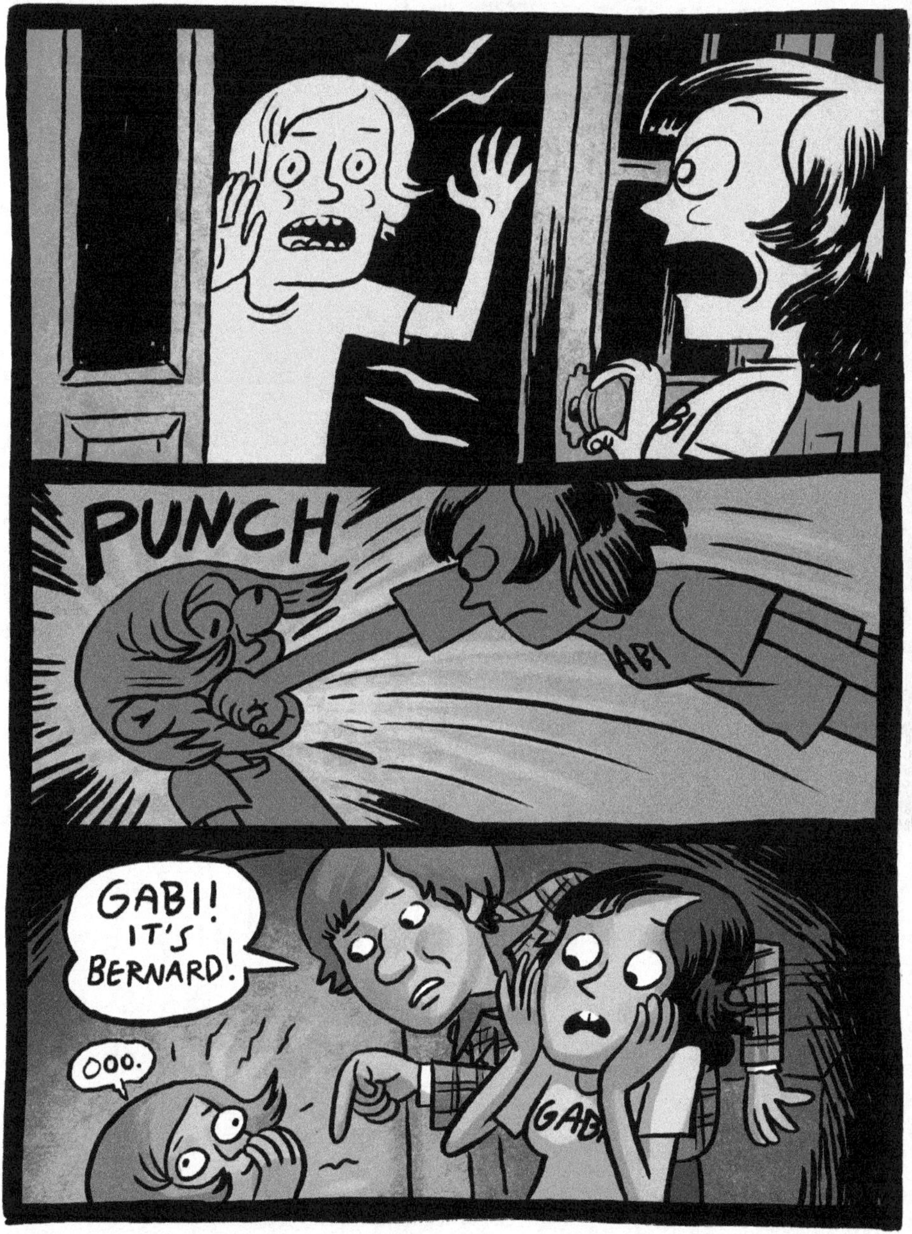
PUNCH
GABI! IT'S BERNARD!
OOO.

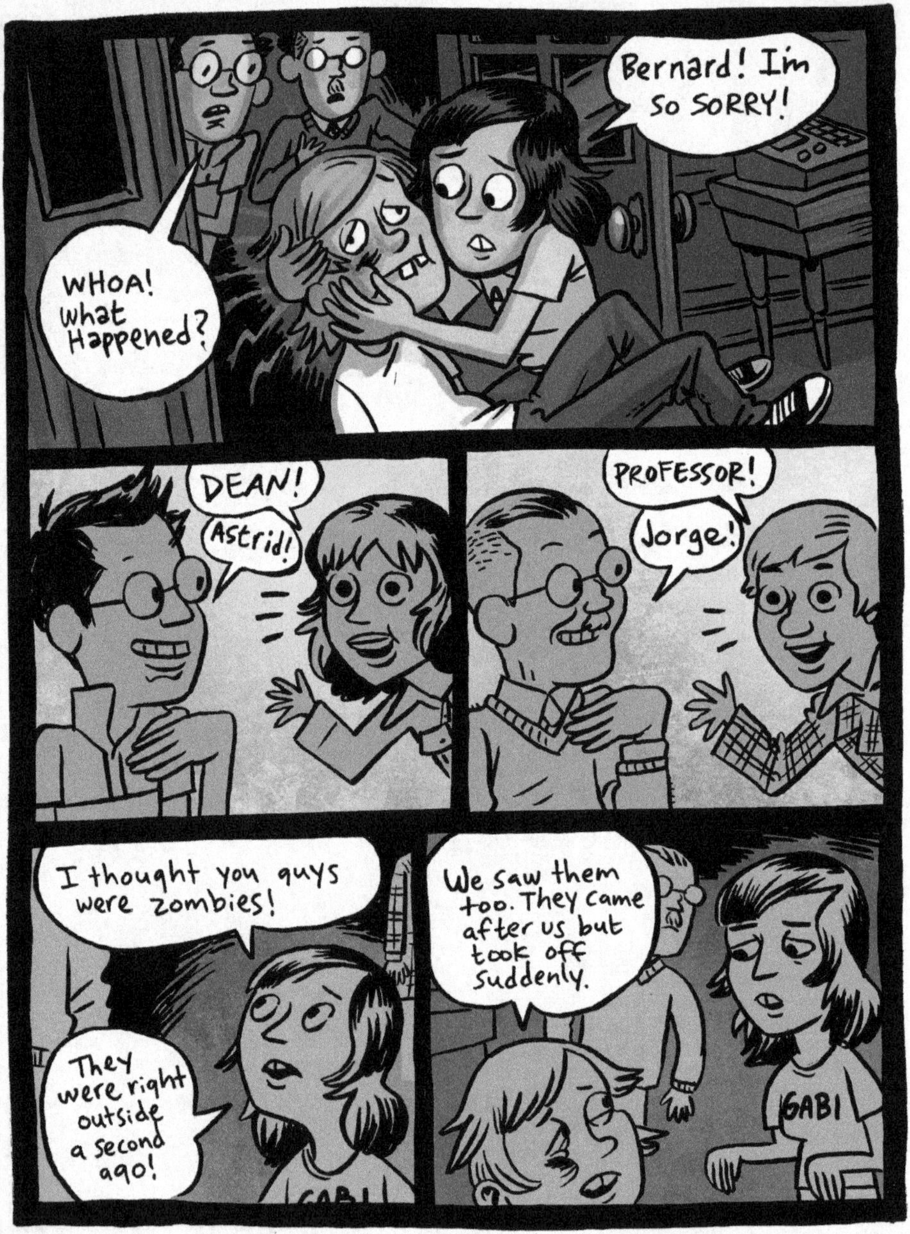
Bernard! I'm so SORRY!
WHOA! What Happened?
DEAN!
Astrid!
PROFESSOR!
Jorge!
I thought you guys were zombies!
They were right outside a second ago!
We saw them too. They came after us but took off suddenly.
GABI

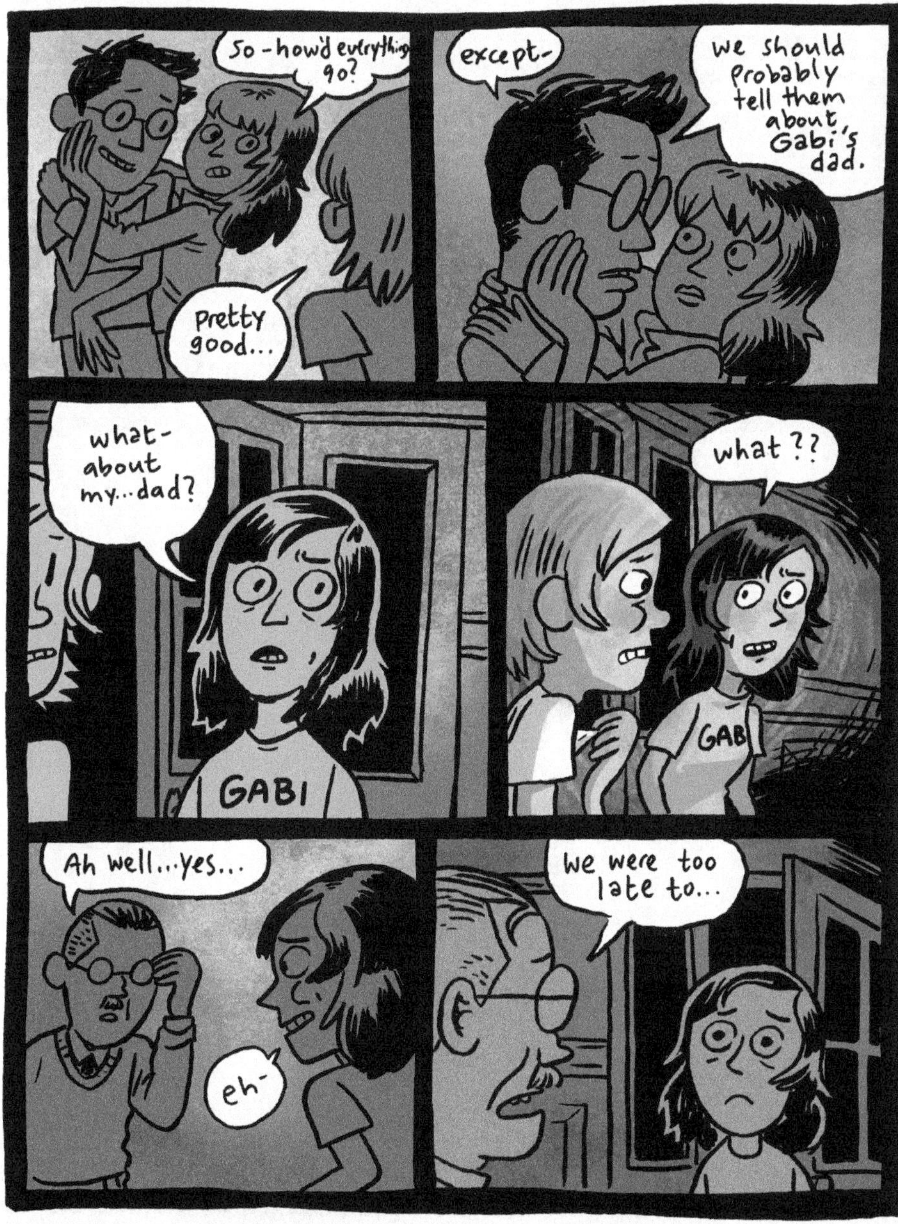
So - how'd everything go?
Pretty good...
except-
we should probably tell them about, Gabi's dad.
what- about my...dad?
GABI
what??
GAB
Ah well...yes...
eh-
We were too late to...

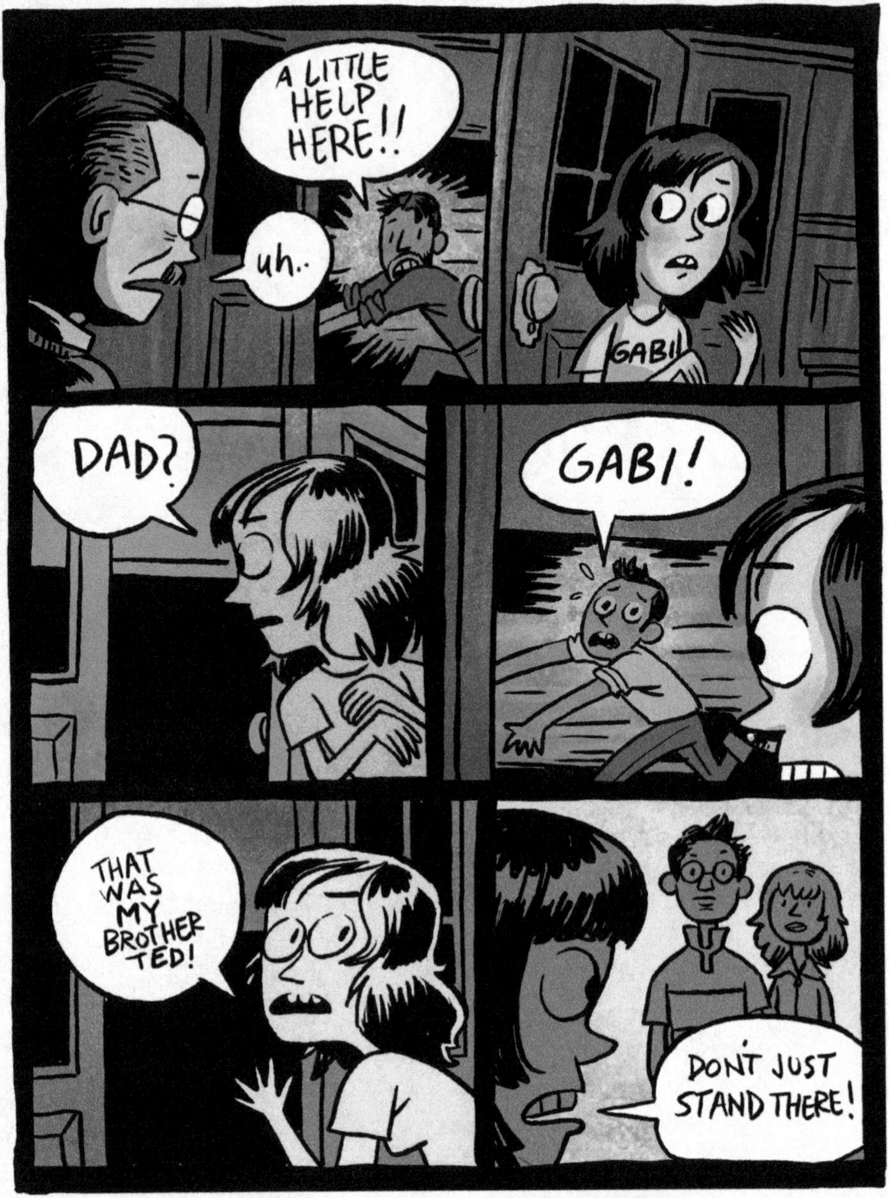
A LITTLE HELP HERE!!
uh..
GABI
DAD?
GABI!
THAT WAS MY BROTHER TED!
DON'T JUST STAND THERE!

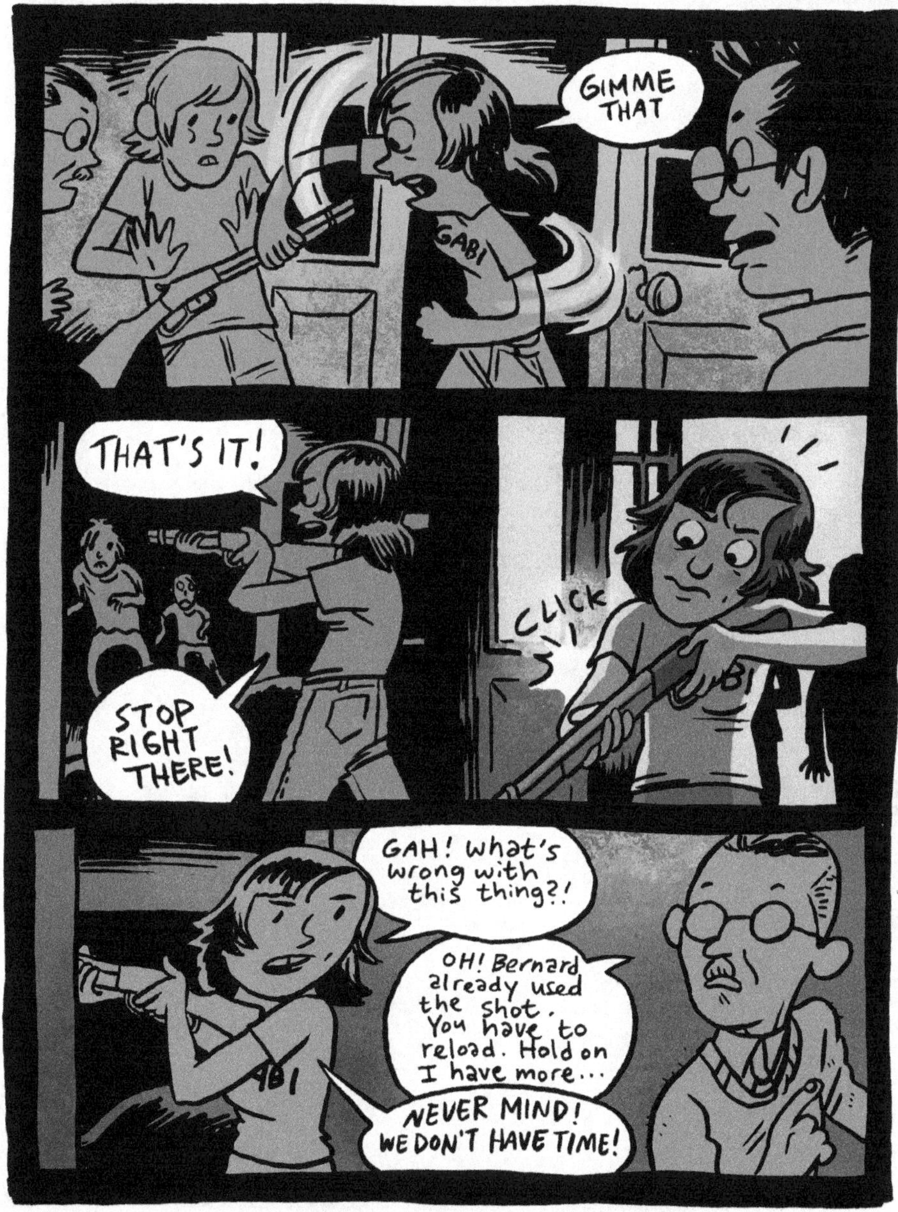
GIMME THAT
GABI
THAT'S IT!
STOP RIGHT THERE!
CLICK
GAH! What's wrong with this thing?!
OH! Bernard already used the shot. You have to reload. Hold on I have more...
NEVER MIND! WE DON'T HAVE TIME!

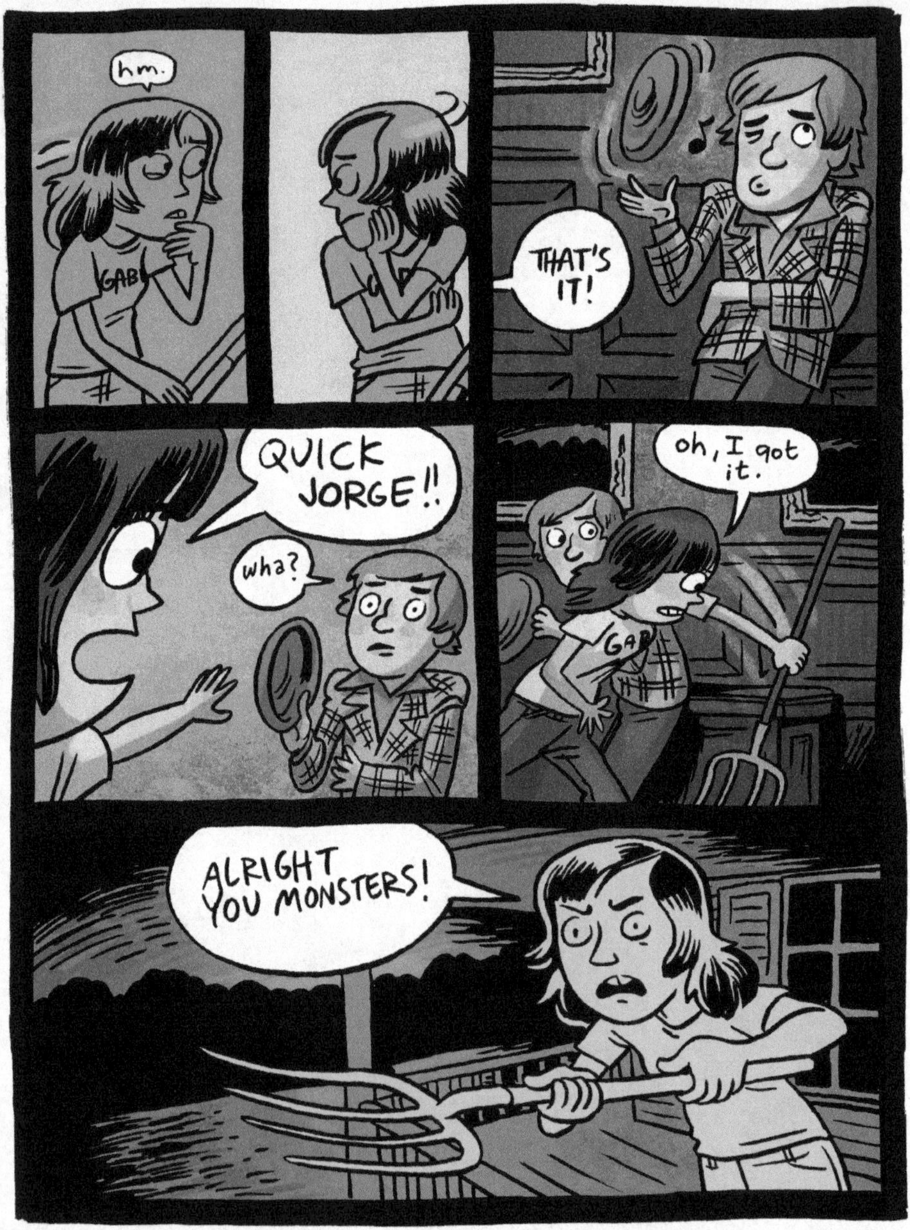
hm.
GABI
THAT'S IT!
QUICK JORGE!!
wha?
oh, I got it.
GAB
ALRIGHT YOU MONSTERS!

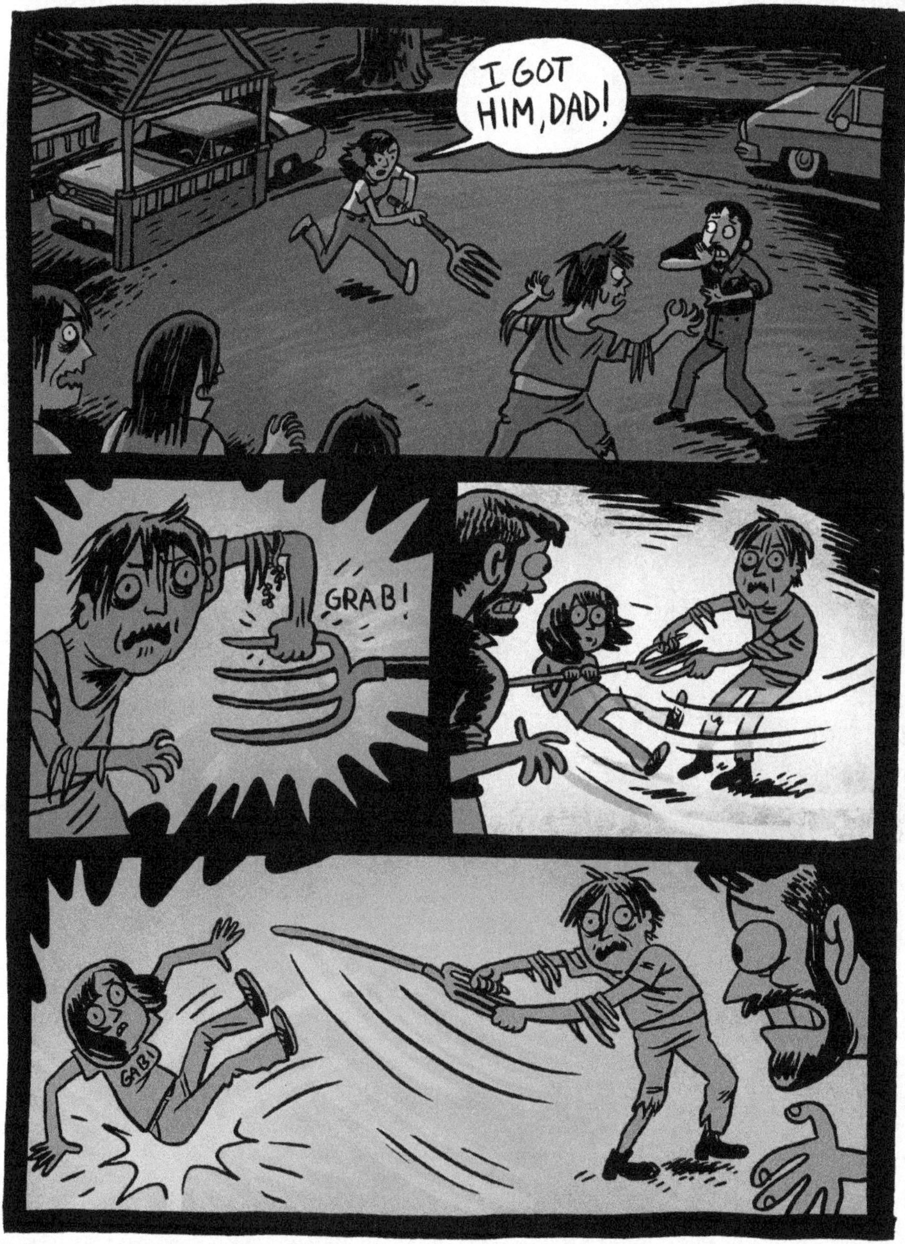
I GOT HIM, DAD!
GRAB!
GABI

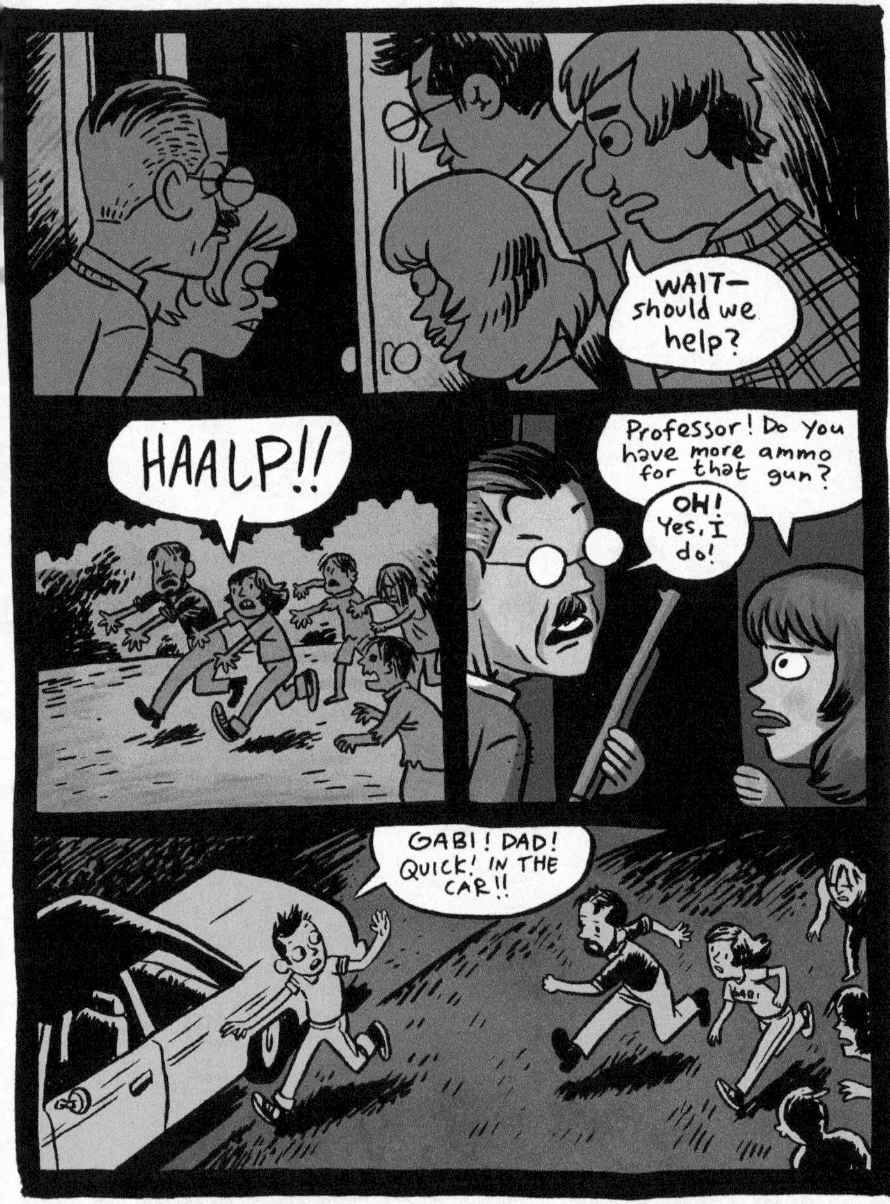

WAIT— should we help?
HAALP!!
Professor! Do you have more ammo for that gun?
OH! Yes, I do!
GABI! DAD! QUICK! IN THE CAR!!

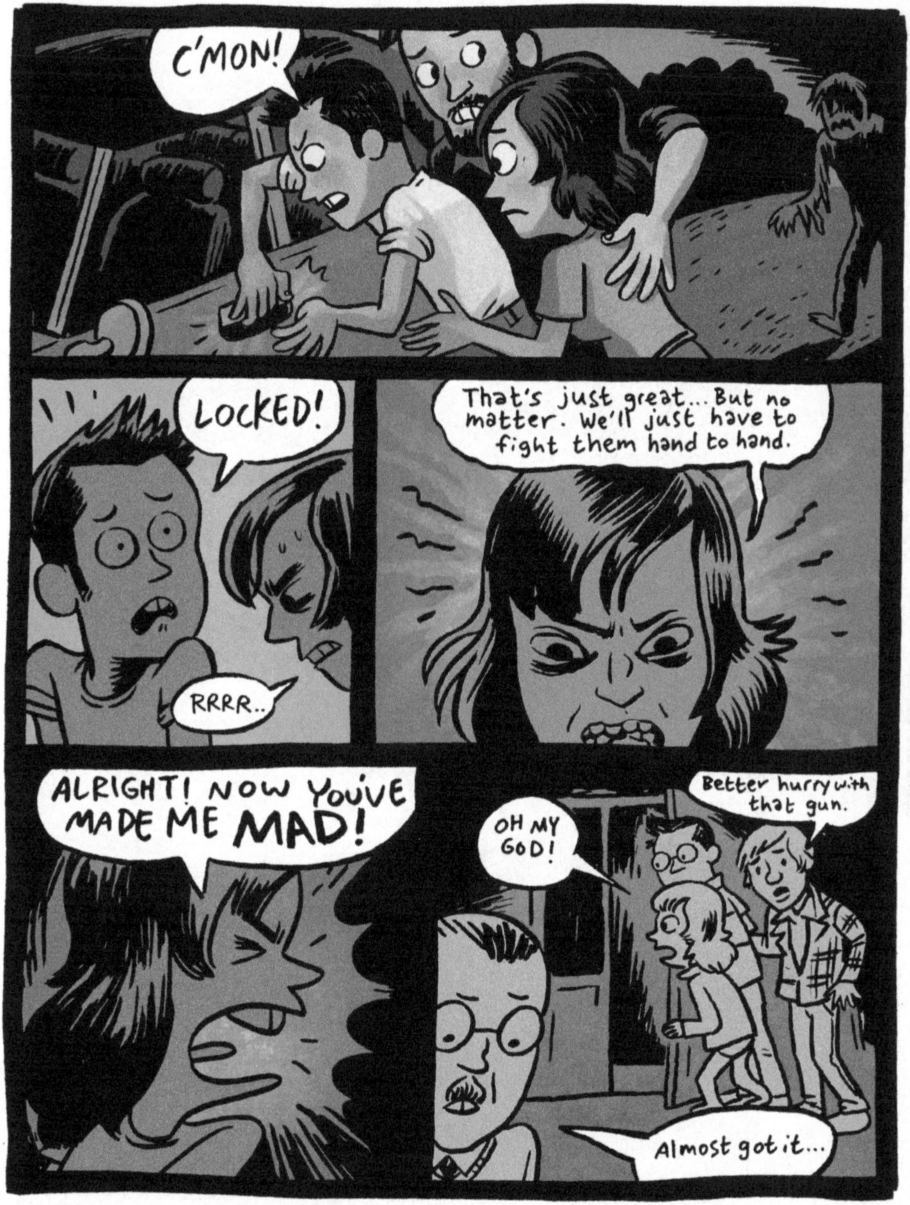
C'MON!
LOCKED!
RRRR..
That's just great... But no matter. We'll just have to fight them hand to hand.
ALRIGHT! NOW YOU'VE MADE ME MAD!
OH MY GOD!
Better hurry with that gun.
Almost got it...

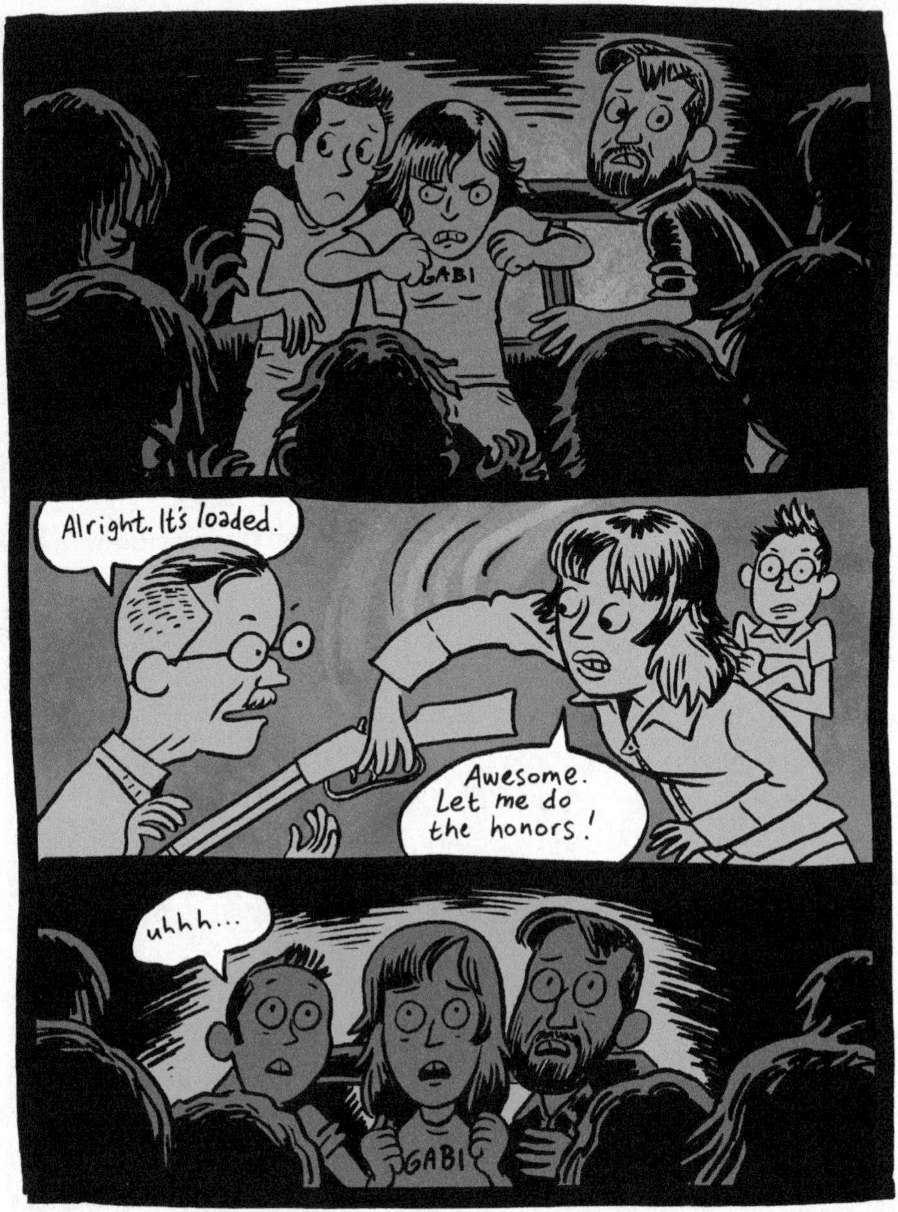
GABI
Alright. It's loaded.
Awesome. Let me do the honors!
uhhh...
GABI

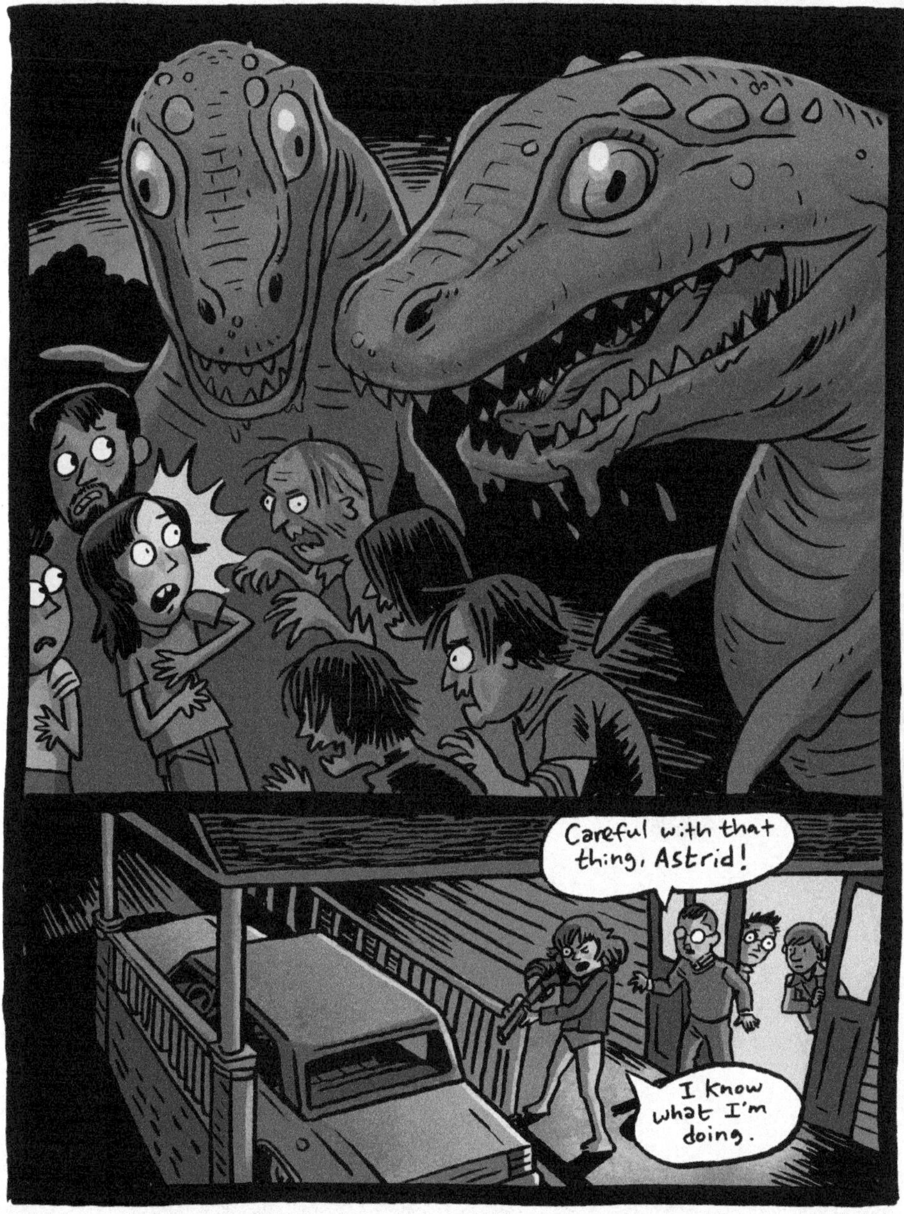
Careful with that thing, Astrid!
I know what I'm doing.

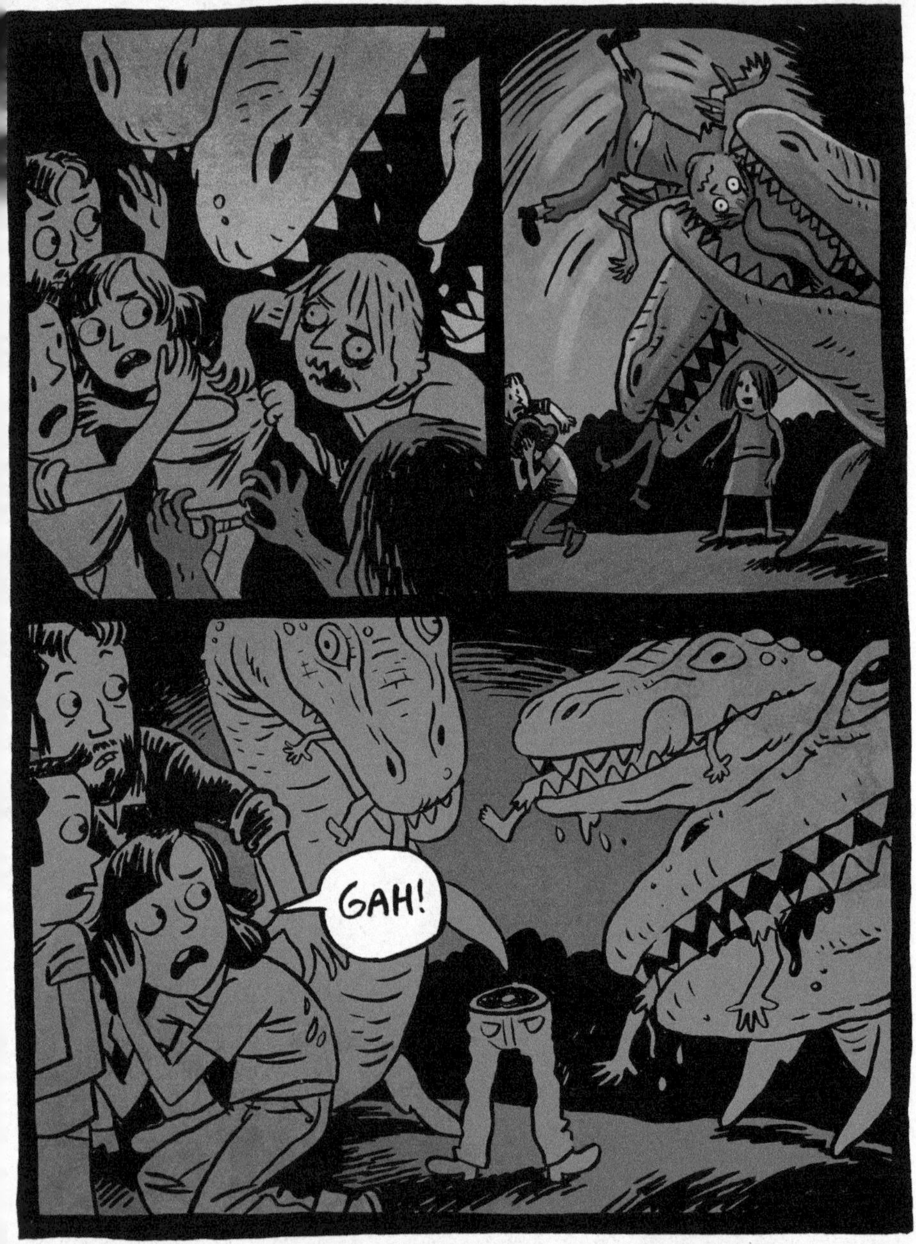
GAH!

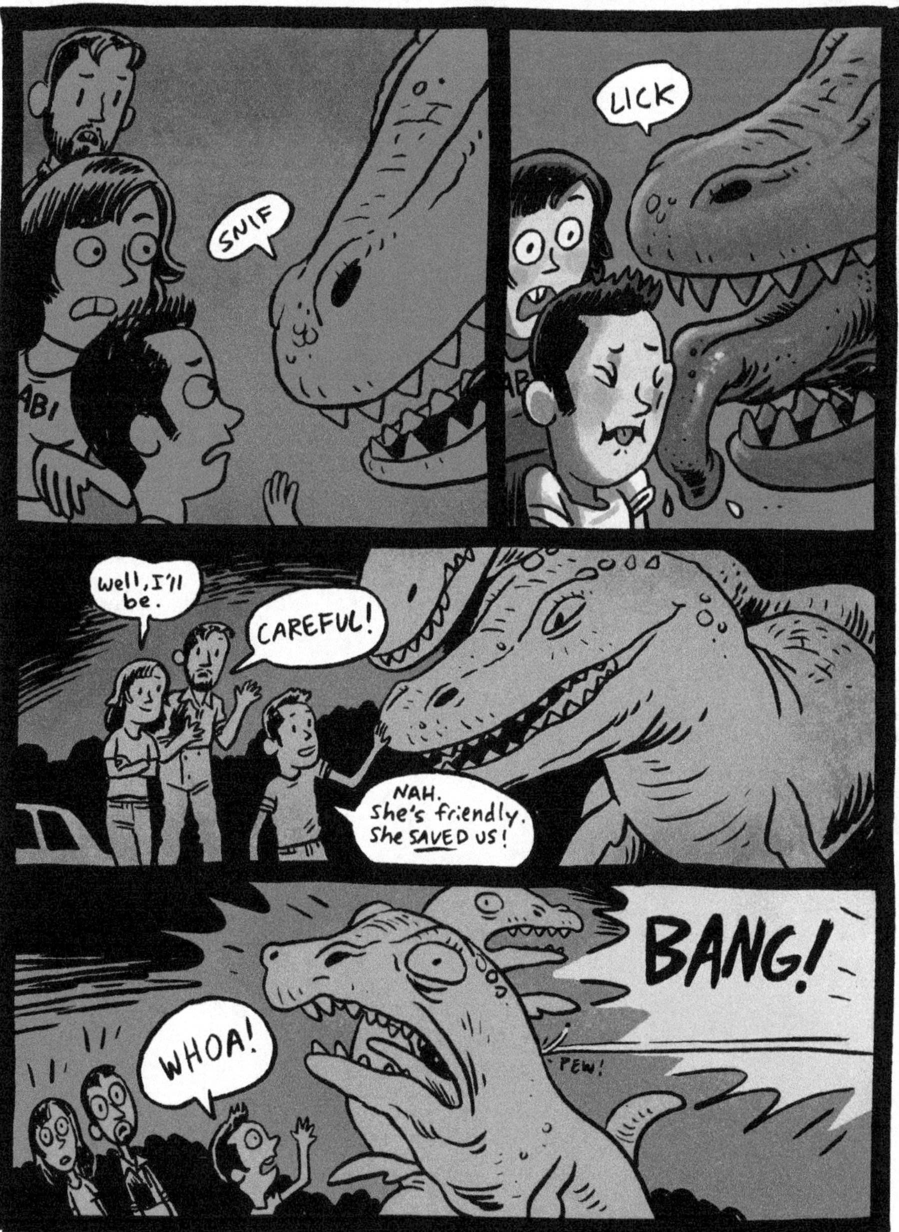
SNIF
LICK
Well, I'll be.
CAREFUL!
NAH. She's friendly. She SAVED US!
BANG!
PEW!
WHOA!

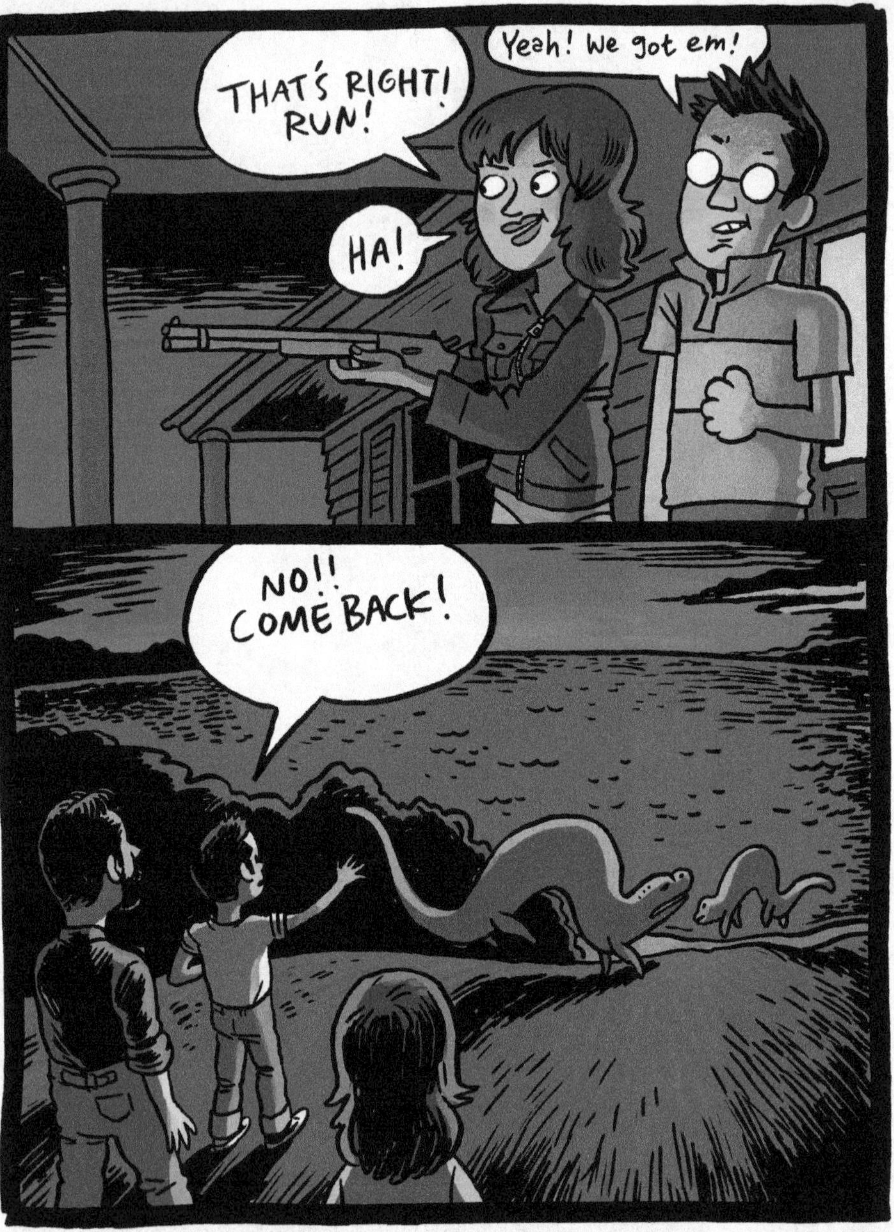
THAT'S RIGHT! RUN!
Yeah! We got em!
HA!
NO!! COME BACK!

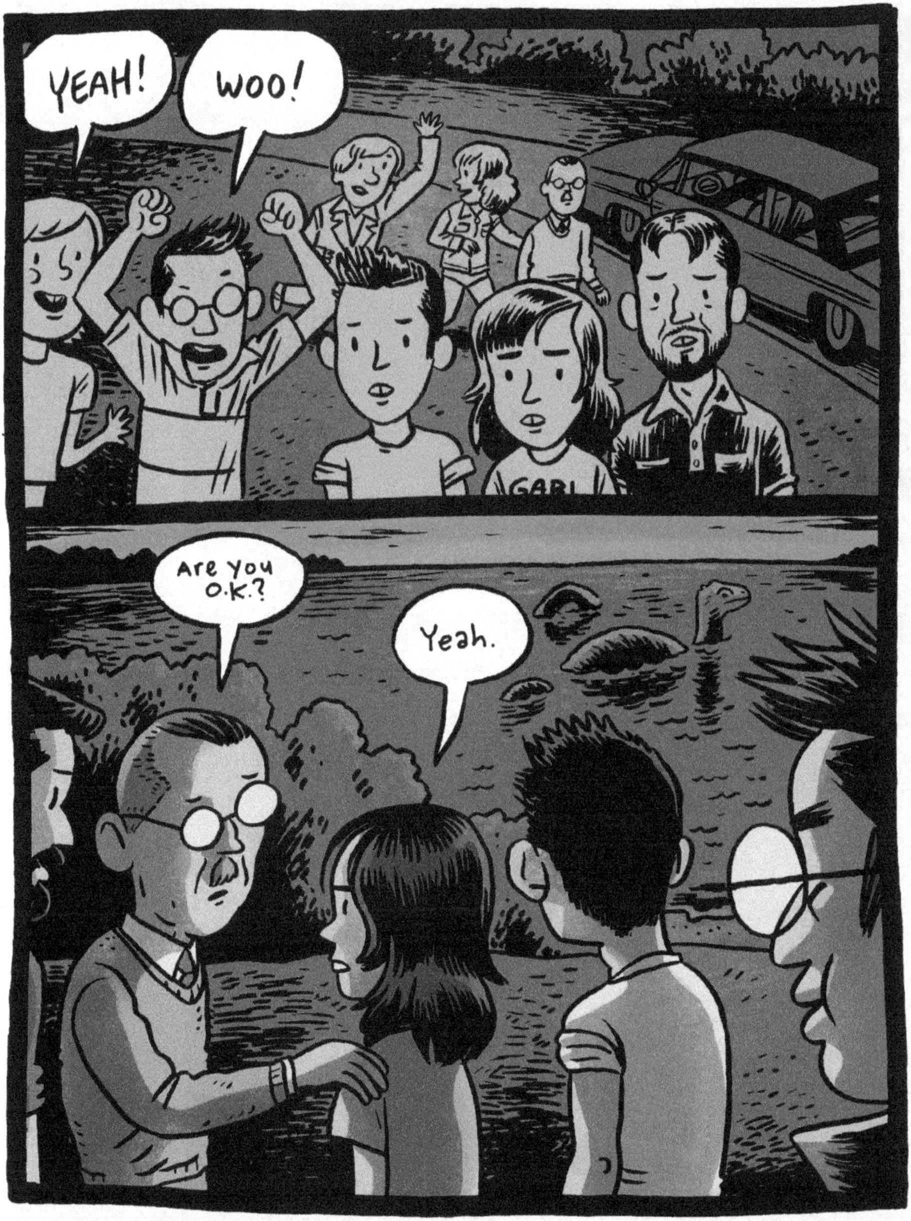
YEAH!
WOO!
GABI
Are you O.K.?
Yeah.

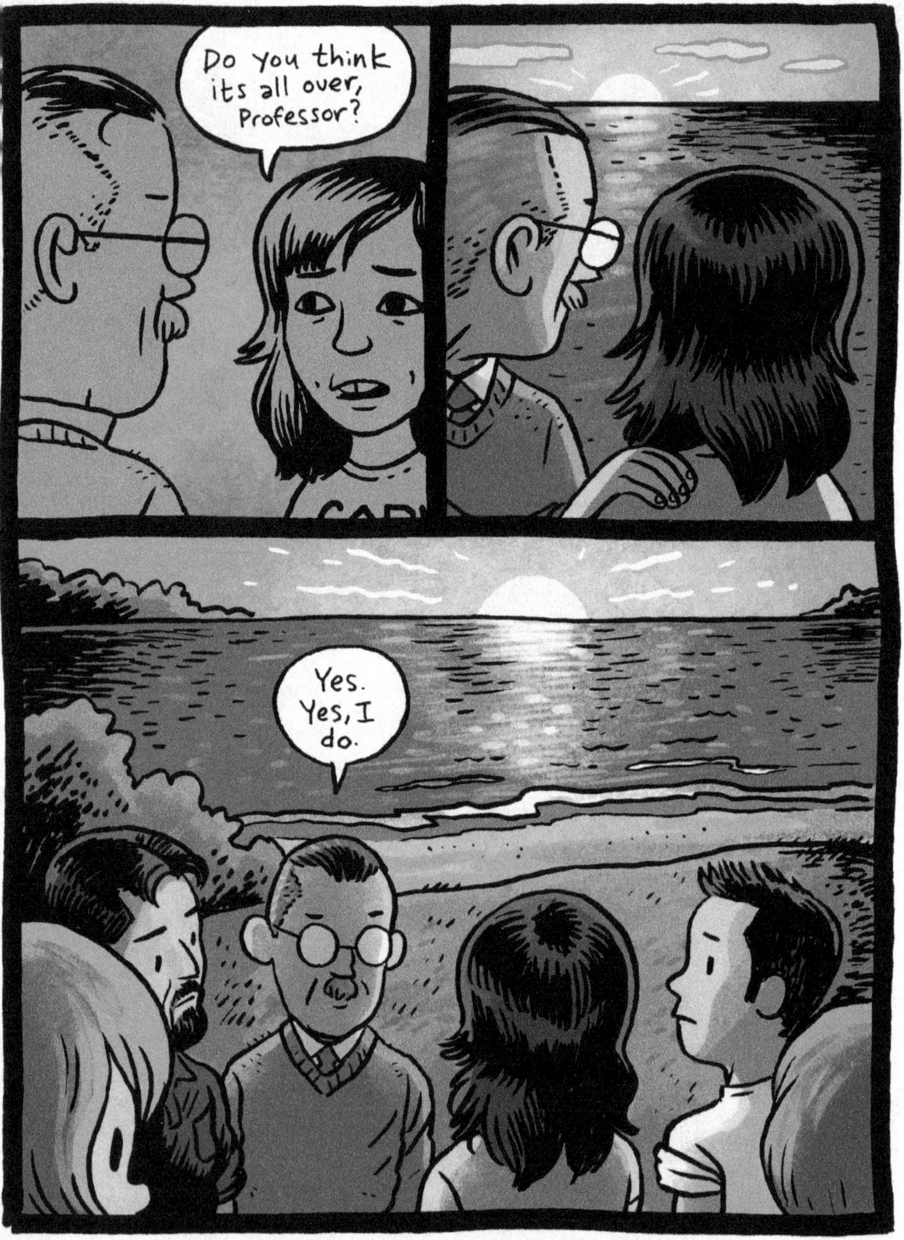
Do you think its all over, Professor?
Yes. Yes, I do.

THE
END